Twin Peaks
FAQ

Twin Peaks FAQ

All That's Left to Know About a Place Both Wonderful and Strange

David Bushman and Arthur Smith

APPLAUSE
THEATRE & CINEMA BOOKS
An Imprint of Hal Leonard Corporation

Published in 2016 by Applause Theatre & Cinema Books
An Imprint of Hal Leonard Corporation
7777 West Bluemound Road
Milwaukee, WI 53213

Trade Book Division Editorial Offices
33 Plymouth St., Montclair, NJ 07042

All images are from the authors' collections unless otherwise noted.

The FAQ series was conceived by Robert Rodriguez and developed with Stuart Shea.

Printed in the United States of America

Book design by Snow Creative Services

Library of Congress Cataloging-in-Publication Data

Names: Bushman, David, 1955– author. | Smith, Arthur, 1971– author.
Title: Twin peaks FAQ : all that's left to know about a place both wonderful and
    strange / David Bushman and Arthur Smith.
Description: Milwaukee, WI : Applause Theatre & Cinema Books, 2016. |
    Includes bibliographical references and index.
Identifiers: LCCN 2015042231 | ISBN 9781495015861 (pbk.)
Subjects: LCSH: Twin Peaks (Television program)
Classification: LCC PN1992.77.T88 B77 2016 | DDC 791.45/72—dc23
LC record available at http://lccn.loc.gov/2015042231

www.applausebooks.com

For Lynch/Frost . . . and Pete Martell,
who found a fish in the percolator.

Contents

Acknowledgments

We rely on the kindness of friends. Mitchel Deltuvia, Lucas Gluszak, Ken Mueller, and Benjamin Myers all aided us with the research and fact-checking for this book. We salute them, plus The Paley Center for Media's Jane Klain, the patron saint of researchers. For their assistance with photographs, we thank also Rob S. Wilson, Ellen O'Neill, Jerry Ohlinger's Movie Materials (especially Dollie Banner), and Photofest (especially Derek Davidson, Todd Ifft, Howard Mandelbaum, and Ron Mandelbaum). We are grateful to everyone who provided images, especially Richard Beymer, who portrayed Benjamin Horne so brilliantly over two seasons and documented the final days on the set with a series of extraordinary photographs, some of which we are fortunate enough to include in this book.

So many people have kept the spirit of *Twin Peaks* alive over the years with their passion and commitment, and no doubt played a significant role in convincing David Lynch, Mark Frost, and Showtime to revive the show. We are especially indebted to the following *Twin Peaks* and/or David Lynch experts for their magnificent work in this field over the decades: Brad Dukes, Craig Miller, Greg Olson, Chris Rodley, John Thorne, and everyone at the Twin Peaks Festival, especially Rob and Deanne Lindley.

A very, very special thanks to Pieter Dom (Welcome to Twin Peaks), Scott Ryan (Red Room Podcast), Mischa Cronin (Twin Peaks Archive), and Andreas Halskov for all their insight and expertise, and for never saying no.

We also extend deep gratitude and appreciation to the following for their counsel and support: Peter Byer, Jay Fialkov, Svetlana Katz, Barry Monush, Maria Pagano, Rebecca Paller, and James Sheridan.

Last, but certainly not least, we thank our families for accommodating all of the demands of this project, and for their unwavering support and inspiration: Mariam, Alex, and Scout (for David) and Jenny and Owen (for Arthur).

Introduction

I'll See You Again in Twenty-Five Years

Are you looking for secrets? Is that it? Maybe I can give you one.

What *Twin Peaks* Means and Why It Still Matters

Once upon a time, a poorly rated (after its brief tenure as a media sensation) show attracted a cult, excited some critics, and vanished quickly. It's a common tale in network television, a uniquely unforgiving medium that ravenously consumes content while fearfully attempting to appease its sponsors, the corporate purveyors of soap and cars and diet soda who care about nothing but return on investment, the highest number of the most demographically desirable viewers. Promising shows are killed in infancy all the time. Why is Showtime bringing the series back to the screen decades after its cancellation? What's so special about *Twin Peaks*? Why, twenty-five years later, do we still care?

Because *Twin Peaks* was unique, and its uniqueness stems from the fact that the series, for all of its reveling in lowbrow genre junkiness, was Art. Art with a capital A. Television, at its best, had certainly been artful before *Twin Peaks*, but never before had prime time featured a work that so thrillingly embraced surrealism, absurdism, and postmodern semiotic playfulness. Never had an American TV show dared such unnerving, alienating elements; such passages of incomprehensible weirdness; such emphasis on mood and texture over narrative clarity; or exalted enigma, formal beauty, and oneiric potency over the comforting tropes that define even its most progressive fellows. *Twin Peaks* snuck a cornucopia of high-culture rigor and experiment onto the tube, disguising its abstractions and disruptions as an

"Diane, 11:30 a.m. February 24. Entering the town of Twin Peaks . . ."

ostensibly familiar soap opera/murder mystery, and demonstrated main-stream, serialized television's potential as a venue for something beyond well-wrought entertainment.

But maybe that's the sort of thing that excites only critics and academics. What explains the show's lingering effect on normal, reasonable people?

Twin Peaks, like much of cocreator David Lynch's work, has the ability to tap directly into the darkest corners of the receptive viewer's subconscious. His faux-naïve, intuitive process bypasses the audience's psychic defenses to provoke primal responses impossible to achieve through conventional storytelling techniques. *Twin Peaks* beguiles with its intriguing oddness, its autumnal beauty, and its cheeky subversion of expectations born of our experience with countless stories of murder, forbidden love, small-town secrets, and heroic knights errant. But the show stays with us because under all of that cleverness and high style, it hits us where we live, rubs up against our most private fears and desires, unsettles us profoundly even as it ensnares us in its gauzy web of seductive lyricism and queasy titillation.

Twin Peaks is a beautiful dream that tells us everything very likely will not be all right, that terrible things will happen and that the world is full of hidden dangers and unspeakable evil. The show is a dark reckoning with an unresolvable mystery: not the identity of Laura Palmer's killer, but the origin of the wickedness and cruelty and chaos that exist everywhere if we but look closely enough, even in such an idyllic little community as Twin Peaks.

It tells us this terrible truth, and we can't get enough. Like Laura Palmer, *Twin Peaks* is an irresistible contradiction, a crucible of beauty and depravity that simultaneously engrosses and repels, delights and disgusts. It gets under your skin and sets up shop in your lizard brain. It haunts you, like a first love lost, the shameful memory of the worst thing you've ever done, a photo in a locket. It's full of secrets, and whispers them close to your ear in a voice both familiar and unsettlingly strange.

Notes on Analyzing *Twin Peaks*: Or How We Learned to Stop Worrying and Love the Mystery

When discussing *Twin Peaks*, it's natural—but unfair—to focus on Lynch's contributions rather than those of his partner Mark Frost. Lynch is after all the marquee name, the rare behind-the-scenes figure as alluring to the press and public as the movie stars enacting his scenarios. And it is Lynch's unique aesthetic that makes *Twin Peaks* a landmark piece of entertainment, elevating a slyly subversive genre pastiche into the realm of high art, worthy of serious academic study and revolutionary in its expansion of the possibilities of the medium of television.

But it's Frost who makes the show work. Much of the pure entertainment value of *Twin Peaks*—the crackling, offbeat dialogue; winking soap opera shenanigans; the procedural investigative aspect of the story and much of the general charming tenor of the town and its residents—comes from Frost. More crucially, his command of more traditional narrative structure gives the story shape and movement, and grounds the viewer in a relatable world (albeit one constructed from a postmodern tangle of cultural symbols and genre tropes) that gives the visionary disruptions of Lynch a context in which they can fully resonate with the viewer. Consider the very mixed reaction to Lynch's version of *Twin Peaks* that did not include Frost: *Fire Walk with Me*. The film is a gut punch of surrealist horror, a searing nightmarish plunge into madness; it's a potent and primal distillation of *Twin Peaks'* most avant-garde and transgressive elements, but its baffling approach to plot, flamboyantly expressionistic presentation, and relentlessly bleak tone clearly could never be sustained over the course of a serial narrative.

That said, in the course of our consideration of the thematic and aesthetic aspects of *Twin Peaks*, we'll largely be focusing on Lynch. For the

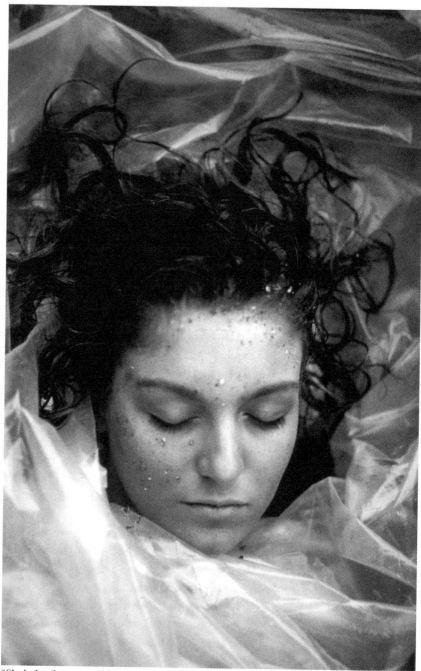

"She's dead, wrapped in plastic." The murdered Laura Palmer in an image dreamlike, beautiful, and heartbreaking.

ABC/Photofest

reasons listed above, admittedly, but here's a better one: the haunting, unresolvable questions, mysteries, and puzzles that kept the series alive in the hearts and minds of its fans are the result of David Lynch's painterly, abstract sensibility colliding with the familiar, predictable narrative rhythms of series television. Frost's work is more readily graspable; we've all grown up watching television dramas, we understand how they behave, and there is not much more to say on the subject after acknowledging the fact that Frost took the basic elements of *Twin Peaks* and made them into a show that worked, and he did it exceptionally well. It's the tension between Frost's more orthodox (and necessary) approach and Lynch's disregard for these storytelling conventions in pursuit of a personal artistic vision that has generated the fodder for so much richly rewarding theorizing, speculation, and armchair analysis since *Twin Peaks'* debut.

And now it's our turn. We love plunging into all of the theorizing, speculation, and armchair analysis as much as anyone; it's why we wrote this book. But before we lose ourselves in the tangled semiotic thicket that is *Twin Peaks*, some prefatory notes might prove helpful:

Embrace the mystery

For Lynch, a mystery is not a problem to be solved, but an opportunity for exploration. He is far less interested in the mechanics of a whodunit than in the possibilities inherent in the unknown. The mystery of who killed Laura Palmer is an invitation to immerse one's self in the world of *Twin Peaks*, not a game to be won with logical deduction.

Lynch cares about story, not plot

Plot is what happens. Story is what those things that happened are *about*. The story of *Twin Peaks* is: A beautiful girl is killed by a terrible monster, and a good man seeks justice for her. The plot of *Twin Peaks* would fill a dozen volumes, and while the plot is necessary to tell the story, it's not the *point*. Spot an inconsistency? Confused about something vague? Hung up on a contradiction? Get over it or learn to live with pain; it really doesn't matter. The plot is like a car taking you to the story: even if the electrical system is wonky and you can't tune the radio in clearly, you will reach your destination, and your trip will be more interesting for the weirdness. The rest is details.

The theme is the thing

For Lynch, more important than plot *or* story is theme.
Twin Peaks is *really* about:

- **Dualities** (light and darkness, Laura and Maddy, evil doppelgängers, White and Black Lodges, and on and on and on. Why do you think it's called *Twin Peaks?*)
- **The mysterious and strange hidden within the mundane** (David Foster Wallace defined Lynch's sensibility as "a particular kind of irony where the very macabre and the very mundane combine in such a way as to reveal the former's perpetual containment within the latter"—and maybe there's our definitive answer to the "Josie in the doorknob" conundrum)
- **Contrast** (dizzy, kitschy comedy abutting graphic horror, iconic Americana touched by the surreally supernatural, the impossibly virtuous Cooper versus the impossibly wicked Bob)
- **Domestic space as nightmare** (chez Palmer and most of the other residences)
- **The evil that men do**

Aesthetics trump logic

The television medium is storytelling at its most intimate, beaming into the privacy of our homes, where we are most vulnerable and unguarded; no wonder Lynch's work, with its pipeline to the unconscious, struck such a nerve in this context. Lynch works with images and sounds to produce aesthetic and emotional effects that transcend the literal meaning of the action he depicts . . . in other words, those tiny letters found under the fingernails of Bob's victims never amounted to much as a plot element, but they provided a supremely creepy detail crucial to the show's overall effect. The economics of television and film production tend to produce very streamlined products; there simply isn't time or money to spend on elements that don't directly contribute to the furtherance of the plot. Lynch couldn't care less—things like the fingernail letters are the entire point. Thus, it can be frustrating for TV-trained audiences to encounter these narrative cul-de-sacs and non sequiturs; surely the attention paid to those letters means they are "important" and "mean something." They are important, and they do mean something, but not necessarily in the way you want them to.

I'll have what he's having: Michael Ontkean and Frank Silva confer with Lynch.

Photo by Richard Beymer

You're going to have to do some work

When Lynch is pressed for explanations of what his more mystifying sequences and details mean, his standard answer has been along the lines of "Whatever you want it to mean." This is more than an evasion: engaging with Lynch's work, with its lack of reassuring narrative payoffs and strict realistic logic, requires interpretive effort on the part of the viewer. It's the depth of this engagement that makes Lynch's work so rewarding, but much of the heavy lifting is up to you. So join us as we penetrate these dark and foreboding woods—we've brought a flashlight, but it's surely not going to provide complete illumination. That's okay; the questions that lack definitive answers are the most compelling. Stay close, here we go.

Twin Peaks
FAQ

It Was Almost Fun Not Knowing

From Concept to Cancellation

Some ideas can arrive in the form of a dream. I can say it again: some ideas arrive in the form of a dream.

Twin Peaks may never have happened if not for Marilyn Monroe. Cocreators Mark Frost and David Lynch first teamed in 1986, paired by Creative Artists Agency (CAA) to adapt Anthony Summers's *Goddess: The Secret Lives of Marilyn Monroe* into a feature film. Lynch was an established film director, with credits including the cult favorite *Eraserhead* (1977); two highly decorated, acclaimed films, *The Elephant Man* (1980) and, most recently, *Blue Velvet* (1986), both scoring Oscar nominations for Best Director; and *Dune* (1984), a colossal critical and commercial bust (Lynch swore never again to make a film without final-cut approval). Frost was more of a TV guy, having scripted two episodes of the juvenile ABC series *The Six Million Dollar Man* in 1975, but burnishing his reputation as a writer/executive story editor on the groundbreaking eighties cop show *Hill Street Blues*, in addition to his work as a playwright, documentarian, and budding screenwriter (*The Believers*, released in 1987).

At first glance, an odd coupling: Lynch, a trained painter with abstract sensibilities, who worshipped at the altar of surrealist filmmakers like René Clair and Hans Richter, and Frost, who dabbled in documentaries and earned his stripes crafting scripts for a gritty, hyperreal television cop show. And yet, it worked: the two hit it off famously, even while running up a streak of bad luck.

Here's what happened to *Venus Descending*, their thinly veiled fictionalization of Summers's book: nothing.

Here's why, at least according to Frost and Lynch: the production company bailed after discovering the script's suggestion that Monroe was murdered, and that Robert Kennedy was behind it.

Next up for Lynch-Frost: *One Saliva Bubble*, set to star Steve Martin and Martin Short, a "dumb" (Lynch's word, not ours) comedy about the impact of a freak accident (a saliva bubble infiltrates, then short-circuits a weapons system at a top-secret military base) on a small Kansas town—also never produced, this one because of financial turmoil at Dino De Laurentiis's company, Lynch's backer, which eventually went belly up.

Undeterred, Lynch and Frost turned their attention to the small screen, encouraged by CAA agent Tony Krantz. Their first pitch, *The Lemurians*, followed law-enforcement officials grappling with the leakage of the evil essence of the sunken, mythical continent of Lemuria, caused when Jacques Cousteau accidently bumps up against a rock during one of his early undersea expeditions. NBC, ruler of the prime-time roost in those days thanks to ratings juggernauts like *The Cosby Show*, *Cheers*, and *L.A. Law*, passed (in Brad Dukes's *Reflections: An Oral History of Twin Peaks*, Krantz says that Brandon Tartikoff, the network's programming whiz, was willing to commission a two-hour telefilm, but Lynch insisted on a series).

Worth noting: Every single one of these scenarios—troubled young woman is murdered, malfunctioning electricity wreaks havoc on small town, law-enforcement officials battle the essence of evil—wound up figuring prominently in *Twin Peaks*. But our real point is this: If any one of these projects had been greenlighted, we might never have had *Twin Peaks*.

But they weren't, and we did.

Easy as A-B-C

The lore is this: Batting around ideas one day at Du-par's, an LA coffee shop, Lynch and Frost were mutually intrigued by the image of the nude body of a murdered woman washing up on the craggy shore of a small-town lake. For Frost, the inspiration was personal: his grandmother used to spook him with stories of a young woman murdered not far from their lakeside vacation home in upstate (Taborton) New York back around the turn of the century, whose ghost was said to be roaming the woods ever since (man, why couldn't *we* have a grandma like that?). More than likely this was Hazel Drew, whose body was pulled from Teal Pond in Sand Lake on July 13, 1908, the murderer never apprehended.

As Lynch and Frost tell it, the unsolved murder was intended as a MacGuffin rather than as the focal point of the series—a portal into a town populated by idiosyncratic characters enmeshed in secret, tangled relationships (think *Winesburg, Ohio*, but noir). Keep in mind that *Hill Street Blues*, from whence Frost came, had famously infused the prime-time police procedural with soap-opera tropes (high melodrama, fractured narrative, yada yada); plus, Lynch himself was a soap fan, having viewed countless hours of *Another World* and *The Edge of Night* while printing engravings at Rodger LaPelle's Philadelphia shop in the late sixties, supporting himself and his expectant wife.

Originally, the show was to take place in North Dakota, as Lynch and Frost were intrigued by the idea of setting the story in the Great Plains, far away from the rest of the world, but ultimately felt the region lacked the mystery and darkness of the heavily forested Pacific Northwest, where Lynch had spent a hefty chunk of his childhood.

This time, Krantz arranged a meeting with the folks at ABC, a smart move. The "Alphabet Network" was in the midst of reinvention, chafing under NBC dominance, yes, but also, like all broadcasters, dwindling audiences, as cable, VCRs, and other alternative forms of home entertainment ascended. ABC's strategy was valorous: the network recast itself as home to innovative, critically embraced shows with upscale demos, like *Roseanne*, *Moonlighting*, *China Beach*, *thirtysomething*, and *The Wonder Years*, banking that profits would follow.

ABC liked the pitch, and one meeting led to another. Lynch famously unfurled a town map he had drawn in charcoal, delineating key locations—a lumber mill here, a sheriff's station there, even the homes of key characters. Lynch and Frost had even versed themselves in the town's topography, and could relate its history going back a hundred years (later on, when the network sought more details, they created the *Twin Peaks Gazette*, a newspaper laying out further details). ABC was expecting a *"Peyton Place* for the nineties" (per Frost), and even sent them episodes of that sixties prime-time soap to watch, but Frost and Lynch had something entirely different in mind. Chad Hoffman, vice president of drama series, ordered first a script, which Lynch and Frost delivered in ten days (bearing the original title of the show, *Northwest Passage*—that title was being used by another project, however, and Frost suggested *"Twin Peaks"* instead), then a feature-length pilot, written by Frost-Lynch and directed by Lynch, shot over "twenty-two and a half days" (per Lynch) in February-March 1989, largely in the Snoqualmie Valley region of Washington State, in the shadow of Mount

Si, about thirty miles east of Seattle (in bitter-cold temperatures, everyone recalls). Also filmed during this window was an alternative ending to the pilot, crafted specifically for European home-video and possibly theatrical release, which provided a resolution to the mystery of who killed Laura Palmer; though different from the solution American TV viewers would eventually see, this eighteen-minute segment, improvised by Lynch at the eleventh hour, wound up defining the most crucial elements of the series' mythology as it developed over the course of two seasons.

Un-Suit-able for ABC?

Twin Peaks was developed originally for the fall of 1989, but like Donald Rumsfeld once said, "Stuff happens." More precisely, both Hoffman and his boss, ABC entertainment prez Brandon Stoddard, ankled the network; Stoddard's successor, Robert Iger, championed the pilot, but it tested poorly, and network suits were troubled by the commercial prospects, fearing it was just too weird for mainstream America (*Variety* famously reported that one ABC executive likened it to "Norman Rockwell meets Salvador Dali").

Stymied, Lynch and Frost launched a guerrilla campaign, hoping to pressure ABC into ordering a full series. Public screenings were held, and copies of the pilot shipped off to media outlets. The press pounced: Avant-garde filmmaker David Lynch, the creative genius behind one of the weirdest movies ever made (*Eraserhead*), and also one of the most disturbingly twisted (*Blue Velvet*), is coming to television! Yay! (While numerous other film auteurs, including Steven Spielberg, Michael Mann, John Sayles, and Robert Altman, also were embracing television at about this time, none was as outré as Lynch.) *Connoisseur* ran the first major magazine piece, in September 1989, calling *Twin Peaks* "the series that will change TV forever." No pressure there. Countless others followed—*TV Guide, Entertainment Weekly, Details, Film Comment*, etc.—all before even a single episode of *Twin Peaks* had aired, indeed, before any but the pilot had been filmed.

Eventually, ABC ponied up, ordering seven additional, one-hour episodes and slotting *Twin Peaks* in as a midseason replacement, though still without a premiere date. The gang reassembled, filming from October to December 1989, this time mostly at specially built studios in a former ball-bearings factory in the San Fernando Valley, plus locations around the area, with extensive second-unit work back in Washington. The entire first season of *Twin Peaks* wrapped before a single minute of the series had appeared on television—a situation Frost, in his foreword to the 2011 reissue of the companion book *The Secret Diary of Laura Palmer*, fondly recollected as toiling in "splendid isolation." Lynch helmed the second one-hour episode (including the famous dream sequence, with the dancing dwarf who moved and spoke backward), then went off to shoot his next theatrical film, *Wild at Heart*, leaving Frost in charge on-site, though the two had already broken the main story for the run of the season. To ease the load, Frost brought in Harley Peyton and Robert Engels, both of whom would go on to play crucial roles over the course of the series.

Launching an extensive promotional campaign of its own, ABC announced that winter that it would air the pilot without national commercials (though local spots would run), at a projected loss of over $1 million in revenue—even though the network had yet to announce an airdate.

As *The Wire*'s Omar Little would say, "All in the game, man."

On the Air

Finally, the big night arrived: *Twin Peaks* premiered on ABC on Sunday, April 8, 1990, from 9:00 to 11:00p.m., and it's hard to imagine a more jubilant scenario. Nearly 35 million viewers watched, accounting for one-third of all the television sets in use during that two-hour period, making it the fifth-highest-rated show of the week. Not too shabby. Critics gushed, orgiastic over this staggering demonstration of what television *could* be: compelling, inventive, atmospheric, challenging, fun. So many "Lynchian" trademarks! Visually elegant! Quirky characters! Absurd humor! Languorously paced! Uncanniness! Frost's experience with fractured narratives on *Hill Street Blues* paid off richly, with so many storylines to juggle, and Angelo Badalamenti's peripatetic score enhanced every crazy mood Lynch and Frost could conjure.

"It's the best thing I've seen on television since 'The Singing Detective,' and the strangest, most surrealistic weekly TV series since 'The Prisoner'—and that was 22 years ago. Basically, it's must-see, must-tape television: watchable, likable and definitely collectible."
—David Bianculli, *New York Post*, April 6, 1990

"This series vaults to the top as the most entertaining and provocative new series since 'Hill Street Blues' on the strength of Lynch's quirky preoccupation with developing a host of beguiling and off-the-wall characters."
—Daniel Ruth, *The Chicago Sun-Times*, April 6, 1990

"If you give yourself over to the dense and languorous mist of Twin Peaks, a slumbering mill town where time seems suspended and nothing's as it seems, you're in for the kind of sensual sensation TV almost never bothers to offer."   —Matt Roush, *USA Today*, April 6, 1990

The mystery begins tonight.

Who killed Laura Palmer?
What's the FBI doing here?
Who videotaped Donna
and Laura in the woods?

Special Preview New Series
▲TWIN PEAKS▲
Like every town you've ever seen.
And no place you've ever known.

9:00PM ⓐⓑⓒ⑦⑧°

In the beginning: *TV Guide* ad promoting the much-anticipated (and much-delayed) feature-length premiere of *Twin Peaks* on April 8, 1990.

It's been said that in the end, *Twin Peaks* was more phenomenon than hit, and who are we to argue? With its army of oddball characters—dancing dwarf, Log Lady, One-Armed Man, friendly giant, creepy killer, coffee-swilling G-man—plus the reluctant mystery at its core—Who killed Laura Palmer?—*Twin Peaks,* especially in the early days, emitted a vibe unlike any television series that had come before, fed by a media frenzy of staggering proportions, not just within the United States but internationally (our personal favorite: *Rolling Stone*'s October 1990 "Babes in the Woods" cover photo of Lara Flynn Boyle, Sherilyn Fenn, and Mädchen Amick in matching denim-and-tank-top outfits, revealing three pairs of dazzling blue eyes, among other things). Any credible history of fan culture would have to give *Twin Peaks* its due, as *Peaks* freaks staged viewing parties, catered with doughnuts, pie, and coffee in honor of FBI Special Agent Dale Cooper (Kyle MacLachlan); zealously embraced the Internet, just then emerging as a potent fan force; created newsletters; gobbled up collectibles; and shopped for *Twin Peaks*-inspired wardrobes, at Bloomingdale's and else-where. Whenever *Twin Peaks* teetered on the brink of cancellation, they rallied the troops, deluging ABC execs with doughnuts, logs, chess pieces, and other allusionary objects; Citizens Opposed to the Offing of Peaks (COOP) rounded up over two hundred people at a demonstration of support in Washington, D.C., in the winter of 1991, after ABC placed the show on hiatus.

And yet, while all of this was going on, the ratings were telling a different story: On April 12, four nights after the pilot premiered, the series moved to its regular time slot: Thursdays at 9:00 p.m., going up against the *Cheers-Grand* leg of NBC's "Must-See TV" lineup—a challenging assignment for even the stoutest of soldiers (Frost had lobbied for 10:00 p.m. Wednesdays, against CBS's *Wiseguy*, NBC's *Quantum Leap*, and local news on the Fox stations, and reports surfaced that the deadly time slot was devised by East Coast executives, including Capital Cities/ABC Inc. chairman Thomas S. Murphy, who disliked the show and had no confidence it would succeed).

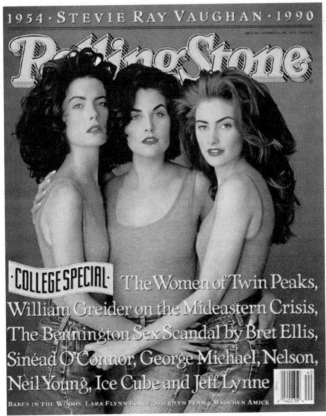

Three babes in the woods.
Copyright © Rolling Stone LLC 1990. All Rights Reserved. Used by Permission

As expected, ratings dipped, but remained impressive (battled *Cheers,* clobbered *Grand*). Not expected: they kept dropping, alarmingly; *Twin Peaks* was bleeding viewers week to week, before finally leveling off at a rate of nearly 50 percent lower than the April 8 premiere. By the penultimate episode of season one, *Twin Peaks* was the fortieth-ranked prime-time show on network television. The first-season finale, directed by Frost, was moved to Wednesday, just to avoid NBC's lineup. On May 21, two days before it aired, Frost and six cast members—Mädchen Amick, Piper Laurie, Dana Ashbrook, Sheryl Lee, Eric Da Re, and Peggy Lipton—appeared on *Donahue,* the daytime talk show, with host Phil Donahue referencing *Twin Peaks* as "the most talked about, most written about, most controversial show on television this season" (in one unintentionally hilarious moment, Donahue inadvertently addressed Amick as Dana, to which Ashbrook replied, "I'm Dana; that's Mädchen").

Twin Peaks got a welcome boost from the National Academy of Television Arts & Sciences, earning fourteen Emmy nominations, more than any other show that year, but wound up bagging just two statues, and neither in a major category: one for editing and one for costume design. It was a major dis, and the attendant publicity didn't help.

By the time ABC was constructing its 1991 fall schedule, there was serious debate within the ranks over whether *Twin Peaks* would even be renewed for a second season—an unthinkable quandary just months earlier.

The good news: it was (Frost announced the renewal live on *Donahue,* saying he just had received the phone call from ABC before stepping out on stage; even the cast members didn't know).

The not-so-good news: ABC relegated it to Saturday nights (along with *China Beach,* another critically acclaimed but ratings-challenged drama), the black hole of TV programming, especially when you're targeting young, hip viewers who . . . we don't know . . . might be doing other things on Saturday nights? Zen moment: What happens if a watercooler show airs and there's no watercooler to gather around the following morning?

Peaks-a-Boo

In anticipation of the new season, ABC reran the entire series to date, beginning in August 1990. On September 14, sixteen days before the second-season premiere, Alan Thicke, star of the ABC sitcom *Growing Pains,* hosted a behind-the-scenes look at *Twin Peaks* and *Cop Rock,* a new, musical cop drama from Frost's old boss at *Hill Street Blues,* Steven Bochco (which could

Finally.
Tonight, find out
who killed
Laura Palmer.
Really.

▲TWIN PEAKS▲

10:00 abc⑦□

The end is here: ABC ballyhoos the November 10, 1990, episode of *Twin Peaks*, which revealed Leland Palmer as Laura's killer, with this *TV Guide* ad.

easily be the subject of its own book). Talk about a kiss of death! *Cop Rock* was inarguably the season's splashiest bust, lasting eleven episodes.

Meanwhile, Lynch and Frost launched their own promo blitz, releasing *"Diane" . . . The Twin Peaks Tapes of Agent Cooper,* an audiobook performed by MacLachlan, assembling Cooper's recordings to his never-seen secretary during the first season, plus new material, and *The Secret Diary of Laura Palmer,* written by Jennifer Lynch, David's daughter, which quickly cracked the *New York Times's* best-seller list. Also during this hiatus MacLachlan guest-hosted on NBC's *Saturday Night Live.*

None of which helped: Ratings continued to plummet (the first half-hour of the highly touted season-two opener ranked fourth in its time slot,

"We are lovers turned to discontent. The bloom has so profoundly fallen off America's romance with 'Twin Peaks' that we have become as vitriolic as respondents in a divorce case. . . . All stories—whether on the page or the big or small screens—must have a beginning, middle, and end. 'Twin Peaks,' one of the most original and innovative shows ever to appear on the tube, seems stuck in its middle like a skipping record."

—Rick Kogan, *Chicago Tribune*, October 12, 1990

behind first-run made-for-TV movies on CBS and NBC, plus Fox's *Married . . . with Children,* and the following ninety minutes overtook Fox only), and many television critics were soon abandoning ship, griping loudly and persistently that Lynch and Frost were manipulating viewers by refusing to unmask Laura's killer. (*PrimeTime Live* even ran a ten-minute segment on viewer dissatisfaction with the show, which aired on the same network!) Typifying this apoplexy was Ed Bark of the New York *Daily News*, who wrote that Lynch-Frost "fell victim to their own cosmic conceits, treating viewers as string-along puppets willing to buy any contrivance."

Frost mixed it up with ABC, accusing the network of fibbing when it said Laura's murder would be solved in the season-one finale, and ABC spokesman Bob Wright issued a mea culpa, saying, "From now on, I will not be making any promises about *Twin Peaks*." Frost even claimed that he deliberately withheld the identity of the murderer, as leverage for renewal, telling reporters that "Our sole strategy was survival." This comment appears to contradict Frost's assertion on *Donahue* that the season-one ending viewers wound up seeing—with Cooper being shot, but without resolution of Laura's murder—was "one of several that we worked on, depending on whether we got picked up for the fall or not. I wanted to polish it off or not polish it off." Frost even added that in view of the phone call from ABC, the creative team was "working feverishly not to polish it off right now." Here Frost appears to be saying that the open-ended season-one finale was a *result* of renewal, rather than a gambit to encourage it.

Lynch and Frost had been determined from the get-go to position Laura's murder as background to the other characters and their stories; Lynch even compared *Twin Peaks* to *The Fugitive*, the sixties ABC drama about Dr. Richard Kimble (David Janssen), falsely convicted of murdering his wife, who escapes from authorities and tries to track down the One-Armed Man he saw leaving the scene of the crime, though Kimble's search typically took a back seat to the human-interest story of the week as the good doctor traversed the country. Still, TV critics in particular were having none of it, obsessing over the identity of Laura's killer from day one. At the

January 6, 1990, ABC Winter Press Tour (before *Twin Peaks* had aired even a single episode or even had an airdate), the first three questions critics posed after viewing the pilot centered on when Laura's killer would be exposed. Toward the end of the press conference the subject came up again: "Has there come a point where you feel that this murder eventually has to be resolved? Like if this goes on for seven years, I mean, people are going to demand that this murder has got to be solved at some point." Lynch's response drew guffaws, but we're not sure he was kidding: "It's got to be solved within seven years."

Swayed by the media (imagine!), ABC suits began exerting relentless pressure on Lynch-Frost to resolve Laura's murder, which particularly irritated Lynch, who had no plans to do so any time soon. Alas, the black hats won; the killer (Laura's father, Leland, inhabited by the super creepy evil spirit Bob) was revealed on November 10, 1990, in the seventh episode of the second season, directed by Lynch from a script by Frost (too late for crotchety critics like Jerry Krupnick of New Jersey's *Star-Ledger*, who moaned, "We don't care who killed Laura anymore"). "We," Jerry? Two installments later the Palmer arc wrapped for good when Leland died in police custody (nope, nothing to do with that). Creatively, the show blundered immediately after, introducing a handful of widely (and rightly)

Killer Bob: I'll be your mirror.   *Photo by Richard Beymer*

derided arcs involving characters and scenarios (Little Nicky, Evelyn Marsh, Lana Budding Milford, Ben Horne's Civil War delusions) nobody cared about, except to loathe—my God, man, Cooper wore a flannel shirt!—but resurged about midway into the second season with the introduction of Cooper's stark-raving-mad former FBI partner Windom Earle, who arrived in Twin Peaks searching high and low for like the evilest place ever, the Black Lodge, which—as luck would have it—was right there smack in the middle of the Twin Peaks woods.

Final (Red) Curtain

Small problem: almost nobody cared anymore; the February 9 episode ranked eighty-fifth for the week, among a total of eighty-nine shows. ABC yanked the series a week later, saying it would air the remaining six installments at an unspecified time later in the season. Lynch and Frost mobilized, staging a press conference on the set of the Great Northern hotel, urging fans to write ABC entertainment president Robert Iger to reinstate the show, but for God's sake, not on Saturdays! (Iger's first name wasn't lost on *Peaks* fans, who started chattering about two Killer Bobs.) "We're in trouble, and we need help," Lynch told the assembled crowd.

The show did in fact come back the following month, once again on Thursdays, but the die was cast. Cancellation was announced in May, and the last two episodes aired back-to-back, after another hiatus, this one of about two months, on Monday, June 10, 1991, as an *ABC Movie of the Week*. "'Twin Peaks' Finale Draws Low Ratings," ran the headline in the subsequent three-paragraph *New York Times* article, which went on to report that it had finished a distant third in its time slot, bested by CBS reruns of *Murphy Brown*, *Designing Women*, and *Northern Exposure*, plus (ouch!) NBC's rerun of the movie *Original Sin*.

Lynch returned to direct the final hour, tossing out huge chunks of the script he had been handed by Frost, Peyton, and Engels because he found the ending "completely and totally wrong," and bringing

"From sizzler to fizzler. Red-hot flame-out. Think 'Twin Peaks,' first and foremost among TV's long list of faded glories. Morton Downey Jr., the 'Batman' series, Erik Estrada, Barbara Feldon—all burned brightly before the public blew them out. But 'Peaks' set a new standard for hot gone cold in a flash. ABC is playing the final two hours of 'Peaks' in a finale tonight that will find lawmen Dale Cooper and Harry S. Truman rushing to the Black Lodge to stop demonic Windom Earle from murdering Miss Twin Peaks. Sorry to bore you."
—Ed Bark, *Daily News* (New York), June 10, 1991

back favorite characters—like the dancing dwarf and the Log Lady—whom the triumvirate had strangely omitted. This highlights the friction that had developed between the two creators over the course of the torturous second season, but also can be seen as Lynch's opening move in reasserting his

David Lynch attends an exhibition of his artwork at the Pennsylvania Academy for the Fine Arts in September 2014, less than a month prior to the announcement that *Twin Peaks* would be returning on Showtime.

Photo by Pieter Dom

Showtime serves its coffee black as midnight on a moonless night.

vision over the world of *Twin Peaks,* followed by the 1992 theatrical film *Twin Peaks: Fire Walk with Me,* which Lynch directed, and cowrote with Engels (without any involvement from Frost), and, in 1993, his decision to pen introductory comments to every single episode (delivered on camera by the Log Lady) as they were rerun on the cable channel Bravo, under the umbrella title "TV Too Good for TV."

Now, the journey continues with news that Showtime has commissioned brand-new episodes of *Twin Peaks,* to be written by Frost and Lynch and directed by Lynch. All of them. The announcement came in 2014—twenty-five years after the events in *Twin Peaks* were supposed to have unfolded on-screen. The timing was impeccable, considering that the last *intelligible* words Laura Palmer spoke to Agent Cooper in the series (excluding "Meanwhile") were "I'll see you again in twenty-five years."

Time's up, Laura. It is happening again.

2

All That We See in This World Is Based on Someone's Ideas

Key Creative Personnel

There's a large group of insane men staying on my floor.

David Lynch

David Keith Lynch was born on January 20, 1946, in Missoula, Montana, to Donald, a research scientist who spent his days working in forests for the U.S. Department of Agriculture, and Edwina, who taught English as a tutor. Though the family moved often, as Donald was assigned to posts in Idaho, Washington, North Carolina, and Virginia, Lynch has reported that his childhood was a happy and stable one. He has two younger siblings, John and Martha. Lynch has often reflected on the influence of his early memories of idyllic small-town life on his work; as he told John O'Mahony in *The Guardian*: "My childhood was elegant homes, tree-lined streets, the milkman, building backyard forts, droning airplanes, blue skies, picket fences, green grass, cherry trees . . . But on the cherry tree there's this pitch oozing out—some black, some yellow, and millions of red ants crawling all over it. I discovered that if one looks a little closer at this beautiful world, there are *always* red ants underneath. Because I grew up in a perfect world, other things were a contrast."

So, here we have this wholesome, all-American boy—an Eagle Scout, yet—who found himself seduced by the life of the artist. A dreamy, intuitive kid of no academic distinction who loved to draw and paint, Lynch attended the School of the Museum of Fine Arts in Boston in lieu of a traditional college education, but the iconoclastic Lynch lasted only a year, abandoning the institution for an abortive trip to Europe to study with the painter Oskar Kokoschka. Unfortunately, Kokoschka proved unavailable, and Lynch returned to the U.S. with no fixed plan or prospects on the horizon.

His friend Jack Fisk, who would later become an acclaimed set designer and husband of the actress Sissy Spacek (who went on to appear in Lynch's film *The Straight Story* in 1999), suggested Lynch join him at Philadelphia's Pennsylvania Academy of Fine Arts. He found the scene more congenial than Boston and stuck with it, though life in the squalid and crime-ridden Philadelphia neighborhood where he lived with his wife Peggy and young daughter Jennifer was less than rosy. Lynch has returned to the atmosphere of that environment many times in his work—the crumbling industrial landscape, unpredictable danger, and abject misery (as Lynch perceived it) of Philadelphia have haunted many Lynch projects.

Lynch began his filmmaking career in 1967 at the Pennsylvania Academy, producing over the next several years shorts including *Six Men Getting Sick* (which featured illness and fire, recurring Lynch motifs), *The Alphabet* (an ostensibly sweet childhood vignette ending in sanguinary horror), and *The Grandmother* (in which a neglected child grows a loving caretaker from a seed). The films were mixtures of stop-motion animation and live action, dreamlike, moody, largely abstract, and disturbing. Sound designer Alan Splet first collaborated with Lynch on *The Grandmother*, crafting an auditory cognate to Lynch's dangerous visions, and the two collaborated closely thereafter on many key Lynch projects.

The Grandmother was funded by the nascent American Film Institute, and in 1971 Lynch and his family moved to Los Angeles, where he began studies at the AFI Conservatory. This would be the incubator for his first feature, *Eraserhead*, a landmark in independent cinema that would establish the young director as an original, audacious talent—but it wouldn't be easy. Working with friends and family (frequent Lynch cinematographer Frederick Elmes came aboard here) on a shoestring budget, Lynch would labor for five years getting *Eraserhead* just the way he wanted it. The result was a nightmarish, blackly comic meditation on the horrors of fatherhood, featuring future *Twin Peaks* stalwart Jack Nance as the hapless, shock-haired Henry, struggling to adapt to his freakish new offspring in a disintegrating industrial hellscape inspired by Lynch's feelings about Philadelphia.

Eraserhead (1977) was a trip, a beguiling and unique plunge into the unconscious that became a staple on the midnight movie circuit and got Lynch noticed by no less a personage than comedy legend Mel Brooks, who at the time was involved in film production. Brooks was flabbergasted by

Eraserhead's off-kilter genius, and approached Lynch with an eye toward collaboration. Their first try, an abstract ode to electricity (another continuing preoccupation of Lynch's) titled *Ronnie Rocket*, never made it past the script stage. Instead, they would make *The Elephant Man*, a biopic based on the real-life tribulations of Joseph Merrick, a hideously deformed man who gained fame in Victorian England as a curiosity offered for the delectation of the upper class.

The Elephant Man (1980) successfully married Lynch's painterly sensibility (the director has continued a serious painting career concurrent with his filmmaking work) and feel for the inchoate, atmospheric, and uncanny with a conventional emotionally resonant narrative, and the film was a hit, earning eight Academy Award nominations, including Best Director and Best Adapted Screenplay, for Lynch.

From the sublime to the ridiculous: the success of *The Elephant Man* led to offers as heady as possibly helming a *Star Wars* installment; instead, Italian movie mogul Dino De Laurentiis hired Lynch to adapt the sci-fi classic novel *Dune* for the big screen. *Dune* the film (1984) was a disaster (though we stubbornly maintain it is misunderstood and underrated): critics and audiences complained it was incomprehensible, boring, awkward, impenetrably dense, and just plain too weird. It flopped spectacularly, but it introduced Lynch to Kyle MacLachlan, who starred in the film as a kind of psychic space messiah. Their next collaboration would go much differently.

De Laurentiis owed Lynch another film, and this time the director had carte blanche to do whatever he liked, however he pleased. He responded with *Blue Velvet*, a bracing shock to cinema and pop culture in general that confirmed Lynch's genius and stands as one of the most significant films of the eighties. *Blue Velvet* (1986) is Lynch's subversion of the small-town ideal he cherished from childhood; in it, MacLachlan returns to sleepy Lumberton in the wake of family crisis and becomes embroiled in a mystery that brings him face-to-face with the unspeakable depravity and evil that lie just below the surface of this Norman Rockwell paradise.

Blue Velvet divided critics (Roger Ebert famously trashed it, while Pauline Kael hailed it as a masterpiece), dominated think pieces, and established Lynch as the industry's premier enigmatic artist—Lynch's personal eccentricities and skewed charisma were media catnip, and he became the rare director as famous as his movies; it is in the *Blue Velvet* era that "Lynchian" became a common descriptor for entertainments that were luridly strange, abstract, or disquietingly peculiar. *Blue Velvet* earned Lynch a second Academy Award nomination for Best Director.

Shortly after this triumph, Lynch met television writer Mark Frost, and the two collaborated on some projects that failed to get off the ground (including a biopic about Marilyn Monroe and a comedy called *One Saliva Bubble*) before creating *Twin Peaks* (1990), another sensation that redefined a medium: after making the suburban cineplex safe for surrealism, Lynch, aided by Frost, did the same for television. This book explores the

On Location: David Lynch, in Snoqualmie Valley, Washington.

production, themes, aesthetics, and cultural impact of that landmark work in some detail.

Lynch returned to film with the hyper-violent black road comedy *Wild at Heart* (1990), which again drew mixed reactions from critics and fans (it did net the Palme d'Or at Cannes, as well as angry protests), following it with a film prequel to *Twin Peaks* called *Fire Walk with Me* (1992), about which we have much to say in the following pages. In a nutshell: it was wildly divisive, critically panned, and an absolutely fascinating example of a unique filmmaking sensibility given its full head.

Lost Highway arrived in 1997, another sinister and otherworldly crime story distinguished by Lynch's extraordinary visuals and narrative puzzles. He followed it with a complete left turn: *The Straight Story* (1999), an economical and affecting tale of an elderly man who goes to extraordinary lengths to visit an ailing brother. It featured nary a doppelgänger or grinning maniac, and the critical reception was warm. Lynch returned to his former full glory (as far as critics were concerned) with his masterful, melancholy Hollywood fantasia *Mullholland Dr.* (2001), a complete return to form that boasted all of the emotional power, unsettling strangeness, and lush, perverse romanticism of *Blue Velvet*. The film wowed critics and audiences, but the victory had a bitter edge: ironically, the project was initially planned as a television series, but ABC—the network that brought *Twin Peaks* to the air—turned it down. He was again nominated by the Academy for Best Director, and won Best Director awards at the Cannes film festival and the New York Film Critics Association.

Lynch has continued to follow his muse, painting, sculpting, composing music, and making films, such as the mystifying, formally rigorous *Inland Empire* (2006). He has married and divorced several times, fathered children, dated international supermodel Isabella Rossellini, written and drawn the comic strip *The Angriest Dog in the World*, and proselytized for Transcendental Meditation. In 2014 Lynch announced plans to revive *Twin Peaks* on the Showtime cable network.

Mark Frost

"The Other Peak," the *Los Angeles Times* called him in July 1990, acknowledging the obvious: in the media frenzy surrounding *Twin Peaks*, Mark Frost had been consumed by the imperial shadow of David Lynch. We get it: Lynch was one of America's most charismatic filmmakers, with a repertoire ranging from avant-garde to mainstream studio film to mega-budget sci-fi to psycho thriller. Critics loved him or loved to hate him, but were never indifferent. Frost was . . . you know . . . the TV guy.

So unjust.

By every inside account, Frost was as integral to the identity and success of *Twin Peaks* as anyone, and not just logistically. Yes, as the experienced television producer he was point man with ABC executives, which involved, among other things, hurdling network-imposed obstacles. But Frost is a creative guy, and that's where his imprint is most pronounced. He wrote five of the first season's eight episodes—the first three (including the pilot) with Lynch, a process that he compared, in an April 8, 1990, *New York Times* article, to the Vulcan mind meld: "You throw your minds up toward the ceiling and they meet somewhere near the light fixtures. The script becomes written by a third party. The author is someone called Lynch-Frost" (even Frost gives Lynch top billing!). Frost directed the season-one finale, and has teleplay credit—singly or jointly—on six of the second season's twenty-two installments. But *Twin Peaks* writers interviewed over the years have without exception stressed Frost's complete immersion in the scripting process: mapping out stories, bouncing around ideas, tapping writers, providing outlines (especially detailed in the first season, when the creative team had the luxury of time), conversing with Lynch, and finally reviewing and editing scripts, not just scene by scene, but line by line. Among actors Frost wins kudos for his snappy, sophisticated dialog, and his voice is especially channeled through so-called verbal characters—in other words, those who like to talk, like Benjamin Horne and Albert Rosenfield (or, on *Hill Street Blues*, where he worked previously, redneck Officer Andrew Renko and silver-tongued Sergeant Phil "Let's Be Careful Out There" Esterhaus). Kyle MacLachlan touts Frost's dry, offbeat sense of humor and deadpan delivery, saying he tapped into both (along with numerous Lynchian quirks and mannerisms, of course) in bringing Dale Cooper to life.

Everyone praises Lynch for concocting the Red Room, Killer Bob, and the dancing dwarf (and rightly so—all strokes of genius), but Frost's abiding interests in theosophy (the Black and White lodges), Sherlock Holmes (Windom Earle), and Arthurian legend (Glastonbury Grove) figure just as prominently in the mythology of the series. Plus, Frost recruited so many behind-the-scenes contributors, including Harley Peyton and Robert Engels, writer-producers who went on to play hugely influential roles in the evolution of *Twin Peaks'* narrative and characters (Engels even cowrote *Twin Peaks: Fire Walk with Me* with Lynch).

"Other Peak?" We prefer "Twin Peak."

Cocreator Mark Frost, playing a television news reporter in the first season of *Twin Peaks*.

Frost had been writing for television on and off for fifteen years by the time *Twin Peaks* premiered in 1990. Initially raised in New York (where his father, Warren—Doc Hayward on *Twin Peaks*—was stage-managing and acting on live early-television anthology dramas), Frost moved to Los Angeles at a young age, then spent his high school years in Minneapolis, while his father taught acting at the University of Minnesota. Mark Frost moved on to Carnegie Mellon University in Pittsburgh, studying acting, directing, and playwriting, but left school early to join fellow Carnegie Mellon alumnus Steven Bochco at Universal Pictures in Los Angeles, landing a writing gig at ABC's *The Six Million Dollar Man*, the action/adventure/sci-fi series starring Lee Majors as a bionic former NASA astronaut (Frost wrote two episodes, both airing in 1975, and earned college credit doing it, so that he was able to graduate). He also wrote for NBC's *Sunshine*, a short-lived half-hour series about a musician widower and his young stepdaughter, and *Lucas Tanner*, starring David Hartman as a former pro baseball player turned English teacher in Webster Groves, Missouri (a St. Louis suburb that was the subject of a very famous, and very controversial, 1966 CBS documentary called *16 in Webster Groves*). Finding the work unsatisfying—go figure—Frost returned to Minneapolis, working as a literary associate and playwright at the Guthrie Theater and writing, producing, and directing documentaries for the local PBS outlet, including *The Road Back*, about a rehabilitation program for juvenile felons.

Frost returned to the City of Angels in 1982, accepting an invitation from Bochco to write for the groundbreaking police procedural *Hill Street Blues*, where he worked until 1985, earning an Emmy nomination and a Writers Guild of America Award (during this time he also scripted a single episode of NBC's *Gavilan*, another instantly forgettable TV drama, this one starring Robert Urich as a former spy turned oceanographer—how do they come up with these ideas?). Frost ankled *Hill Street* with the intention of crafting more personal work, and though he wrote two episodes of the well-regarded CBS crime drama *The Equalizer* that aired in 1986 ("Wash Up" and "No Conscience"), it was around this time that he teamed with Lynch to adapt Anthony Summers's *Goddess: The Secret Lives of Marilyn Monroe* into a thinly veiled biopic titled *Venus Descending*. While that project, and two others with Lynch, never saw the light of day, the pairing, of course, led to *Twin Peaks*, as well *American Chronicles*, a short-form-documentary series airing briefly on Fox in 1990, and *On the Air*, a criminally underappreciated 1992 sitcom about a hilariously incompetent television network in the 1950s, whose stars included *Twin Peaks* alum Ian Buchanan (Dick Tremayne), Miguel Ferrer (Albert Rosenfield), and David L. Lander (Tim Pinkle)— seven episodes were made, but, sadly, only three aired. Although credited as an executive producer on the Lynch-directed 1992 theatrical film *Twin Peaks: Fire Walk with Me*, Frost was not involved in the making of the film, which he has attributed to a disagreement with Lynch over its timeline: Frost wanted to pick up where the TV series had left off, while Lynch was intent on making a prequel.

While Frost took a break from TV in the aftermath of *Twin Peaks* and *On the Air*, he later returned, exec-producing *Buddy Faro*, a 1998 CBS crime drama (which he also created), and *All Souls*, a 2001 horror show for UPN, both short-lived.

Frost launched his feature-film career with the screenplay for the 1987 occult film *The Believers*, directed by John Schlesinger (*Midnight Cowboy*). *Storyville*, a New Orleans-set political thriller starring James Spader and Jason Robards—written and directed by Frost—was released in 1992, though Frost had worked on it extensively during the second season of *Twin Peaks*, leaving some members of the cast dismayed that he wasn't around as often as in season one (they felt the same way about Lynch). Ironically, the

It's a hit: *Twin Peaks* merchandise for the fans.   *Photo by Pieter Dom*

film was championed by Lynch's old nemesis Roger Ebert, who awarded it 3.5 out of 4 stars, and even here couldn't resist taking a shot at Lynch: "With Lynch's recent work, it's as if he wants you to know he's superior to the material. Frost doesn't mind being implicated—he likes this kind of stuff, and plunges into the dark waters of his plot with real joy." That same year Frost executive-produced a documentary about *Playboy*'s Hugh Hefner, titled *Once Upon a Time*. Later film work includes the 2005 adaptation of his own nonfiction book about golf, *The Greatest Game Ever Played*, plus the screenplays for two Fantastic Four movies (*Fantastic Four*, 2005, and *Fantastic Four: Rise of the Silver Surfer*, 2007).

Frost also boasts a flourishing authorial career, with nonfiction books about golf and baseball, but also several novels, including two occult-themed yarns of particular interest to *Twin Peaks* deconstructionists, since they present themes and characters evocative of *Peaks* mythology: *The List of Seven* (1993) and its sequel, *The Six Messiahs* (1995). The protagonists in both books are Arthur Conan Doyle, the creator of Sherlock Holmes, and a fictional character named Jack Sparks, clearly modeled after Holmes.

What They Really Wanted to Do Was Direct

Unsurprisingly, David Lynch directed more episodes of *Twin Peaks* than anyone else: a total of six, including the feature-length pilot, which set the template for all other directors to follow (Lynch, of course, also helmed the 1992 theatrical prequel *Twin Peaks: Fire Walk with Me*). When all cylinders were running, the process went like this: directors were handed their script, which they read, followed by a meeting with Lynch and Frost, and then off they went to shoot the episode. Lynch would view their work during the sound mix, which would leave enough time to repair anything that needed fixing. As Frost told Brad Dukes in *Reflections: An Oral History of Twin Peaks*: "I think everyone understood that was the assignment: work with the house style and the mood that David had so brilliantly created and then bring whatever you can of yourself to add to that."

More surprising is who comes in second: Lesli Linka Glatter, with four episodes (five, ten, thirteen, twenty-three). Though today a veteran TV director with over sixty credits, including many of the small screen's most distinguished dramas (*Homeland, Mad Men, The Walking Dead,* and *The West Wing* among them), Glatter was relatively unknown when tapped for her *Twin Peaks* debut, having helmed just three installments of the NBC anthology show *Amazing Stories* (created by Steven Spielberg, plus the *St. Elsewhere/Northern Exposure* team of Joshua Brand and John Falsey) and a long-forgotten TV movie titled *Into the Homeland* (with a cast including *Twin Peaks'* Leo Johnson, Eric Da Re, as "Male Surfer #1"). Like Lynch, Glatter is a graduate of the American Film Institute, and it was her 1985 Oscar-nominated short film *Tales of Meeting and Parting* that brought her to Spielberg's attention and launched her TV career.

Caleb Deschanel, Duwayne Dunham, and Tim Hunter all directed three episodes of *Twin Peaks*. Deschanel (episodes six, fifteen, and nineteen) also was an inexperienced television director when tapped for his first episode of the series, but had two feature films to his credit (*The Escape Artist, Crusoe*). He too attended the American Film Institute, concurrently with Lynch. Today he is one of Hollywood's most accomplished cinematographers, with Oscar nominations for *The Right Stuff, The Natural, Fly Away Home, The Patriot,* and *The Passion of Christ*. Deschanel's daughters, Emily and Zooey, are both established television stars (*Bones* and *New Girl*, respectively), and his wife, Mary Jo, portrayed Eileen Hayward on *Twin Peaks*.

Dunham (episodes one, eighteen, and twenty-five) was a neophyte director, but landed the choice assignment of helming episode one ("Traces to Nowhere")—the first director not named David Lynch to take on a *Twin*

Peaks assignment. Dunham had edited the pilot, and later the season-two opener, both Lynch-directed episodes. He possessed some shiny film-editing medals as well, including two little films called *The Empire Strikes Back* and *Return of the Jedi*. As an editor he had worked with Lynch on *Blue Velvet* and was editing *Wild at Heart* as the first season of *Twin Peaks* was airing.

Hunter (episodes four, sixteen, and twenty-eight) had attended AFI with Lynch and Deschanel; he was one of the bigger-name directors to lend his skills to *Twin Peaks*, having made a splash with the 1986 theatrical film *River's Edge*, which helped launch the careers of Crispin Glover and Keanu Reeves and earned Hunter an Independent Spirit Award nomination. Like *Twin Peaks*, *River's Edge* pivots on the murder of a high school girl, found, well, at the river's edge. Having also helmed episode twenty-eight ("Miss Twin Peaks"), Hunter is the last person not named David Lynch to have directed an installment of the series.

Tina Rathborne and Todd Holland each directed two episodes of *Twin Peaks*. Rathborne (episodes three and seventeen) had directed Lynch in his first significant acting role, in *Zelly and Me* (1988), which starred his then-girlfriend Isabella Rossellini, who was originally tapped for the role of Andrew Packard's wife (a character that eventually mutated into Josie Packard, portrayed by Joan Chen), but had to bow out due to scheduling conflicts.

Holland helmed two season-two episodes (eleven and twenty); the former ("Laura's Secret Diary") features one of the series' most inventive opening scenes, in which the camera burrows inside the acoustic tiles of the walls in the interrogation room at the sheriff's station as Leland Palmer confesses to the murder of Jacques Renault. Holland dreamed that one up himself; the only direction in the script was that Leland was being questioned. Holland had previously helmed episodes of *Amazing Stories* and *Max Headroom*, and today is a major TV director, with Emmys for his work on *Malcolm in the Middle* and *The Larry Sanders Show*.

Each of the following directed a single episode of *Twin Peaks*: Mark Frost, Graeme Clifford, Uli Edel, James Foley, Stephen Gyllenhaal, Diane Keaton, and Jonathan Sanger.

Aussie Clifford had three theatrical films on his *résumé* by the time he joined *Twin Peaks* for episode twelve ("The Orchid's Curse"), including the critically acclaimed 1982 biopic *Frances*, earning Jessica Lange an Oscar nomination for her portrayal of troubled actress Frances Farmer.

Edel, helmer of episode twenty-one ("Double Play"), had directed a number of television programs in his home country, Germany, before tackling the 1989 film adaptation of Hubert Selby Jr.'s controversial novel *Last Exit to Brooklyn*, about emotionally wounded Brooklynites teetering on the edge of society. Edel's connection to Lynch was that he had directed the German trailer for *Dune*.

Foley was an accomplished Hollywood film director by the time he joined *Twin Peaks* for episode twenty-four ("Wounds and Scars"), having worked—separately—on both sides of the Madonna-Sean Penn equation, with *At Close Range*, *Who's That Girl*, and *Madonna: The Immaculate Collection*, plus the 1990 neo-noir adaptation of Jim Thompson's *After Dark, My Sweet*.

Gyllenhaal was an established TV director when arriving at the tail end of the series to direct episode twenty-seven ("The Path to the Black Lodge"), whose credits included the 1990 telepic *A Killing in a Small Town*, based on a real-life Texas murder, earning actress Barbara Hershey a Golden Globe. He is the father of actors Maggie and Jake Gyllenhaal.

Keaton was an Oscar-winning actress best known for *Annie Hall* and other collaborations with Woody Allen, plus her appearances in *Reds* and the *Godfather* movies, by the time she joined *Twin Peaks* for episode twenty-two ("Slaves and Masters"), which blissfully concludes the much derided James Hurley-Evelyn Marsh arc. Keaton had little directing experience up to that point, though she had helmed an episode of ABC's *China Beach*, plus the documentary *Heaven* and a *CBS Schoolbreak Special*.

Jonathan Sanger also had only a handful of episodic television credits when tapped to direct episode twenty-six ("Variations on Relations"), though he was a producer on the 1980 theatrical film *The Elephant Man*, which earned David Lynch an Oscar nomination for Best Director.

The Write Staff

Harley Peyton was the most prolific *credited* writer on *Twin Peaks*, solely or collaboratively contributing thirteen of the thirty scripts. Mark Frost is next, with eleven teleplay credits, though of course Frost oversaw all of the writing and would go over scripts with writers scene by scene. Robert Engels is credited solely or partially with ten teleplays, in addition to coscripting *Fire Walk with Me* with Lynch.

Peyton, born and raised in *Twin Peaks* country (Spokane, Washington), was a writer on the first season of the series, scripting two episodes, one nominated for an Emmy. For the second season he was bumped up to producer. He got his first big break in Hollywood penning the screenplay for the 1987 adaptation of Bret Easton Ellis's novel *Less Than Zero*, starring Brat Packer Andrew McCarthy, plus Jami Gertz and Robert Downey Jr. Peyton attended the Directors Guild of America preview screening of the *Twin Peaks* pilot at the invitation of his friend Mark Frost (the two belonged to the same fantasy baseball league). Peyton's post-*TP* work includes the feature film *Friends with Benefits*, starring Mila Kunis and Justin Timberlake, for which he shares story credit. He created and executive-produced the short-lived *Moonlighting* wannabe *Moon over Miami*, and also was co-executive producer on the 2013–2014 series *Dracula*, starring Jonathan Rhys Meyers, and the 1993 reboot of *Route 66*. He wrote and executive-produced the 2001 theatrical film *Bandits*, directed by Barry Levinson and starring Bruce Willis, Billy Bob Thornton, and Cate Blanchett.

Engels was a made member of the Minnesota mafia Mark Frost rounded up for *Twin Peaks*, which also included Richard Hoover (production designer), Chris Mulkey (Hank Jennings), Kenneth Welsh (Windom Earle), and of course Mark's dad Warren (Doc Hayward) and brother Scott (writer). Engels was credited strictly as a writer on the first season of the series, but was promoted first to executive story editor and then to coproducer on the second. He and Frost went back almost twenty years; Warren Frost was Engels's college adviser at the University of Minnesota, and Engels had trained as an actor at the Guthrie Theater, where Mark Frost had also worked. Engels eventually headed to New York, where he acted in commercials and daytime soaps before shifting to documentary writing for HBO and Showtime. When first writing for *Twin Peaks*, he was concurrently story editing/writing for the CBS crime show *Wiseguy*, which curiously included a "Lynchboro Arc" about a serial killer in the Northwest in the winter of 1990—after the first season of *Twin Peaks* had been shot, but before it aired. Hmmm. After *Twin Peaks*, Engels moved over to the short-lived Lynch-Frost sitcom *On the Air*. Of course, he also coscripted *Twin Peaks: Fire Walk with Me* with Lynch, which they followed up with two never-produced screenplays: *The Dream of the Bovine*, about three erstwhile cows who are transformed into men (we kid you not), and *In Heaven*, about a man forced to marry an unattractive woman who suddenly becomes beautiful. Engels's subsequent TV work includes Gene Roddenberry's *Andromeda* (2002–2005). His wife Jill portrayed Trudy, the waitress at the Great Northern.

Other writers who contributed teleplays to *Twin Peaks* were Barry Pullman (four); Lynch (three); Scott Frost and Tricia Brock (two apiece); and Jerry Stahl (one, though not really, according to all accounts).

Pullman had written for *Shannon's Law* and *Against the Law* before contributing to *TP*, and went on to work as a writer and/or producer on numerous network shows, including *Roswell* and Mark Frost's *Buddy Faro*.

In addition to contributing two teleplays to *Twin Peaks*, Scott Frost wrote the 1991 companion book *The Autobiography of F.B.I. Agent Dale Cooper: My Life, My Tapes*. He went on to write for Gene Roddenberry's *Andromeda*, along with Robert Engels.

Brock (Harley Peyton's first wife) made her network-TV writing debut on *Twin Peaks*, and has gone on to become an established television director, with credits including *The Walking Dead* and *Girls* (odd combo, that).

Stahl struggled on his one assignment for *Twin Peaks* (episode eleven, "Laura's Secret Diary"), being in the throes of heroin addiction at the time (as recounted in his 1995 book *Permanent Midnight: A Memoir*, later adapted into a feature film starring Ben Stiller), and the aberrational teleplay credit reads "Jerry Stahl and Mark Frost & Harley Peyton & Robert Engels." Stahl had written previously for *thirtysomething*, *Moonlighting*, and—believe it or not—*ALF*.

3

In a Dream, Are All the Characters Really You?

Dossiers: Principal Characters

FBI Special Agent Dale Cooper (Kyle MacLachlan)

A cademics love to write about Dale Cooper. "Agent Cooper's Errand in the Wilderness: *Twin Peaks* and American Mythology." "Patterns and Conflicts: An Analysis of the Windom Earle/Dale Cooper Chess Game." "Cooper's Failure as Protector of the Middle Class" (whoa, *huge* burden there).

That's swell, if it's your bent. Around these parts we like to keep things simpler. We think Cooper is awesome (*Blue Velvet*'s Jeffrey Beaumont "all grown up," as MacLachlan likes to say). You might say he likes to wear black and white, but is not himself black and white, except that in the series finale, in the Black Lodge, he *is* black and white, metaphorically speaking. Academic Andreas Blassmann has written of Cooper's "Bi-Part Soul," which Edgar Allan Poe had evoked with respect to C. Auguste Dupin in "The Murders in the Rue Morgue," but fortunately we are not academics and therefore not required to explain this concept any further.

Here's why Cooper is *the* (G-)man:

Cooper is portrayed by Kyle MacLachlan: Cooper was the first role cast, the third collaboration between MacLachlan and Lynch (*Dune, Blue Velvet*). Everyone involved in his depiction agrees Cooper is an amalgam of MacLachlan, Lynch, and Frost, but MacLachlan told Brad Dukes in *Reflections: An Oral History of Twin Peaks* that he was especially channeling Lynch in mannerisms and speech. Frost, though, penned many of Cooper's monologues. MacLachlan bummed out *Peaks* fans by initially refusing to reprise the role in *Fire Walk with Me*, but it worked out great, because we wound up with

Chet Desmond, and MacLachlan eventually accepted a smaller role anyway. Win-win. Only wish we could have seen Cooper and Desmond in a scene together (Showtime, are you listening?).

Cooper is kooky: Cooper's no babe in the woods—after all, the woman he loved died in his arms from stab wounds inflicted by her husband, whom the two of them were cuckolding—but he's infectiously childlike, boundlessly curious, and guilelessly enthralled by everything he can hear, see, smell, taste, and touch, from Douglas firs to snowshoe rabbits to coffee, doughnuts, and pie. He dictates every detail of his life into a mini-tape recorder, to some woman named Diane who we conclude is his secretary, though we never see her, and you have to wonder why she would even care about the price of his tuna fish sandwich on whole wheat. He actually says things like "There's nothing quite like urinating out in the open air." When he asks Annie Blackburne out a date, it's a nature study. Working undercover on the Palmer investigation at One Eyed Jacks, he *thanks* an escort for propositioning him (and declines, of course). We could go on, but you get the point.

Ich bein ein **Cooper:** Roughly translated: We are Cooper. Cooper is us. Outsider. Truth-seeker (somebody has to be in this serpentine town). Stranger in a strange land. Continental Op in Poisonville. He falls in love with Twin Peaks as much as we do. Sure, he stirs up a mess o' trouble poking at hornets' nests. Jean Renault tells him so: "Before you came here, Twin Peaks was a simple place." Now it's a simple nightmare. "Maybe you brought the nightmare with you," Renault says. Not exactly true, but not exactly false either. Josie Packard pumps three holes in him because she's sick and tired of his meddling. Windom Earle's murder spree, Annie's abduction . . . would any of this have happened if not for Cooper? Never mind that Renault is himself a nightmare (liar, drug dealer, murderer; that's just above the fold). The point is that Cooper's arrival in Twin Peaks coincides (more or less) with our own; his journey is ours, and whatever impact he has on the town we do as well, by proxy.

Cooper is brilliant: So much has been written about Cooper's deviation from ratiocinative Western detectives like Dupin and Sherlock Holmes through his embrace of higher-consciousness techniques like dreams, intuition, the Tibetan rock throw (not to mention magic and luck), but Cooper is proficient in the art of reckoning, too. We see this especially in the early episodes, when he serially astounds Harry by decoding who is sleeping with whom ("body language"), and also when he deduces that Laura and Donna were videotaped at the picnic by a biker, after spotting the reflection of a motorcycle in Laura's eye. Elementary? Yeah, right.

Cooper is honorable: Essential for any pantheonic investigator, of course. We know this because Raymond Chandler said so, and if Chandler said so, it's true. "Down these mean streets a man must go who is not himself mean, who is neither tarnished nor afraid," Chandler wrote in "The Simple Art

A second-season romance was brewing between Audrey and Cooper, until Kyle MacLachlan or then-girlfriend Lara Flynn Boyle kiboshed it.

of Murder." Cooper goes down mean streets, mean dreams, mean lodges. Lots of meanies in Twin Peaks. Uncommon? You bet. Weird, you might say. Uncommonly perceptive, attentive, noble, heroic. But common, too. He protects the middle class, for Pete's sake! (Or tries to.) His disregard for wealth and status—witness his disdain for Ben Horne—would make any flinty shamus proud. Unafraid? We acknowledge the debate, given the Black Lodge debacle in the series finale, but the guy offers to sacrifice his soul for the woman he loves. We call that fearless. Tarnished? See following entry. But bottom line: you *have* to be an honorable man to rebuff Audrey Horne on principle when she's laying buck naked in your bed, right?

Cooper is imperfect: "You know, there's only one problem with you: you're perfect," Audrey Horne tells Cooper. Close, but no cigar. If Cooper were perfect, he'd be unbearable. He makes mistakes. (We're not gonna talk about the flannel shirts. In fact, we're not gonna talk about the flannel shirts at all.) The biggest mistake Cooper ever made has haunted him every day of his life ever since: He carried on with Caroline Earle, the wife of his then-partner, Windom Earle. We're not rendering moral judgment on Cooper's role in Caroline's extramarital affair—after all, they loved each other, and Windom was a batty hatter—but he endangered her welfare, and she wound up dying in his arms. (Cooper tells Audrey he doesn't have secrets, but this is untrue, as we discover in the latter half of season two, when the narrative swerves from Laura's secrets to Cooper's.) Cooper suffers from J. J. Gittes syndrome, named after the snakebit gumshoe in Roman Polanski's (no relation to Ronette Pulaski) 1974 retro-noir *Chinatown*, who fails to protect the woman he loves—twice. We're thinking his obsessive need for order is the direct result of that moment in time four years prior when it totally eluded him.

Cooper is empathetic/compassionate/decent: Whereas Albert Rosenfield antagonizes everyone in Twin Peaks with incessant putdowns about "chowder-head yokels" and "blithering hayseeds," Cooper goes the opposite route, meeting people on *their* terms, eventually coming to appreciate the town so much he contemplates putting down roots there. He backs Sheriff Truman over Albert—a fellow J. Edgar—even while there's no denying Truman walloped Albert in the face, because—let's face it—Albert had it coming. It's the right thing to do. Note how Cooper tenderly restores Laura's arm to its rightful place in the morgue in the immediate aftermath of the Rosenfield-Truman bout, or how accepting Cooper is of DEA Agent Dennis/Denise Bryson's transgenderification. Above all, think of Cooper navigating a dying Leland Palmer "into the light" and toward redemption from Laura, drawing from the *Bardo Thodol* (*Tibetan Book of the Dead*), or consoling a bereft Sarah Palmer in the prelude to Leland's funeral, ending with, "Mrs. Palmer, I would be honored to drive you." What a mensch!

Cooper is gifted: This we know because Major Briggs says so, and Major Briggs is like the Raymond Chandler of Air Force officers: if he says so it must *be* so. "You sir, were blessed with certain gifts," he says. Margaret Lanterman also knows this, and she is the Raymond Chandler of log ladies. Even Albert Rosenfield knows it! Near the end of the Laura Palmer case Albert Rosenfield tells Cooper he has no clue where the trail leads next, but "the only one of us with the coordinates for this destination and its hardware is you."

So exactly what are these gifts? Cooper is, as Martha P. Nochimson and numerous other scholars and critics have pointed out, a boundary-crosser, (how appropriate then that he is summoned to Twin Peaks because Ronette Pulaski steps out over the state line). He is willing to step outside the lines himself—both physically, as when he crosses over into Canada to interrogate Jacques Renault, and again to rescue Audrey Horne, and metaphysically, by embracing unconventional methods of detection. He has visions, precognitive dreams even. His Tibetan dream endowed him with "the deepest level of intuition." Whereas early on he is reluctant to ask the Log Lady's log for help with the Palmer investigation, by season two he is asking not only the log for help, but also a giant and an inhabiting spirit with one arm.

Everyone talks to Cooper, even if half the time we have no idea what they're talking about. Audrey prays to him. Laura tells him who killed her. At the end of *Fire Walk with Me*, Laura celebrates her liberation, presumably in the White Lodge, with her guardian angel, which makes sense, but Cooper? She never even met the guy, other than in dreams. Only two types of people see Bob, says the One-Armed Man: the gifted and the damned. Cooper is both, poor guy.

Laura Palmer (Sheryl Lee)

Laura Palmer, the all-American dream girl—beautiful, blonde, charitable, industrious, the iconic small-town homecoming queen immortalized in that haunting framed photo (an actual relic of actress Sheryl Lee's high school career) that would become one of the signature images of *Twin Peaks*—

was hiding so very much. Laura was also a drug addict, prostitute, secret girlfriend to bikers and businessmen, and, most crucially, a victim of sustained, horrific abuse. Laura's public and private lives connected her to every aspect of Twin Peaks society, from the Meals on Wheels program to the revels at the bordello/casino One Eyed Jacks, and for this reason, her murder, the inciting event of the entire series, affects the community of

The iconic image of Laura Palmer, Twin Peaks golden girl and tragic victim. The photo was a relic of actress Sheryl Lee's actual high school days.   *ABC/Photofest*

Twin Peaks on a molecular level. Everyone has a stake in Laura's death, and in the secrets she harbored.

Before turning to *Twin Peaks*, Lynch and Frost were working on a project (never completed) about the tragic life of Marilyn Monroe, and many elements of Monroe's story would inform the creation of Laura Palmer (although the name "Laura" is likely a reference to the 1944 Otto Preminger film of the same name, which concerns the fallout following the presumed murder of a beautiful young woman, who is apparently killed before the action of the movie; see sidebar on *Laura* in Chapter 5), including her beguiling beauty and sex appeal, her disarming mixture of girlish innocence and carnal availability, her exploitation at the hands of powerful men, and the lurid mystery and speculation surrounding her untimely death. It's an archetype tailor-made for Lynch, a stark example of light/dark duality and the horrors hidden in the everyday and familiar.

As the story begins with Laura dead, wrapped in plastic, the viewer becomes acquainted with the young woman through indirect means. We see her in home movie footage, frolicking with her best friend, the virtuous Donna Hayward (the footage is shot by her secret biker boyfriend, James Hurley), we hear her voice on audiocassettes sent to her therapist, and we see the effect her loss has on those who knew and loved her, in many cases inspiring outsized outpourings of bathos that tread that thin Lynchian line separating the disturbingly strange and the grotesquely funny. It's a canny strategy; Laura functions in the narrative as a kind of repository for the community's fantasies and collective guilt—she was not wholly seen or understood by anyone, and these fleeting glimpses and hints allow the viewer to likewise construct the persona of Laura Palmer according to his or her own lights. She is like a still pond under moonlight, hiding its mysterious depths beneath the reflection of whoever's looking.

Over the course of the series (and the prequel film, *Twin Peaks: Fire Walk with Me*, which puts Laura—and Lee's devastating, no-holds-barred performance—front and center), we learn that Laura has been the victim of sexual abuse from girlhood, and that her image as the perfect high school student masked her proclivities for cocaine and selling sex, urges emanating from the intense self-hatred and desire for oblivion that are the fruits of her degradation. She "officially" dated popular jock Bobby Briggs, but secretly loved brooding biker James Hurley, and she lived with unspeakable horror and pain. Most shockingly, we discover that Laura's abuser and murderer was her own father—and that he committed these abominable acts while under the influence of the malevolent spirit called "Bob," who had long fixated on Laura. The abrupt resolution of the storyline (the timing mandated by ABC programming executives fearful of alienating the audience), after such an enigmatic unfolding of the mysteries surrounding Laura's life, disappointed many, including Lynch himself, who relished the continuation of the mystery as a conduit for the exploration this "place most wonderful and strange."

As *Twin Peaks* blossomed into an unlikely media sensation, "Who killed Laura Palmer?" became the series' hook line, reminiscent of the "Who shot J.R.?" phenomenon of an earlier TV generation's nighttime soap opera obsession. But unlike *Dallas*, an enjoyably shallow exercise in melodramatic archetypes and absurd plot mechanics, *Twin Peaks* had other things on its mind. *Who* killed Laura Palmer wasn't at all the point. *Twin Peaks* is not the story of a murder investigation, and Laura Palmer is not a plot device. She is a catalyst, a window into another, stranger world that is disturbingly similar to our own, and she is full of secrets.

Leland Palmer (Ray Wise)

If Laura Palmer is the heart of *Twin Peaks*, her father, Leland, represents its sick, divided soul. On the surface, Leland is one of the community's most solid, respectable citizens, a successful attorney (he handles Ben Horne's legal work) and devoted family man. Of course, he is also the host for the sadistic and murderous Bob, apparently a spirit of pure evil, who periodically possesses Leland to perpetrate rape and murder—most horrifically, of Leland's own daughter, Laura.

So, Leland good, Bob bad? It's not that simple. Leland and Bob go way back—it's implied that Bob (a neighbor) molested Leland himself in Leland's boyhood—and it can be difficult to determine to what extent Leland is directly controlled by a demonic entity versus his conscious participation in a cycle of abuse. For instance, when, in *Fire Walk with Me*, Leland plans an orgy with some high school–aged prostitutes, only to flee in panic when he recognizes Laura as one of the participants, it certainly doesn't look like the reaction feral Bob would have; it looks like the furtive terror of a guilty father. Likewise, it's Leland's bloodlust driving the action when he murders the helpless Jacques Renault. But what Leland knows and doesn't know (or chooses to know and not know) is one of *Twin Peaks'* unsettling, unanswerable questions. His increasingly unhinged behavior in the aftermath of Laura's killing, which features manic, compulsive singing and dancing, can be read as an unconscious indicator of guilt: he's been "performing" the

Father, monster, victim: Leland Palmer.

part of upstanding husband and father for years, and at this crisis point his performance becomes literalized as desperate song and dance routines, a grotesquely exaggerated burlesque of a man putting on a show.

Wise's performance is astonishing in its range and power: Leland is by turns tragicomic in his eccentric paroxysms of grief and terrifying when under the influence of Bob—his murder of his niece Maddy is one of the most wrenchingly traumatic sequences in the history of network television. And yet, even at his most abject and monstrous, Leland remains heartbreakingly human, as Wise's expressive face and raw, fearlessly emotional performance constantly remind us that Leland is a man in constant, overwhelming pain, as lost, corrupted, and damaged by the crimes he has committed as his victim, Laura. Leland's death is both horrific and redemptive: the tormented man kills himself by bashing his head into the wall, a final, desperate, self-sacrificing attempt to thwart Bob.

A noble and fittingly cathartic conclusion to the tragic life of Leland Palmer . . . but in *Twin Peaks*, every ray of light casts an equivalent shadow: we see Leland—or his doppelgänger, to be precise—once more, in the Red Room, where he tells Cooper that he never killed anybody. If this is Leland's evil, Bob-possessed aspect (and if he's telling the truth), the implication here is that Leland's crimes were in fact committed by Leland himself, under his own control. Is Bob an autonomous hijacker of earthly bodies, a metaphor for the evil contained in the human soul, or a psychologically constructed evasion to protect Leland from the truth about himself? Which answer is the most disturbing? And who, really, killed Laura Palmer?

Sheriff Harry S. Truman (Michael Ontkean)

Yes, Harry is a true man and a steady man (original name: Dan Steadman). Yes, the buck stops with Harry, and yes, Harry gives 'em hell. But those are all cheap jokes, and we would never stoop so low. In a 1990 ABC-TV special previewing *Twin Peaks'* second season, Ontkean says he's always thought of Harry (the last major character cast) as the designated driver. He's got that Will Kane vibe going on, and not just because of the cowpoke hat. He's equable, just, loyal, valiant, and decent, which is no small thing in Twin Peaks. Harry has just one weakness, and her name is Josie Packard. As weaknesses go it's a bad one to have, since she is a liar and a murderer. Josie dies, and Harry goes on an epic bender. He trashes the Bookhouse and yells at Cooper. This is so not like Harry, but we all have bad days. He nearly dies when Thomas Eckhardt's assistant, Jones, tries to strangle him in the midst of straddling him, in retaliation for loving Josie. On the plus side it distracts him from his rage. Harry goes back to work, helping Cooper confront the cosmic mysteries of Twin Peaks. Harry feels like Dr. Watson to Cooper's Holmes. We know this because Harry says he feels like Dr. Watson to Cooper's Holmes. Who doesn't love Dr. Watson? Harry is a Bookhouse Boy. The Bookhouse Boys are cool. They fight the evil in the woods. When Cooper needs someone to fly wingman on his furtive mission across the Canadian border to rescue Audrey Horne, who do you think it is? Harry!

Did we mention that Harry is valiant? When Cooper is suspended and the agent in charge of the investigation solicits Harry's cooperation, Harry says, "I suggest you take that cooperation and stuff it." Harry waits hours and hours and hours for Cooper to return from the Black Lodge, never leaving Glastonbury Grove (not even for a bathroom break, as best we can tell). Did we mention that Harry was loyal? When Albert tries to drill a hole in Laura Palmer's head in order to conduct an autopsy instead of releasing the body to the family for the funeral, who do you think punches Albert in the face? Harry! Did we mention that Harry was decent? When Leland Palmer is finally unmasked as Laura's killer and Bob kind of pops out from inside of him in the interrogation room, so that Leland is acting like a psycho-killer, who do you think it is who can't wrap his head around the notion that Leland was demonically possessed? Harry! Did we mention that Harry was pragmatic? Little-known fact: Ray Wise, who wound up portraying Leland, auditioned for the role of Harry first. Did we mention that casting director Johanna Ray was a genius?

Bobby Briggs (Dana Ashbrook)

Is Bobby Briggs a villain? He certainly begins the series looking like a total creep, an abusive bullying jock and low-level drug pusher who cheats on his homecoming queen girlfriend with a married woman. In fact, he was the blackguard who provided Laura Palmer with cocaine! On closer inspection, young Mr. Briggs reveals hidden depths. True, he worked with truly vile men like Jacques Renault and Leo Johnson to bring drugs over the border . . . but only because Laura needed him to do so to ensure a steady supply for herself. His fraught relationship with Shelly Johnson is alternately sordid (adultery/attempting to exploit her brain-damaged husband) and sweet (bravely intervening to save Shelly from the murderous Leo, and industriously applying himself as Ben Horne's assistant in an effort to support them when their insurance scheme fizzles). Most tellingly, in unguarded moments of high emotion Bobby reveals a truly sensitive side, railing against the town's hypocrisy at Laura's funeral and welling with tears when his upright military father expresses his boundless love and high expectations for his wayward son. Major Briggs is no fool; does he foresee a Prince Hal–like transformation in store for Bobby? Dana Ashbrook, a lanky, handsome young actor with arguably the show's most era-specific hairstyle, was one of *Twin Peaks'* most dynamic and exciting performers, an unpredictable live wire equally convincing barking like a mad dog to intimidate James, vibrating with lust and wild romanticism in Shelly's arms, and tearfully recounting the accidental shooting of his drug connection (also Laura's fault). In the final analysis, Bobby is bad with a lowercase "b," a rude and intelligent "aimless youth" whose faults—selfishness, impulsiveness, sneering contempt for the niceties of small-town society—pale in significance compared with the determined, sadistic degeneracy of Bob. Initially a prime suspect in Laura's murder, Bobby Briggs is a red herring in the mystery around who killed Laura Palmer. He's a bad kid, not an evil man.

Donna Hayward (Lara Flynn Boyle/Moira Kelly)

Laura Palmer's straitlaced, level-headed best friend, Donna Hayward squarely—in both senses of the word—occupies a central place in the investigation of Laura's murder. Lacking her doomed friend's fascinating complexity, Shelly Johnson's frisky sexuality, or Audrey Horne's effortless chic charisma, Donna is distinguished among the showier female teen characters by her steely gravitas and pure-hearted devotion to finding justice for Laura. Her forbidden romance with Laura's grieving boyfriend James Hurley was a major romantic hook early in the series, and it's a reasonably effective one despite James's terminal blandness, but we prefer Donna on her own, doing her downbeat Nancy Drew routine. She provides leadership and an emotional center to the teenage investigative team she forms with James and Maddy Ferguson, and her courageous willingness to confront the darkest aspects of humanity is all the more heroic when one considers her cozy, cloistered, wholesome upbringing. Donna's a good girl for sure, but she's not a drag; in Lara Flynn Boyle's series performance (Moira Kelly assumed the role in *FWWM*, about which more later), Donna is sharply perceptive and intelligent, and possessed of a dry, deadpan wit; she's not worldly, but neither is she anyone's fool. She is also a striking beauty, cat-eyed and willowy, but so common is this condition among the women of Twin Peaks that this is not much remarked upon. Donna does reveal a darker side as the case progresses and terrible secrets are uncovered, mostly by smoking and wearing sunglasses. Her zeal for finding answers claims some collateral damage in the form of fragile Harold Smith's suicide, which isn't great, but we guess you can't make an omelet without breaking some eggs. After the mystery of Laura's death is resolved, Donna becomes fixated on the truth about her paternity, which results in yet more trauma and turmoil. Donna reminds us that truth and justice come at a high cost indeed; when exposed to the light, some hidden things bite.

Donna vs. Donna

Nothing stokes *Twin Peaks* fans like the debate over which actress is the definitive Donna Hayward: Lara Flynn Boyle, who portrayed her throughout the series, or Moira Kelly, who took over in *Fire Walk with Me* when Boyle bailed (lots of conflicting, unsubstantiated rumors as to why, and we're not going to solve that here).

Here's your answer: Lara Flynn Boyle, hands down.

Lara Flynn Boyle, the definitive Donna Hayward: Solemn, sensible, sweatered.

Yes, the Donna-James romance can be a drag.

Yes, the Ben-Horne-Is-Not-My-Daddy storyline is afflictive.

Yes, Boyle antagonized writers and many of the faithful by, according to some reports, nixing a second-season romance between Audrey Horne and Agent Cooper, portrayed by then-boyfriend Kyle MacLachlan; other reports say it was MacLachlan who put the kibosh on that idea. We say thank you kindly to whoever it was, because we *really* didn't want to see Cooper dating a high school coed.

And yes, she disappointed *Twin Peaks* fans by spurning *Fire Walk with Me* (available or not, and who really knows?).

Still, every iconic image of Donna Hayward summons up visions of Boyle, and not just because she logged so many more hours in the role. That voice (so husky)! Those eyes (so feline)! Those freckles (so freckly)! Boyle's Donna was all over the place, really, especially in season two—virtuous, vixenish, petulant, adoring—but so what? Ice and fire, baby. Kelly's a terrific actress in her own right, but her puppy-dog Donna lacks dynamism; she's so overwhelmed by Sheryl Lee's Laura Palmer that she practically evaporates on-screen.

Here, then, are highlights of Lara Flynn Boyle's Donna Hayward:

Pilot, classroom, crying scene: Donna intuits something horrific has happened to Laura even before anyone tells her. Her breakdown is brutal . . . but we mean that as a compliment. The audience, knowing that Laura has been murdered, is one step ahead of her all the way, as we watch her mind piece together the clues around her, finally reaching the devastating conclusion that her best friend is gone forever.

Donna visits James in the holding cell: Donna starts off season two new and possibly improved, depending on whether you prefer good girls or bad; here she's

Dreaming is free: Moira Kelly as Donna Hayward in *Fire Walk with Me.*

not just wearing Laura's sunglasses, but channeling her dead friend's mojo. Poor James is confused, as usual: both aroused and befuddled, he doesn't know how to react.

Donna pays a visit to Laura's grave: Even in death Laura casts her imposing shadow over Donna, and the fact that James is falling for Laura's look-alike cousin isn't helping. Here Donna drops by the cemetery and tells Laura exactly how she feels about it; the soliloquy starts off tender, ends up resentful, and tells us quite a bit about Donna Hayward in between.

Donna skinny-dips (OK, not actually, but she *remembers* skinny-dipping, relating the story to Harold Smith): Yowsa! Graeme Clifford, who directed this episode, told Brad Dukes in *Reflections* that he was so engrossed in this scene he forgot to yell cut. That's our girl!

Donna reads the missing page from Laura's diary: We love the odd tripling here—just Donna, Cooper, and Deputy Andy Brennan—but there's a lot going on beyond that, namely the decompartmentalization of Laura's worlds. Though Laura's best friend, Donna never had any notion of Laura's torturous immersion in the harrowing world of Bob, the Man from Another Place, and the Red Room . . . until now.

We'd also include the Donna-James-Maddy rendition of "Just You" here, but that scene is deconstructed elsewhere in this book (Chapter 20).

Donna's single finest moment: lip-syncing to "Rockin' Back Inside My Heart" at the Roadhouse. Resist this and you're not human.

Donna's single worst moment: "You're my daddy!" Not once, but thrice. Nobody's perfect.

Audrey Horne (Sherilyn Fenn)

Audrey Horne slinks coquettishly along the good/bad dividing line . . . she's a troublesome girl, given to mischief, but her transgressions are more the product of restlessness and excessive high spirits than malice. Audrey is Ben Horne's daughter (so no surprise she's morally flexible), and seems to be regarded as a disappointment by her father. Audrey wasn't part of Laura's inner circle, but secretly appreciated her devotion to her developmentally disabled brother, and begins her own investigation into the murder; boredom and an infatuation with the dashing new FBI agent in town are additional motivations. Audrey begins the series as a classic teensploitation bad girl, all insolent smoking, naughty schoolgirl wardrobe, and teasing innuendo; she gleefully sabotages a major business deal of her father's, blackmails her way into a job, and surprises Agent Cooper with a naked visit to his hotel room. Cooper's reaction—a gentle rejection couched in honest affection and respect—brings Audrey's better nature to the fore, revealing a passionate and idealistic young woman beneath the juvenile delinquent facade. A romance was initially planned for the two, and the chemistry between the actors is perhaps the series' fizziest, but MacLachlan nixed the idea, arguing such behavior would be in violation of Cooper's strict code of ethics (conventional wisdom has it that MacLachlan was also pressured by his then-girlfriend, Lara Flynn Boyle, to refrain from an on-screen relationship with Fenn). Instead, a warmer, sweeter dynamic emerges: Cooper recognizes Audrey's value and clearly has her best interests at heart, providing the healthy paternal attention so lacking from her own father. Audrey remains a pistol after their heart-to-heart (her infiltration of One Eyed Jacks and survival of the Freudian nightmare *that* turned into displays massive pluck), but she gains dimension as the show progresses, becoming more serious-minded and concerned with her place in the world (her tepid romance with cipher John Justice Wheeler was a snooze, but bad storylines can happen to the best characters). Fenn, blessed with Old Hollywood glamorous good looks and a witty, lively intelligence, is dazzling as Audrey, and the character is a firm fan favorite—she made such an impact, in fact, that Lynch's film *Mulholland Dr.* was initially conceived as a spin-off featuring Audrey. Her infamous cherry stem trick, a truly innovative job interview stratagem, counts as one of *Twin Peaks'* most memorable moments, but for our money, the iconic image of Audrey remains her dancing alone in a romantic reverie at the Double R, seduced by a dreamy tune, swaying scandalously in a sensible sweater and plaid wool skirt.

Benjamin Horne (Richard Beymer)

Ben Horne is the richest man in town, but this ain't Bedford Falls, and Horne's no George Bailey. From his base of operations at the Great Northern hotel, Horne oversees an empire that includes both Twin Peaks' nicest department store and one of Canada's most exclusive brothels. Tall, handsome, eloquent, and sophisticated, immaculately turned out in swanky low-slung double-breasted suits (Ben Horne is the rare Twin Peaks resident who doesn't take his fashion cues from circa 1955), Horne epitomizes the hated yuppie, a cultural trope from the go-go eighties that found its ultimate satirical expression in *American Psycho*'s Patrick Bateman. Horne isn't *that* bad, but he's not that great, either: he engaged in a sexual (and, surprisingly, deeply emotional) affair with Laura Palmer, his daughter's high school classmate; he arranged the arson at Packard Sawmill and the attempted murder of his lover and coconspirator Catherine Martell; he runs and frequents a creepy bordello where he enjoys "breaking in" the young new girls; and he constantly smokes enormous cigars. Despite these glaring flaws, Ben, like his daughter, Audrey, hides a finer nature beneath his veneer of unctuous villainy. Unfortunately, viewers had to suffer through an interminable, ill-conceived arc in which a beleaguered Horne (he cracks when arrested under suspicion of murdering Laura—ironically the one crime he *didn't* commit) delusionally believes himself to be a Civil War general before we got to see it. Upon returning to his senses, Horne gives up graft and cigars and takes up the cause of the endangered pine weasel, remorseful about his sins and dedicated to doing good. He may be going too far, however, when he visits the Hayward home to reveal the truth about Donna's parentage—it is very heavily implied that Ben and Eileen Hayward engaged in an affair, which produced Donna. Doc Hayward understandably takes issue with this little family reunion and savagely attacks Horne, severely injuring and possibly killing him. Karma, Ben. Karma.

James Hurley (James Marshall)

Sigh. Okay. James. Ostensibly one of *Twin Peaks'* leads, particularly early on, James Hurley fit the broad outlines of a potentially entertaining character: the Hoodlum with a Heart of Gold. Surely Lynch, Frost, and company would ring some mind-bending changes on that old cliché! Imagine, James Dean by way of *Blue Velvet*! Not so much: beyond fulfilling some basic plot necessities (as Laura's ex-boyfriend, Donna's new boyfriend, Bobby's rival, and Maddy's crush), the character of James is aggressively bland and forgettable—the heart of gold is in place, as is a mouth of mush, a face of constipated concern, and an air of general uselessness. Basically, they forgot the "hoodlum" part of the equation, leaving us with a lachrymose mope in a leather jacket. James does have an indelible scene: he, Donna, and Maddy record a song together for some reason, a haunting faux-fifties doo-wop ballad shifted more than a few degrees into creepiness by James's affectless falsetto croon. It's a deliciously weird, unexplained interlude, vintage *Twin Peaks* atmosphere. More typical for the character is his disastrously uninvolving "noir" storyline with duplicitous femme fatale Evelyn Marsh, considered by many *Twin Peaks* fans as the show's single worst misstep. After the conclusion of that dismal little affair, James got on his bike and rode away from Twin Peaks, unmourned and irrelevant. Aside from a postcard mentioned in passing, no one saw or heard from him again, or even seemed to register the fact that he had gone.

Catherine Packard Martell (Piper Laurie)

Catherine Martell is the sister of Packard mill owner Andrew Packard, and she runs the business after his apparent death, though the ownership passes to his "widow" Josie—and that arrangement is not a happy one for anyone involved. A fiercely proud, shrewd, forceful, and bitterly thwarted personality, Catherine vents her frustrations on her husband, Pete, a gentle former lumberjack and angling enthusiast bewildered by his wife's hostility. Catherine is conducting an affair with Benjamin Horne and conspiring with him to defraud Josie out of the mill and surrounding land, not suspecting his intention to double-cross and do away with her, taking all the spoils for himself. Academy Award winner Laurie gives an effortlessly authoritative performance—Catherine is a formidable presence, and while she's no Girl Scout, there is also an affecting vulnerability (as seen in her poignant appreciation of the remnants of affection that remain between her and Pete, and in her jealous paranoia regarding Ben's affections) that makes her something more than a stock antagonist. Catherine has no connection to Laura Palmer or the supernatural phenomena haunting Twin Peaks, serving instead as a linchpin in the show's soapier plot mechanics, and she is one of the series' more conventional characters—she is absent any bizarre tics or wardrobe eccentricities and feels like she could comfortably exist in a typical "straight" TV drama. That is, until she, after her apparent death (if you're gonna kill a Packard, make sure you see the body before you assume the job is done), disguises herself as a Japanese businessman to take her revenge on Horne. That was pretty weird.

4

It's Not Really a Place, It's a Feeling

Significant Locations and Landmarks

Something very, very strange in these old woods.

Where Was *Twin Peaks* Shot?

Most of the iconic establishing shots of Twin Peaks' landmarks—including the Double R, the Packard Sawmill, and the Sheriff's Department—shot for the pilot (to be reused as establishing shots in the series) and the film *Fire Walk with Me* were filmed in Snoqualmie and North Bend, Washington, and the surrounding area. Additional exteriors were shot in California, where the series episodes were also filmed on soundstages (inside an erstwhile ball-bearings factory) in Van Nuys.

The Twin Peaks

They have names: White Tail Mountain and Blue Pine Mountain, according to a map hand drawn by David Lynch. The actual

On a foggy day you can see the *real* twin peaks, Mount Si, towering over North Bend, Washington. *Photo by Deanne and Rob Lindley*

mountain whose jagged profile stands in for the titular summits is called Mount Si.

The Packard Sawmill

The first images we see of Twin Peaks proper occur in the show's opening credits sequence and depict the Packard Sawmill and its immediate environs. The primacy of this location is no accident: its smokestacks loom above Black Lake, where Pete Martell makes the terrible discovery of Laura Palmer's body. The mill, surrounded by the lush, primordial Ghostwood Forest, represents man's mechanized mastery over nature, the collision of orderly systems and wild, chaotic life. This tension has long featured in Lynch's work; the oddly beguiling shots of sparking circular saws and streaming chimneys recall his preoccupation with industrial clank and thrum in films such as *The Elephant Man* and *Eraserhead*.

There is also precedent for an interest in forestry and the lumber industry: Lynch's father worked for the U.S. Forest Service as a research scientist in Washington and Montana, and the director has frequently rhapsodized about his early childhood in the Pacific Northwest and the powerful,

The *real* Packard mill was the Weyerhaeuser mill; all that remains today is a single powerhouse and smokestack.   *Photo by Pieter Dom*

mystical allure of the surrounding woods—he has spoken specifically about his fascination with a tree in his backyard that oozed black pitch, swarming with ants, an image of the beauty and revulsion that so often exist cheek-by-jowl in nature that has clear resonances with *Twin Peaks* and many of his other projects. *Blue Velvet's* setting, Lumberton, is (on its surface) a nostalgic, idealized amalgam of Lynch's old stomping grounds.

The Packard Sawmill's significance to the story involves the convoluted machinations of Josie Packard, "widow" of mill owner Andrew Packard, and Catherine Martell, Andrew's sister, for control of the business, and of Benjamin Horne, who schemes to acquire the valuable real estate it occupies. Catherine and Shelly Johnson (her cuckolded husband Leo, an efficient sort, figures to get the maximum yield out of his arson errand and ties her up in a shed) nearly die there when the mill burns. It's an unlucky place—why, once there was even a fish in the percolator! (That incident occurred in the house on the property shared by Pete, Catherine, and Josie, aka Blue Pine Lodge—in actuality, the Kiana Lodge, built in the 1930s, also used for interior shots of the Great Northern.)

Leo Johnson burns the Packard mill down in the series, but the actual site—the Weyerhaeuser Mill, built in 1917—has since been felled by an even greater force: economics. A decline in the local logging industry led to the dismantling of the vast complex . . . only a single powerhouse and smokestack remain standing.

The Double R Diner

Probably the quintessential *TP* location, the Double R is a locus for damn fine coffee and cherry pie; beautiful, troubled women; important conversations and meetings; and impromptu dancing. A throwback to classic fifties eateries, the Double R is a repository of retro-Americana kitsch signifiers, and its centrality to the show (nearly every major character patronizes the diner) suggests the importance of these aesthetic considerations. Owned and operated by beautiful, melancholy Norma Jennings, the Double R is the archetypal American diner: a welcoming, comforting place, a bedrock of small-town tradition, a neutral corner to which to retreat from the uncertainties of the wider world. The actual restaurant used for the Double R was built in 1941 and called the Mar-T Café. It sustained fire damage in 2000, attracting a crazed man armed with a brush and purple paint who claimed God had commanded him to put the *Twin Peaks* restaurant back together.

Twede's Café, known in *Twin Peaks* as the Double R.   *Photo by Pieter Dom*

Sounds about right. It's back up and running under the name Twede's Café, and word has it the pie is very good.

Twin Peaks Sheriff's Department

Drab and functional, the TP Sheriff's Department building provides a respite from the town's more recherché locations; it is a place of order and rational thought, a haven from the chaos and darkness where Cooper, Truman, and their associates are able to soberly and objectively analyze and strategize. There are a few amenities: you're never more than a few steps from a doughnut-laden surface, and there was briefly a mynah bird you could feed, before it was murdered in cold blood. The actual location of the department was an office for the Weyerhaeuser Mill, the real-life Packard Sawmill.

The Great Northern

The Great Northern is one of Twin Peaks' most distinctive locations: The majestic hotel (in real life the Salish Lodge and Spa), with its dramatic cliffside setting above roaring falls (Snoqualmie Falls), vividly evokes the Pacific Northwest in all of its rough-hewn splendor.

Horne Headquarters, home to Dale Cooper during his stay, and destination spot for Scandinavian investors, the grand Great Northern hotel rests at the center of *Twin Peaks'* various intrigues. The interior is striking, all exposed wood and Native American design elements; it resembles the Overlook from *The Shining* crossed with a log cabin. Ben Horne administers his empire from here, glad-handing, wheeling and dealing, and exploring the Kama Sutra in his office with Catherine Martell. Cooper's time at the hotel has its ups and downs: he is kept awake late into the night by singing Norwegians, shot in the stomach by Josie, and experiences really inefficient room service; on the other hand, Audrey, the owner's beautiful young daughter, shows up naked in his bed. All in all it appears to be a pretty nice place to stay, but the drawer pulls are kind of weird.

The majestic Snoqualmie Falls and Great Northern hotel (in reality, the Salish Lodge & Spa).

The Palmer House

An attractive four-bedroom Dutch Colonial, the Palmer residence is the very picture of comfortably affluent, solidly traditional suburban life; it's so wholesome and all-American we half-expect to see Beaver and Wally, or perhaps Archie and Jughead, ambling down the walk. But this house hides terrible secrets, and its very normalcy underscores the depravity of the horror it contains. Inside the house, the idyllic illusion wobbles a bit: ashtrays overflowing with butts are littered about the place (Mrs. Palmer is a chain smoker due to her "nerves," and we can't blame her), and the color scheme in the living room is a sickly mélange of pinks, beiges, and yellows—a sallow, dingy dollhouse pallor. This is where Maddy is killed, Sarah has her visions of the white horse, and Leland waits in the dark, plotting murder. The Palmer house is freighted with such menace that a repeated shot of a ceiling fan at the top of the stairs remains one of the series' most chilling signifiers. Last but not least, we repeatedly see Bob here, creeping through windows, hiding in Laura's room, peering out from mirrors. It's a stark image of violation—the cozy home violently invaded by a ragged bogey-man—that resonates with nauseating vividness. Forget the Red Room, Jacques' cabin, even the abandoned train car—the sunlit Palmer house is Twin Peaks' scariest location.

The Roadhouse

Come for the ethereal song stylings of Julee Cruise; stay for the prophetic visions. A lot goes down at the Roadhouse (as it's colloquially known; its official name is the Bang Bang Bar, an actual tavern in Snoqualmie Valley, Washington). It's a place to meet when the Double R is too small or too public. A hangout for bikers and young lovers, the saloon also serves as an ad hoc courtroom and as the venue for the Miss Twin Peaks pageant, and is a place where the Giant appears to impart information to Agent Cooper. We like the idea that Cruise, a soporific, archly theatrical crooner of gauzy lullabies, apparently enjoys an extended residence as the house chanteuse.

FWWM introduces the Roadhouse's dark twin, the vile, squalid Partyland, located just north of the Canadian border. The film's most arresting set piece, mesmerizing and nightmarish, depicts Donna's attempt to match Laura transgression for transgression, led like Virgil through this Hellish landscape, descending ever further into degradation. It's an oppressive, fetid cavern, with sickening strobe lights flickering over a sticky carpet

A lot went down at the Bang Bang Bar, aka the Roadhouse, which still stands today in Fall City, Washington.   *Photo by Pieter Dom*

of beer bottles and cigarette butts. In place of the luminous and soothing presence of Julee Cruise we have a garish heavy metal band making meaningful conversation impossible, and the atmosphere is rank with sweat, smoke, booze, and predatory lust. The Roadhouse is about community, Partyland is for oblivion.

One Eyed Jacks

One Eyed Jacks, the Twin Peaks–adjacent casino and bordello situated just north of the border of Canada (much to Agent Cooper's eventual chagrin), serves as a crucial location in the series: Ben Horne owns it, his daughter Audrey queasily keeps it a family business, Laura Palmer worked there (recruited, like her colleagues, from the perfume counter at Horne's department store), and Jean Renault's use the den of iniquity as a station in their drug-running enterprise.

A cozily rustic establishment, One Eyed Jacks is visually of a piece with other Twin Peaks settings, its luxe Native American–themed furnishings recalling the atmosphere of the Great Northern and its heavy red drapes echoing those in the Red Room (in fact, the same set of drapes was used to dress both locations). The beautiful young hostesses are evocatively attired in playing-card-themed lingerie, and their elegant madam Blackie rules the roost with cool poise and efficiency. The businessman and tourist clientele understandably find the place a potent attraction, and we see Ben Horne cannily leverage his involvement to help grease the wheels of his real estate dealings.

There are, unsurprisingly, some sly allusions and references going on with the name: *One-Eyed Jacks*, a western starring Marlon Brando, featured *Twin Peaks* actor Hank Worden (our favorite slow-mo room service waiter) in a small part, and, on a bawdier note, a "one-eyed Jack" can be read as a phallic euphemism. Or maybe it's just a nice place to play poker.

The Johnson House

An unhappy home, perpetually under construction, with plenty of raw lumber and plastic sheeting on display (queasily echoing Laura Palmer's final resting place and shroud). Truck driver and all-around criminal sleazeball Leo Johnson stashes his young wife Shelly here while he's hauling freight, legitimate and otherwise. When Leo is home, he enjoys dominating and beating Shelly for minor behavioral infractions—good thing he doesn't know Bobby Briggs keeps his side of the bed warm while he's out on the road. After Leo's shooting, the hapless Mr. Pinkle installs a comically faulty harness to help move the invalid around, and the indignities Leo suffers in the contraption are a mere prelude to the psychological torture Shelly and Bobby undertake out of frustration over caring for the helpless psychopath. Basically, the place is a bummer, dreary and shabby, and nothing good ever happens here.

Horne's Department Store

A lovely place to shop, or to recruit underage prostitutes. Part of the Horne empire, this upscale establishment wears two faces, as per Twin Peaks tradition. The respectable matrons who peruse the makeup and perfume counter never suspect the attractive young women serving them form a "talent" pool from which the odious Emory Battis recruits "hostesses" for One Eyed Jacks—though both cosmetics and prostitution cater to male fantasy and promote the objectification of women. In one of the series' slyest, sickest jokes, we see on the counter a sign promoting a line of products branded

"Invitation to Love." This references both the title of TP's favorite soap opera and the counter's true purpose as a gateway to sexual solicitation. Creepy.

Jacques Renault's Cabin

Remember when grown-ups would warn you against hitchhiking, claiming you'd wind up bound and murdered in some maniac's remote cabin in the woods? This is that cabin. Property of nightlife professional and total degenerate Jacques Renault, this filthy, squalid party pit is the setting for various *Flesh World* porno photo shoots and the orgy that directly precedes Laura Palmer's murder. It's an absolute clue bonanza for Cooper and Truman, who find the broken poker chip and Waldo the Amazing Mynah Bird there—we also learn the meanings of some of Cooper's more recondite dream revelations, such as why there is always music in the air (record player) and why Laura's arms sometimes bend back (Leo tied her up for S&M sex). It's the Palmer house without the veneer of respectability—a place of pain and degradation. Probably smells like creamed corn.

Windom Earle's Cabin

Cooper's former best friend turned nemesis, the psychotic ex-FBI agent Windom Earle, sets up shop in a dilapidated, abandoned cabin to plot his siege of the Black Lodge and his revenge against Cooper. Mostly, though, he uses it as a workshop for his many arts and crafts projects: sculpting a giant plaster chess pawn, making playing-card collages, constructing a Major Briggs–sized crossbow target, and assembling his many, many ridiculous disguises. His faithful servant Leo (rendered tractable by a shock collar) attends to his earthly needs, freeing the brilliant Earle to concoct his fevered plans, listen in on the sheriff's department from a remote microphone, and play long-distance chess with Pete. If you take away the murder and torture, this place is actually kind of fun, like a summer camp for demented genius children who don't like sports.

Owl Cave

This ominous cave is located in Ghostwood Forest and houses the petro-glyph—a wall marking that depicts the location of the Black Lodge and the times at which it is accessible. There are hidden mechanisms in the cave—one accidentally activated by Deputy Andy Brennan with a wild axe swing, another by Windom Earle on a subsequent visit—that reveal further aspects of the petroglyph. The aptly named cave is indeed thick with owls, which are not what they seem, and extreme caution seems warranted, though in times past the cave was a popular destination for locals out enjoying nature.

5

The Usual Bumper Crop of Rural Know-Nothings and Drunken Fly-Fishermen

Dossiers: Locals

Emory Battis (Don Amendolia)

Hard to quibble with Blackie O'Reilly's spot-on description of Battis as a "spineless gas bag"; Jean Renault grows so irritated by his yabbering that he puts a bullet in him, presumably just to shut him up. Up until that development Battis occupies some sort of authoritative position at Horne's department store (director of personnel, going by the script), where he recruits impressionable girls as escorts for One Eyed Jacks, including Laura Palmer and Ronette Pulaski. Battis himself enjoys partaking of Jacks's offerings, as we discover when Audrey Horne disrupts the enactment of one of his fantasies, involving bondage, polished toenails (his), a woman in a cowboy hat and boots vacuuming, and a bucket of ice. What a prince.

Annie Blackburne/Blackburn (Heather Graham)

Trivia question: What's the last word ever spoken on ABC-TV's *Twin Peaks*? Trivia answer: "Annie," as in Annie Blackburne (or Blackburn, as it is inexplicably respelled in *Fire Walk with Me*), pronounced by the Dale Cooper doppelgänger who surfaces from the Black Lodge after the real Cooper has journeyed there to rescue her. The writers scrambled to create the character

Sweet Annie Blackburne, perpetual damsel in distress.   *Photo by Richard Beymer*

after their original idea, for a second-season Cooper-Audrey Horne romance, was nixed, by either Kyle MacLachlan (Cooper) or then-girlfriend Lara Flynn Boyle (Donna Hayward), depending on which version of history you believe. Hence, the fateful arrival, in episode twenty-four ("Wounds and Scars"), of honey-blonde, ethereal Annie Blackburne, Norma Jennings's younger sister, a refugee from a nunnery whose scarred wrist bares a troubled past, involving a torturous high school breakup (oh, youth). A romantic who can quote Heisenberg, Annie soon sweeps Cooper off his feet while serving up piping-hot coffee and generous slabs of pie at her sister's diner, with her social awkwardness, vulnerability, and glittering blue eyes. While Annie never did redeem the series in the eyes of disgruntled critics and viewers at this late date, redemption is exactly what she offered Cooper, still tormented by an ill-fated love affair of his own with Caroline Earle in Pittsburgh. In the series finale, Annie is abducted by Windom Earle, and Cooper, in pursuit, descends into the Red Room, where Annie and Caroline take turns morphing into each other and where Cooper offers to sacrifice his soul to save Annie. Beyond that we have no real idea what transpires, except that Annie ends up lying on the ground in the Twin Peaks woods beside Cooper, her face covered in blood. Annie appears briefly in *Fire Walk with Me,* turning up in a dream sequence, telling Laura she's been with her and Cooper in the lodge and that "the good Dale can't leave," none of which has actually happened yet, which is how things go in the world of *Twin Peaks*. Thanks to a deleted scene released in 2014, we finally learn what happened to Annie immediately post-series: she's at Calhoun Memorial Hospital in a trance, repeating the same lines she voiced in Laura's dream. Interestingly, Annie now wears the same mystical ring that Teresa Banks and Laura Palmer both had in their possession at the time of their deaths, but not for long, as the ring is lifted from Annie's finger by a hospital nurse, apparently with a taste for garish jewelry, especially at that price.

Betty Briggs (Charlotte Stewart)

All you really need to know about Betty Briggs is this: she wears a smiley-face button pinned to her coat at Laura Palmer's funeral. Betty isn't terminally stupid or cheerful, just a poster child for avoidance, and when you live in Twin Peaks and you're Bobby Briggs's mom and Major Garland Briggs's wife, maybe that's a good thing. There are, however, cracks in the armor, moments when you can see the angst, though they dissipate quickly on every occasion save one, when, midway into season two, Bobby comes home one night to find her sitting alone in the dark, distraught over Garland's mysterious disappearance. This leads very neatly into Betty's other defining characteristic: her adoration of her husband—"an extraordinary human being," she tells her son—whose shoulders she is seen massaging when first we meet her, in the pilot (trivial pursuit: twice during the pilot Sarah Palmer refers to Betty as Beth, though the script says Betty). Charlotte Stewart, the actress

Actress Charlotte Stewart shows off Betty Briggs's famous smiley-face button at the 2015 Twin Peaks Festival.

Photo by Pieter Dom

who portrays her, starred with Jack Nance (Pete Martell) in Lynch's outré 1977 feature debut, *Eraserhead*.

Major Garland Briggs (Don S. Davis)

Our favorite description of Major Briggs comes from son Bobby, midway into the second season, after the major has mysteriously vanished: "My father is a deeply weird individual. But he has a lot more going on under his hat than most people, that's for sure." As Johnny Horne would say, "Amen." The major is actually a minor character in season one, a surprising revelation given his eventual prominence (on the DVD commentary for episode three, director Tina Rathborne opines that she initially believed Briggs to be a "blowhard," but was set straight by Lynch). We nominate this scene from season two/episode one—directed by Lynch and scripted by Frost from a story they conceived together—as the turning point, in which Major Briggs coincidentally encounters Bobby at the Double R diner and shares with him his "veranda on a palazzo" vision, which concludes with a "warm and loving embrace, nothing withheld," between father and son, leaving Bobby in tears (one of Frost's favorite moments from the series). Up to this point the relationship between the two had been disputatious, consisting mostly of the major futilely seeking to connect with his son through verbose philosophical lectures on death, rebelliousness, responsibility, and whatever else circumstances seemed to dictate, and Bobby either ignoring them or countering with thundery dismissals. The major typically remains exasperatingly stoic during these exchanges, though there is one anomalous scene at the Briggs dinner table early on in which he slaps Bobby so hard across the face that his cigarette goes flying into Betty Briggs's meatloaf, which didn't look very appetizing to begin with. The diner seems to be a favored hangout for the pie-loving Major Briggs, and in the second episode of season two he has an important encounter there with the Log Lady, his spiritual kin; putting aside for a moment the significant plot implications, this is a precious scene pairing two eccentric characters who don't seem to know each other very well, one (the Major) unfailingly polite, the other willfully oblivious to anything so inconvenient as social refinement. As season two advances, Briggs starts popping up at key moments of the Laura Palmer investigation—it's he who escorts the Waiter to Cooper's revelatory roundup of suspects at the Roadhouse, and he bizarrely emerges from the trees outside the sheriff's office as Cooper and the gang ponder the meaning of Bob after Leland's death, contributing this slight alteration of Hamlet's comment to Horatio: "Gentlemen, there's more in heaven and earth than is dreamt of in our philosophy." A devoted family man with an unbending moral code, the major plays for the good guys, a real shining knight in a world often consumed by wickedness. His subsequent abduction as he and Cooper are out night-fishing in the woods, his work on Project Blue Book (an Air Force initiative to investigate UFOs and other strange phenomena, which also involved Windom Earle), and finally his kidnapping and torture by Earle all unquestionably catapult Briggs to the status of major player in the *Twin Peaks* gallery—not bad for a guy whose earliest dialogue in the series includes the line "You know, dear, I have no idea what's going on here."

The Reverend Clarence Brocklehurst (Royce D. Applegate)

Poor Reverend Brocklehurst must have drawn the short straw when he wound up in Twin Peaks, a haven for sinful, heinous activity that compels us to wonder if God is even paying any attention to this Pacific Northwest Gomorrah. We don't see much of Brocklehurst either, since he shows up exactly twice: once to conduct Laura Palmer's funeral and once to officiate at the wedding of Dougie Milford and Lana Budding. It is a measure of Brocklehurst's sway in town that both events devolve into spectacles that he is powerless to stop, though in fairness to him we are dubious that anyone could have done any better. His sermon at Laura's gravesite—he baptized her and taught her in Sunday school—is actually not terrible, especially if you consider that he apparently had absolutely no clue what was really going on in her life.

Louise Dombrowski (Emily Fincher)

Louise appears in just a single *Twin Peaks* scene, a flashback in episode fifteen, "Drive with a Dead Girl," but who among us will ever forget? With Ben Horne locked up on suspicion of murdering Laura Palmer, brother Jerry drops by to build a defense, and is reminded by the cell's bunk beds of the Hornes' childhood, particularly a glorious moment in time when young Louise Dombrowski danced in the dark with a flashlight on a hook rug in a knee-length skirt and bobby socks, scored to lush fifties pop by Angelo Badalamenti, as the bespectacled Ben and Jerry look on in thrall.

Louise's face never is seen, but she was portrayed by Emily Fincher, sister of filmmaker David Fincher (*Fight Club, Se7ev, Gone Girl, The Social Network*) and also a crew member on season two of *Twin Peaks*.

Eileen Hayward (Mary Jo Deschanel)

Wheelchair-bound (no clue) Eileen Hayward, Doc's wife and Donna, Harriett, and Gersten's mom, is a pretty flavorless character—churchgoer, empathetic friend, supportive spouse, beaming mom, always ready with a hug or term of endearment—until the handful of episodes that end the series, when a new storyline pops up out of the blue strongly suggesting that Eileen and Ben Horne were lovers some twenty years earlier, and that Donna is a product of that conjoinment (that would place the affair several years after the birth of Johnny Horne, suggesting that Ben at least was married). Though confronted more than once by Donna, Eileen refuses to confirm or deny this speculation; the mystery is never resolved, and the arc ends with Will delivering a (possibly fatal) punch to Ben as Eileen, Donna, and Sylvia Horne all look on in horror (in a scene also accountable for the unfortunate Donna Hayward outburst "You're my Daddy! You're my Daddy! You're my Daddy!"). Eileen, who also appears in a deleted *FWWM* scene released in 2014, was portrayed by Mary Jo Deschanel, mother of actresses Emily (*Bones*) and Zooey (*New Girl*) and wife of Caleb, who directed three episodes of *Twin Peaks*.

Gersten Hayward (Alicia Witt)

The younger of Donna Hayward's two sisters, Gersten appears just once in *Twin Peaks*, in the Lynch-directed second-season premiere ("May the Giant Be With You," for those of you who like your titles), dressed in a glittery pink dress, with a silver tiara atop her striking red hair, to commemorate her selection as the fairy princess in her school play. Precocious much? This kid plays Mendelssohn's *Rondo Capriccioso, Opus 14*, in front of not only her beaming parents and sisters, but also the Palmers and Maddy Ferguson. Unfortunately it is Gersten who is at the keyboard when Leland passes out while frenetically warbling "Get Happy," and she is neither seen nor heard from again (except during the anomalous closing-credits sequence of this particular episode, when Gersten virtuosically performs a blues shuffle). The music business is tough. Gersten was portrayed by Alicia Witt, who was discovered by Lynch when he cast her as Alia Atreides in his critically/commercially disastrous 1984 adaptation of Frank Herbert's sci-fi classic *Dune*, starring Kyle MacLachlan (she was nine years old when the film came out).

Harriet Hayward (Jessica Wallenfels)

Middle sisters are complicated. Older than Gersten but younger than Donna, Harriet has the soul of a poet: we meet her just twice (in two Lynch-directed episodes), and both times she's engaged in verse, either writing it (as in the pilot, where she ponders the relative merits of "blossom of the evening" versus "full flower of the evening," before ultimately opting for "full blossom of the evening") or reciting it (as in the second-season premiere, where her poem about Laura Palmer—"It was Laura/and I saw her glowing/in the dark woods . . ."—nearly brings Sarah to tears). Harriet's a wool-sweater-over-turtleneck kind of gal, and while she vows to cover for Donna as her older sister defies a town curfew by slipping out the bedroom window to meet up with James, she caves the minute Dad demands to know where Donna went. She may be a budding English major, but she's not stupid.

Will "Doc" Hayward (Warren Frost)

Twin Peaks' least eccentric resident? Doc Hayward, husband of Eileen, father of Donna (or *is he?*), Harriet, and Gersten (Gersten?), stands as a paragon of rectitude and gentle concern, the loving, solid, incorruptible father figure that Leland Palmer only appears to be. Doc gets along with everybody (with the exception of Albert Rosenfield), and serves as a voice of reason and decency in the face of unimaginable tragedy. He does whatever he can to assist in the investigation of the murder of his daughter's friend and never seems to put a foot wrong or indicate any moral weakness—until Ben Horne, who, by every indication, cuckolded Doc and fathered Donna—drops by the house for a family chat in the series finale. Doc completely loses it and seemingly kills Horne in a fit of rage . . . but we later see him with Sheriff Truman visiting Cooper in his room, so the ultimate disposition of that unfortunate incident remains cloudy. What is clear is that Doc's spasm of violence this late in the story is particularly shocking and dismaying: even a man as noble and pure as Doc Hayward is capable of

Decent, dutiful Doc Hayward.   *Photo by Richard Beymer*

murderous rage when pushed far enough. Maybe Doc is a better man than Leland, or maybe he's just lucky Bob didn't choose him for a host.

Heidi (Andrea Hays)

Giggly Heidi, a waitress at the Double R, appears just twice in *Twin Peaks*, in the pilot and the finale, both, not coincidentally, directed by Lynch, who had a habit of resurrecting characters he particularly enjoyed. A stout German, Heidi wears her long blonde hair in a braid and, like Teresa Banks, can't seem to get to work on time, which confuses Bobby Briggs, who's under the belief that Germans are necessarily prompt, as he articulates to her in both of the scenes in which she appears. In fact, the dialogue in the two scenes—set twenty-nine episodes apart—is almost identical: both times Heidi shows up late for work, Shelly ribs her about it, Bobby opines about Germans, and Heidi can't stop giggling. Whatever the intent—if in fact there even was one—the effect is provocative, because it compels us to ponder the enormity of the changes that have unfolded in Twin Peaks in the intervening time, even if Heidi appears exactly the same. She seems to have existed in some hermetically sealed world where time stands still, oblivious to all of the horrors that have unfolded. Heidi appears very briefly in *Fire Walk with Me*, sitting at a Double R booth with a bloody nose, so that Shelly has to step in and help Laura pack up the Meals on Wheels station wagon

(Shelly's reluctance to do so being a function of the fact that she is sleeping with Laura's boyfriend).

Jerry Horne (David Patrick Kelly)

The manic id to his brother Ben's (Ben and Jerry, get it?) cultivated super-ego, Jerry Horne pursues life's material pleasures with childlike glee and abandon, ecstatically reveling in food, drink, and women, his boundless appetites contrasting amusingly with his short, slight frame. The little man takes up a lot of space with his overbearing manner and flamboyant ward-robe, but Jerry is not merely a clown: he is the Horne brother drumming up business internationally, pressing the flesh and charming investors through sheer overwhelming force of will. Despite their starkly different public personas, Jerry and Ben are peas in a pod (witness their weirdly touching childhood reminiscence while sharing a jail cell); it's just that Jerry, flitting about the globe, can display his true nature more freely, while Ben, holding down the fort at home, must project a more sober countenance. Kelly is an off-kilter delight as the voluble younger Horne; B-movie devotees will surely remember him fondly as the iconic bottle-clinking, sneering villain from the 1979 drive-in classic *The Warriors*.

Johnny Horne (Robert Davenport/Robert Bauer)

Johnny was portrayed by two actors over time—Robert Davenport in the pilot and Robert Bauer in the four ensuing episodes in which he appeared. According to his sister, Audrey, Johnny is twenty-seven years old, but with the intellect of a third-grader, and he doesn't change much over the two sea-sons: when we first see him he's wearing pajamas and an American Indian headdress, banging his head against a toy house inside the Great Northern, distraught that Laura Palmer hasn't shown up for their tutoring session; in his final appearance, toward the end of season two, he's wearing full Indian regalia and practicing archery with a toy bow and arrow outside Horne central, so at least he's getting out more. His big moment comes at Laura's funeral, where he punctuates the Reverend Brocklehurst's sermon with two "Amens," unintentionally triggering Bobby Briggs's rant against hypocrisy and a near rumble between Bobby and James. Clutched in Johnny's arm at the funeral is a used first-edition copy of *Peter Pan*, which speaks volumes about the character. Say what you want about Johnny, but it can't be easy being a Horne.

Sylvia Horne (Jan D'Arcy)

Benjamin Horne's wife Sylvia is forever *verklempt*, but who can blame her, being married to that amoral, philandering cad? Plus she's coping with an emotionally stunted son and intellectually stunted brother-in-law (or is it the other way around?). Sylvia appears in just four episodes, always on the precipice of exploding at Ben, including the series finale, in which she is one of several characters brought out of mothballs by Lynch (she hadn't appeared in *Twin Peaks* since episode two, and wasn't in the original script for the finale either). Lynch liked Sylvia enough to write her into *Fire Walk with Me*, though not so much as to preserve her appearance, which was eventually clipped.

"Big" Ed Hurley (Everett McGill)

Poor ol' Big Ed Hurley. Key member of the Bookhouse Boys, uncle to dreary James, husband to nutty Nadine, lover of tragic Norma, and proprietor of something called a "gas farm," Ed just can't catch a break. The senior Hurley is one of *Twin Peaks'* most overtly "soapy" characters—blandly noble, manfully stoic, tall and ruggedly handsome—who seems to exist only to suffer romantically. McGill, a soap veteran, handled these familiar story beats expertly, but also brought a sneaky, rueful humor to many of the clueless Ed's big scenes: witness his alarming flirting and sad-sack lucklessness at One Eyed Jacks. Norma correctly pegs Ed as being too nice to ever get anything he wants, and indeed, at series' end, despite a glimpse of happiness with Norma, Ed dutifully recommits to his insane, one-eyed, superhumanly strong spouse. McGill previously appeared in Lynch's *Dune*, playing a worm-riding desert terrorist with a tube in his nose. So . . . upgrade?

Nadine Hurley (Wendy Robie)

What can you say about a woman who possesses both sexual maturity and superhuman strength? Nadine is one of Twin Peaks' more flamboyantly eccentric residents (a crowded field). We first encounter the flame-haired, eyepatch-sporting matron hysterically determined to perfect her invention: completely noiseless curtain runners. Nadine's see-sawing mania and suicidal despair hover somewhere between heightened melodrama and outright camp; her loopy intensity, unusual appearance, and ill-defined super strength (Doc Hayward says something about "adrenaline") are chiefly comic fodder, wacky window dressing for the show's parodic soap

One Harley, two Hurleys: Gas Farm proprietor Big Ed and his endlessly charismatic
nephew James.

opera elements. Nadine hits the familiar daytime drama story beats of
a) serving as third wheel in a tragic love triangle, b) surviving a suicide
attempt, and c) amnesia. Mentally regressed to adolescence, she reenters
high school, joins the wrestling team, and pursues a romance with teenage
creep/Bobby Briggs associate Mike Nelson, only to regain her memories
and lose her enhanced muscle power after a blow to the head. All pretty
ridiculous, and it's tempting to write Nadine off (despite Robie's funny and
touching performance) as an example of weirdness for weirdness's sake, a

gratuitous dollop of absurdity with no deeper purpose than to poke fun at the narrative conventions of a disreputable genre. But Nadine, like so many *Twin Peaks* characters, hides a deep well of sadness, and her insecurity, stemming from her knowledge that Ed would prefer Norma and stays with Nadine out of guilt and obligation (he accidentally caused the injury that cost her her eye), is legitimately affecting. *Twin Peaks* thrives on this tension between profound emotional turmoil and the bizarrely comic distortions such pain can produce in human behavior; it is a compelling but deeply uncomfortable fact of life not often depicted on TV, but an absolutely essential component of the series' unique power.

Dr. Lawrence Jacoby (Russ Tamblyn)

Headshrinker Dr. Lawrence Jacoby (PhD, MD, Individual and Family Counseling) might be a kook—*is* a kook—but he's no quack. Yes, he sticks golf balls in his ears, then extracts them from his mouth. He dresses eccentrically and wears eyeglass lenses tinted two different colors. His obsession with Hawaii seems, at times, unnatural. But Jacoby is astute and effective. Exhibit A: He dissuades Johnny Horne from wearing an Indian headdress to Laura's funeral. Exhibit B: He forces Bobby Briggs to confront his demons. Exhibit C: He eases Ben Horne out of his Civil War obsession (if only he had done it sooner and spared us all the pain of that arc). Exhibit D: He understood Laura Palmer, a patient for six months, perhaps as well as anyone, telling Cooper and Truman she was living a double life and, in the end, had finally achieved peace by welcoming death. When Cooper sternly counters that Laura didn't commit suicide, Jacoby says, "No, no, but maybe she allowed herself to be killed." Exactly, Doc. Jacoby loved Laura profoundly, probably not such a great idea given their professional relationship (not to mention the age difference), but as far as we know it was chaste (likely *her* doing). Jacoby may be yet another Twin Peaks resident named after someone from Otto Preminger's 1944 noir *Laura,* in which the title character's portrait is painted by an artist named Jacoby (pronounced differently), who was madly in love with his subject. Despite his jolly front, our Jacoby is uncommonly self-aware, as demonstrated in one of our favorite scenes from the series, when Cooper visits the fog-enshrouded cemetery at night and encounters Jacoby in dapper cowl and hat, placing a bouquet of flowers at Laura's gravesite, leading to this soliloquy, in which he explains why he hadn't attended the funeral earlier that day: "I'm a terrible person, Agent Cooper. I pretend I'm not, but I am. Oh, I sit and listen to their problems day after day. These people think of me as their friend. The truth is, I really don't care. I thought nothing, no one, could ever reach me again. Laura changed all that. I couldn't come today, I just couldn't. I hope she understands. I hope she forgives me." If an in-studio poll taken during the May 21, 1990, installment of *Donahue* devoted to *Twin Peaks* (featuring Mark Frost and six cast members—though not Tamblyn—as guests) was any indication, viewers agreed with his self-assessment, as 31 percent of the audience tapped him as Laura's killer, making him the leading vote-getter. According to Frost, the role of Jacoby was intended as minor, but was expanded once they cast Tamblyn, a veteran Hollywood actor who had starred in the 1961 film version of the Broadway musical *West Side Story* along with Richard Beymer (Benjamin Horne). Unfortunately, Jacoby also is a coconspirator in one of the most wretched moments in *Twin Peaks* history, a duet of "Dixie" with Benjamin Horne. Look away, indeed.

Laura: Noir as Midnight on a Moonless Night

Before Laura Palmer there was Laura Hunt, whose facility at arousing *amour fou* in members of the opposite sex apparently extended to David Lynch and/or Mark Frost. This Laura, the title character in Otto Preminger's stylish film noir from 1944, is young (though beyond her impossible years), pulchritudinous, and charismatic, effortlessly beguiling all manner of men intent on imbuing her with their own notions of idealized femininity ("The best part of myself, that's what you are," one tells her). She's deceased even before the film begins, or rather reputed to be, yet manages to dominate the narrative from the get-go by the sheer force of her magnetic reputation, assisted by a haunting, mournful theme song bearing her name and an iconic framed portrait exerting powerful, beckoning vibes.

Sound familiar?

Like Lynch and Frost with *Twin Peaks*, Preminger tussled with executives over the making of the film, especially 20th Century Fox cofounder and production honcho Darryl F. Zanuck, who first refused to let him direct (relenting eventually, after recognizing that early dailies, from director Rouben Mamoulian, were a disaster), then tried to impose an alternate ending on the film (finally giving in when his pal, puissant newspaper columnist Walter Winchell, told him he didn't get it).

Laura opens in the aftermath of Laura Hunt's apparent shotgun murder in her New York apartment, the victim's face mutilated beyond recognition. Gotham copper Mark McPherson (Dana Andrews) spends the next sixteen minutes or so getting inside her skin through testimonials from her closest "friends," as well as letters and—get this, *Twin Peaks* fans—a private diary. Watching these events

The famous portrait of the murdered Laura (or . . . was she?), Ms. Palmer's namesake, from Otto Preminger's 1944 film of the same name, portrayed by Gene Tierney.

unfold, we're reminded of David Lynch's famous comment about Laura Palmer: though she appears in *Twin Peaks* just momentarily (and even then, only as a corpse), her presence is felt in every scene of every episode over the two seasons of the series.

Finally, we meet Laura Hunt through an extended flashback, and soon after that discover that she was not in fact the victim—in actuality an unfortunate business acquaintance (Diane Redfern, a model) who happened to be in the wrong place at the wrong time (and by that we mean in Laura's apartment, wearing Laura's negligee and slippers, and with Laura's fiancé, a scalawag by the name of Shelby Carpenter, portrayed by future horror-meister Vincent Price). Then Laura herself shows up, after a weekend in the country, totally oblivious to reports of her demise (given the well-dissected similarities between *Laura* and *Twin Peaks* back when the TV series was originally airing, this turn of events led to bouts of speculation that Laura Palmer too was still alive, and would suddenly reappear, or even that look-alike cousin Maddy Ferguson, played by the same actress, Sheryl Lee, was really Laura in disguise. Wrong, and wrong).

Laura Palmer is one of four *Twin Peaks* characters named after folks from *Laura*. Robert Lydecker, the never-seen veterinarian whose beatdown at a Low Town bar brings good buddy Phillip Gerard, the one-armed shoe salesman and vessel for the otherworldly Mike, to Calhoun Memorial Hospital, and thus to Cooper's attention, and Waldo the mynah bird, one of Dr. Lydecker's patients, are both nods at Waldo Lydecker (Clifton Webb), the acrid, persnickety newspaper columnist/radio commentator whose creepy fixation with Laura Hunt eventually mutates into homicidal rage ("I don't use a pen," he tells Laura in one early scene. "I write with a goose quill dipped in venom"). Twin Peaks' resident lunatic headshrinker, Dr. Lawrence Jacoby, suffering from a dire bout of Laura Palmer-itis, shares a surname with the similarly smitten painter (John Dexter) of the iconic Laura Hunt portrait hanging above the fireplace, though their appellations are pronounced differently (you say Ja-*co*-by, I say *Jack*-o-by). Waldo Lydecker may grumble that Laura Hunt's Jacoby "never captured her vibrance, her warmth," but the painting casts a powerful spell over McPherson, who finds himself becoming infatuated with a supposedly dead woman largely because of it, and even submits a bid to purchase it (accurate or not, the portrait certainly evokes Laura Palmer's framed homecoming-queen photo proudly displayed in the trophy case at Twin Peaks High School). While *Twin Peaks*' Agent Cooper never pines romantically for Laura Palmer in the way that McPherson does for his Laura, his determination to expose and apprehend her killer borders on obsession; whereas McPherson is convinced only he can spare Laura Hunt from the decadent, self-absorbed, morally bankrupt leeches who circle in her orbit, Cooper takes personal responsibility for restoring Laura's dignity in death, and honoring her memory.

Like *Twin Peaks*, *Laura* is about identity, and the interplay between reality and perception (yup, the "D" word again: duality). Both are soaked in oneirism, with a hypnagogic vibe that can make it tricky to distinguish wakefulness from hallucination. The prominence of dreams in *Twin Peaks* is explored elsewhere in these pages, but in *Laura* the title character's "return from the dead" stirs McPherson from a nap, so at first we wonder whether it is even really happening, rather than the fantasy of a man possessed. Later the flatfoot tells her, "Get some sleep. Forget the whole thing, like a bad dream." Lydecker's deranged farewell radio commentary pointedly quotes from Ernest Dowson's best-known poem: "They are not long, the days of wine and roses/Out of a misty dream/Our path emerges for a while, then closes/Within a dream," suggesting that life itself is merely a fleeting dream.

Interesting footnote: *Laura* was rather notoriously adapted for television in January 1968 by *Twin Peaks*' own network, ABC, as a vanity project for Lee Bouvier, Jacqueline Kennedy's sister, who was married to a Polish prince at the time and also went by the married name of Princess Lee Radziwill, though her on-screen credit is Bouvier. This adaptation was co-penned by Thomas W. Phipps and Truman Capote, Bouvier's buddy (TV critic Jack Gould of *The New York Times* dubbed Capote the "Professor Higgins of the jet set"), and overseen by celebrity producer/talk-show host David Susskind. Whatever else one might think of Susskind, he was a consummate showman, and certainly savvy enough to recognize a publicity bonanza when it was staring him in the face; he got everything he could have dreamed of out of Bouvier in *Laura*—an avalanche of clippings and ratings up the roof (38 million viewers, or 43 percent of all television sets in use at the time)—except for one thing: critical appreciation, and we're pretty sure he wasn't exactly taken aback by that. Typical of the reaction by our nation's esteemed television critics was this, from *Variety*: "Lee Bouvier was a disaster in the title role—a crucial failing for the show. . . . Miss Bouvier is neither good nor bad, she is just not an actress."

Ouch!

Norma Jennings (Peggy Lipton)

The kind, beautiful, world-weary proprietress of the Double R bakes a mean cherry pie and radiates melancholy resignation. Norma threw over her longtime high school boyfriend Big Ed Hurley for the exciting and dangerous Hank Jennings and regretted it bitterly after Jennings's criminal habits landed him in prison. Her reignited, now adulterous relationship with Big Ed hits one roadblock after another, and her own mother, a prominent restaurant critic, impugns her professional reputation. In other words, Norma is essentially another soap opera trope: the good woman constrained by impossible circumstances, suffering in silence. Lipton suffers very prettily indeed, and her natural gravitas lends Norma a feeling of significance that is not borne out by the plot; aside from securing Hank's parole, she doesn't

The incandescent Peggy Lipton as Double R honcho Norma Jennings (named for Norma Jean Baker?).

really affect any of the major characters' actions. Lipton's presence in the role is one of *TP*'s many references to bygone television; as the distaff member of *The Mod Squad*, (she briefly reunites with fellow *Mod Squad* cast member and *TP* guest star Clarence Williams III in an amusing scene), the actress epitomized counterculture cool. . . and now she's behind a lunch counter. Zing!

Shelly Johnson (Mädchen Amick)

Lovely Shelly Johnson works as a waitress at the Double R. She is married to Leo Johnson, who abuses her, and is engaged in a dangerous sexual affair with high school hoodlum Bobby Briggs. Shelly is tangential to the Laura Palmer case: her husband and boyfriend were both sexually/romantically involved with Laura and enablers of her drug habit, and both were suspected of her killing, but Shelly essentially had no role in Laura's life or death (Lynch was so taken with Amick he expanded her part on the show—see Gordon Cole's, played by Lynch himself, infatuation with Shelly, referenced below). Arguably Twin Peaks' most beautiful resident, Shelly struggles with low self-esteem—witness her taste in men—and a fatalistic acceptance of her drab lot in life, expressing surprise when Bobby suggests she enter the Miss Twin Peaks contest. In this way she resembles her employer, Norma, another gorgeous, defeated woman who fell for an exciting bad boy and wrecked her life because of it. Shelly can be a little tricky to pin down; she mostly appears to be a pleasant, essentially decent person caught up in a bad situation, but it is her undeniable attraction to the shadier side of the street that put her there. She reveals a cruel streak when the helpless, brain-damaged Leo is returned to her care after being shot, and she is morally slippery enough to participate in Bobby's medical fraud scheme without undue soul-searching. But perhaps we are meant to take a cue from Cole, Cooper's FBI superior, who takes an instant and immense shine to Shelly . . . he seems like a good judge of character. On the other hand, she really is just *that* pretty.

Irene Littlehorse (Geraldine Keams)

If you ever attend the annual *Twin Peaks* fan festival, be on the lookout for this trivia challenge: Name the two Irenes who appear in *Twin Peaks*. One is Irene the waitress at Hap's Diner, who appears in *Fire Walk with Me*, and the other is this Irene, the real-estate agent who takes Cooper to visit Dead Dog Farm in episode nineteen ("The Black Widow"), while he is suspended by the FBI and considering buying property in Twin Peaks. No matter how many times we watch this episode we can't stop thinking of Irene as a Native American iteration of the comedian Roseanne Barr, except way cheerier. Irene doesn't even want to show Cooper Dead Dog Farm ("It's worse than it sounds"), but as fate would have it, a coin that Cooper flips to decide which of two other properties to see first lands instead on a photo of this bucolic fixer-upper, as Cooper generously describes it to Diane, which turns out to be an extremely fortuitous development, since Cooper winds up discovering traces of cocaine on the property, leading eventually to his takedown of Jean Renault and his reinstatement to the bureau. Turns out Irene's expertise extends not only to real estate but also to local lore, as, after driving Cooper to Dead Dog Farm in her nondescript Buick sedan, she fills him in on the legend behind the place: "Of all the people in the world, the best and the worst are drawn to Dead Dog, and most turn away. Only those with the purest of heart can feel its pain, and somewhere in between the rest of us struggle." Sounds Black Lodge–connected to us, but the writers never really went anywhere with it.

The Log Lady: aka Margaret Lanterman (Catherine E. Coulson)

Arguably the most eccentric character in a town creeping and crawling with them, the Log Lady (real name: Margaret Lanterman) is rude and prickly,

The Log Lady never went anywhere without her ponderosa pine (the subject of Lynch's father's thesis).

but a valuable ally to have, especially if you've run up against a brick wall while conducting a murder investigation. Margaret's singular gift is that she communes with a hunk of ponderosa pine, which she carries around with her whenever she goes, cradling it in her arms like a baby. Some have suggested that within the log resides the spirit of her deceased husband, a lumberjack who perished under mysterious circumstances (involving a flash of light and an owl call) in a fire soon after their wedding, which may or may not accurate, but Margaret is sure convinced the log possesses preternatural wisdom, and given everything that happens over the course of two seasons, it's hard to argue. She and Cooper get off to a rocky start—he can't quite bring himself to converse with her log when first invited to do so, and it is some time before he knows how to act and what to say in her presence (she even slaps his hand once, when he reaches for a cookie without waiting for the tea)—but eventually they develop a profound bond, and her Cassandra-like talents are crucial to Cooper's investigation (it is Margaret who, channeling her log's recollection of events in the woods on the night of Laura's murder, suggests the presence of a mysterious Third Man, someone other than Jacques and Leo, who turns out to be Leland/Bob, Laura's killer). Their shared gift as receptacles of supernatural knowledge is highlighted in the Roadhouse scene where the Giant tells Cooper "It is happening again" as, across town, Leland/Bob is brutalizing Maddy: everyone in the room freezes as the Giant speaks except for Cooper and Margaret (look closely and you'll see her hands moving over her log). Like so many of the oddballs who roam this neck of the woods, the Log Lady prefers to speak in code, pregnant with meaning—who knows if her comment that "Fire is the devil hiding like a coward in the smoke" is as good an explanation as we'll ever get of "Fire walk with me"? Like the Giant, she seems preoccupied with owls, as when she assures Cooper, Harry, Hawk, and Doc Hayward that "the owls won't see us in here" (meaning her cabin in the woods), or when she translates her log's account of events overheard and seen on the night of Laura's murder ("The owls were flying. . . . The owls were near. . . . The owls were silent"), or when, just hours before Maddy's demise, she searches out Cooper at the sheriff's station and tells him, "We don't know what will happen or when, but there are owls in the Roadhouse." During the Windom Earle arc, the Log Lady keeps a lower profile, but eventually reveals a pair of marks on the back of her right leg—they look like twin mountain peaks, and are a souvenir from a walk in the woods when she was seven years old and disappeared for a day—that play a crucial role in Cooper's eventual discovery of the petroglyph in Owl Cave, a map to the Black Lodge. Margaret is among the Lynch-favored characters resurrected by the director for the series finale after being omitted from the original script, in her case to explain one of the series' nagging mysteries: the significance of the scorched engine oil odor detected by Ronette Pulaski, Laura Palmer, Maddy Ferguson, and Dr. Jacoby, all while in the presence of Bob. Margaret shows up at the sheriff's station with a jar of oil and, at Cooper's prompting, reports that her husband brought it home one night shortly before his death, claiming it was "an opening to a gateway." True dat, as a pool of the stuff is located in Glastonbury Grove, by the entrance to the Black Lodge. The Log Lady also makes a very brief but crucial appearance in *Fire Walk with Me*, approaching Laura Palmer one night as she is about to enter the Roadhouse. Placing her right hand on Laura's forehead, Margaret cautions the girl against yielding to her darker impulses: "When this kind of fire starts, it is very hard to put out. The tender boughs of innocence burn first, and the wind rises, and then . . . all goodness is in jeopardy." Profoundly touched, Laura examines

Jack Nance and his iconic hairdo in Lynch's feature-film debut, *Eraserhead*.

her reflection (and surely her soul) in the Roadhouse door, and once inside begins sobbing, but the sudden appearance of Donna seems to overwhelm whatever hope she had summoned, and so the debauchery begins. The Log Lady was portrayed by Catherine E. Coulson, who was an assistant director on David Lynch's first feature-length film, *Eraserhead* (1977), in which she also briefly appears, and was married to that film's star, Jack Nance (Pete Martell in *Twin Peaks*), from 1968 to 1976. According to lore, it was during the filming of *Eraserhead* that the director first came up with the idea of casting Coulson as a single woman who carries around a log after her husband was killed in a fire, originally for a show that would have been titled *I'll Test My Log with Every Branch of Knowledge* (if it helps, Lynch's dad was a scientist for the federal government whose job involved examining trees for signs of disease). In 1993, when Bravo began airing repeats of *Twin Peaks*, Coulson was recruited in the guise of the Log Lady to read the brand-new Lynch-penned intros. The only one who *really* had a problem with Margaret was Norma Jennings, who scolded her for sticking chewed gum on the counters and walls at the Double R diner. Coulson's death in September 2015—she was already set to appear in the Showtime relaunch—devastated the *Twin Peaks* community.

Dr. Robert (Bob) Lydecker (None)

Yes, another Bob, and while this one never actually appears in *Twin Peaks* or *Fire Walk with Me*, he does play a Rosencrantz-and-Guildenstern-like role in the events that unfold in the series. Beaten into a coma outside a bar in Low Town on February 25, Lydecker is brought to Calhoun Memorial Hospital, where he's visited by good friend Phillip Michael Gerard, the One-Armed Man who had a featured role in Cooper's Red Room dream and whom Hawk spots wandering the hallways at Calhoun. Thus it's Lydecker who indirectly introduces Cooper to the man who eventually leads him to Killer Bob. That alone rocks, but there's more: Lydecker, a veterinarian, treated a mynah named Waldo, who belongs to Jacques Renault and who, Cooper eventually discovers, was present at Jacques's cabin on the night of Laura's murder. Sadly, Bob Lydecker's fate is never revealed to us. He, like Waldo, was named after dandyish newspaper columnist Waldo Lydecker, a character from the film noir *Laura*, whose title character also may have some connection to *Twin Peaks* (wink).

Pete Martell (Jack Nance)

"She's dead . . . wrapped in plastic." That chilling pronouncement became a macabre catch phrase that somehow distilled the specific weirdness of *Twin Peaks* into a single disturbing, weirdly funny sentence. The line derives most of its impact—certainly its uncomfortable humor—from the affectless drawling delivery of Jack Nance, an actor whose eccentricities Lynch had employed to unforgettable effect in his landmark film *Eraserhead*. The image of a shock-haired Nance's staring, haunted visage has become an icon of independent cinema, and his skewed charisma is put to excellent use here in the form of the kindly, confused, peace-craving fisherman Pete Martell. Married to an unhappy, verbally abusive shrew, Pete paternally dotes on Josie and mostly tries to keep a low profile. He is incidental to the series' plots until the point at which his prodigious chess skills become useful in Cooper's deadly game with Windom Earle. Pete is a joy whenever he appears, a warm, avuncular presence with a distinct but pleasant oddness, a sensibility that seems to hover somewhere between *Field and Stream* and the rings of Saturn. No one else could make such a meal of the line "there was a fish in the percolator," and we're really ticked off that he accompanied Andrew on that fatal errand to the bank. Nance passed away in 1996, at the age of fifty-three.

Dell Mibbler (Ed Wright)

Creaky Dell Mibbler, the antediluvian loan manager at Twin Peaks Savings and Loan, is having just another day at the office in the series finale (his lone appearance in the series, though he does turn up in a deleted *FWWM* scene) until Audrey Horne shows up to protest the Ghostwood development project by chaining herself to the vault, after which he winds up at least kerfuffled, and possibly dead. Dell escorts Andrew Packard and Pete Martell to safety deposit box 14761, where, unbeknownst to all, Thomas Eckhardt has planted an explosive device, the force of which upon detonation propels Dell's oversized black glasses all the way onto one of those magnificent Douglas firs that Cooper is always chattering about (at least we think they're Dell's glasses). The fates of Dell, Andrew, Peter, and even Audrey were left unknown. Dell hoards over sixty seconds of uninterrupted airtime shuffling to and from a water cooler to fetch Audrey a drink, and director Lynch soaks up every glorious bit of it, evoking the similarly glacially paced scene with Señor Droolcup (the Waiter), Cooper, and the glass of warm milk in the second-season opener. Mibbler was portrayed by Ed Wright, who had appeared as the unnamed desk clerk in Lynch's 1990 film *Wild at Heart*.

The Milfords (John Boylan/Tony Jay/Robyn Lively)

Hoary Twin Peaks Mayor Dwayne Milford (Boylan) pops up briefly in the series pilot, presiding over the town hall meeting arranged by Cooper in the wake of Laura's murder, but is quickly shunted aside when he can't figure out how to work the microphone (Luddite!). Dwayne disappears then for sixteen episodes before returning midway into season two; better he should have stayed away forever. The occasion for his resurfacing is Leland Palmer's wake, where he and his likewise ancient brother Dougie (Tony Jay), owner of the *Twin Peaks Gazette*, engage in fisticuffs over Lana Budding (Robyn Lively), the fetching teenager who's about to become Dougie's fifth wife, despite being a tiny fraction of his age. Dougie's licentious lifestyle is an irritant to Dwayne, and this newest spat is just the latest manifestation of a feud that erupted some fifty years earlier for nebulous reasons having something to do with an old flame in a rumble seat, as Doc Hayward reports it. Sadly Dougie doesn't survive the morning after his marriage, dying of a heart attack "with his boots on," as Sheriff Truman phrases it, after what looks to have been a busy night of sexual high jinks. This provokes outrage from Dwayne, who brands Lana a "murdering hussy" who slayed his brother with sex. More accurately, Lana's a conniving vixen, dripping in French perfume and Southern honey, with the power to bewitch any man who circles within her orbit, including, eventually, Dwayne—a gift she shamelessly exploits by seducing Miss Twin Peaks judge Dick Tremayne and refusing to elope with Dwayne unless he arranges for her to win the pageant, which, sadly for Dwayne's sake, she doesn't (losing to Annie Blackburne).

Nicholas "Little Nicky" Needleman (Joshua Harris)

Demon seed or rambunctious child? That is the question Dick Tremayne and Deputy Andy Brennan set out to answer after Dick becomes convinced that Little Nicky is the devil, "or at the very least homicidal in the first degree." Let's take a step back: Dick, trying to woo a pregnant Lucy, claims to have undergone an epiphany, concluding that he is a "terrible, crashing bore" who needs someone in his life to care for (we could have told him that *eons* ago). That someone turns out to be Little Nicky, an orphan who—according to his case manager (portrayed by future Not Ready for Prime Timer Molly Shannon)—has been victimized throughout his brief life by "persistent random misfortune," including the mysterious death of his parents. After being subjected to multiple instances of annoying behavior by Nicky, and then nearly being crushed by a car while changing a wheel as Nicky looks on, Dick becomes convinced of Nicky's satanic roots, and is certain the boy had something to do with his parents' death, none of which turns out to be true, of course. For a character who functions largely as comic relief, Nicky turns out to have a terribly tragic backstory, as Doc Hayward finally explains to Lucy's two hapless suitors, who are driven to tears upon hearing it (which is exactly how we felt watching the bulk of this broadly comedic storyline).

Herbert Neff (Mark Lowenthal)

This prematurely balding, tweed-jacket-wearing life-insurance peddler—named after Fred MacMurray's hard-boiled sap in Billy Wilder's 1944 adaptation of the classic James M. Cain noir *Double Indemnity* (the plot of which the *Twin Peaks* writers essentially appropriated for the calamitous season-two arc involving James and Evelyn Marsh)—is, judging by appearance, about as bland and straight-arrow as they come, but as things turn out he is, like so many of the residents of Twin Peaks, a morally dubious chap with grand ambition (we know this because when Catherine Martell flat out asks him if he is an ambitious man, he replied, "One likes to think so."). Neff calls on Catherine one night at Blue Pine Lodge to collect her signature on a $1 million life insurance policy that names Josie Packard as her beneficiary—and that Catherine knows absolutely nothing about. Turns out the policy was purchased by Josie and Ben Horne, which is both eye-opening and devastating to Catherine, who all this time was thinking that Ben not only was in cahoots with her to wrestle the mill from Josie, but also that he might actually have felt something for her emotionally (they *were* poking each other, but come on; this is Ben Horne we're talking about!). What's interesting about Neff is that he could have made a mint off the policy by agreeing to let Ben Horne "collect" (read "forge") Catherine's signature, no questions asked, but insisted instead on checking in with her himself, at the risk of losing the sale. This seems at first a noble choice, but it turns out Neff is angling for something bigger and better, which becomes clear when he offers to lend Catherine his assistance with the policy "or anything at all," and then responds receptively to her query about his ambition. James M. Cain would be proud of this guy.

Mike Nelson (Gary Hershberger)

Mike Nelson. . . even the name rings generic. In season one, Mike is almost exclusively seen in the company of best buddy Bobby Briggs; biker Joey Paulsen/Paulson even derides them as Mutt and Jeff during the pilot's Roadhouse rumble scene. Physically, Mike emits a much softer vibe (Bobby's color scheme is black, as in his leather jacket and hair; Mike's a strawberry blonde who for all we know sleeps in that red varsity jacket), and he is sufficiently functional to adapt his behavior for adults if beneficial to his cause (a skill Bobby develops over time), but there's no denying that he, like Bobby, has embraced the dark side, dealing drugs to high school students on behalf of the truculent Leo Johnson. Mike, whom Bobby affectionately calls Snake, is further distinguished by his Neanderthal approach to women, in particular Donna Hayward, whom he barks at like she's his indentured servant, once even manhandling her by the lapels to impress upon her the depth of his dissatisfaction (not that she cares). In season two, Mike is pure comic relief, object of desire for superhuman Nadine Hurley ("He has the cutest buns"), and irony notwithstanding, it's not a proud moment for anyone.

Andrew Packard (Dan O'Herlihy)

Hear this, a dead man's tale: Andrew Packard, reputedly deceased, makes a surprise appearance at the end of episode eighteen ("Masked Ball"), and frankly it takes us all of about five seconds to recognize him for what he is: a cold-hearted bastard. Sometime within the year prior to the advent of the series, Andrew, owner of Packard mill and perhaps the most powerful man in Twin Peaks ("Andrew Packard practically built this town," Sheriff Truman tells Cooper), was supposedly killed in a boat explosion rigged by Hank Jennings, who was paid $90,000 for the job by Andrew's wife Josie, upon orders from Andrew's Hong Kong–based former business associate Thomas Eckhardt after their relationship had soured. However, Andrew, aided by his sister Catherine, sussed out the scheme, faked his death, and went into hiding in Pearl Lakes, all the while patiently plotting revenge, an especially ominous development for everyone involved, as Andrew is accustomed to getting what he wants. Hence, the trail of dead bodies he winds up leaving in his wake, including Josie's and Eckhardt's, even if he never pulls the trigger himself (Andrew is more of an "idea man"). Andrew has a jocose gene that he enjoys indulging with Pete —boys will be boys—which drives the humorless Catherine mad, but make no mistake: he's a pitiless, sadistic shark in a world swimming with them. On the plus side, he's a spiffy dresser and speaks beautifully.

Josie Packard (Joan Chen)

Exotic, mysterious, beautiful Josie Packard, the embattled owner of the Packard Sawmill (as played by the luminous Joan Chen), was a last-minute addition to the series; the part of the alluring foreign woman was originally conceived for Isabella Rossellini. Chen's stunning beauty and effortless sensuality make Josie a superficially appealing presence, and her affection for kindly Pete and romantic relationship with Sheriff Truman cue us to consider her one of the "good guys"; why, that mean old Catherine Martell wants to cheat the poor woman out of her inheritance! Ah, but Josie is also a prostitute, con artist, thief, and murderer, cat's-paw of the vengeful Thomas Eckhardt, orchestrator of the murder attempt on Andrew Packard, point-blank shooter of Agent Cooper, and, ultimately, a haunted knob on a dresser. Don't judge a book by its cover, we guess is what we're saying. Josie has no strong connection to the Laura story (Laura tutored the Chinese

Duality imagery, a melancholy, mysterious, beautiful woman: Josie Packard regards the mirror, the first character seen in *Twin Peaks*.

national in English)—she's a classic femme fatale, caught up in the Martell/ Horne/Packard/Packard Sawmill/Ghostwood Estates intrigues—so it comes as a particular surprise when her death (from fear) summons Bob and the MFAP, who consign her to her confounding fate.

Sarah Palmer (Grace Zabriskie)

With her staring, haunted eyes, blasted nimbus of frizzy hair, and features drawn into a permanent rictus of pain, Sarah Palmer, mother of the abused and murdered Laura, wears the face of grief itself. Sarah's frequent bouts of inconsolable sobbing keep the horror of Laura's death front and center— it is through her devastation that we are most strongly reminded that Laura's death is not just a mystery, but a tragedy. Even before her daughter's murder, Sarah suffered from nerves, filling countless ashtrays with the cigarettes she chain-smoked, suggesting she knew or sensed something of the horrific sexual abuse perpetrated by her husband against their child. She also seems touched by the supernatural: Sarah Palmer experiences visions, including the gruesome visage of Bob, the discovery of Laura's necklace, and, most

Sarah Palmer, shattered by grief and terror.

perplexingly, the image of a majestic white horse standing in her living room. It is perhaps this psychic talent that allows Windom Earle to use her as a vessel, channeling his voice to inform Major Briggs of Agent Cooper's new residency in the Black Lodge. This sensitivity is not a gift; Sarah Palmer is a woman who has seen too much and learned truths too difficult to bear. The terrible cost of this knowledge is apparent in her ravaged visage and shell-shocked demeanor: a soul rent to pieces by grief and fear.

Joey Paulson/Paulsen (Brett Vadset)

This ponytailed biker/Bookhouse Boy shows up thrice, twice in season one and once in season two, and the poor guy's name is listed on-screen differently every time: he's Joey in the pilot, Joey Paulson in episode two, and Joey Paulsen in episode thirteen ("Demons"). Hey, how about a little respect? Joey's one of the good guys: in the pilot, he sneaks Donna out of the Roadhouse rumble so she can meet up with James in the woods, and in a later episode stands guard over Bernard Renault so Harry and Coop can pump the hapless Canuck with questions. Shouldn't loyalty work both ways?

Tim Pinkle (David L. Lander)

Yes, *Laverne & Shirley*'s Squiggy (David L. Lander) bagged a recurring role in *Twin Peaks*, though not much of one, appearing briefly in three second-season episodes as Tim Pinkle: once as a weaselly salesman peddling defective home-care contraptions to Shelly and Bobby for the vegetative Leo; once as a weaselly soldier in Ben Horne's Stop Ghostwood crusade, disrupting the benefit fashion show when the real (pine) weasel in his care escapes and runs amok; and finally as a weaselly choreographer overseeing the dance segment at the Miss Twin Peaks pageant, cumulatively demonstrating beyond any reasonable doubt that Tim Pinkle is utterly devoid of talent or charisma.

Jeanie Pombelek (None)

Never-seen employee at the Clean-and-Save dry-cleaning outlet that Pete Martell visits in episode twenty-two ("Slaves and Masters") to pick up Josie's clothes, which is problematic only in that Jeanie doesn't speak a drop of English and the only Hungarian words Pete knows are "paprika" and "goulash." This is significant in that when Pete unloads the dry cleaning back at

Blue Pine Lodge in order to take a phone call, Cooper surreptitiously lifts a couple of items, allowing Albert to eventually connect the powder residue on Josie's glove to the gun used to shoot him in the season-one send-off.

Eric Powell (Craig MacLachlan)

Hmmm, MacLachlan . . . sounds familiar, no? Craig is Kyle's brother, whose sole contribution to *Twin Peaks* was as a production assistant until he got tapped for the lifeless, thankless role of Eric Powell, the ex-merchant marine/vagrant stabbed to death by Windom Earle and left in the sheriff's station along with a chessboard during the Earle-induced blackout, a black pawn stuffed inside his taped-shut mouth. Eric's crime? His surname, same as the maiden name of Windom's late wife Caroline, whom Earle killed after discovering that she and Cooper were lovers.

Janek and Maria/Suburbis Pulaski (Rick Tutor/Alan Ogle; Roberta Maguire/Michele Milantoni)

Stout, hardy folk who worship at the altar of flannel, Ronette Pulaski's parents seem like decent enough people, though their daughter sure turned out a mess. Janek Pulaski appears briefly and silently in the pilot, portrayed by Rick Tutor; his wife, originally named Maria, didn't make the cut, and thus actress Roberta Maguire is listed in the end credits without ever actually appearing in the series, at least discernibly. By the following episode both parts had been recast (with Alan Ogle and Michele Milantoni) and Mrs. Pulaski renamed Suburbis, of all things. They appear just briefly, sitting vigil outside Ronette's hospital room as Hawk pumps them for clues.

Ronette Pulaski (Phoebe Augustine)

Ronette spends the entire first season comatose and utters only a handful of intelligible lines throughout the series (more in *Fire Walk Me*), yet rates among the most important characters in *Twin Peaks*, being Laura's companion on the night of her murder and the only eyewitness to her abduction and torture ("One person saw the Third Man," the Giant cryptically advises Cooper). That alone would suffice, but Ronette's fugue-state traversing of the state line in the immediate aftermath of her ordeal in the train car is what brings Laura Palmer's murder to the attention of the FBI, and hence accounts for Cooper's dispatch. We know only the barest of details about her, yet the picture that emerges isn't pretty: Ronette's an extremely troubled young woman who travels in the same debauched circles as Laura, for reasons that are never made clear, as her parents seem like decent enough folks. Ronette consumes copious amounts of drugs and alcohol, touts herself in *Flesh World* classifieds, freely copulates with the hideous Jacques and Leo (among others), and indulges in sex for hire (in *Fire Walk with Me*, Teresa Banks arranges for a four-way "party" involving Ronette, Laura, Leland, and herself, though Leland skips out at the last minute, after learning that one of the girls is Laura). Like Laura, Ronette works the perfume counter at Horne's department store, where both are recruited by the odious Emory Battis for One Eyed Jacks, a notorious den of sin secretly owned by Benjamin Horne. For those who like their analysis deeper, it's been said that Ronette is the yin to Donna Hayward's yang, each representing an aspect of Laura's duality: typical of Lynch-Frost, it is the lighter-haired Ronette who personifies the corrupted Laura, the dark-haired Donna the idealized one. Makes sense to us. In *FWWM* Ronette meets up with Laura at Partyland, where Jacques Renault refers to them as the "party twins . . . my high school sandwich," as gross as that is. Here Ronette informs Laura that Teresa Banks had, at the time of her death, been blackmailing somebody, which Jacques confirms, revealing that Teresa called to ask for descriptions of each of the two girls' fathers, after Leland skipped out on the foursome. Here too Jacques extends his fateful invitation to the two girls to visit his cabin on Thursday, which turns out to be the last night of Laura's life. Ronette has the misfortune of being at the wrong place at the wrong time, and is dragged from the cabin to the abandoned train car along with Laura by Leland/Bob, where she pleads for forgiveness, and is visited by a guardian angel. Apparently Leland/Bob leaves Ronette for dead after belting her and tossing her out of the train car as he spots her trying to escape. Ronette trivia: In the original, "Northwest Passage" script, the character's name is Sharon Pulaski. In the revised script, her first name is spelled Ronnette, which is also the case in the end credits to the series finale, as well as in Jennifer Lynch's *The Secret Diary of Laura Palmer*.

Jack Racine (Van Dyke Parks)

Singer-songwriter/Brian Wilson confederate Van Dyke Parks appears in a single episode of *Twin Peaks* (season two, episode five), as Leo Johnson's attorney, and it's pretty low-key. Parks's Racine (same surname as William Hurt's lawyer character in the 1981 neo-noir *Body Heat*) argues that prosecuting Leo for the multiple crimes he stands accused of committing would constitute a "mockery of the justice system," given the medically established fact that Leo is brain dead (in a literal sense). He wins.

Harold Smith (Lenny Von Dohlen)

A lonely soul. Gentle, retiring, and agoraphobic, Harold Smith is a romantic, housebound young man who befriended Laura Palmer in the course of her duties as a Meals on Wheels delivery volunteer. Harold raises orchids and is a bit of a hothouse flower himself, fragile, tremulous, and totally isolated from the wider reality of Twin Peaks, which makes him essentially invisible to the likes of Bob. Laura finds a refuge in Smith's lair, and entrusts him with her secret diary . . . which is a shame, because Donna's later theft of said diary drives the unstable Smith to suicide. Too pure for this world, Harold Smith dies among his beloved blooms, and whatever secrets he kept die with him.

Judy Swain (Molly Shannon)

Future (1995–2001) Not Ready for Prime Time Player Molly Shannon appears in just one *Twin Peaks* scene (episode nineteen, "The Black Widow"), as Judy Swain, caseworker from the Happy Helping Hands organization, which regrettably links her to the dreadful Little Nicky arc that stained the series in the immediate aftermath of the resolution of the Laura Palmer murder. Swain's specific function is to freak out Dick Tremayne with news that even in his brief life to date Nicky has been the victim of "persistent random misfortune," which presumably doesn't involve having to watch these episodes, but does include the fact that his parents were killed under "mysterious circumstances." This news eventually plays a role in convincing the clueless Dick that the boy is a demon seed (untrue, of course), whereas our own conclusion is that it is Dick himself who is in league with the devil. The most notable thing about Shannon's performance here is her nifty red-and-black plaid blazer. And speaking of Dick Tremayne . . .

Dick Tremayne (Ian Buchanan)

Tremayne is a divisive figure in *Twin Peaks* fandom; while Ian Buchanan's portrayal of the unctuous, pretentious menswear salesman is undeniably droll, the character largely exists to drive some of the series' least loved plotlines, including the "who's-the-father" imbroglio among himself, Andy, and Lucy, and the disastrous Little Nicky adoption arc, which feels like a strained joke that never quite comes off. Still, Tremayne's catastrophic failure hosting a charity event for the endangered pine weasel is a comic highlight of the series, and the character's flamboyantly dandyish sartorial sense contributes greatly to *Twin Peaks'* striking use of fashion to evoke character, setting, and mood.

Waldo (None)

"Where we're from, the birds sing a pretty song . . ." Waldo is a mynah character (some jokes are hard to resist), but a crucial one; Jacques Renault's Gracula religiosa (commonly known as a hill mynah bird), he was present at Jacques's cabin on the night of Laura's murder, and thus witnessed the sexual debauchery that unfolded among Laura, Ronette, Jacques, and Leo immediately before the two women were dragged to the abandoned train car where Laura was murdered. Mynah birds being gifted mimickers of the human voice, Coop and the gang are hopeful Waldo has something pertinent to say, so he leaves his voice-activated mini-tape recorder on overnight at the sheriff's station, where Waldo is being temporarily caged, in case the bird decides to start yapping. As we learn from Jacques, it was Waldo who generated the bite marks on Laura's shoulders, having pecked away at her after Jacques liberated him from his cage; Laura's protests prompted Leo to stuff a One Eyed Jacks poker chip in her mouth, telling her to "Bite the bullet, baby!" Waldo meets a tragic end, picked off by a shotgun-wielding Leo, who's fearful he'll spill the beans about that night, his blood spilling like jelly onto a tableful of doughnuts. Waldo's last words: "Laura? Laura? Don't go there. Hurting me. Hurting me. Stop it. Stop it. Stop it. Leo, no! Leo, no!" Waldo is the namesake of Waldo Lydecker, a character from the Otto Preminger noir *Laura*.

6

The Quiet Elegance of the Dark Suit and Tie

Fashion in *Twin Peaks*

> *The casual indifference of these muted earth tones is a form of fashion suicide, but, uh, call me crazy—on you it works.*

Twin Peaks is, among other things, an immersive exercise in world-building: every element of the show, including the music, sets, hair, and makeup styling—pretty much everything you can see or hear—works in concert to suggest an aesthetically consistent, wholly contained reality. A major component of this "unity of effect" (Edgar Allan Poe's term, for all you lit majors out there) is the characters' wardrobe. *Twin Peaks'* hazy fifties/eighties postmodern twilight zone of references found exuberant expression in clothing, and style mavens quickly singled out the show's potent retro-chic sartorial glamor as a major component of its appeal. In fact, several fashion houses—including Suckers Apparel and Spain's TitisClothing—have issued clothing lines directly influenced by and referencing *Twin Peaks* style.

The rightness of the show's clothing choices goes beyond the juxtaposition of fifties and eighties style cues, though the melding of those curiously rhyming eras, with their emphasis on mythic Americana and capitalist optimism, could not be more on the money. *Twin Peaks* achieves the rare feat of making its characters' clothing feel completely authentic and specific to their situations and temperaments—the apparel seems to have been hanging for decades in their owners' closets rather than from a rack in a wardrobe trailer.

Longtime David Lynch collaborator Patricia Norris dressed the cast for the pilot, but wardrobe duties would be handled by Sara Markowitz for the duration of the series. Below, we single out some of the more distinctively attired denizens of Twin Peaks and take a closer look at what they're wearing.

Agent Dale Cooper

Cooper's look is aggressively correct, the image of moral rectitude and government authority. Cooper's simple black suits, solid dress shirts, and conservative striped ties mark him as a straight-arrow company man and invest him with a baseline gravitas somewhat at odds with his gee-whiz boy's adventure demeanor. His trench coat is straight out of the Noir Detective Handbook, and it's easy to imagine him late at night in his room at the Great Northern, scrupulously shining his sensible black oxfords by lamplight.

When Cooper is suspended from the Bureau in season two, he leaves the suit in the closet and goes native, dressing in plaid flannel and heavy twill trousers. This instantly visually strips him of roughly 89 percent of his perceived power and authority—he appears diminished, "Dale who eats at the diner" rather than "Agent Cooper of the F.B.I." Actually, so immaculately handsome and poreless is MacLachlan that he hardly looks human in this getup, more like some kind of "Northwoods Ken" doll companion to Barbie. Thank goodness he's back in "the quiet elegance of the dark suit and tie" before the series ends.

Audrey Horne

The vixen, the good/bad girl, Lolita of the pines . . . Audrey Horne oozes style. Pairing tight sweaters with full wool skirts, alternating Sunday School saddle oxfords with trashy red heels, Audrey literally wears her divided nature on the outside, and looks amazing doing it. Her wardrobe is both retro and timeless, suiting her old-Hollywood glamorous good looks—she's Elizabeth Taylor in the Twilight Zone, a pinup queen who's joined the Junior League, Bettie Page gone Ivy League. She's intoxicating is what she is, a style legend, the quintessence of *Twin Peaks'* queasily nostalgic and dangerously potent erotic allure.

Audrey Horne's iconic saddle shoes— the production crew was unable to locate a pair of these schoolgirl classics in Snoqualmie, so they altered a pair of plain white oxfords with black paint.

Dick Tremayne

There are fashion victims, there are fashion casualties, and then there is Dick Tremayne. So unctuous he's almost a fossil fuel, the menswear salesman affects a nauseatingly fussy style, layering vests and jackets and shirts and ties sporting clashing tartans and plaids, extraneous belts and buckles, and a general effect of complete overkill. Taken individually, the elements of his wardrobe are all rather nice, natty, British sportsman–inspired classic pieces that would make Ralph Lauren weep. But Tremayne piles it on indiscriminately, and elegance and style curdle into precious, dandyish affectation. Gross.

Pete Martell

An absolute (albeit unwitting) style success—Pete may be the best-dressed man in town. With classic country-gentleman tweeds and knits; handsome,

Pete Martell, silver fox and the best-dressed man in town.

masculine plaids; and a rare knack for pulling off a fedora, Pete is an Orvis catalog illustration come to life, the epitome of outdoorsy tradition and sylvan élan. Pete unconsciously dresses in the rustic but gentlemanly manner Dick Tremayne tarts up into eye-assaulting pretension, and always looks great.

The Log Lady

Mrs. Lanterman definitely has some Earth shoes in her closet—she tends toward earth tones in general (they match her chief accessory, a log), and her eccentric art professor look, with oversized red spectacle frames, voluminous cardigans, severe bobbed haircut, and nature-referencing pins and brooches, suggests a hippie past. One of the series' most visually iconic characters, the Log Lady is a popular choice for *TP* cosplayers.

Benjamin Horne

Twin Peaks' leading entrepreneur is an archetypal yuppie, sporting low-slung double-breasted suits, polka-dotted ties against striped shirts, and gold-rimmed glasses. He's more Gordon Gekko than Mark Trail, and as such is distinguished visually as an anomaly in Twin Peaks—his look, like his brother's, is pure eighties (although a more subdued take), suggesting he is the rare man in town disposed to buying new clothes, a vain man concerned with image and status. He does switch up his look after suffering a nervous breakdown, harkening back to the sixties—the 1860s—with a Civil War general's uniform.

Jerry Horne

The diminutive younger brother of Benjamin, Jerry compensates for his small stature with a flamboyant dress sense that suits his rapacious and boisterous personality. Jerry commits many sartorial sins particular to the eighties: ugly designer spectacles, wild geometric patterns, linebacker shoulder pads, boxy blazers, flashy two-toned shoes, bolo string ties . . . he's a garish disaster, but it works for him. It also marks him as essentially an outsider; Twin Peaks may be home, but Jerry is a "sophisticated" citizen of the world, and it only figures his clothing choices would reflect that.

Benjamin Horne, channeling *Wall Street*'s Gordon Gekko.

Dr. Jacoby

Jacoby's eccentric ensembles, featuring loud Hawaiian shirts and sunglasses with mismatched red and blue lenses, reek of affectation; he's a sharply perceptive psychiatrist, despite his clownish appearance, and we wonder if his look is deliberately cultivated to keep others off guard.

James Hurley

Work shirts, jeans, leather jacket: standard fifties Brando biker apparel, which the mopey, soft-eyed James utterly fails to carry off; he's so clearly a sensitive marshmallow in bad boy drag. Still, he instantly registers visually as the iconic juvenile delinquent he's meant to represent, so the clothes work as far as that goes.

Annie Blackburne

Poor Annie. Actress Heather Graham is a pneumatic bombshell, but vulnerable, damaged Annie Blackburne, when not in her utilitarian Double R uniform, dresses like a refugee from the Wilder family, far from her little house on the prairie. Full sleeves, high ruffled necks, massive skirts . . . Annie came to Twin Peaks straight from a convent, and it shows.

Nadine Hurley

Open-toed sandals with socks, shiny leotards, piratical eyepatch, cheerleader uniform: genius. Nadine, never change.

7

Another Great Moment in Law Enforcement History

Dossiers: Lawmen

Deputy Andy Brennan (Harry Goaz)

The comic relief. Clumsy, gormless, slow-witted, Deputy Andy Brennan was *Twin Peaks'* most dependable comic engine, an endearingly disastrous collision of pratfalls and good intentions wrapped in a gangling frame and set off by Goaz's melancholy low warble of a voice. Andy does display competence from time to time: his sketch of Bob based on Mrs. Palmer's description is a perfect likeness, and he puts his marksmanship tutorials to effective use when his quick shooting saves Harry from the treacherous Jacques Renault. Even Andy's clumsiness pays dividends, as when a loose board reveals a large cache of cocaine as the hapless lawman receives a bonk on the noggin, or when his wild axe swing activates the petroglyph in Owl Cave. Most of Andy's screen time involves his tortured relationship with receptionist Lucy Moran, for good and ill; his hangdog lilt and her nasal chirp combine in delightful duets of absurdist badinage, but the love triangle with Dick Tremayne and the saga of Little Nicky generally rank low on most fans' lists of favorite storylines. Perhaps Andy's most important quality is his innate, unshakable decency—in the often abject world of *Twin Peaks*, Andy stands as a rare beacon of uncomplicated goodness, and it is his helpless teary breakdown upon the discovery of Laura Palmer's body that informs the audience of the emotional seriousness underpinning the show's more flamboyantly outré conceits.

Deputy Tommy "The Hawk" Hill (Michael Horse)

The steady, stoic backbone of the Twin Peaks Sheriff's Department and Bookhouse Boy in good standing, Deputy Hawk serves and protects with quiet, unfailing competence and provides a useful counterbalance to the well-intentioned but fragile Deputy Andy Brennan. Not just a rock-solid lawman, Hawk also possesses expert tracking skills and easily navigates the occult and mythic lore aspects of the Laura Palmer case (he groks the concept of the White and Black lodges from the jump), as befits his Native American heritage, but he's also one of Twin Peaks' most down-to-earth and practical residents, a man who can really appreciate a Brandeis-trained veterinarian.

The Bookhouse Boys, including honorary member Agent Cooper . . . because *somebody* had to fight the evil in those old woods. *ABC/Photofest*

Truman and Doc Hayward examine Pete's gruesome discovery.

Lucy Moran, winsome heartbreaker of the Twin Peaks Sheriff's Department.

Lucy Moran (Kimmy Robertson)

The helium-voiced receptionist at the Twin Peaks Sheriff's Department, Lucy Moran keeps the officers updated—constantly—with breathless and comically overcomplicated briefings over the office intercom. Childlike, literal-minded, and moody, Lucy is played for comic relief, particularly in scenes with her boyfriend, the clumsy, sensitive, depressive Deputy Andy Brennan. Their fractious relationship is a hoot, but pays diminishing returns when the caddish Dick Tremayne becomes a rival suitor (the less said about the Little Nicky fiasco the better). Robertson imbues Lucy, often a difficult and frustrating personality, with enormous offbeat charm—imagine the love child of Droopy Dog and Carol Kane—and her unique nasal squeak is one of *Twin Peaks'* most instantly recognizable and fondly remembered elements.

8

Let's Rock

The Music of *Twin Peaks*

Where we're from, the birds sing a pretty song, and there's always music in the air.

Twin Peaks Theme

Composer Angelo Badalamenti's contribution to the seductive spell cast by *Twin Peaks* cannot be overstated. Just the opening notes of the show's haunting, lovely theme are enough to immerse the viewer in the peculiar emotional landscape of the story—it's a bit kitsch (that tremulous fifties rock ballad guitar), mysterious, and surprisingly emotionally affecting.

Badalamenti is Lynch's simpatico, longtime collaborator (the two met when the composer gave *Blue Velvet* star Isabella Rossellini singing lessons), and has composed scores for *Wild at Heart*, *Fire Walk with Me*, *Lost Highway*, *Mulholland Dr.*, and *The Straight Story*. Their first joint effort was born of necessity: unable to afford the rights to Tim Buckley's "Song to the Siren" (Lynch's favorite song), the director had to come up with an original tune as a replacement to include in a key role in his landmark film *Blue Velvet*. He reluctantly came up with some lyrics—a set of naïve, romantic sentiments and images tinged with Lynch's signature uncanny *je ne sais quoi*—and gave them to Badalamenti, who set them to a quivering, ethereal tune that suggested the Shangri-Las on barbiturates.

The result was "Mysteries of Love," sung by chanteuse Julee Cruise, a delectable slice of mesmerizing dream pop. The sound recalls classic girl groups, but the lush synthesizer beds and weirdly disconnected beauty of Cruise's affectless schoolgirl warble puts it in a category of its own, allusive, hypnotic, timeless, and original.

The song gained a bit of a cult, and the trio decided to continue a good thing by collaborating on Cruise's album *Floating into the Night*. One of that record's songs, "Falling," would be repurposed (minus the vocals) as the *Twin Peaks* theme.

Badalamenti won the 1990 Grammy Award for Best Pop Instrumental Performance for his *Twin Peaks Theme*, and the series' soundtrack featuring it sold over two million copies, the first 40,000 within the first two weeks of its U.S. release.

The Love Theme

Badalamenti's *Love Theme* recurs in the series as a leitmotif—sometimes at ostensibly inappropriate but emotionally resonant moments, including the identification of Laura Palmer's corpse—and is as intrinsic a part of the show's aesthetic DNA as eerily flickering lights, immaculate slices of cherry pie, sumptuous red drapes, and sensible saddle shoes.

Angelo Badalamenti, *Twin Peaks* composer and David Lynch's longtime secret weapon.

That theme, with its florid emotionalism, recalls the swelling schmaltz of classic soap opera scores ("*Blue Velvet* gone *Peyton Place*" was an early Lynch note), but the indelible melody's aching emotional core and the arrangement's shifts from swooning romanticism to sinister drones transcend pastiche. The *Love Theme* distills the essence of *Twin Peaks*—that beguiling, postmodern collision of retro camp, formal beauty, raw feeling, and an air of inchoate, sinister dread—into a concise piece of timeless music. Lynch was so excited upon hearing it that he exclaimed to Badalamenti, "You just wrote seventy-five percent of the score. It's the whole mood of the piece. It is *Twin Peaks*."

All in a day's work for Badalamenti—actually, make that twenty minutes. The *Love Theme* was composed (with coaching from Lynch) in less than a half-hour. The composer and director are true collaborators, with the musically inclined Lynch actively contributing to the process with descriptions of moods and feelings he wishes Badalamenti to evoke.

Cool Jazz

Badalamenti coined this appellation for the loping, finger-snapping lounge music that provides a sort of audio "seam" that helps to stitch many of *Twin Peaks'* tonally disparate scenes into a cohesive whole. It lays on the hipster kitsch heavily, with its deliberately synthetic evocation of bygone cool seeming to mock the noir seriousness of much of the show's action. This is the music (with variations) the Man from Another Place shuffles to, but for our money its most memorable occurrence is its accompaniment of Audrey's slow solo dance at the Double R diner, an iconic moment that perfectly captured *Twin Peaks'* cockeyed glamor; swaying in a private reverie, Audrey asks, "Isn't it too dreamy?"

It is.

Sycamore Trees

This torchy ballad, stunningly performed by legendary jazz vocalist Jimmy Scott, appears in the series' final episode as a sort of musical greeting to Agent Cooper upon his arrival in the Red Room via the portal at Glastonbury Grove. The song references the stand of trees encircling this ingress point, and it's a fittingly creepy paean to that ominous locale. Lynch's lyrics are characteristically simple and direct in an almost childlike manner, and while nothing untoward is specifically articulated, the effect is chilling. Badalamenti's lachrymose composition is partly responsible, as are the flickering lights that accompany the song, but most of the credit goes to Scott, famed for his eerily androgynous and passionately expressive voice. The scene bears some resemblance to Dean Stockwell's woozily riveting lip-synch to Roy Orbison's "In Dreams" from *Blue Velvet*, but this sequence has an austere chill all its own.

Just You

More faux-fifties rock balladry from Badalamenti and Lynch. In season two's "Coma," Donna, James, and Maddy take a break from their murder investigation to, for some unexplained reason, record a demo of this Ricky Nelson-esque love ballad in Donna's living room. It's one of those weirdly indelible scenes that seems to exist in its own discrete bubble, and recalling it feels like trying to remember some half-forgotten dream. There is some archness going on here: the sappy lyrics are pointedly relevant to the increasingly awkward love triangle formed by the trio, a sly acknowledgment

Julee Cruise, the Roadhouse Singer, is not amused by your requests for "Freebird."

of the clichéd nature of their soapy entanglement. But the hushed, almost sacramental demeanor of the performers, the atmospherically reverberant electric guitar, and James's disaffected, uncannily androgynous (giving Jimmy Scott a run for his money) croon push the sequence into classic "I'm unsettled and not sure why" *Twin Peaks* territory. The voices heard on the track are the actors' own; maybe James grew up to be Chris Isaak?

Julee Cruise

The otherworldly voice of Julee Cruise graces several Badalamenti/Lynch compositions over the course of *Twin Peaks*: "Falling" (the instrumental version is the series' theme; Cruise performs the version with lyrics in the pilot), "The Nightingale," "Rockin' Back Inside My Heart," "The World Spins," and "Into the Night." Cruise herself appears in the pilot episode performing "Falling" and "The Nightingale," and in season two's "Lonely Souls," singing "Rockin' Back Inside My Heart" and "The World Spins" at the Roadhouse, where she also essays "Questions in a World of Blue" in *FWWM*.

Badalamenti and Lynch also composed the songs for her albums *Floating into the Night* and *The Voice of Love*, and Lynch featured her singing several

TP numbers, including "Into the Night," "Rockin' Back Inside My Heart," and "The World Spins," in his video installation *Industrial Symphony #1: The Dream of the Brokenhearted.*

The Soundtracks

There are three official releases collecting the music of *Twin Peaks*: *Soundtrack from Twin Peaks* (1990), *Twin Peaks: Fire Walk with Me* (1992), *and Twin Peaks Music: Season Two Music and More* (2007).

9

Break the Code, Solve the Crime

Dossiers: G-Men

DEA Special Agent Dennis/Denise Bryson (David Duchovny)

Count Denise Bryson as one of season two's narrative non sequiturs . . . but an interesting one. A pre-fame David Duchovny portrays transgender DEA agent Denise (formerly Dennis) Bryson as an entirely reasonable and sympathetic investigator looking into allegations of malfeasance on the part of Dale Cooper. Bryson proves invaluable to Cooper's cause, helping to clear his name and coming to his aid at Dead Dog Farm. While at first glance the inclusion of a transgender character might raise concern that the show was callously exploiting the "weirdness" of a trans woman (at a time when transgender people were marginalized nearly out of existence when it came to popular culture), Bryson is in fact presented as a completely "normal," competent, principled person who easily commands the respect and admiration of her peers. Also, Bryson's "double nature" (she occasionally resumed her Dennis identity when going undercover) chimes with the series' overriding theme of duality and fluid identity. Duchovny would, of course, go on to portray one of television's most famous FBI agents: Fox Mulder of *The X-Files*.

FBI Regional Bureau Chief Gordon Cole (David Lynch)

David Lynch himself portrays FBI Regional Bureau Chief Gordon Cole, Special Agent Dale Cooper's hearing-impaired immediate superior and trusted friend. Cole (named for a studio executive minor character in *Sunset Blvd.*, a Lynch favorite), with his large, outdated, malfunctioning hearing aid, misheard questions and responses, and obliviously blaring voice, is mostly played for comedy. In one of *Twin Peaks'* most purely delightful minor

I'd like to buy a vowel: a forensic puzzler, tiny letters placed beneath Laura Palmer's fingernails.

storylines, Cole has a discombobulating reaction to the supernaturally attractive Double R waitress Shelly Johnson, falling into instantaneous helpless infatuation and engaging in adorable old-school flirting. It transpires that Cole can hear her, and only her, with complete clarity, and his half-serious pursuit of her affections, including an audacious kiss in full view of seething boyfriend Bobby Briggs, is hilarious and weird in that uniquely Lynchian fashion. Thematically, Cole's lack of comprehension and convoluted, often inscrutable communication style (unaccountably comparing Cooper to a "small Mexican Chihuahua," briefing Desmond and Stanley with arcane gestures rather than explicit information) are of a piece with *Twin Peaks'* assertion that the truly compelling mysteries defy rational explanation . . . the fact that series cocreator Lynch plays an authority figure who can't or won't explain anything surely isn't an accident.

FBI Special Agent Chester "Chet" Desmond (Chris Isaak)

Chester Desmond, portrayed by rockabilly musician Chris Isaak (Lynch had directed one of his music videos), is the FBI agent dispatched to Deer

Meadow, Washington, to investigate Teresa Banks's murder in the opening segment of *Twin Peaks: Fire Walk with Me*. According to Robert Engels, who cowrote the script with David Lynch, the character's name was an amalgam of Chet Baker, the jazz trumpeter, and Norma Desmond, the central character in the 1950 film noir *Sunset Blvd*. Unlike Sam Stanley, his partner on the Banks case, Desmond is never referenced in the television series, and doesn't even appear in the early draft of the *FWWM* script. The character was added after Kyle MacLachlan—who had portrayed Special Agent Dale Cooper in the series and was supposed to lead the Banks probe—balked at reprising the role in the feature film (though he later relented, winding up with a reduced but still significant role). Note that Desmond's initials are Cooper's flipped, lending credence to the theory that Deer Meadow is the mirror-image of Twin Peaks (bad sheriff, bad diner, bad coffee, trailer park instead of luxury hotel, yada yada), though Engels has denied this intention. Like Cooper, Desmond is intuitive, but he emits a more terrestrial vibe. He's a cool cat, soft-spoken, unflappable, and dauntless, but not in an obnoxious way, and why shouldn't he be? Look at the way he whoops Sheriff Cable's butt back out yonder by the sheriff's station in that deleted scene, released among the "Missing Pieces" in 2014. If Desmond were a ballplayer, they'd say he leads by example, but lead he does. He's dogged and determined, but there's artistry here; his M.O. is idiosyncratic enough for Gordon Cole to make a point of referencing it to Stanley right off the bat. Desmond isn't exactly a laugh a minute, but he cracks himself up when, at Hap's diner, he asks Stanley for the time, knowing full well that Sam will wind up pouring hot coffee all over himself when he turns his wrist to check his watch (he does). Interestingly, this scene was inserted into the script *after* MacLachlan dropped out, meaning it was written specifically for Desmond. Desmond's competence is so pronounced that it comes as a real shock when, at the conclusion of the initial Deer Meadow segment, he reaches for Teresa Banks's ring, sitting in a mound of dirt beneath a Fat Trout trailer, and vanishes into thin air, never to be seen or heard from again (at least not yet).

Diane (None)

Peaks freaks love a mystery, and it's true the TV series never explicitly identifies Diane, to whom Cooper addresses the dictation into his trusty pocket tape recorder beginning with our very first sighting of him, in the pilot ("Diane, 11:30 a.m., February 24th, entering the town of Twin Peaks"). However, Scott Frost's book *The Autobiography of F.B.I. Special Agent Dale Cooper: My Life, My Tapes* unequivocally establishes Diane as Cooper's secretary, beginning with the December 19, 1977, entry, in which Cooper describes her as a cross between a saint and a cabaret singer. The *Fire Walk with Me* press packet reaffirms this, reporting that Cooper is "shooting streams of consciousness—and torrents of trivia—back to his unseen secretary." In a deleted *FWWM* scene, Cooper converses with Diane (unseen by the audience) while performing isometric exercises against a door frame, telling her she looks "sensational" (the two even briefly date, according to Scott Frost's book). Still, there *was* plenty of mystery surrounding Diane back in the day, when reports kept surfacing that she would appear on-screen. During a Museum of Broadcasting (now The Paley Center for Media) panel in March 1990, Mark Frost told the audience that the producers had given a lot of thought to the issue of whether viewers would ever get a glimpse of Diane, adding that "it's very possible you might see her if we get picked up" for a second season. As the first season was airing, Liz Smith, the doyenne of New York gossip columnists, inaccurately reported that Carol Lynley had been signed to portray Diane in the second season, in what was probably a career-promotion gambit by Lynley. On an installment of the daytime talker *Donahue*, airing two days before the season-one finale, Frost stated unequivocally that viewers "will see parts of Diane in upcoming episodes" (given the show's preoccupation with the sixties drama *The Fugitive*, which starred David Janssen in the title role, it is not unreasonable to wonder if this notion was inspired by another Janssen show, *Richard Diamond, Private Detective*, in which certain body parts belonging to Diamond's answering-service operator, portrayed by Mary Tyler Moore—most notably her gams—were depicted, though never her full body or face). Needless to say, none of these developments ever happened. Mystery over.

Windom Earle (Kenneth Welsh)

The Big Bad Wolf of the second half of season two, Earle is a demented genius: brilliant, deranged, and unrepentantly malignant. Once upon a time, back in the Pittsburgh days, Earle was Cooper's partner, mentor, and friend—at least Cooper *thought* so ("He taught me everything I know about being a special agent," he tells Audrey Horne), though details emerge over the course of season two confusing Earle's entire history, even suggesting he had been hiding his psychosis since the mid-sixties, when the FBI loaned him out to the Air Force to help on Project Blue Book, and he became obsessed with the Black Lodge. What's clear is that *somewhere* along the way, Earle went stark raving mad, and that four years prior to the events of *Twin Peaks* he killed his wife, Caroline, and seriously wounded Cooper, with whom she was having an affair. Earle, however, dodged suspicion by feigning madness born from grief, which worked, landing him a room at the local "laughing academy," as Albert Rosenfield puts it. In episode two of season two, Albert delivers news that Earle "flew the coop, Coop," and it isn't long before he's sending Cooper chess moves (back in Pittsburgh Earle and Cooper had played a match every day for three years) and tape-recorded messages reaffirming that he is (1) bonkers and (2) viperous, and soon after that he touches down in Twin Peaks with a diabolical plan to exact revenge and gain entry to the Black Lodge, involving killing lots of people in some sort of human chess game, plus treating Leo Johnson like a lap dog with the aid of a shock collar. Earle's mind is "like a diamond," per Cooper—"cold and hard and brilliant"—and the madman was clearly modeled after Professor Moriarty (Mark Frost, a devout Sherlockian, presented Arthur Conan Doyle as the protagonist in two of his novels, *The List of Seven* and *The Six Messiahs*). Though he reputedly is a master of disguise, his trickery looks pretty flimsy to us, and there's something so gleefully over-the-top about his turpitude that he comes across at times like a comic-book villain, as when he is prancing around his cottage in the woods (or "verdant bower," as Earle calls it) in long johns, tooting away on his bamboo shakuhachi flute, which he then uses to beat Leo into submission. Don't be fooled: Earle's a sulfurous monster (fear is his favorite emotional state, though only in others), and it is he who lures Cooper into the Black Lodge in the series finale by abducting Annie Blackburne. Lynch reportedly found the character painfully unsubtle and uninteresting, which makes sense, since he practically gutted him from the Red Room/Black Lodge scenes in that finale, tossing out the original script and improvisationally rebuilding the segment as a showdown between Cooper and Bob (or, really, Cooper and himself), rather than Cooper and Earle.

Pittsburgh

What happens in Pittsburgh stays in Pittsburgh . . . not.

As viewers of the TV series know, four years before arriving in Twin Peaks, Dale Cooper worked out of the bureau's Pittsburgh office, where horrific, life-altering events occurred: an Oedipal drama in which Cooper fell in love with Caroline Earle, the wife of his partner/mentor, Windom, who wound up stabbing both of them, killing Caroline and seriously wounding Cooper, though neither Earle nor anyone else was ever charged with the crime. Earle himself? Loony-bin time.

Early in season two, the writers were already foreshadowing life after Laura Palmer, which would feature Earle as the "Big Bad," to appropriate a coinage from TV's *Buffy the Vampire Slayer*. Earle is first mentioned in the second episode of the season, when Albert Rosenfield reveals that "Your former partner flew the coop, Coop." Four episodes later, Gordon Cole delivers an anonymous note to Cooper containing a chess move, which Cooper correctly deduces is from Earle. The plot thickens.

Still later, Cooper, once again deflecting romantic overtures from the smitten Audrey Horne, reaffirms that he will never again become romantically entwined with anyone involved in a case he's working on. It happened once before, Cooper says, and the woman "died in my arms," even though he and Windom Earle had been assigned to protect her after she witnessed a federal crime. Cooper is convinced his failure was a direct result of his having fallen in love with the witness, causing him to lose focus. Even here Cooper withholds crucial information: that the object of his affections was Caroline Earle, who was married to his partner at the time of their dalliance.

Eventually, Earle himself touches down in Twin Peaks, seeking vengeance against Cooper, but also entrée into the Black Lodge. About two-thirds of the way into the season, with Earle having killed once already and threatening to strike again, Cooper finally fully fesses up, telling Sheriff Truman he's "brought some baggage to town." This is Cooper's first admission that he had an affair with his partner's wife. Cooper is convinced Earle not only wounded him and killed Caroline, but also committed the (unidentified) crime that she had originally witnessed, and that he feigned insanity from grief afterward only to escape suspicion. This is eventually confirmed by Gordon Cole, who reports that "When Earle went boy-yoy-yoing, the doctors discovered he was on haloperidol"—the same drug injected by the One-Armed Man Gerard to suppress the inhabiting spirit Mike—to fake insanity ("definite schizoid maneuvering," Cole calls it).

Earle's backstory becomes even more convoluted later on, when details emerge tracing his insanity back even further, to a two-year (1965 to 1967) loan from the bureau to the Air Force, where he worked on Project Blue Book, exploring UFOs and other strange phenomena. Major Garland Briggs, a veteran of the same project, reports that when focus shifted from outer space to the wooded area surrounding Twin Peaks, Earle became possessive, obsessive, and, eventually, violent, so was booted from the team. Briggs produces a videotape in which Earle rants about evil sorcerers—dugpas—and the Black Lodge.

There are other references to Pittsburgh in the TV series, including this whopper: In the ninth episode of season two ("Arbitrary Law"), as Leland/Bob confesses to murdering Laura and Maddy Ferguson, he says, "I have this thing for knives. Just like what happened to you in Pittsburgh that time, huh, Cooper?" This retort unnerves Cooper, who has never discussed Pittsburgh with Leland or with anyone likely to have shared that information with him, implying that Bob himself must somehow have knowledge of the events that unfolded there, and possibly even facilitated them. This is never again referenced in the series, though there are multiple hints in *The Autobiography of F.B.I. Special Agent Dale Cooper: My Life, My Tapes* that it might be true. The book delves far deeper into the events in Pittsburgh than the series does. However, while sanctioned by the Lynch-Frost team, *My Life, My Tapes* was written before season two was fully plotted, and also before *Fire Walk with Me* was conceived, and includes numerous inconsistencies with both the series and the film. For example, with respect to Pittsburgh, the book records the events as having transpired in 1979, six years prior to the time frame established by the series. Hence, it is impossible to consider the book canon, leaving us with yet another unsolved *Twin Peaks* mystery. The more the merrier, we say.

Caroline Powers Earle (Brenda E. Mathers)

Windom Earle's late wife is at the epicenter of the "baggage" Cooper brings to town, as he fesses up to Harry once Earle has embarked upon his murder spree in Twin Peaks. Coop remembers Caroline as a "very beautiful, very gentle woman," and she must have been something to lure Cooper from the straight and narrow: four years earlier, the two fell in love in Pittsburgh, which is all fine and good except that she was still married at the time to Earle, Cooper's FBI partner and, as it turns out, a raving madman. Caroline's subsequent death at the hands of her husband is the defining event of Cooper's adult life; he's plagued with guilt not only for failing to protect her, but for becoming romantically entangled in the first place—hence, his repeated deflection of overtures from a flirtatious Audrey Horne while asserting his strict prohibition against dating anyone connected to a case (plus, she's a teen, for God's sake). Caroline was portrayed by Brenda E. Mathers, who appears in just two episodes (though we also see her photo, which Cooper still carries in his wallet), both during the second season: one in which her superimposed image pops up on-screen as Cooper recalls the events in Pittsburgh for Harry, and again in the series finale, when Caroline and Annie Blackburne transmogrify into each other during Cooper's ill-fated sojourn in the Black Lodge.

FBI Special Agent Roger Hardy (Clarence Williams III)

Hard-ass Hardy is the FBI Internal Affairs agent who busts Cooper for crossing into Canada on two separate trips to One Eyed Jacks, once to chat with Jacques Renault and once to rescue Audrey Horne, without authorization, among other, trumped-up charges, so therefore is the guy we hold fully responsible for Cooper's flannel-shirt fashion faux pas in the middle to late stages of season two. When Cooper declines to mount a defense, saying he is convinced of the rightness of his actions, Hardy does what any adamantine macho man would do: he impugns his masculinity, opining that any FBI agent who doesn't "stand up for himself . . . may be packing feathers where his spine is supposed to be." Hardy was portrayed by Clarence Williams III, who had costarred alongside Peggy Lipton (Norma Jennings) and Michael Cole in ABC's *The Mod Squad* (1968–1973), and Hardy's redemption comes in his final scene, when he stops in at the Double R for a slice of cherry pie served by Norma, thus reuniting two of the three stars of the iconic counterculture cop show for one brief, shining moment.

FBI Special Agent Phillip Jeffries (David Bowie)

One of the most puzzling characters in all of *Twin Peaks* lore, Phillip Jeffries, portrayed by the late rock icon David Bowie, appears in *FWWM* only, suddenly showing up in Regional Bureau Chief Gordon Cole's Philadelphia office after a long and unexplained absence, in a brief and totally bizarre sequence of events unfolding after Desmond's disappearance in Deer Meadow and before the story transitions to Twin Peaks. Nothing that Jeffries says during this entire sequence makes any sense whatsoever—whether he is babbling on about some unidentified entity named Judy ("Well, now, I'm not going to talk about Judy. In fact, we're not going to talk about Judy at all. We're gonna keep her out of it."), impugning Cooper's identity ("Who do you think this is there?"), or recounting his attendance at a meeting with Bob, the Man from Another Place, the Tremonds, and a whole menagerie of other aberrant characters, plus heaping bowls of creamed corn ("It was a dream. We live inside a dream"). The general weirdness of this all is exacerbated by the sights and sounds of the erstwhile glam rocker masquerading as a white-suited G-man with an unsteady gait and a weird, indecipherable accent as Lynch the director repeatedly dissolves between the two locales, the FBI office in Philly and the meeting room, said by Jeffries to be located above a convenience store. When he has finally said his piece, Jeffries ups and vanishes again, and the security desk reports that he never

Lil the Dancer and her famous blue rose, in *Fire Walk with Me*.   *New Line Cinema/Photofest*

even entered the building in the first place. In the *FWWM* press kit (in which he wholeheartedly endorses working with the "delightfully bonkers" David Lynch), Bowie described his character as an "intensely over-traveled upholder of the law" who has "seen too much and has little ability to do much about it. Not dissimilar to the perspective of a rock god, really." Blissfully, the deleted scenes released in 2014 give us more Jeffries—because, really, can we ever get enough of Bowie playing an FBI agent in a David Lynch movie?—and shed *some* light on the character, though not much (this *is* Lynch, after all). Here we learn that Jeffries found "something"—possibly the Owl Cave ring—at Judy's place in Seattle, which may have led him to the convenience-store meeting, and that at some point he winds up in a swank Buenos Aires hotel, from which he vanishes into thin air, though later reappearing just as mysteriously, so spooking a bellhop in the process that he defecates himself and screams at Jeffries, "Are you the man? Are you the man?" Duh . . . of course Bowie is the man.

Lil the Dancer (Kimberly Ann Cole)

Lil appears in *FWWM* as a colleague of Gordon Cole's who briefs agent Desmond on the investigation of the murder of Teresa Banks. Lil strikes a bizarre figure with her bright red hair and dress (and blue rose; see Chapter

12), vivid makeup, pinched expression, and bizarrely stylized body movements; it transpires that Lil's appearance and contortions contain a multitude of nonverbal signifiers about different aspects of the case. Why employ this convoluted and unsettling method to convey information? If we take as read that things in the *Twin Peaks* universe just tend to be weird, we wonder if Lil's stilted communication style has something to say about the way in which information can confuse as much as enlighten, and about the tendency of mysteries to contain an ever-widening series of even deeper mysteries. We know for sure that Lil exemplifies Lynch's talent for evoking horror without anything objectively horrible happening on-screen. Lil's ostensibly one of the good guys, but she scares the hell out of us and we're not sure why.

FBI Special Agent Albert Rosenfield (Miguel Ferrer)

Pugnacious, haughty, master of the eloquent putdown, FBI forensic examiner Albert Rosenfield makes up in investigative acumen what he lacks in interpersonal skills. Held in high professional esteem by Cooper, Rosenfield immediately alienates all and sundry upon his arrival in Twin Peaks with his reflexive rudeness and lacerating criticisms of the abilities of the local medical and law enforcement communities. So obnoxious is Rosenfield that the usually even-keeled Sheriff Truman is moved to strike him, and the cynical FBI man seems poised to assume the role of bureaucratic antagonist to Cooper and company . . . until Rosenfield, in an emotional speech, contextualizes his abrasiveness as part and parcel of his zeal for peace and love, as practiced by his heroes Gandhi and Martin Luther King Jr. It's a stunning reversal, both touching and funny, and one of *Twin Peaks'* more playful dualities: the hateful man of love. Actually, Albert is downright endearing in his interactions after this revelation, warmly hugging Truman and proclaiming his love for the nonplussed lawman. He retains his sharp tongue, happily, and his status as one of *Twin Peaks'* most quotable characters. For instance: "I've had about enough of morons and half-wits, dolts, dunces, dullards, and dumbbells—and you, you chowder-head yokel, you blithering hayseed. You had enough of me?" Never, Albert, never.

FBI Agent Sam Stanley (Kiefer Sutherland)

Unlike Special Agent Chester Desmond, his comrade in the Teresa Banks investigation in *Fire Walk with Me,* Sam Stanley *is* referenced in the TV series, though just once, and not very flatteringly: in the pilot, when Cooper

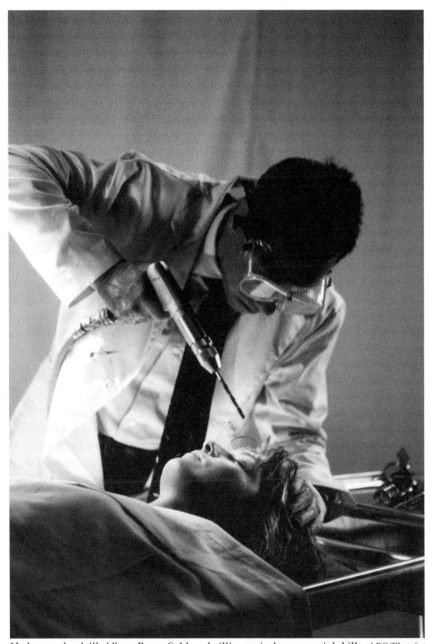

He knows the drill: Albert Rosenfield . . . brilliant mind; poor social skills. *ABC/Photofest*

instructs Diane to assign the Laura Palmer case to Albert Rosenfield and his forensics team. "Don't go to Sam," Cooper adds. "Albert seems to have a little more on the ball." Limned against type by Kiefer Sutherland (already an established film star and erstwhile fiancé of Julia Roberts, though still nine years away from his breakout performance as macho man Jack Bauer in TV's *24*), the dorky, bowtie-wearing Sam is a facts-and-figures guy, antithetical to the intuitive Desmond and the mystical Cooper, and also to David Lynch, who famously ignores interviewers' prompts to concretize his abstractions (Sam's completely out-of-the-blue comment that the entire Deer Meadow Sheriff's Station is probably worth around $27,000—Desmond looks at him like he's mad—seems like an obvious allusion to Hollywood suits who prioritize commerce over content). Still, Sam's no slouch when it comes to forensics, whatever Cooper says about him (and his uncharacteristically pronounced distaste for Stanley is reinforced in a deleted scene released in 2014, their sole interaction as it turned out, though originally Cooper and Stanley were supposed to investigate the Banks murder together): Gordon introduces him to Desmond as "the man who cracked the Whitman case" (though spelled "Whiteman" in the script, it is pronounced "Whitman" in the film, and is never explained), which clearly has won him renown within the bureau, and it's Sam who recognizes the ring mark on Teresa's left hand and extracts the letter "T" from beneath the nail of her left ring finger (plus, he picks up on the fact that Lil the Dancer's dress has been tailored, which impresses even Desmond). Compared with his exceptionally poised fellow G-men, Brylcreemed and nattily attired, Stanley is an aberration, with quivering hair and a spasmodic tic, and unlike Desmond and Cooper he wears a wedding band, but even more tellingly he seems to be the one agent excluded from the blue-rose club, as both Desmond and Cooper (in the deleted scene) refuse to tell him what it means. In another deleted scene, Sam and Desmond speculate about why Jack, the owner of Hap's diner, is fixing a lamp: is it for aesthetic purposes or practical ones? When Desmond opines the latter, Sam responds: "Aesthetics are subjective, aren't they, Agent Desmond?" In other words: out of Sam's league.

10

Take Another Look, Sonny

Totems, Themes, Motifs, and Other Significant Recurring Details

It's gonna happen again.

Electricity

Electricity, like everything else, behaves eccentrically in *Twin Peaks*. Lights flicker and strobe, microphones squeal, and music plays unexpectedly; TV static "snow," swaying power lines, and a lonely traffic light number among the series' most potent visual motifs.

Theories abound regarding the significance of these electrical manifestations, the consensus being that electrical displays indicate the machinations of the White and Black lodges, and that electricity is the medium through which lodge spirits enter the mundane world. Perhaps; Leland significantly starts a ceiling fan before attacking Laura, presumably summoning Bob. In *FWWM*'s confounding "convenience store" scene, one of the creepy figures present enunciates "e-lec-tric-i-ty!" with exaggerated significance, perhaps indicating the element's value as a commodity in the spirit realm, along with creamed corn and Formica.

On a subtextual level, the unreliability of electricity and electronic tools supports some of *Twin Peaks'* key themes: the flickering lights are a stark representation of the show's fascination with duality—light and dark, alternating in less than the space of a second.

Considered further, the trope suggests the ultimate futility of attempting to uncover or communicate the "truth" in the face of the world's essential mystery. An electric light may partially illuminate, but its flickering obscures and disorients more than it reveals. An amplified public address drowns in feedback. A video camera records a figure that is no longer there.

Intercoms and hearing aids fail repeatedly. Technology is nothing against the impenetrable secrets of this world and the next, akin to a candle guttering in a hurricane.

Aesthetically speaking, flickering lights very effectively imbue their scenes with an atmosphere of unease and tension. It's an elegantly simple tactic straight from the *Twin Peaks* playbook, but its first appearance was not by design; when filming the pilot episode's scene in which Cooper first examines Laura's body, the fluorescent bulb above the gurney began to die . . . and one of *Twin Peaks'* signature effects was born. Lynch liked it so much he wound up flickering the light himself.

The Traffic Light

It's a lovely, unaccountably haunting image, recurring in the series seemingly at random: a single traffic light, suspended in the dark space of night, slowly cycling through its mute color-coded commands.

What does it mean? Maybe it's nothing more than an atmospheric detail, a visual bit of punctuation helping to stitch together disparate scenes into an aesthetically consistent whole. Or perhaps it's meant to function as a caesura, or rest, does in a piece of music.

In the story, this location marks Laura and James's last encounter, in which Laura makes her choice to turn away from James (understandable), and to enter the woods and ultimately meet her grisly end. It makes sense thematically for the scene to play out here: Laura stands at an intersection, and makes a wrong turn.

For us, however, there seems to be a little more to it; why do we feel a little mournful toward, a bit chilled by, this utterly mundane object when it appears? It's a lonely-looking thing, a solitary sentinel swaying in the chill wind, seemingly unseen and unheeded in the small hours of a Twin Peaks night, and maybe that's the thing that pulls at us.

It's a symbol of authority and order, of protection from chaos and violence, blindly executing its function, mechanically, pointlessly, protecting no one. The law won't save you; witness its forsaken beacon, quietly failing to push back the dark.

Coffee, Pie, Doughnuts

Forget wood from the Packard Sawmill; Twin Peaks' most important commodities are caffeine and pastry. The sheriff's office is absolutely infested with heaping stacks of assorted doughnuts, characters consume oceans of coffee, and the pie at the Double R drives sober men to heedless gluttony.

The emphasis on comforting sweets and simple honest java is undoubtedly meant to poke satirically at the exaggerated wholesomeness of Twin Peaks' surface quasi-1950s atmosphere (and perhaps at Lynch's own sweet

Coop, Truman, and a cop's best friend: doughnuts.

tooth—he has referred to sugar as "granulated happiness"). Cooper's bottomless enthusiasm for the treats is interesting, suggesting even our incorruptible straight-arrow hero may be tempted by ultimately harmful sensual pleasures.

This being *Twin Peaks*, can we tease out some more sinister implications from the town's sweets-and-coffee jones? We posit that the ostensibly benign mind-altering substances glucose and caffeine represent another duality: they are socially sanctioned stimulants that the "good" people of Twin Peaks depend on to get through the day, as opposed to the cocaine brought in over the border under cover of night that fuels the transgressive actions of the community's less upstanding element.

Or maybe they're just that delicious.

Owls

"The owls are not what they seem."

So goes one of *Twin Peaks'* signature gnomic pronouncements, this one courtesy of the Giant, who periodically offers assistance to Cooper in the form of puzzling, seeming non sequiturs. Of course, not much in Twin Peaks is exactly as it seems—perhaps the Giant was simply urging Cooper to dig beneath the surface of the town's rustic charms. Or, the owls may serve the lodges in some way: theories hold the owls may be emissaries or hosts for Bob and his Amazing Friends, as their presence is mentioned or seen in conjunction with a number of horrific events, including the murder of Laura Palmer. The sagacious Mrs. Lanterman will, in fact, only talk to Cooper inside, where the owls won't see them.

Also noteworthy: the petroglyph unlocking the mystery of the lodges is found in Owl Cave, and Major Briggs reports that his abduction included a vision of a giant owl. Oh, and Cooper sees an owl while relieving himself. So the owls are clearly linked to the spirits and lodges somehow . . . but their specific nature and function remain a mystery, which seems appropriate.

Owls are common symbols in Native American folklore, so their significance makes sense in the context of the other indigenous myths that contribute to *Twin Peaks'* supernatural tapestry. They are most frequently thought to represent messengers from the spirit realm or harbingers of death—both functions relevant to the inhabitants of the lodges (they are also used to depict intuition and the ability to see beyond the here and now—looking at you, Cooper). The owl glyph used in the series closely resembles a symbol used by the Wishram Indians, a tribe native to American Northwest.

Red Drapes

Twin Peaks (not to mention other Lynch locations, including *Blue Velvet*'s Lumberton and *Lost Highway*'s nightmare LA) is lousy with crimson window treatments. They, along with the black/white zigzag floor pattern, define the Red Room, and they appear among the sycamores in Glastonbury Grove when the portal to the lodges is in service. On the earthly plain, they also grace the Roadhouse, One Eyed Jacks, and Jacques Renault's cabin. What's the common thread? Each of these locations can be read as a sort of staging area, which ties in with the theatrical association of red velvet drapes—the Miss Twin Peaks pageant is held in the Roadhouse, Jacques's cabin was the site of pornographic photo shoots, and One Eyed Jacks features a veritable chorus line of courtesans. Note that these various "stages" all concern the sexual objectification of women, from the ostensibly wholesome beauty pageant to the more explicitly erotic arenas of pornography and prostitution.

And speaking of women and eroticism, well, ahem, red drapes pretty clearly carry a lot of Freudian freight, but perhaps that area would be better explored in another kind of book.

Angels

Not much to unpack here: the angels that appear (and disappear) over the course of the story seem to carry their traditional meaning of salvation, goodness, protection, and grace. One might scoff at the lack of subtlety in depicting angels in this literal manner, but Lynch's canny exploitation of the power inherent in such primal symbols obviates any concern over their obviousness. We see an angel in the fatal train car when Ronette is miraculously freed from her bonds, and, troublingly, the image of an angel disappears from the painting on Laura's wall (which depicts the heavenly messenger ministering to desperate, abandoned children—now, that's barely even a metaphor) when she is at her most hopeless. Finally, the appearance of the angel at the end of *FWWM* suggests that Laura has been freed from her torment.

There are no mentions of angels in the *FWWM* shooting script—were they a last minute inspiration of Lynch's? They recall his use of Glinda the Good Witch in his film *Wild at Heart*, a fairy-tale-like reaffirmation of the possibility of love and goodness in a blighted world; and disturbingly, of the dubious spiritual comfort provided by *Eraserhead*'s Lady in the Radiator, a deformed angelic presence who listlessly and unconvincingly sings of the promise of heaven, where "everything is fine."

Masks

One of the oldest and most profound tools of drama—the mask—plays a significant role in the construction of *Twin Peaks'* thematic carapace. Like angels, masks are rather obvious symbols; they evoke concealment, double natures, and the mutability of identity.

Figuratively, many of the key players present "masks" to the world: Laura Palmer plays the golden girl paragon; her father Leland the respectable family man; Benjamin Horne the legitimate businessman; Josie Packard the embattled, grieving widow; Hank Jennings the reformed swain; and on and on and on. The very persons of Leland and, at various times, Gerard (Mike), Dale Cooper, and others possessed by lodge spirits are masks for the entities animating them.

Literal masks and disguises also appear with great frequency: consider the thousand faces of Windom Earle, or Catherine Martell's extended performance as Mr. Tojamura. The monkey who intones "Judy" wears a mask, and Audrey Horne conceals her identity at One Eyed Jacks with a fetching cat mask. Earle sends Cooper the death mask of Caroline Earle (less fetching).

The most striking masks—crude, white, phallic-nosed—adorn the Tremond grandson and the convenience store's Jumping Man. The Jumping Man's mask has slits for his eyes and mouth, while the Tremond boy's features are completely covered; we're not sure what this symbolizes, but the "Fire walk with me" invocation includes the lines, "In the darkness of future past/The Magician longs to see." Is the grandson the Magician? We know he studies magic, as his grandmother explained when he made a handful of creamed corn disappear. Young master Tremond tells Laura that "The man behind the mask is looking for the book with the pages torn out." Bob? Leland? Himself?

Who was that masked man?

Fire

Fire has been a longtime source of fascination for Lynch—he got into trouble as a kid for his pyromaniacal tendencies, and fetishistic evocations of flame have graced most of his works, from his early short *Six Figures Getting Sick* (also known as *Six Men Getting Sick*, and which depicted burning, vomiting heads), turning up in *Blue Velvet*'s guttering candle, the close-ups of flaring matches that recur in *Wild at Heart*, the permanently blazing shack in *Lost Highway*, and on and on. Beyond its immediate and striking qualities as a purely visual element, fire is rich with symbolic possibilities: it is a transformative element, and contains many contrasts and oppositions that neatly chime with *Twin Peaks'* pet themes.

Fire warms and illuminates even as it consumes and destroys—the "Fire walk with me" incantation can be understood as a request for a light to penetrate the "darkness of futures past"—but *Twin Peaks* more often features the negative aspects of this wild element: for example, the sawmill burns down, nearly killing Catherine and Shelly; the Log Lady's husband died in a fire; the smell of burned engine oil indicates the presence of Black Lodge spirits and mayhem; and Windom Earle's head explodes into flame when Bob claims his soul. The Log Lady, who lost her lumberjack husband in a forest fire, equates fire to the devil, "hiding like a coward in the smoke."

Fire and electricity seem to have some sort of relationship as mediums for the evil forces contained in the Black Lodge, and they seem to be placed in opposition to wood and water, other elements that feature heavily as visual motifs that might represent the White Lodge, but the specifics as to how all of this works are, as ever, elusive.

Doubles

Twin Peaks announces its preoccupation with doubles and *doppelgängers* in its very title. This theme, often associated with Alfred Hitchcock (the blonde/brunette, Laura/Maddy dichotomy owes something to Kim Novak's character in Hitchcock's *Vertigo*—Maddy shares a first name with one of the Novak character's incarnations, and her surname, Ferguson, is shared with Jimmy Stewart's protagonist in that film), is one of the central pillars of Lynch's work. Doubles offer a trove of narrative and subtextual opportunities, including explorations of fluid identity, instances of high contrast, and playful cultural references. Following is a partial list of the many doubles to be found in the funhouse mirror world of *Twin Peaks*.

- Laura Palmer/Maddy Ferguson (dark and light aspects of the girl next door)
- Bob and Mike/Bobby Briggs and Mike Nelson (Black Lodge spirits and earthly hoodlums)
- Norma Jennings/Shelly Johnson (pretty girls who threw their lives away on bad men)
- Jacoby's mismatched blue and red spectacle lenses
- Twin Peaks/Deer Meadow Sheriff's Departments (rural outposts of the law, one welcoming and sympathetic, one hostile and threatening)

- Black Lodge/White Lodge (Manichean repositories of good and evil)
- The Roadhouse/Partyland (saloons, one communal and welcoming, one bleak and annihilating)
- Town/Forest (corrupt civilization and primal nature, cheek by jowl)
- Dale Cooper/Windom Earle (brilliant mystical government men, one enlightened and kind, one evil and twisted)
- Double R/Hap's Diner (archetypal charming small-town eatery vs. rancid, unfriendly roach haven)
- Giant/MFAP (Lodge spirits of distinctive, contrasting heights)
- Dennis Bryson/Denise Bryson
- Benjamin Horne's Civil War obsession (a country divided, in opposition to itself)
- The two sets of ledgers for the Packard Sawmill
- Laura's two diaries
- Two halves of Laura's heart necklace

. . . And on and on and on.

Vertigo and Twin Peaks

David Lynch rarely expounds on his cinematic inspirations, but Alfred Hitchcock's *Vertigo* (1958) is a notable exception—Lynch has frequently acknowledged *Vertigo* as a favorite, and hosted a screening of the suspense classic at New York's IFC Center in 2006.

Vertigo concerns the efforts of a detective, Scottie Ferguson (James Stewart), to discover the truth about an enigmatic blond beauty, Madeleine Elster (Kim Novak), who, after establishing an intense romantic connection with Ferguson, apparently dies; enter Judy Barton (also Novak), a dead ringer for Madeleine, apart from her dark hair. Ferguson, obsessed with the deceased Madeleine, compels Judy to change her hair and wardrobe to more closely resemble the dead woman, and his mad fixation ultimately leads to tragedy.

There are some obvious surface connections to draw here between the film and *Twin Peaks*: Laura, a mysterious blond, is murdered; an emotionally invested detective dedicates himself fully to her case, and his dreams about her contain hidden clues as to her fate; and an uncanny doppelgänger of Laura—apart from her dark hair—soon arrives in the form of Maddy Ferguson, Laura's identical cousin. Maddy's first name is derived from Mrs. Elster's, while she shares a surname with Detective Ferguson. Maddy, Donna, and James concoct a plan using Maddy, disguised as Laura, as bait, just as Scottie Ferguson does with Judy.

Lynch would repeat the blond/brunette doubling theme with Patricia Arquette's dual roles in *Lost Highway*, and both *Blue Velvet* and *Mulholland Dr.*

James Stewart and two faces of Kim Novak, from Alfred Hitchcock's *Vertigo* (1958).

feature blond and brunette female character pairs who function as contrasting poles of femininity. It's a potent archetype, familiar from many popular culture iterations; the identical-save-hair-color Betty and Veronica from *Archie* comics spring to mind, as does an advertising campaign featured in *Mad Men* that posited all women were either a "Jackie" (Kennedy) or "Marilyn" (Monroe). *Twin Peaks* capitalizes brilliantly on the trope, reveling in its cheesy obviousness and iconic power simultaneously.

Clearly, themes of doubles and doppelgängers are central to *Twin Peaks*—again, look no further than the name—as are references to classic cinema and a fascination with kitschy narrative genre mechanics. In *Vertigo*, Hitchcock, like Lynch, employs expressionistic devices (lurid washes of color, vertiginous camera effects) to subvert and deepen pulp conventions in the service of evoking overwhelming emotion. By using such a primal and immediately graspable idea (blonde and brunette women as dual sides of one personality), Lynch, like Hitchcock, is free to construct ever more abstruse stylistic frames for it; of course, even grounded in such a familiar archetype, the strangeness of *Twin Peaks* is enough to make you dizzy.

Fathers and Daughters

Twin Peaks has an Electra complex. The father/daughter relationship is a consistently fraught dynamic on the show; the horrific abuse and betrayal suffered by Laura Palmer at the hands of her father Leland is the most extreme example, but we see tension in this filial bond touch each of the young women at the core of the story: Benjamin Horne disapproves of his daughter Audrey (who seeks affection and approval from older men, like Cooper and John Justice Wheeler), and his romantic attachment to and idealization of Laura, by contrast, had disturbing incestuous overtones of misplaced paternal devotion. When Audrey goes undercover at One Eyed Jacks, she narrowly escapes a sexual assignation with Benjamin, who loves nothing more than breaking in the new girls—Audrey's presence literalizes the creepily paternalistic aspect of this chore, which concerns the efforts of a worldly older man ushering his female charges into a twisted sort of "maturity." Finally, Donna Hayward was secure in the knowledge that her father Will was a good man . . . until it became pretty clear that she was in fact the product of an affair her mother had with Benjamin Horne (that guy gets around).

Whether this motif is simply more grist for the psychosexual mill or has some personal significance to the creators, we can't say—but it is interesting/disquieting to note that Lynch assigned the authorship of *The Secret Diary of Laura Palmer*—which detailed Laura's molestation and rape by her father—to his daughter, Jennifer.

Shaking Hands

A mysterious palsy afflicts several Twin Peaks residents in the late season-two episode "The Path to the Black Lodge"; Cooper, Pete Martell, and an unidentified woman at the Double R suffer brief twitching spells in their right hands. This phenomenon is never explained (shocking, we know!), but a chilling scene from the episode's climax may provide a clue: we see Bob's right hand emerge from the curtains behind the sycamores in Glastonbury Grove. Perhaps the twitches were premonitions shared by "the gifted and the damned" regarding the imminent incursion of Bob (we can stretch and say Pete is damned to tag along on Andrew Packard's fatal visit to the bank—no idea what the woman's story might be)? Other theories hold that the tremors indicated Bob's attempts at possessing new hosts, but we can only speculate.

Utility Pole

At the Fat Trout Trailer Park, there is a utility pole affixed with a sign bearing a large "6," plus a series of additional numbers, that repeatedly serves as a harbinger of inexplicable events (such as Carl Rodd's trance and Special Agent Phillip Jeffries's unorthodox travels). Does the pole, clearly associated with electricity, a key Twin Peaks motif, contain

Six Appeal: "E-lec-tri-ci-ty!" Strange things—like Carl Rodd's trance and Agent Desmond's disappearance—seem to happen whenever this utility pole at Fat Trout Trailer Park turns up. We have no idea what it means, either.

deeper meaning? Did it zap Chester Desmond into the Black Lodge? Is that why we hear the war whoop sound when it is shown? Does the number 6 on the sign mean anything? Hmm, six dots on Hank Jennings's domino . . .

We like it as a resonant detail of the dreary trailer park at least, an ugly, functional expression of technology . . . its starkness suggests something of the desolate isolation of contemporary rural spaces, and it just feels "right" when it pops up, so we'll leave it at that (until somebody comes up with a better explanation).

Circles

Circles loom large in *Twin Peaks'* visual grammar, representing, among other things, the cyclical nature of much of the story: Bob abuses Leland, Leland abuses Laura; we will see Laura again "in 25 years"; Cooper and Windom Earle play out their earlier dynamic; Mike remembers, "Bob and I, when we were killing together. There was this, this perfect relationship: appetite, satisfaction, a golden circle."

A circle is a closed system: enter at any point and you will inevitably come around to that same point again; in the case of this story, the murder of Laura Palmer. In the convenience store, the MFAP intones that "everything will proceed cyclically." He should know.

Below, some examples of the copious circle imagery of *Twin Peaks*:

- The Palmers' ceiling fan
- Spinning records, in both the Palmer home and Jacques Renault's cabin
- Roulette wheel at One Eyed Jacks

- Various rings: the owl rings, also jewelry worn by Cooper, Audrey, and Donna
- Circle Brand boots, as sold by Gerard
- "Golden circle," as described by Gerard
- Circle of sycamores in Glastonbury Grove
- Coffee cup rims, doughnuts
- Astrological symbols on the black puzzle box
- Traffic light indicators
- The Tremond boy's ambulatory pattern in the parking lot
- Owl eyes

Mirrors

"Yes, look in the mirror. What do you see? Is it a dream, or a nightmare? Are we being introduced against our will? Are they mirrors?" So asks the Log Lady, and they are pertinent questions. Mirrors abound in *Twin Peaks*—they are a natural symbol for the show's overriding theme of dualism, and, in practical terms, they are the conduit through which various characters are able to view Bob (see the entry on Bob to discover how a mirror landed Frank Silva the role). Mirrors appear so frequently in *Twin Peaks* that it is pointless to attempt to enumerate them all (the very first image in the show features Josie gazing at her reflection), but one instance stands out in particular: in the series' finale, Cooper, inhabited by Bob, studies his reflection in the bathroom mirror at the Great Northern—he sees the demonic, gleeful image of Bob staring back, and he smashes his head against the glass, repeating "How's Annie?" with mounting hilarity. It's one of *Twin Peaks'* most indelible images, crystallizing the show's Manichean philosophy and obsession with twinning (and there is a lot to say here as well about the theories of psychoanalyst Jacques Lacan, but this isn't an advanced lit theory class . . . *officially*) that, in typical *TP* fashion, makes a certain kind of perfect sense but explains nothing definitively. And why on earth did Leland bring a mirror with him into the train car on that terrible night? We'll let Mrs. Lanterman have the last word: "What is a reflection? A chance to see two? When there are chances for reflections, there can always be two—or more."

You May Be Fearless in This World, but There Are Other Worlds

Dossiers: Spirits and Other Mysterious Entities

"Who are you? Who are you really?"
—*Laura Palmer, to Bob, in* Fire Walk with Me.

Bob (Frank Silva)

We'll tell you who: Bob is a nightmare, semiologically as well as literally. *Twin Peaks* is an endless maze of mysteries, but none as profound as this. The irony is that of all of *Twin Peak's* unearthly spirits, none is as transparent as Bob when it comes to intent: he is as evil as they come, and makes no bones about it.

First, some background: As essential as Bob is to the core mythology of *Twin Peaks*, his mere presence in the series is attributable to an astounding stroke of luck (or fate, depending on your philosophical bent).

The story is well reported: Frank Silva, the actor who portrayed him, was a set decorator working on the pilot; one day, he accidentally trapped himself behind a chest of drawers in Laura Palmer's bedroom as Lynch was shooting a scene there. As Lynch recounts it, someone on the crew shouted out to Silva, and "the image of Frank locked in that room popped into my head." Lynch offered him a role on the spot, without knowing what specifically it would be. When the time came for a panning shot of Laura's room, Silva was instructed to crouch down by the foot of her bed, and Lynch captured the image on film—still unsure of how he would use it

"He is Bob/Eager for fun."

(this scene would eventually appear in the first hour-long episode, "Traces to Nowhere," directed not by Lynch but by Duwayne Dunham, during one of Sarah Palmer's visions). Wait . . . there's more. In the penultimate scene of the pilot, Sarah wakes up with a jolt following a vision in which the gloved hand of some unidentified person (Dr. Jacoby, we later learn) digs up James's half of Laura's necklace from under a rock in the woods, where he and Donna have buried it. During the filming of this scene, Silva was standing across the room with a handful of cigarettes, waiting to pass a new one to Sarah (Grace Zabriskie) with each succeeding take. When the scene wrapped, cameraman Sean Doyle pointed out to Lynch that Silva's reflection was inadvertently captured in the living-room mirror, located just above Sarah's head. Lynch took a look in his eyepiece and loved it. No need to reshoot, he said—still unclear in his own mind how Silva would figure into the story. (Silva's reflection flashes by so quickly that it's difficult to perceive at normal speed, but freeze-frame it and by golly, there it is.)

After wrapping the pilot, Lynch was reminded of his contractual obligation to deliver a closed-end version for the European home market, in which Laura's killer was unmasked. *Voilà!* With one day left to shoot, Lynch filmed the alternate ending, with Silva appearing as Killer Bob. Though the resolution put forth here differs substantially from the solution American viewers would eventually see, Silva's role as Killer Bob never changed. Ultimately he appears in nearly a dozen episodes—sometimes briefly, in someone's vision or as a reflection in a mirror (intentional now)—and sometimes for painfully longer stretches, as when he brutally murders Maddy Ferguson, as well as in the theatrical film *Twin Peaks: Fire Walk with Me.*

Interesting note: While so much of *Twin Peaks* was a collaborative venture between Lynch and Mark Frost, Bob was specifically a Lynch creation, though clearly the character permutated over time as other members of the creative team became involved.

Another interesting note: While there's disagreement over whether the character was truly named after Bob's Big Boy, which had been one of Lynch's favorite eateries for seven years, give or take (2:30 every day, after the lunch crowd, chocolate shakes and lots and lots of coffee with lots and lots of sugar, stimulating "granulated happiness" and a rush of ideas), as so many people like to say (including the press team for *Fire Walk with Me*, which included that tidbit in its packet of information), everyone seems to be in agreement that the achromatic name effectively comments on the banality of evil. Let's face it: "Bob" isn't exactly "Beelzebub" or "Mephistopheles."

Now, back to our original question: Who, or what, is Bob? Theories abound. Here are six of them:

1. Bob, who in the course of *Twin Peaks* inhabits two bodies (FBI Agent Dale Cooper and attorney Leland Palmer), both male and both highly regarded members of society, symbolizes the misogynistic patriarchal violence lurking beneath the facade of the respectable male figure. This theory is of course particularly popular with feminist scholars.

2. Bob as Gothic "monster," as posited in 1993 by scholar Lenora Ledwon. Like Frankenstein, Mr. Hyde, or Dracula, Bob is the crystallization of his environment's darkest impulses (and believe us, in Twin Peaks there are plenty). Here, Bob is inadvertently created by the very people he terrorizes, and functions as a mirror image of the town (how appropriate, given that Bob is so often depicted as a mirror image), thus exposing its flaws and compelling the people to acknowledge and confront them.

3. Bob's existence is specific to Laura or to Leland; that is, he is an imaginary being summoned up as a means of repressing an unbearable truth (in Laura's case, that she is being raped by her father; in Leland's, that he is raping his daughter). This is a problematic proposition (aren't they all?). First, Bob's existence extends beyond the deaths of both Laura and Leland. Second, multiple characters other than Laura and Leland appear to see the exact same physical manifestation of Bob that they do, including Cooper (in his Red Room dream, and then again in series finale, in the Black Lodge), Sarah Palmer, and Maddy Ferguson (while it is impossible to say whether Bob's appearance in Maddy's murder scene is depicted through her own eyes, his apparition at the Hayward house on the night Maddy, James, and Donna gather there to perform "Just You" clearly is).

Also, Andy's sketch of Bob, based on Sarah's description ("filthy, gray-on-gray long hair"), resonates with both Ronette Pulaski—who saw Bob not in a vision or a dream, but in actuality (though certainly extremely traumatized), on the night of Laura's murder—and with Mike, who specifically says, "This is his true face." The conclusion of that statement—"but few can see it: the gifted, and the damned"—suggests a possible counter-counterargument: What if all the gifted and damned are cosmically linked, so that they all share the same visions; thus, even if Bob was specifically Laura's or Leland's summoning, they would all share the same physical representation of him (we know, for example, that Cooper and Laura shared the same dream).

Whoa, heavy!

In *Fire Walk with Me*, Bob is much more of a privately shared Laura-Leland experience, though even here his presence in the convenience-store scene as recounted by Phillip Jeffries is problematic in the context of this interpretation, as is the confrontation with Mike during the stalled-traffic scene. If Bob is merely a figment of Laura's or Leland's, imagination, what the dickens is Mike talking about (or is he just a crazy person?)? Also, Bob does appear post-Laura's death, both at the lake and in the Red Room/Black Lodge; Leland, however, is present on both occasions. In the Red Room/Black Lodge scene, Leland and Bob actually appear as two separate physical manifestations, which proves . . . nothing.

The notion that Bob is strictly a figment of Leland's imagination is essentially the wishful thinking that Sheriff Truman expresses in the aftermath of Leland's death: "Now this Bob, he can't really exist? I mean, Leland's just crazy, right?"

4. Bob is extraterrestrial, visiting from another planet. Seriously. This idea has been floated by Robert Engels, a writer/producer on the series and coscripter with Lynch of *Fire Walk with Me*. In multiple interviews, Engels has said that one concept bandied about by him and Lynch in the writers room had Bob and Mike hailing from a planet covered with creamed corn, and that the two of them had a falling-out when Bob stole a can of corn from Mike, with the chase eventually leading to Twin Peaks (reference to an argument between Bob and Mike over embezzled corn does indeed find its way into *FWWM*, during the stalled-traffic scene). This planet of corn is ruled by—Ho, ho, ho!—the Green Giant (OK, that part, not seriously). In fairness to Engels, he did eventually say that "place" might be a more appropriate word than "planet." Still, an intriguing idea, but like David Lynch says: If it isn't on the screen it didn't happen.

5. Bob is a demonic inhabiting spirit, a transcendent evil discrete from anyone's psyche, residing in the Black Lodge (or some alternate hellish locale), manipulating his human hosts (Leland/Bob uses the word "vehicle" in the interrogation room scene, after Leland is arrested) into committing heinous acts, all so that he can feed on the pain and sorrow (garmonbozia) this produces. There's nothing wrong with enjoying *Twin Peaks* as a good old-fashioned supernatural "possession" yarn, in the mold of *The Exorcist*, and a bounty of evidence exists in support of this theory. In the penultimate episode, for instance, Sheriff Truman specifically asks Cooper if there's a connection between Bob and the Black Lodge, to which Cooper replies, "Harry, I think that's where he comes from" (on the other hand, if the entire Black Lodge is a product

of an individual's psychic state, then the Bob who resides there could be a psychosomatic byproduct, right?). In the series, Mike refers to Bob as a parasite requiring a human host, who feeds on "fear . . . and the pleasures." Mike adds here that Bob was once his "familiar"—a term meaning one supernatural entity in service of another, which makes sense, since Laura writes in her diary that Bob has shared with her that he is afraid of just one man, and that man is Mike. In this reading, Bob would be one of multiple nefarious spirits residing in the Black Lodge—note that in his last breaths, Leland Palmer repeatedly uses the pronoun "they" when referencing the forces that compelled him to kill Laura and Teresa Banks.

Mark Frost harbored his own thoughts about Bob, which buttress the notion of Bob being a discrete supernatural entity, telling the fanzine *Wrapped in Plastic* that he was based on an evil spirit rooted in Pacific Northwest Native American mythology dating back to ancient times.

6. Bob is the physical manifestation of "the evil that men do," as FBI Special Agent Albert Rosenfield, of all people, phrases it. Lynch himself seems to endorse this notion in an interview with Chris Rodley, stating that Bob was an abstraction in human form (kudos to Rodley, as Lynch rarely publicly interprets his own work). Albert's comment is the coda to one of *Twin Peaks'* truly great scenes, which cuts to the heart of this conundrum, as he, Cooper, and Truman retire to the woods in the immediate aftermath of Leland's death to ponder the weirdness of everything they have just witnessed (met there, for some inexplicable reason, by Major Briggs, bathed in sunlight). Pragmatist that he is, Harry can't wrap his head around Leland's transformation, which he calls "way off the map" (Harry and the others have just seen Leland act in a manner that was exceedingly bizarre, but he did not transform physically into Bob until the others left the room). Cooper, who on multiple occasions has demonstrated an openness to mystical phenomena, responds noncommittally, but in a way that suggests he would prefer to believe in the supernatural origin of evil, because it allows him to believe in the essential goodness of Leland Palmer and, by extension, humankind: "Harry, is it easier to believe a man would rape and murder his own daughter? Any more comforting?" Days later, Cooper seems to endorse this position, telling Sarah Palmer that Leland was an "innocent and trusting" victim of "dark and heinous" forces, adding: "Leland did not do these things." However, Cooper's next comment to Sarah is ambiguous, and can be interpreted as denying Leland total absolution: "Not the Leland that you knew."

This notion of Bob as "the evil that men do" can seem dissociative, but on a more personal level can be presented as the evil that *we* do—our own Hyde-like impulses, which we constantly struggle to suppress (again, appropriate given Bob's frequent depiction as a mirror image). Here, Bob is the darkness within Leland (and all of us), including his lust for Laura; Leland's possession forty years prior by the "gray-haired man who lived next door" to his grandparents' lakeside home becomes Leland's acknowledgment of these repressed impulses, and his surrender to them. This approach condemns Leland rather than absolves him.

This quandary over determining the full extent of Leland's responsibility for Bob's transgressions surfaces in the series once Laura's killer is unmasked, but is especially challenging in *Fire Walk with Me*, where Lynch and Engels clearly provide Leland with a motive (blackmail) for killing Teresa Banks, and at no time during her death scene is he physically depicted as Bob (unlike with Laura and Maddy). Yet in *his* death scene, in the series, Leland specifically says, "They had me kill that girl Teresa," absolving himself of responsibility. Leland uses the same pronoun, "they," when saying he was forced to kill Laura, but the difference is that in the train car scene from *Fire Walk with Me* we actually see Leland transform into Bob while stabbing Laura to death.

The interrogation-room scene in episode sixteen ("Arbitrary Law"), in which Leland, finally apprehended, confesses to the murders of both Laura and Maddy, includes one of the most provocative lines of dialogue from the series, opening a line of inquiry into Bob's nature that, sadly, is never pursued: "I have this thing for knives," he says, "just like what happened to you in Pittsburgh, that time, huh, Cooper?" Leland/Bob's knowledge of the events in Pittsburgh four years earlier, involving Cooper's tragic affair with the wife of then-partner Windom Earle, so ruffles the FBI man that he takes a step backward, away from Leland/Bob. Since Cooper has never shared the details of that history with Leland or with anyone who is likely to have informed Leland about them, we are compelled to wonder how Bob has come to know them. One obvious possibility is that Bob has had his eye on Cooper for decades, and that the FBI man was his original target all along (a notion reinforced by Scott Frost's 1991 companion book, *The Autobiography of F.B.I. Special Agent Dale Cooper: My Life, My Tapes*, though there is no evidence that Lynch ever read this book or cared about its contents, and there are multiple discrepancies between the book and series). Another theory holds that Bob, being a demonic entity unbound by natural law, can tap into the thoughts and feelings of the people around him, and has telepathically registered the roots of Cooper's guilt. A third possibility: that Bob *is* the thoughts and feelings of the people around him, particularly fear, in human form.

The answer to Laura's question above? Blowing in the wind, just like the traffic light at Sparkwood and 21.

Very sadly, Frank Silva passed away on September 13, 1995, at the age of forty-five.

Chalfonts

(see Tremonds)

Convenience Store Coterie

A woodsman, electrician, and man in a red suit and white mask walk into a room. . . . The setup to a long, rambling joke, right? Wrong. Rather, key components—along with Bob, the Man from Another Place, the Tremonds, multiple bowls of creamed corn, and . . . a monkey—of the oneiric mise en scène with which we are presented in the so-called "convenience store scene" from *FWWM*, as recollected by long-lost FBI Special Agent Phillip Jeffries upon his sudden surfacing at the Philadelphia office of Regional Bureau Chief Gordon Cole. People may *claim* they know what this scene means, but take it from us: they don't. Nobody does. They can't; it's not possible. Even Ken Scherer of Lynch/Frost Productions couldn't figure it out, as he told Charlotte Fraisse, for her *Twin Peaks: Fire Walk with Me Official Shooting Diary*, adding, "I know it's going to be a great moment." He's right about that: the scene is a blast. (A slightly extended version appears among the "Missing Pieces" released in 2014; for more on that see the *Fire Walk with Me* section.)

The "convenience store" reference evokes the One-Armed Man's comment in Agent Cooper's dream from the second episode of the TV series (lifted from the European ending to the pilot) in which he reveals that he used to bunk with Bob back in the old days, when both were marauding agents of evil: "We lived among the people. I think you say . . . convenience store. We lived above it." Those days apparently are already history as this scene unfolds, as Mike is nowhere to be found. Bob and the Man from Another Place sit alone in the foreground, at a Formica table covered with bowls of creamed corn, perhaps suggesting a hierarchy among these deviants, the rest of whom are off in the background with just a single measly bowl of corn among them (if in fact it is corn inside that bowl by the feet of the Tremond bowl; hard to tell at that distance). There appears to be some (unexplained) connection between this room and the Red Room, and hence perhaps to the Black Lodge (some refer to this alternately as the Black Lodge scene), as toward the end we are presented with the familiar black-and-white zigzag floor and red curtains, which Bob parts as he and the Man from Another Place exit, destination unknown. Further linking this scene to the Red Room is that the characters speak in reverse, with the cameras rolling backward.

The Electrician (Calvin Lockhart) keeps a pretty low profile, but the Woodsman (there actually are two, Woodsman and Second Woodsman, but we speak here only of the former)—a dark-haired lad with a Rapunzelian beard—does get to move his left arm up and down in distorted motion (for no discernible reason), and is portrayed by German actor Jürgen Prochnow, who had previously appeared in David Lynch's *Dune*. Prochnow was prominent enough at the time of filming that his on-screen credit appears at the beginning of the film, even though he never utters a word and is neither seen nor heard from again after this scene (he does have two lines in the shooting script—"We have descended from pure air" and "Our world"—but neither made the cut). Some wags have speculated that this Woodsman is actually the Log Lady's deceased husband, who was indeed a logging man and died under mysterious circumstances, but really, who knows, and why would he be associating with these creeps anyway? Even more puzzling perhaps is the Jumping Man (Carlton L. Russell)—the aforementioned man in red suit and white mask, with a conical nose and slits exposing his eyes and mouth—so called because at one point during the proceedings he jumps backward onto a platform (for no discernible reason). In his right hand he holds an unidentified object that resembles a slingshot, but this too is never explained (for more on the Jumping Man, see separate entry below). Worth noting: the Jumping Man isn't the only one of these aberrants to don a mask: the Tremond grandson is briefly seen lifting a similar white mask of his own twice, first revealing his own face and second the face of the aforementioned monkey, who interestingly does not appear in any version of the *FWWM* script but who makes a far more celebrated, also unscripted appearance near the end of the film when he utters a single word: "Judy," for—you guessed it—no discernible reason. For more on this, see the "Judy" entry in Chapter 12.

The Giant (Carel Struycken) and the Waiter (Hank Worden)

What's this, a narrative poem by Lewis Carroll? "The time has come, the Giant said, to talk of many things: of smiling bags and chemicals, of owls and of rings." These two otherworldly folks are crucial to Twin Peaks, grouped here because there's ample reason to believe they are, as the Giant so memorably phrases it in the Red Room scene from the series finale, "one and the same" (a line not in the original script for the episode, but likely added by David Lynch when he tore up the script), though this is never proven conclusively (like anything in *Twin Peaks* ever is). This theory posits that the Giant is, like Bob and Mike, an inhabiting spirit, who for some reason unknown to mankind has selected as his vessel the Waiter—quite possibly the oldest human being on the planet.

Four times Cooper encounters the Giant immediately after interacting with the Waiter, though on the flip side the Giant twice appears in episodes in which the Waiter never shows. Four of the Giant's six appearances, and three of the Waiter's four, are Lynch-directed, and we know the Giant at least sprung from Lynch's fecund mind because Mark Frost said as much years ago to *Wrapped in Plastic*, the *Twin Peaks* fanzine: "One day David rushed in and said, 'Mark! There's a giant in Cooper's room!'" In the scheme of things these two blokes rarely show up, and when they do they don't stick around for long, but their appearances are invariably pivotal, and one might even argue that the Waiter is as important as anyone in cracking the Laura Palmer murder probe, just by offering Cooper a stick of gum. The Giant is hugely helpful in his own right, and also gets to recite several of the series' most iconic lines, including "He points without chemicals," "It is happening again," and "The owls are not what they seem."

Conventional wisdom holds that Giant is a potent force of good, an emissary perhaps from the White Lodge, dispatched to Twin Peaks to help facilitate the Laura Palmer investigation. A contrary point of view, which also makes the rounds among *Twin Peaks* deconstructionists, is that he, like the other spirits who visit town, are all part of a conspiracy to maneuver Cooper to exactly where he ends up at the end: inside the Black Lodge. (Carel Struycken, who portrayed the Giant, has described his character as a "psychiatrist from outer space," but says he received little direction from Lynch about his origin or motives, though he *was* instructed to talk more slowly.)

Both characters are introduced in the Lynch-helmed second-season opener, in a scene notorious for its exceptionally languorous pace at a time when ABC was pleading with Lynch and Frost to cut to the chase. It's the

Waiter who discovers Cooper sprawled on the floor of his Great Northern hotel room after being shot by Josie Packard. No spring chicken—one episode hence, Special Agent Albert Rosenfield will dub him "the world's most decrepit room-service waiter" and, even more famously, "Señor Droolcup"— the Waiter doesn't exactly dive into action. What he does do, over the course of a whopping four and a half minutes, is this: deliver a warm glass of milk to Cooper's bedside table, hang up the telephone (despite Deputy Andy Brennan pleading on the other end for affirmation that everything is OK), hand the prostrate Cooper a bill to sign, inform Cooper his reputation precedes him, offer him a thumbs-up, and, finally, leave, all the while remarkably unalarmed by the fact that the G-man is lying on the floor in front of him bleeding profusely. Struycken has commented multiple times on his uneasiness during the filming of this scene because the Waiter (Hank Worden) was taking so long to cross the room. When Lynch yelled cut, Struycken felt certain the director would instruct Worden to pick up the pace, but instead encouraged him to play the scene even more slowly, as if he were a hundred and twenty years old.

Within seconds of the Waiter's departure, the Giant materializes out of thin air, assuring Cooper he is a friend and that "we want to help you." Only to a point, however, because he's not divulging any information about where he emanates from or who "we" are. What he does share are three cryptic clues, intended to help crack the Palmer investigation:

1. "There's a man in a smiling bag."
2. "The owls are not what they seem."
3. "Without chemicals, he points."

Not exactly "Leland Palmer is the killer, he's possessed by a demonic spirit named Bob, now go out and get him before he kills again," but hey, this is *Twin Peaks*, and Cooper is nothing if not open-minded, so he plays along, even surrendering his ring to the big guy, who promises to return it "when you find these things to be true" (though, truthfully, Cooper hasn't yet ruled out the possibility that he's hallucinating).

Apparently even otherworldly beings experience memory lapses, because the Giant returns the following night, informing Cooper that he had neglected to share certain vital pieces of information, among them the Zen-like counsel that "a path is formed by laying one stone at a time," but also the more practical news that "one person [as in Ronette Pulaski] saw the Third Man. Three have seen him, yes, but not his body. One only. Known to you. Ready now to talk." Last, the Giant does his damnedest in his own oblique way to remind Cooper that he has yet to open a note from Audrey Horne, informing him she has gone undercover at One Eyed Jacks, which he had been about to read when he was shot, though why the Giant chooses to convey this message via the words "One more thing: you forgot something" instead of "Read the note from Audrey Horne already!" is beyond us even now, and it is several episodes before Cooper finally makes the connection.

The duo returns for more weirdness in the seventh episode of season two; the Waiter occupies a seat at the Roadhouse bar next to Bobby Briggs—talk about odd couples!—as Cooper, Truman, and the Log Lady listen to Julee Cruise sing "The World Spins" (lyrics by Lynch, music by Angelo Badalamenti), while over at the Palmer house Leland/Bob is beating Maddy Ferguson to death. "It is happening again," the Giant, materializing once again out of ether, tells Cooper, as everyone else in the room (other than the Log Lady) freezes in time. Once reanimated, the Waiter shuffles over to Coop, pats him on the shoulder, and says, "I'm so sorry."

Two episodes on, with Maddy's recent death weighing heavily upon him, Cooper visits the One-Armed Man Gerard in his room at the Great Northern and presses for information, hoping to unlock the secret of his season-one dream so that he can finally recall the identity of Laura's killer. When talk turns to the Giant, Gerard says, "He is known to us here," suggesting that whatever world Gerard, Bob, and the Man from Another Place hail from, the Giant graces as well. After Gerard tells Cooper that the Giant can help him find Bob, but that he must ask him first, Cooper walks out in the hallway and crosses paths with the Waiter, again carrying a tray of warm milk. "I know about you," the Waiter tells him again, as he did in the hotel room, after Cooper was shot. "That milk'll cool down on you, but it's getting warmer now," he says. Cooper interprets this a clue that he is on the right path.

Later in the same episode, Cooper assembles the suspects at the Roadhouse on a dark and stormy afternoon; as the clock strikes three, he announces that someone is missing, at which point Major Garland Briggs appears, escorting the Waiter. Cooper's response—"Major, you're right on time"—leaves unclear whether he was anticipating the arrival of Briggs or the Waiter, or both. Briggs explains that he was on his way home, and the Waiter flagged him down, asking for a lift to the Roadhouse—no explanation asked for or given as to why he would be heading to the Bang Bang Bar in the middle of a stormy afternoon. It's here he offers Cooper the stick of gum, an act observed by Leland Palmer, who comments, "I know that gum. I used to chew it when I was a kid. That's my most favorite gum in the world."

Hearing this, the Waiter responds with the exact same phrase used by the Man from Another Place in Cooper's dream: "That gum you liked is going to come back in style." Suddenly, everything clicks for Cooper, who finally remembers the words Laura whispered into his ear: "My father killed me." The Giant appears, delivering on his promise to return Cooper's ring "when you find these things to be true." Exiting the Roadhouse, Cooper salutes the Waiter with a thumbs-up; beaming, the old man waves back.

In episode twenty-seven ("The Path to the Black Lodge"), the Giant returns briefly for a solo gig, sans Señor Droolcup, appearing once again to Cooper only, immediately after Annie shares the news that she'll be competing in the Miss Twin Peaks contest. Waving his arms and mouthing "No," the Giant appears to be warning Cooper against it.

The Giant and the Waiter make their farewell appearances in the Red Room scene from the series finale; worth noting is that neither appears in the scripted version, which was ripped up by Lynch when he arrived to direct. After the Man from Another Place announces to Cooper that "some of your friends are here," the first to appear is Laura Palmer, or some iteration thereof, acting suitably weird. Next up: the Waiter—it's almost as if the MFAP is hosting a talk show, with rotating guests occupying the chair immediately to his left. The old man taps his fingers against his mouth, makes multiple "whooping" sounds, like a child pretending to be an Native American (this is the same sound made by the Man from Another Place in Laura Palmer's dream in *FWWM*), and exchanges "Hallelujahs" with the MFAP. He rises, placing a cup of coffee on a table to Cooper's right, before transforming into the Giant, who here makes the comment "one and the same."

The presence of these two characters in the Red Room confuses many, because the venue is typically associated with the Black Lodge, a place of pure evil. One clue may lie in the Man from Another Place's description of the Red Room as "the waiting room," suggesting perhaps that it is a sort of purgatory, leading to either Door One (the Black Lodge) or Door Two (the White Lodge), depending on how things play out.

Our response: Who the hell knows?

Jumping Man (Carlton L. Russell)

The Jumping Man appears only in *Twin Peaks: Fire Walk with Me* and is never identified by name (though he *is* identified as the Jumping Man in the end credits, a designation clearly derived from the fact that he jumps around on a crate during the one scene he appears in, popularly known as the convenience-store scene, a flashback accompanying the incoherent ramblings of Special Agent Phillip Jeffries at FBI headquarters in Philadelphia). This enigmatic character not only never appears in the TV series, but doesn't even exist in the original film script (ditto for the monkey and the Electrician, who appear in the same scene). There's much speculation that the Jumping Man is another Black Lodge spirit, along with Bob and the Man from Another Place, who are present at the same meeting. The Jumping Man never speaks. He wears a white mask similar to the one worn by Pierre Tremond/Chalfont (though different in that it includes slots for the mouth and eyes), and holds in his hand an unidentified object resembling a slingshot similar to the one Pierre is later seen holding outside the Red Diamond Motel, where he too is jumping around, leading to rampant speculation that these two characters share some important (unknown) connection. The Jumping Man wears a red suit, similar to that worn by the Man from Another Place, leading to bizarre Internet conjecture that he is some other part of Mike's body, just as the Little Man is his arm. We warned you this could get crazy. Third theory: that the Jumping Man is the court jester among these wild and crazy guys, a tummler of sorts (his jumping halts abruptly once Bob claps his hands, suggesting—perhaps—some sort of subservience). The truth is . . . we may never know the truth, and that's fine with us.

Man from Another Place: aka Little Man (Michael J. Anderson)

Little man, BIG mystery. Exactly who is this "midget in a red suit," as Cooper describes him to Harry and Lucy following his star-making role in Cooper's Red Room dream from episode two ("Zen, or the Skill to Catch a Killer"), which had pop culture-istas buzzing? Well, we know he can dance. He hangs out with some pretty strange dudes. He's chatty, but speaks in riddles—"fortune cookie Dadaisms," Owen Gleiberman dubbed them in his *Entertainment Weekly* review of *Fire Walk with Me* (not to mention backward, a skill that Michael J. Anderson, the thirty-seven-inch-tall former NASA computer programmer and disco dancer who played the Little Man, had mastered in childhood; the dialogue was then reverse-projected, so that it approximates normal speech, but distorted): "When you see me again it won't be me." . . . "Where we're from, the birds sing a pretty song, and there's always music in the air." . . . "With this ring, I thee wed." This is particularly exasperating because no one seems to spend as much time hanging out with Bob, or feels so comfortable around him, as this little guy, suggesting that he could decode so many of the most confounding riddles Cooper confronts, if only he were better at sharing! Almost everything we know about him derives from two Red Room scenes in the series, first during Cooper's dream and later in the series finale, plus a pair of key scenes from *Fire Walk with Me:* the so-called convenience-store meeting, as recollected by Phillip Jeffries, and Laura's dream. He is among the otherwordly entities who pop in and out of *Twin Peaks*, along with Bob, Mike, the Giant, the Waiter, and the Tremonds, and he was David Lynch's creation; Mark Frost told a PBS interviewer in 1990 that he was skeptical at first and wanted to know more, like why he was dancing.

Bottom line: Is he a Black Lodge spirit, a White Lodge spirit, or neither (like, maybe just a talk-show host on good terms with both sides: the David Letterman of the spirit world)? Let's examine the clues:

1. His comment to Cooper in the Red Room dream that "I've got good news. That gum you like is going to come back in style," though impenetrable at the time, eventually unlocks Cooper's memory, when repeated by the Waiter at the Roadhouse in episode sixteen ("Arbitrary Law"), empowering him to solve the Palmer investigation. Score one for the good guys.

2. Immediately after Josie's death in episode twenty-three ("The Condemned Woman"), Cooper has a vision first of Bob, then of the Man from Another Place, hoofing it up on Josie's bed. This can't be good, can it? Score 1-1.

3. In the series finale, he doesn't emit a particularly sinister vibe at first, asking Cooper if he'd like some coffee and informing him that some of his friends are there, as Laura Palmer, the Waiter, and the Giant pop in for conversation (such as it is). He smiles a lot. However, his unfortunate "Fire walk with me" comment kind of puts a damper on the proceedings, as the screen bursts into huge, billowing flames, a woman screams, the strobe lights start kicking in, and truly, it is all downhill from there. By the time Cooper starts ducking in and out of the different rooms, the Little Man has undergone a radical transformation, and not for the better, barking "Wrong way!" at Cooper at one point and making disturbing, guffawing sounds. His eyes now have that opaque look associated with doppelgängers in the *Twin Peaks* universe ("doppelgänger," in fact, is the last word the MFAP ever speaks in the series), an interesting development considering that none of the other spirits known to us ever seem to appear in doppelgänger form. One point for each side. Score: 2-2.

4. Moving on to *Fire Walk with Me*, a particularly convoluted conundrum. In the convenience-store scene, the Man from Another Place is seated in the foreground at a green Formica table along with Bob; on the tabletop are four bowls of creamed corn, which the Little Man references as "garmonbozia." Six characters are either seated or standing in the background, only two of whom—the Tremonds/Chalfonts—we have met before. Based on their positions in the shot, the Man from Another Place and Bob seem to be equals, the others subordinate. Bob and the MFAP appear to be at peace with each other. Score 2-3, because while we have no clue what is transpiring here, we're supremely discomforted by the Little Man's apparent closeness to Bob (they even leave the room together, parting the red curtain).

5. In Cooper's Red Room dream in the series, Mike (the One-Armed Man) tells Cooper that he, like Bob, has been "touched by the devilish one," but had his entire left arm severed once he saw the face of God. Hence, arm = evil. In Laura's *Fire Walk with Me* dream, the MFAP asks Cooper if he knows who he is. When Cooper shakes his head no, the Little Man replies, "I am the arm." If arm = evil and MFAP = arm, does not MFAP = evil? Score 2-4, for the bad guys.

6. In that same *FWWM* dream, the Man from Another Place holds out the Owl Cave ring to Laura. Don't take it, Cooper says. The ring, we know, was in Teresa's possession when she dies and will later be in Laura's possession when she dies. Agent Chet Desmond disappears reaching for it. Phillip Jeffries may have disappeared after finding it. Conclusion: the ring is bad news. If the MFAP is urging Laura to take it, doesn't that mean he plays for the bad guys? On the other hand, consider the possibility that Laura is actually better off taking the ring, so that she can finally end her misery—and thwart Bob's desire to possess her—through death, in which case the MFAP is actually doing her a favor, and Cooper is mistaken in urging her not to take it. On a third hand, if we had one . . . nah. Score 2-5, bad.

7. During the train car scene, in which Laura is brutally murdered, there are two fast cuts to the Little Man. Is he laughing? Screaming? Indecipherable. Score: Still 2-5.

8. After Leland/Bob kills Laura, he parts the curtains in Glastonbury Grove and winds up back in the Red Room. Seated there are Mike and, to his left, on the side of the missing arm, the Man from Another Place. Leland and Bob—now two entities instead of one—stand before them (Leland suspended in the air), as if summoned to judgment. The Little

Man walks over to Mike and places his right hand on his shoulder; together they say, "Bob, I want all my garmonbozia." Like all Red Room dialogue, this comment is subtitled, and appearing parenthetically next to "garmonbozia" are the words "pain and sorrow." These otherworldly folk do seem to like their creamed corn (save Mrs. Tremond, who wants no part of it). Here it appears Mike and his left arm have been reunited at last, and it feels so good. But united in evil or in goodness? Keep in mind that this scene—like all of *Fire Walk with Me*—occurs *before* the events of the series, and thus before Cooper encounters either Mike or the Man from Another Place. Score: Totally lost track. But who cares? Embrace the mystery.

Mike: aka *Phillip/Philip Michael Gerard aka the One-Armed Man (Al Strobel)

Any fan of the sixties TV show *The Fugitive,* in which Dr. Richard Kimble spent four seasons eluding law-enforcement officials after being unjustly convicted of murdering his wife, will recognize the intertextual allusions at play here: the cop who tracks Kimble with Javert-like zeal is Philip Gerard, and the actual killer, whom Kimble crisscrosses the country in pursuit of, is known as the One-Armed Man because, well, he has only one arm. Unfortunately, our One-Armed Man is more complicated than that, beginning with the fact that he isn't strictly a man, but rather an inhabiting spirit from another world, whose arrival in Twin Peaks is likely inspired by his antagonistic relationship with Killer Bob, though his motives ultimately are murky, and there seems to be a disconnect between his iterations in the TV series and the film. What we can state confidently is that Mike is an otherwordly spirit who has inhabited the body (or "vessel," as Mike calls it) of a one-armed shoe salesman named Phillip Michael Gerard. Cooper and Truman first encounter him briefly in an elevator at Calhoun Memorial Hospital in the series pilot, as they descend to the morgue to examine Laura Palmer's corpse. No words are exchanged, and the chance meeting is unremarkable at the time, but two episodes later he turns up in Cooper's Red Room dream (though he himself doesn't actually appear in the Red Room), and from that point on he's a rock star. "In another time, another culture, he may have been a seer, a shaman priest," Cooper says. "In our world, he's a shoe salesman and lives among the shadows."

Mike's value to Cooper is his familiarity with Bob: once upon a time the two were roomies, living above a convenience store, of all things (think of the robbery-prevention benefits). Like Bob, Mike had been "touched by the devilish one," but he "saw the face of God" and was reborn, severing his left arm to commemorate this transformation (which apparently mutated into the Man from Another Place, who expressly states in *Fire Walk with Me* that "I am the arm"). In the original script for episode two ("Zen, or the Skill to Catch a Killer"), in a segment lifted straight from the European ending of the pilot, Mike calls Cooper at the Great Northern and tells him he knows who "did" Teresa Banks; they meet up at the hospital, where Mike further reveals that he has been searching for Bob for a year, and has finally located him in the basement of the hospital. Mike winds up fatally shooting Bob, but in so doing reveals some sort of bizarre symbiosis between the two, as it apparently results in his own death as well: as Bob dies, the script reads, "Mike clutches a pole and twists to the ground, in agonizing sympathetic pain." None of this transpires in episode two as filmed.

Following the dream, Cooper becomes obsessed with locating the One-Armed Man (the One-Armer, Gordon Cole calls him), whom Hawk eventually tracks to the Timber Falls Motel, where he's registered as Gerard, the shoe salesman (two-day delivery guaranteed) who claims to have lost his left arm—tattooed "Mom," he recalls, sobbing—in a traffic accident. He denies knowing anyone resembling Deputy Andy Brennan's sketch of Killer Bob, based on Sarah Palmer's vision. However, several episodes hence he shows up at the sheriff's station peddling his wares, and has a radically different reaction upon spotting a "Have You Seen This Man?" poster of Bob: severely disoriented, he makes a mad dash for the men's room, but is unable to shoot up in time to suppress the emergence of Mike, who exits the stall muttering, "Bob, I know you're near. I'm after you now." Mike slips out of the sheriff's station unnoticed, but Hawk eventually tracks him down again (though as Gerard once again), and this time Cooper—finally piecing together the One-Armer's dependence on the drug haloperidol, used to treat schizophrenia, with the Giant's clue that "Without chemicals, he points"—withholds the medicine, yielding great dividends: Mike reemerges, revealing significant chunks of information about both himself and Bob, including these two very juicy tidbits:

1. Once upon a time, Bob was Mike's "familiar"—a term used, in supernatural circles, to describe a demon subservient to a higher being. (Later in the series, we learn, from Laura's secret diary, that Bob is afraid of only one man, and that man is Mike.)
2. Mike continues to inhabit Gerard's body for a single purpose: to stop Bob.

Sadly, Mike refuses to divulge anything about the world from which he and Bob emanate, but throughout the remainder of the Palmer investigation he drops in and out, endearing himself to Cooper with crucial clues as to Bob's location and identity. The logical conclusion, based on Mike's appearances in the television series, *seems* to be this: Mike has renounced evil and, having "seen the face of God," is intent, out of pure goodness, on stopping Bob before he kills again.

Now comes *Fire Walk with Me,* which rather convincingly upends this premise.

First, note that Mike does *not* turn up in the convenience-store scene, unlike Bob, the Man from Another Place, and numerous other spirits from their world, just as he doesn't appear in any of the Red Room sequences in the television series (though, in the *FWWM* script directions, the Man from Another Place is twice interchangeably referred to as Mike in the convenience-store scene). So, his disembodied left arm—possibly representing his severed evil side, possibly not—*is* present, but Mike is not, which *could* mean this is a gathering of black spirits, and Mike is no longer a member of the club, but if that is the case what are the Tremonds doing there, or are they also evil?

Never mind.

When Mike finally does appear in *FWWM* (almost ninety minutes in), he's in a foul mood, far angrier than we have ever seen him. After pursuing Leland and Laura in a tense car chase, he pulls up beside Leland's open convertible, stopped at a crosswalk, and screams: "You stole the corn! I had it canned over the store!" To Laura, he adds: "And miss, the look on her face when it was opened! There was a stillness, like the Formica table top!" These comments are indecipherable, but the references to corn, a store, and the Formica table clearly evoke the convenience-store scene from earlier in *FWWM,* even though Mike was nowhere to be seen during it. Finally, Mike appears to be alerting Laura to the fact that Leland and Bob are one and the same: "It's him! It's your father!" (Hmmm . . . If Mike knows that Leland is Bob in *FWWM,* why does he have so much trouble identifying him for Cooper in the series, which takes place *after* the film?) As he yells this, we see the Owl Cave ring—heretofore associated with Teresa Banks's death and Agent Chet Desmond's disappearance—on his right pinky.

Two additional mysteries surface in this traffic scene: One: during his rant, Mike says to Leland: "The thread will be torn, Mr. Palmer! The thread will be torn!" The meaning of this comment is unclear, and never explained. Second, Laura tells Leland that Mike looks familiar to her, though as far as we know the two have never met, in either the film or, of course, the TV series, since Laura is already dead by the time the series opens.

We meet up with Mike again on the night of Laura's murder, running through the woods "like a madman," as the *FWWM* script phrases it, presumably to stop Leland/Bob from killing Laura and Ronette. By the time he reaches the derelict train car, Leland has locked himself and the girls inside. Mike demands to be let in, to no avail. Ronette manages to slide the door open, and as Leland/Bob tosses her out, the ring goes flying in, landing on the floor of the train car, where Laura sees it, picks it up, and places it on her finger. The *FWWM* script further confuses the issue: Mike leans into the partially opened train car and laughs, yelling at Bob: "That's his own daughter you're killing!" He continues to laugh, then runs from the train car. There is no mention whatsoever here of the ring. Nevertheless, the scene as filmed raises numerous questions: Is this an act of beneficence on the part of Mike, recognizing that since he can't stop Laura's murder he can at least offer her the ring so that she can end her suffering through death? Is the ring actually a gift, preventing Bob from possessing Laura? Does it inadvertently simply fall off his finger? Or is Mike promoting still some other agenda, of which we are unaware?

Never mind.

Even if, like us, you are clinging to Mike's goodness up to now, what ensues has to unsettle you. Keep in mind that the following scene occurs *before* the events of the TV series, perhaps shedding doubt on Mike's forthrightness in his dealings with Cooper: When Leland/Bob descends into the Red Room after killing Laura, he finds the Man from Another Place and Mike seated side by side—Mike's first appearance in the Red Room in either the film or the series. The dwarf sits to Mike's left, where his arm would be. The Little Man stands up and walks over to Mike, placing his right hand on Mike's shoulder. In unison, they say, "Bob, I want all my garmonbozia," meaning, we are advised by subtitling, "pain and sorrow" (in the script, this line is preceded with "Bob, you're not going home without me," but the line was dropped). Are Mike and his evil arm reunited? Are they feasting on pain and sorrow? Are they angry at Bob not for the act of killing itself, but for hoarding pain and sorrow? Is all of this simply about a can of corn Bob stole from Mike while they roomed together above the convenience store? Is it all part of some plot eventually luring Cooper to the Black Lodge?

Never mind.

* Postscript: In the *FWWM* script, Gerard's first name is spelled Philip (one "l"), which deviates from the spelling throughout the series (Phillip).

Tremonds/Chalfonts (Frances Bay; Austin Jack Lynch/Jonathan J. Leppell)

Who doesn't love the Tremonds? On the other hand, who *are* the Tremonds? Black Lodge? White Lodge? A little of this, a little of that? Prevailing wisdom—at least, *our* wisdom, which prevails here—is that the Tremonds are guides, shepherding Laura and Cooper along the path to resolution and reward . . . or is it all part of some nefarious plot to trap Cooper in the Black Lodge? Don't they lead Donna to Harold Smith, who produces the missing page from Laura's diary, thus triggering Cooper's realization that he and Laura shared the same dream? Still, why are they hanging out in that room above the convenience store in *Fire Walk with Me*, with Bob, the Man from Another Place, and all those other evil-looking dudes? We are so confused.

The Tremonds—an old woman and her young grandson—show up just once in the TV series, in episode nine ("Coma"), written by Harley Peyton and directed by a fella by the name of David Lynch, but play a pivotal role in the resolution of the Palmer murder investigation, and figure even more crucially (and enigmatically) in *Fire Walk with Me*. In the series they are verbally referenced (by Donna, the only person to see them) as Tremond,

The mysterious Tremonds/Chalfonts present Laura with a painting, in *Fire Walk with Me*.

New Line Cinema/Photofest

though even that identity is later impugned; in the film they are never directly addressed by name, but comments by Carl Rodd, manager of Fat Trout Trailer Park, suggest they were known as the Chalfonts while inhabiting Deer Meadow. The grandson, portrayed by David Lynch's son Austin Jack Lynch in the series and Jonathan J. Leppell in the film, is never referenced by first name in the series or the film (either verbally or in the credits), but is dubbed Pierre Tremond in *The Secret Diary of Laura Palmer* and in the collectible card series issued by Star Pics in 1991, and the name seems to have stuck, canon or not. Lynch scholars have likened the Tremonds to characters in the director's 1970 short (thirty-four-minute) experimental film *The Grandmother*, about a young boy (like Tremond, fond of tuxedos) with a bed-wetting problem who, living with an abusive father and a kook of a mom, literally (perhaps) *grows* a kind, loving grandmother from a seed (the film has obvious connections to the Laura-Leland arc of *Twin Peaks* as well).

While meeting with Maddy Ferguson at the Double R diner in episode eight ("May the Giant Be with You"), Donna Hayward receives an anonymous note advising her to "Look into the Meals on Wheels," the aid program Laura had organized with Norma Jennings. The source of this note is never definitively established, though theories abound. Immediately after Donna and Maddy read the note, the camera cuts to the Log Lady, occupying another booth at the diner, suggesting that the note may have come from her. Margaret's Cassandra-like gifts are demonstrated multiple times in the series, and she clearly evinces a desire to help uncover the identity of Laura's murder. However, many *Peaks* geeks alternatively believe that the note was sent by Harold Smith, a shut-in on the MOW route and someone Laura was particular close to; for evidence, they point to a comment Donna makes during a phone conversation with Harold in the following episode ("I received yours," she says, in an apparent reference to the note). However, as far as we're concerned, this suggests only that Donna *believes* the note came from Harold, not that it in fact did. A third theory is that the note came from the Tremonds, who will soon demonstrate an interest in furthering the investigation by connecting Donna to Harold, and who appear capable of all sorts of acts defying rational explanation.

Turns out the Tremonds are among the stops on Laura's route, as Donna soon discovers, having decided to take it over, in full Nancy Drew mode. She raps on the Tremond door, is instructed to enter, and finds Mrs. Tremond sitting up in her bed, wearing a nightgown. She's frail, sickly. Initially Donna doesn't notice the grandson, seated in an armchair off in the background, but he calls to her and says, "Sometimes, things can happen just like this," snapping his fingers. Mrs. Tremond is alarmed to discover creamed corn on her plate: "Creamed corn? Do you see creamed corn on that plate?" Donna answers affirmatively. "I requested no creamed corn," Mrs. Tremond says. "Do you see creamed corn on that plate?" she asks again. Donna looks; the creamed corn is gone. She glances over at the grandson, now holding the corn in his cupped hands. Donna looks back at the plate, then back at the boy—the corn has vanished again. The boy is studying magic, Mrs. Tremond offers, helpfully.

Old Mrs. Tremond says she didn't know Laura well, but suggests Donna reach out to Harold Smith, who resides next door. The grandson shares a parting comment: "J'ai une ame solitaire" ("I am a lonely soul"). Meaningless at the time, this statement turns out to correspond exactly to the suicide note Harold Smith will leave behind; Donna overhears Deputy Andy Brennan reciting it at the Double R diner, inspiring her to share details of her visit to the Tremonds with Agent Cooper. However, when Donna returns to the house with Cooper and Andy, the woman claiming to be Mrs. Tremond (now portrayed by Mae Williams) looks nothing at all like the previous iteration, and has no idea what Donna is talking about. She does, however, hand over an envelope from Harold, found among her mail the morning after his suicide and addressed to Donna; inside is the missing page from Laura's diary, in which she recounts her Red Room dream of February 21, identical to the dream Cooper had in the first season.

On now to *Fire Walk with Me:* Our first sighting of the Tremonds comes during the convenience-store gathering, as recollected by Agent Phillip Jeffries upon his return to the Philadelphia office of the FBI after a two-year, unexplained absence, one of the most inscrutable scenes in all of *Twin Peaks.* In the foreground, Bob and the Man from Another Place sit at a green Formica table, atop which are four bowls of . . . what else? Creamed corn. No wonder the old woman hates it! In the left background stands the character known as the Jumping Man, wearing a white mask with a conical nose. Behind him sit a row of, shall we say, mysterious entities: the Electrician, Mrs. Tremond, her grandson, and two characters known as the Woodsmen (there are two empty seats as well). At the grandson's feet is a bowl of something, possibly creamed corn. Between them the Tremonds speak just once in this scene, as the grandson points at someone or something off camera (apparently in Bob's direction) and says, "Fell a victim." Later in the scene, the grandson too is wearing a white mask with a conical nose, though different from the Jumping Man's; he doffs it twice, the second time revealing the face of a monkey.

Later in the film, Cooper is dispatched to Deer Meadow, Washington, in search of missing colleague Chester Desmond. At Fat Trout Trailer Park, where Desmond has last been seen, Cooper observes a vacant lot; Carl Rodd, manager of the park, tells him the family who last lived there—an old woman and her grandson—were named Chalfont, and that the family before that also was named Chalfont (our conclusion: The Tremonds are in reality neither the Tremonds nor the Chalfonts, but rather simply assume the name of whoever lives at the abode they are borrowing at the time). This is the same trailer that Desmond was diverted to on his last trip to Fat Trout, under which sat Teresa Banks's ring.

The next time we see the Tremonds is in Twin Peaks, when they appear outside the Double R diner as Laura Palmer loads up the station wagon for her Meals on Wheels run. Mrs. Tremond beckons her over, gifting her with a painting of an empty room with an open door, commenting that "This would look nice on your wall" (the grandson has ditched the tux, replaced by a suit and tie, but still wears the white mask). "The man behind the mask is looking for the book with the pages torn out," the boy tells Laura, apparent references to Laura's diary and to Bob, hiding behind the mask of Leland. "He is going towards the hiding place. He is under the fan now." Laura, alarmed, scurries home, where she discovers Bob lurking in her bedroom, screams, and bolts from the house. Hiding in the bushes outside, she observes Leland exiting the house, poking at any repressed notion that Bob and her father are one and the same. That night, Laura hangs the picture on her bedroom wall and, dreaming, is beckoned inside the room by Mrs. Tremond. The grandson snaps his fingers; Laura suddenly has entered the Red Room, along with the Man from Another Place, who brandishes Teresa's ring, and Cooper, who urges her not to take it.

The grandson appears one last time, during Leland's flashback to his planned motel tryst with Teresa and two of her friends; realizing at the last minute that one of them is Laura, Leland scurries away before his daughter can see him, and as he does so the Tremond boy emerges from the bushes outside the motel. In his white mask, he bounds aimlessly around, a stick grasped in his right hand—strongly evoking the Jumping Man for the second time—before finally vanishing into thin air, as any self-respecting spirit would do.

Those are the facts, but what to make of them? Debate rages over whether the Tremonds hail from the White Lodge or Black (or neither). In the series, Mrs. Tremond seems to aid Donna by directing her to Harold Smith, who ultimately shares information vital to the Laura Palmer murder investigation. Cooper is galvanized by the discovery that he and Laura shared the same dream, made possible only because someone, believed to be Harold, coughed up the missing page from Laura's diary. In *FWWM*, Pierre Tremond's warning to Laura that Bob is looking for her diary figures integrally in her eventual acknowledgment that Bob and Leland are one and the same. Central to the mystery of which team the Tremonds play for is this whole issue of the creamed corn. In *Fire Walk with Me,* creamed corn is equated with "garmonbozia," which, subtitles tell us in the final Red Room scene, represents "pain and sorrow." What seems apparent is that Black Lodge spirits consume this for nourishment, so if Mrs. Tremond rejects the creamed corn in the scene with Donna Hayward, does that exclude her from membership (unless, of course, she is a Black Lodge spirit forbidden to eat the corn, which, by all accounts appears to be such a prized possession, perhaps reserved for the special few)?

On the other side of the ledger, there's much that disturbs us about the Tremonds, particularly their link to Teresa's ring (alternately called the Owl Cave ring), which seems unequivocally cursed—Teresa and Laura both die with it in their possession, and Desmond disappears while reaching for it (under the Tremond/Chalfont trailer, let's not forget). What draws Desmond to that particular trailer in the first place? In the *Fire Walk with Me* script, Desmond gets a "strange feeling" while walking around Deputy Howard's trailer: He looks past Teresa's trailer to the far edge of the park, and sees a hand appear in the window of the Chalfont trailer. Then the hand disappears, and Desmond approaches. Curiously, in the film itself the hand is not visible, but the implication remains that someone or something is drawing him to that trailer. Who could it have been if not the Chalfonts? Further, the painting that Mrs. Tremond/Chalfont gifts to Laura outside the Double R diner serves as a portal to the Red Room, where Laura is offered the ring by the Man from Another Place.

Of course, the possibility exists that the Tremonds are trying to guide Laura to the awareness that the ring is her salvation: by wearing it she will become Bob's next victim, finally freeing her from his torment and degradation.

If you believe that is the power of the ring.

Which we do.

12

The Magician Longs to See

The Mystery and Mythology of *Twin Peaks*

> *Even with complicated languages used by intelligent people, misunderstanding is a common occurrence.*

Black Lodge/White Lodge/Red Room

Color us confused.

Somewhere along the lost highway, *Twin Peaks* mutates from murder mystery to cosmic battle between good and evil, as symbolized by the White and Black Lodges. The lodges have no presence whatsoever in season one, but soon after the Palmer murder case is cracked, Cooper accompanies Major Briggs on a night-fishing expedition, during which the major asks if he has ever heard of the White Lodge (he hasn't). In the conversation following, Briggs foreshadows themes that loom large in the episodes ahead, as the lodges become more prominent, especially the question of how one confronts evil. Essentially, Briggs says there is great evil in the world, and that those who confront that evil with fear become vulnerable to it.

Briggs vanishes from sight before he can elaborate, but Cooper learns from Sheriff Truman and Hawk that the White Lodge is an old local legend, which Hawk, a Native American, describes as "a place where the spirits that rule man and nature here reside." Hawk also introduces Cooper to the legend of the Black Lodge, "the shadow self of the White Lodge," adding: "The legend says that every spirit must pass through there on the way to perfection. There you will meet your shadow self. My people call it 'The Dweller on the Threshold.'" Echoing Major Briggs's earlier reference to fear, Hawk concludes: "But it is said, if you confront the Black Lodge with imperfect courage, it will utterly annihilate your soul."

Shadow self . . . Dweller on the Threshold . . . This notion of a "doppelgänger" (literally German for "double-goer") dovetails neatly with the whole theme of duality that runs throughout *Twin Peaks*. In actuality the term Dweller on the Threshold was coined not by Native Americans, but by the nineteenth-century British writer Edward Bulwer-Lytton (best known perhaps for the opening to his 1830 novel *Paul Clifford*: "It was a dark and stormy night."). In the 1842 novel *Zanoni*, Bulwer-Lytton wrote of a Dweller *of* the Threshold, a menacing specter guarding the ingress to a world of higher, mystical learning. This term also features prominently in the teachings of theosophist Alice Bailey, a huge influence on Mark Frost, who described the Dweller as an "elemental form" embodying a person's evil nature, and posing the final test of courage as he seeks entry to a "sacred portal."

Our other expert on the lodges is Windom Earle, who conducted research on the subject in the mid-sixties, during a two-year stint with the U.S. Air Force (on loan from the FBI); Earle became dangerously obsessed with the Black Lodge and eventually was booted off the project (and the bureau welcomed him back why exactly?). Our point: Earle is hardly a reliable narrator. His description of the White Lodge drips with sarcasm; he speaks disdainfully of "gentle fawns" gamboling "amidst happy, laughing spirits. The sounds of innocence and joy filled the air, and when it rained it rained sweet nectar that infused one's heart with the desire to live life in truth and beauty." Earle's consistent use of the past tense here has led to speculation that the White Lodge is extinct, an argument we find unconvincing: not only does Major Briggs believe he was taken to the White Lodge during his disappearance, but it can be persuasively argued that *Fire Walk with Me* ends there, with Laura Palmer celebrating her liberation from a life of relentless torment, in the presence of Cooper and her guardian angel.

By contrast, Earle's evocation of the Black Lodge is gleeful, and wholly (even holy) in the present tense, describing it as a "place of almost unimaginable power, chock-full of dark forces and vicious secrets." If harnessed, Earle says, the dark spirits that reside "in this hidden land of unmuffled screams and broken hearts will offer up a power so vast that its bearer might reorder the Earth itself to his liking."

Major Briggs (having safely returned from the White Lodge, or wherever it was he had disappeared to) tracks down video from Earle's lunatic days on Project Blue Book, and it isn't pretty: Mad Man Earle (his surname is lifted from the character "Mad Dog" Earle in the 1941 Humphrey Bogart film

Mad Man Earle: No wonder he got booted off Project Blue Book.

Photo by Richard Beymer

High Sierra) rants about evil sorcerers called dugpas, who "cultivate evil for the sake of evil, nothing else," affording them entry to a secret place called, yes, the Black Lodge.

Over time, Cooper develops his own notions of the Black Lodge; this, he suspects, is where Bob hangs out, and the fountainhead of what Truman, earlier in the series, had referred to as a "sort of evil" emanating from the woods surrounding Twin Peaks. "There's a source of great power there, Harry, far beyond our ability to comprehend," he says.

Responsibility for constructing this mythology fell primarily to Frost, who, in his edacity to tackle the conflict between good and evil, and ponder the possibility of evil made manifest, was strongly influenced by theosophists like Bailey and Dion Fortune, and by the Hermetic Order of the Golden Dawn, a late-nineteenth/early-twentieth-century fraternity devoted to the study and practice of mystical and paranormal activities. None of these terms—White Lodge, Black Lodge, dugpa—were invented for *Twin Peaks.* Helena Petrovich Blavatsky, the doyenne of theosophy (and a character in Frost's 1993 novel *The List of Seven*), referenced Tibetan black sorcerers as dugpas; the White Lodge was a fraternity comprising highly evolved spiritual masters, and the Black Lodge, naturally, their enemies, committed to evil. Author Talbot Mundy appropriated all of these terms in his pulp novel *The Devil's Guard,* even describing dugpas as sorcerers who "cultivate evil for the sake of evil"—in 1926, sixty-five years before Windom Earle spoke the same exact line (just one of numerous similarities between *Twin Peaks* and *The Devil's Guard*).

The Black Lodge emerges at the epicenter of the second half of season two because of Earle's master plan to locate it (easier said than done; it's not like there's a map, you know . . . . Oh, wait, there is), breach it, and harness the power within. Cooper votes nay. Racing against each other, they discover that fear (Black) and love (White) open the portal to the lodges, which are located in the woods out at Glastonbury Grove, and can be opened only during the conjunction of Saturn and Jupiter. That would mean, like, now.

Earle arrives first, using the fear of his kidnap victim, Annie Blackburne, to wedge his way in. Cooper follows, setting up one of the most controversial series finales in television history—frequently inscrutable, though never dull (you either love it or you hate it). This is largely the work of Lynch, who directed the episode and, dissatisfied with the script penned by Mark Frost, Haley Peyton, and Robert Engels—he told interviewer Chris Rodley he found it "completely and totally wrong"—discarded huge chunks, improvising his revisions on set and in the process creating what we now think of as the Black Lodge.

What irked Lynch so? Let's explore:

In the original, scripted version, Cooper journeys through multiple virtual venues—a shabby motel office, a "dark, ominous version of the Great Northern," the Red Room (known to us from Cooper's episode-two dream), even a dentist's office—encountering a handful of characters, some familiar, some not, including: someone called the Guardian (in Bulwer-Lytton's *Zanoni,* the Dweller of the Threshold is referred to as a "grisly and appalling guardian"); a desk clerk with a "bizarre orthopedic brace" and tracheotomy tube; an old man who resembles his father but refuses to acknowledge Cooper as anything other than a motel guest; and his own double. Here and there are evocations of Cooper's tragic past: his love affair with Caroline Earle, Windom's wife, followed by both their stabbings, Caroline's fatally, at the hands of Mr. Earle. Earle performs—yes, performs!—musical numbers, including Cole Porter's "Anything Goes" (in top hat and tails!). Annie transforms into Caroline, who transforms into Annie, who transforms into Caroline, and so on. Eventually, Annie turns up dead in the arms of Cooper's double, except she's not dead. Cooper demands Earle release her; Earle consents, but only if Cooper—a "good human being"—voluntarily offers up his soul, apparently required for Earle to grab the dark powers he so desperately craves. Cooper agrees, but just then Killer Bob shows up—wearing a white dentist's smock!—announcing that Earle will be punished for breaking the rules by coercing Cooper into sacrificing his soul rather than requiring him to voluntarily surrender it. First, however, Bob must deal with Cooper; just as he is about to assault him with a giant syringe for "extracting" something (the soul?), Laura Palmer intervenes, putting an end to that idea. Bob looks alarmed, energies collide, a white light fills the room. End Black Lodge scene.

Now, Lynch's version: The Glastonbury Grove portal opens with the parting of red curtains. This leads to a hallway, leading in turn to the Red Room. The Little Man tells Cooper: "When you see me again, it won't be me." Here's where things really start to go south. "Fire walk with me," the Little Man says, and when is that ever a good thing? The screen erupts into brilliant, billowing flames, followed by flickering blackness and a woman's screams. Black Lodge, anyone? Here, in Lynch's vision, there appear just two identical rooms (though sometimes furnished, sometimes not), located on either side of the hallway, each enterable only through a set of red curtains. Cooper, in search of Annie, navigates his way back and forth between them, confronting doppelgängers galore, including not just the Little Man's (so *that's* what you're talking about!), but also Laura's, Leland's, even his own—perhaps, if we are still buying into Hawk's explanation, his Dweller on the Threshold, meaning Cooper's test of courage looms. Like in the scripted version, it will involve Caroline and Windom Earle, evoking the Pittsburgh tragedy. Suddenly, Cooper finds himself stabbed and bleeding. Annie morphs into Caroline, who morphs into Annie, yada yada. Earle demands Cooper's soul in return for setting Annie free. Cooper agrees. Earle stabs Cooper. Bob appears, chastising Bob to Cooper—"He can't ask for your soul. I will take his." Bob kills Earle. Cooper is chased by his own doppelgänger, who eventually catches him, though not before curiously turning to the camera to show us that his eyes are no longer opaque, like those of the other doppelgängers, and that instead he looks exactly like the real Cooper.

Both scenarios end the same way, with the good Cooper trapped in the lodge, the evil one footloose and fancy-free, in all likelihood about to terrorize Twin Peaks. What no one has ever satisfactorily explained is how exactly Cooper failed, even after offering to sacrifice his soul for Annie and saving her life. Sure, some argue that his courage was imperfect, as he turned and fled from his doppelgänger; in other words, that he failed to confront and conquer the evil within him, But let's not confuse courage with stupidity. Cooper's primary goal was to save Annie—and he was even willing to sacrifice his soul to do it. Anything else was a distraction. Why *shouldn't* he run?

The Red Room is virtually irrelevant to the scripted version, yet integral to Lynch's. Keep in mind that Lynch invented the Red Room, in the process of ad-libbing a closed ending to the European home-video version of the

Lynch spins his magic, directing Annie and Cooper in the abstruse Red Room segment of the series finale.   *Photo by Richard Beymer*

pilot, which he and Frost had contracted to provide for financial reasons (a whole chunk of this ending was later appropriated for Cooper's dream sequence in episode two). Interestingly, there's nothing in that sequence to suggest that the Red Room—weird and disorienting as it is, with a dancing dwarf, the spirit of a dead girl whose murderer Cooper is hunting, and a dialect all its own—is particularly dangerous or associated with pure evil, and in fact it is here that Cooper learns the true identity of Laura's killer (never mind that he immediately forgets). Lynch has been asked multiple times about the significance of the room, and while he is generally loath to respond to any queries about the meaning of his work, he has been surprisingly open on this particular matter. His answer, essentially, is that he isn't certain himself: it was created out of necessity, without the luxury of time, and hence not particularly well thought out. He admits to borrowing the floor pattern from his first feature-length film, the cult favorite *Eraserhead*, but everything else about the room he attributes to instinct and intuition. Lynch leaves open the possibility that the Red Room exists in an otherworldly dimension, perhaps a waiting room "between two worlds"—our world and the world of Bob, Mike, the Man from Another Place, and all the other spirits who pop in and out of Twin Peaks. But Lynch also defines the Red Room as a physical manifestation of an individual's psychological state of being, meaning that the Red Room Cooper encounters is reflective of his psyche only, and looks and sounds different from what it would for anyone else.

What's missing here is any consideration of the Black Lodge, which, again, was Mark Frost's creation, and didn't even surface in *Twin Peaks* until well into the second season, during a period of time when Lynch was significantly less involved in the show, due to other considerations. Yet the entire narrative thrust of the second half of the season had led to this showdown in the Black Lodge between Cooper and Windom Earle, leaving Lynch, as director, in a real pickle.

Obviously, Lynch's solution was to attempt an integration of the two mythologies. Hence, the portal to the Black Lodge leads not to limitless black space, from which a shabby motel office materializes, as it did in the scripted version, but to the Red Room, raising the question of whether Lynch was suggesting that the Red Room and the Black Lodge were one and the same, or whether they were connected in some other fashion (worth noting: in *Fire Walk with Me*, written by Lynch and Engels, but not Frost, the word "lodge" is spoken just once, when Annie tells Laura, "The good Dale is in the lodge and he can't leave." However, the final scripted scene, with

Laura sitting on Cooper's lap, which blessedly was junked, describes the setting as "BLACK LODGE/RED ROOM," suggesting that by this point, even Lynch was confused). The Man from Another Place perhaps answers for us, telling Cooper: "This is the waiting room," which might explain the subsequent presence of the Giant, the room-service Waiter from the Great Northern, and Laura Palmer, all of whom helped guide Cooper to the truth during the hunt for Laura's killer, and seem unlikely candidates for permanent Black Lodge residency ("Some of your friends are here," the Little Man says). If we accept this interpretation, Cooper's actual entry into the Black Lodge appears to coincide with the Little Man's recitation of the line "Fire walk with me."

We could argue forever whether Lynch successfully merges these two concepts, but what he clearly did achieve was a radical restructuring of the final showdown, which in the scripted version of the series finale is essentially a confrontation between Cooper and Earle, despite Bob's late cameo. In the filmed version, it's Cooper against himself, his dark side in pursuit of his virtuous one, with evil triumphing—at least for now.

Blue Rose

A rose is a rose is a rose, except when it's not. In *Fire Walk with Me*, FBI agents Chester Desmond and Sam Stanley are briefed on the Teresa Banks murder investigation at a private airport in Portland by the eccentric Lil (or Lil the Dancer, as she is known), who communicates not in words but in coded actions and wardrobe choices. On the ensuing drive to Deer Meadow, Desmond decodes all of Lil's messages for Sam except one: the blue rose pinned to her dress. "I can't tell you about that," he says. Sam lets it go then and there, but presses for an explanation later on, just before returning to Portland with Teresa's body as Desmond plans one last look-see at Fat Trout: "Are you going back to the trailer park for the blue rose?" he asks. Desmond smiles, but ignores the question. In one of the deleted scenes finally released in 2014, Cooper, before heading off to Deer Meadow in search of the missing Desmond, powwows with Sam, who tells him Desmond wouldn't reveal the meaning of the blue rose. "Neither will I," Cooper replies. Poor Sam! Why is everyone being so cagey? Many wags think "blue rose" simply designates particularly vexing mysteries with paranormal implications, since blue roses themselves are naturalistically impossible (X-Files, anyone?). Still, that answer seems overly obvious to us, and it's hard to believe Lynch and coscripter Robert Engels didn't have something more in mind, given all of the secrecy between investigating agents. Here's what we think: "blue rose" is just a metaphor for all of the unanswered mysteries of *Twin Peaks* (and all of Lynch's work, really), and the refusal by Desmond and Cooper to explain its meaning equates to Lynch's famous antipathy for imposing his own interpretations of his work on others. In other words, "blue rose" means whatever you think it means, and stop asking me about it. Worth noting: the blue rose was *not* in the first draft of the script, when it was Cooper heading up the Banks investigation, but was added once Kyle MacLachlan opted out of the film (later rescinding that decision, and winding up with a smaller part) and was supplanted by Desmond. Engels told the *Wrapped in Plastic* fanzine that he had no recollection of why it was added. And Lynch? Yeah, right. Funnily enough, there's a report going around the Internet that Greg Olson, author of *David Lynch: Beautiful Dark* (2011), claimed that Lynch lived on Blue Rose Street in Los Angeles, but it isn't true, and Olson himself says he has no recollection of ever making any such comment, though if he did it would have been intended as a metaphor, meaning that Lynch loves mystery.

Creamed Corn/Garmonbozia

Creamed corn appears in exactly one scene in ABC-TV's *Twin Peaks*, in episode nine ("Coma"), written by Harley Peyton and directed by David Lynch. Donna Hayward, having taken over Laura's Meals on Wheels route as she searches for clues as to the identity of her killer, delivers a plate of chicken, rice, and creamed corn to a mysterious old bird named Mrs. Tremond, who exhibits supreme agitation upon discovering the corn on her plate. "I requested no creamed corn," she says. The corn magically disappears into the cupped hands of Mrs. Tremond's grandson, sitting in an armchair across the room, then vanishes altogether. Mysterious, but so what? Throughout *Twin Peaks* Lynch, Frost, and the rest of the creative team infuse typically benign objects like corn with talismanic significance. Never again in the television series is creamed corn even mentioned. So imagine our wonder when it turns out, in *Fire Walk with Me*, that corn may be at the root of all the supernatural evil committed in *Twin Peaks*.

Before contemplating *FWWM*, one interesting note: Lynch typically revised whole sections of scripts for episodes he directed, improvising on set, which drove Frost and the other writers on the series crazy, because Lynch's spontaneity rarely took into account their plotting (at a 1990 gathering of TV critics, Lynch said, "To me, a script is a blueprint . . . but when you get on the set, you get a lot of ideas, and those sometimes can be extremely

Mark Frost contemplates other worlds (made of creamed corn?).
Fox Broadcasting Company/Photofest

exciting and can jump the thing up to another level"). Peyton's "Coma" script makes far less of a fuss over creamed corn than the version that aired: Mrs. Tremond does indeed say, "I requested no creamed corn," and, after Donna apologizes, adds, "We detest yellow food." However, that's the end of that. Hence, it seems possible at least that Lynch already had grander plans for these tasty little kernels of Zea mays, as he eventually demonstrates in *FWWM*. In his introduction to "Coma," delivered on air by the Log Lady when Bravo reran *Twin Peaks* in its entirety in 1993, Lynch wrote: "Where does creamed corn figure into the workings of the universe? What really *is* creamed corn? Is it a symbol for something else?" Thanks for clearing that up, DKL.

FWWM includes three significant appearances and/or references to corn:

- In the so-called convenience-store scene, four bowls of creamed corn are placed atop a green Formica table; seated to our right is Bob and to our left the Man from Another Place. In the background are six additional characters, including Mrs. Tremond and her grandson, at whose feet sits another bowl, though its contents are undetectable from a distance. The first word uttered by the Man from Another Place is "garmonbozia"—a nonexistent word, unexplained here but followed by a close-up of creamed corn.

- Leland, while driving Laura to a breakfast meeting with Sarah, is pursued by the One-Armed Man, Gerard (Mike), who finally catches up to them during a traffic jam and yells at Leland: "You stole the corn! I had it canned above the store!" Then, to Laura he adds, "Miss, the look on her face when it was opened. There was a closeness. Like the Formica table." This encounter, impenetrable as it may be to us, severely agitates Leland, triggering flashbacks to his tryst with Teresa Banks and a near unintended sexual encounter with Laura and Ronette Pulaski.

- Near the end of the film, after murdering Laura, Leland/Bob enters the Red Room, where Mike and the Man from Another Place await. In unison, they say, "Bob, I want all my garmonbozia" (the scripted line that immediately precedes this comment, "Bob, you're not going home without us," is deleted). Here, finally, the term "garmonbozia"—a perversion of ambrosia, perhaps?—is explained, parenthetically in subtitles: "pain and sorrow" (again, a variation on the script, in which it is the word "corn" that appears parenthetically). How weird is this? An actual annotation from a filmmaker who religiously eschews explanation. Approximately fifteen silent, uninterrupted seconds of screen time follow, devoted to a close-up of someone—perhaps the Man from Another Place—eating creamed corn. (Just to demonstrate how obsessive *Twin Peaks* fans can be, some of them were recording the word "garmonbozia" and playing it backward—shades of "Paul is dead"!—and coming up with all sorts of coded messages.)

So, where does this leave us? To recap: Garmonbozia, meaning "pain and sorrow," is physically manifested as creamed corn. These otherwordly spirits appear to derive sustenance from it (though maybe not Mrs. Tremond), possibly even committing heinous acts of violence like rape and murder specifically to cultivate it (Bob "feeds on fear, and the pleasures," Mike tells Cooper in the TV series, and it is fear that leaves one vulnerable to the Black Lodge). Mike is miffed at Bob for stealing his corn. Mike and the Man from Another Place want their garmonbozia.

Now we get it.

Robert Engels told the fanzine *Wrapped in Plastic* that when he and Lynch were writing the *FWWM* screenplay, they chewed over the possibility that these spirits hailed from another world, one made up of creamed corn, but this concept never came to fruition. Under this scenario, Bob and Mike had a falling-out over a can of corn—this conflict did eventually find its way into the film—and the chase led them to Twin Peaks, where they're trapped. Now all they wanted was to return home. Or, Engels has said, maybe the whole thing was a dream.

Sound familiar?

After all, there's no place like home.

Dreams

In 1984, David Lynch told *Rolling Stone* magazine that he loves dreams, ambiguities, and absurdities. Two crucial dream sequences occur in *Twin Peaks* and *Fire Walk with Me*—one by Laura Palmer and one by Dale Cooper—and take it from us, they're rife with ambiguity and absurdity.

Both unfold largely within the confines of the mysterious Red Room. In fact, until the latter half of season two, dreams seem to be the *only* way into the Red Room, suggesting that in its original interpretation at least, the Red Room might have existed as some sort of limbo world between dreaming and wakefulness ("One chants out between two worlds . . .").

Of course this notion eventually becomes indefensible, once Cooper, Major Briggs, and Windom Earle start talking about fear and love as the keys to, respectively, the Black and White lodges, entrance to which seems to pass through the Red Room, and indeed it is Annie Blackburne's fear—rather than any dream—that ultimately wins Earle entry in the series finale (on the other hand, who knows how Cooper gets in as he pursues them). Even Lynch has articulated uncertainty over the essence of the Red Room, but he has suggested that it is the physical manifestation of the psyche of whoever has entered. If this is true, it would seem impossible that the Red Room could appear the same to any two individuals, though this is exactly what happens in a dream shared by Laura and Cooper, five days apart (for more on that dream, look below, under "Cooper's Dream").

Here's a look at the two dreams:

Laura's Dream

In *FWWM*, Mrs. Tremond/Chalfont presents Laura Palmer with a painting of a barren room with an open door leading to a second room. That night, she hangs the painting on her bedroom wall; it has been an especially trying day: that afternoon she had found Bob in her bedroom, searching for the secret diary, and Leland exiting the house immediately after, surely upsetting whatever suppressed notions she had of a connection between her father and Bob. That evening, at the dinner table, Leland had excoriated her for her "filthy" hands, and after that, feeling remorseful, had visited her in her bedroom to tell her how much he loved her. By this point, Laura is a wreck.

In her dream, Laura moves inside the painting (everything we view in the Red Room is through the subjective camera, so that we never see Laura, only her point of view), through the open door and into the second room, where she finds Mrs. Tremond/Chalfont beckoning her forward, past yet another open door and into yet another room. There, she's greeted by the second half of the Tremond/Chalfont tag team, the grandson, who snaps his fingers; suddenly, we are in the Red Room (we'd know those billowing curtains and Escher-like geometric floor pattern anywhere) and come to an ornate table, atop of which is the green Owl Cave ring—the same ring that Teresa Banks once wore and that Agent Chet Desmond found at Fat Trout Trailer Park immediately prior to his disappearance.

Agent Dale Cooper, whom Laura has never met—and never will meet in the waking world—parts the curtains and enters. The Man from Another Place waits for him, as always in the Red Room (though dressed a bit more formally this time—red suit and shirt, of course, but also a red tie). Cooper approaches. They stare. "Do you know who I am?" the Little Man asks. Cooper doesn't. "I am the arm," the dwarf says. "And I sound like this. . . ." Here he makes a whooping sound, tapping his hand back and forth against his mouth—language and behavior we have seen once before, from the old waiter in the series finale. Cooper observes, intently but silently.

The Little Man picks the ring up from the table, holds it out for Laura, and turns to Cooper, who finally speaks, uttering what have become two of the most debated lines in the entire film: "Don't take the ring, Laura. Don't take the ring."

Cut to Laura, in bed. We now assume the dream is over, but we assume wrong. In a somnambular state, Laura sits up and turns to her right, holding her left wrist with her right hand (the script reads that her left arm has fallen asleep). The camera follows Laura's gaze to her right, stopping at her bedroom door, then to her left, where she finds, lying in bed beside her, a blood-drenched Annie Blackburne, who says: "My name is Annie. I've been with Dale and Laura. The good Dale is in the lodge, and he can't leave."

This is a precognitive vision, as Annie's Black Lodge ordeal from the series finale has yet to happen.

Laura looks again at her bedroom door, then at her bed, but Annie is gone. She opens her left fist; there, in her palm, is the Owl Cave ring. Laura gasps. She rises, walks to the bedroom door, opens it, peers outside into the stairway; empty and quiet (this action appears without context in the film, though in the script it is written that she is hearing her mother call out to her). Laura turns back to look at the painting, and now sees herself inside of it, also standing at a door—-two Lauras, just as earlier in the film we had seen two Coopers, one in the security room and one in the hallway as captured on a closed-circuit monitor at the FBI offices in Philadelphia. Cut back to Laura, this time in bed, sleeping, and dissolve to morning. Laura opens her fist again; no ring. Dream over. Laura removes the painting from the wall and places it face down on her desk.

Plenty of mystery here, folks: Why was Mrs. Tremond/Chalfont so determined that Laura have the painting? Why did the Man from Another Place dangle the ring in front of her? Was Cooper right or wrong in urging her to rebuff? While Laura had been living a double life at least since the age of twelve, when Bob first "visited" her, is the dichotomous imagery here meant to signify that Laura has emerged from this dream a different person from the one who entered?

Answers? Not so many. The Tremonds' motives remain puzzling, as always. We *can* state unequivocally they have dreadful taste in companions. The Little Man? As bizarre as it sounds, his "I am the arm" proclamation can mean only one thing, right? He *is* Mike's severed arm, which, considering that Mike chopped it off once he saw the face of God, would seem to equate to his evil, Bob-like impulses. If in fact the rings marks Bob's next victim (which is arguable in and of itself), the Little Man is big trouble. Cooper, who knew the ring belonged to Teresa Banks—assuming this dreamworld iteration possesses the same knowledge as the real-world Cooper at this particular point in time—logically counseled her against accepting. Yet at the end of the film, when the ring falls into the train car, Laura grabs it and puts it on, triggering her own death (and thus preventing possession by Bob). If she had accepted the ring earlier, how much heartache would have been avoided? At least he meant well. But did the Little Man?

Finally, the two Lauras: Some argue that this dream transforms Laura into a new person—more fatalistic? assertive? aware?—but this is a tough assessment to prove or disprove. Surely her downward spiral accelerates soon after with the trip to the Roadhouse and Partyland, yet it is soon after this that she finally confirms Bob's true identity and asserts control by donning the ring, putting an end to her torment and to her life.

Cooper's Dream

Yes, we call this "Cooper's Dream," but in fact he and Laura shared it (while we never see Laura's version, we do hear about it as Donna reads from a missing page in her diary, establishing that Laura had the dream on February 21, five days before Cooper).

At the conclusion of episode two, Cooper has a Red Room dream of his own. These scenes are excerpted from the ending to the European home-video version of the pilot, never seen on American television (however, the Red Room scene as it appears in the European ending is never identified as being part of a dream). The European ending is approximately eighteen minutes; the dream sequence from episode two runs only a third as long—it is a quirk of the series that in the following episode, when Cooper recounts his dream for Harry and Lucy, he describes multiples scenes that occur in the European ending but not in the dream as we have just seen it.

This dream opens with a much older iteration of Cooper seated in an armchair in the Red Room. Within the room are three dark upholstered deco chairs, standing lamps, and a white Grecian statue of a female nude. The floor has the familiar zigzagging pattern, but appears here to be colored burnt sienna and amber, rather than the familiar black and white of later iterations (perhaps a lighting inconsistency?). The Man from Another Place stands off to his left, facing the red drapes, his entire body shaking. We faintly hear Sarah Palmer call out to her daughter, then see Sarah descending the steps in the Palmer house. The following images flash by quickly: Bob crouching at the foot of Laura's bed; a bloody corpse at the abandoned train car, wrapped in plastic; a close-up of Laura at the morgue. We meet Mike, the spirit inhabiting the One-Armed Man Gerard, who recites the "Fire walk with me" poem, then explains that he and Bob once were roomies and soulmates, living above a convenience store. "I too have been touched by the devilish one," Mike says. "Tattoo on the left shoulder. Oh, but when I saw the face of God, I was changed. I took the entire arm off. My name is Mike. His name . . . is Bob." Cue Bob: "Mike, Mike, can you hear me? Catch you with my death bag. You may think I've gone insane, but I promise, I will kill again."

Next, a ring of twelve lit candles, extinguished all at once. Back in the Red Room, Cooper sees a woman who looks exactly like Laura Palmer, seated in another chair, dressed in a low-cut black evening gown, smiling radiantly. The Little Man finally turns around, and says: "Let's rock" (Cooper had seen these same words on the windshield of Chet Desmond's car in *Fire Walk with Me,* after Desmond has disappeared). The Little Man takes a seat between Cooper and Laura. Laura touches her right index finger to her nose; the shadow of what appears to be a bird flies across the red curtains.

"I've got good news," the Man from Another Place says. "That gum you like is going to come back in style." Cooper stares at Laura Palmer. The Little Man sees. "She's my cousin. But doesn't she look almost exactly like Laura Palmer?" he says. Isn't she Laura Palmer? asks Cooper. "I feel like I know her," the woman says, "but sometimes my arms bend back." The Little Man says the Laura look-alike is "filled with secrets," then adds, "Where we're from the birds sing a pretty song, and there's always music in the air." Music plays. He dances. Strobe lights flash. Laura rises, approaches Cooper, kisses him on the lips (Coop likes). She whispers something into his ear. End of dream.

As creepy and discombobulating as the Red Room feels in this dream, it is nowhere near as threatening as in subsequent iterations. In fact, the portion of the dream that unfolds within this room is loaded with crucial, if oblique, clues to the identity of Laura's killer, like the shadow of the bird (foreshadowing Waldo, Jacques Renault's mynah), "Let's rock" (a link to Desmond's disappearance), "She's my cousin" (Maddy Ferguson, Laura's cousin, is Bob's next victim), "sometimes my arms bend back" (Laura's arms were tied behind her back), music in the air/the dancing dwarf (Leland, following Laura's death, was overcome with the urge to sing and dance), "That gum you like is going to come back in style" (which turns out to be the final nail in Leland's coffin), and, of course, the actual identity of the killer, whispered by Laura to Cooper, even if he does forget upon awakening. Cooper himself recognizes this the next morning, telling Harry and Lucy, "Break the code, solve the crime."

Judy, Jeffries, and the Convenience Store (Plus the Monkey)

Slushy, anyone?

Twin Peaks may be "filled with secrets," as the Little Man says about Laura Palmer, but we challenge anyone to identify a more confounding sequence of events than the *Fire Walk with Me* scenes involving Phillip Jeffries, the long-lost FBI agent portrayed by the late rock legend David Bowie, and the meeting in the room above the convenience store. The entire sequence, from the moment Cooper marches into Gordon Cole's office to announce the date and time to Cole's rhetorical query as to the location of the recently vanished Agent Chet Desmond, runs a little over four minutes, but has sparked febrile debate and speculation for over two decades.

The "Missing Pieces" released in 2014 shed *some* light on all this, but not so much.

Here's a recap of the scene as it appears in the 1992 theatrical version of *FWWM:*

Cooper enters Cole's office, reporting that it's 10:10 a.m. on February 16; he's worried because of a dream he discussed earlier with Cole (unspecified). Cooper ducks back and forth between the hallway and a surveillance room lined with closed-circuit monitors. Everything's copacetic, until the security-room Cooper sees the other Cooper still standing in the hallway, even though he has left the hallway and is back in the security room. Suddenly, two Coopers at once, just as in the finale of the television series, where he's split in two in the Black Lodge. Jeffries emerges from an elevator and marches into Cole's office, Cooper trailing. Cole introduces them, establishing that—as far as he knows, at least—they have never met before. Jeffries, a little wobbly, informs the others (Albert Rosenfield is also in the room) that he won't talk about Judy. He points at Cooper and says, "Who do you think this is there?"

Next, we transition to the room above the convenience store—viewers of the TV series will recall that Mike once told Cooper he and Bob were roommates above a convenience store, before Mike "saw the face of God" and repented. Jeffries continues to offer commentary throughout, via voice-over (not that it helps). The first character we see is a man in a red suit, wearing a white mask with a conical noise and holding a stick (aka the Jumping Man). Also in the room: the Man from Another Place and Bob, seated in the foreground at a table, atop of which are four bowls of creamed corn, plus, in the background, the Jumping Man, the Electrician, the Tremonds, and two woodsmen, referenced in script as the First Woodsman and the Second Woodsman (interesting to note which spirits are *not* present, like Mike and the Giant). At the feet of the Tremond boy is another bowl, its contents undetectable.

"Garmonbozia," says the Man from Another Place (this word was invented for *FWWM*, and though it isn't explained here—much later in the film it is identified as "pain and sorrow"—Lynch closes in on a bowl of creamed corn immediately after the Little Man says it). "This is a Formica

Star Man: Is there a more mysterious figure in *Twin Peaks* than Agent Phillip Jeffries?

table. Green is its color." That we knew! What we don't know is why the Tremond boy, apparently pointing at Bob, then says, "Fell a victim," or what the Little Man means when he says, "With this ring I thee wed," especially as there is no ring anywhere in sight.

"Listen all, listen carefully," Jeffries says. "I've been to one of their meetings." Bob claps his hands above his head, and the Jumping Man leaps backward onto a platform. The room's barren walls are transformed into the curtains of the Red Room. Jeffries makes a comment that sounds like, "Elga, baby, damn no! I found something" (the Blu-ray missing-scenes version captions the first part of this comment as "Hell, God, baby, damn no!"—since the line isn't scripted, we can't know for sure). Close-up on Mrs. Tremond's grandson, now also wearing a white mask, also with a conical nose, and with a stick protruding from the forehead. He removes the mask once, puts it back. "And then there they were," says Jeffries. The mask is removed again; this time revealing . . . the face of a monkey.

This scene ends with Bob and the Man from Another Place parting the red curtains, through which we see more red curtains on the opposite side of the hallway. This too evokes the series finale, where Cooper ducks back and forth between rooms with black-and-white zigzag floors, bordered by red curtains, and establishes what has to be considered a clear link between the room above the convenience store and the Black Lodge (not so surprising, since Mike said he and Bob lived here together *before* he rejected the touch of the "devilish one").

Jeffries screams. He's seated in a wooden chair in Cole's office, then he isn't. "He's gone! He's gone! Albert, call the front desk," says Cole. Albert complies, then reports that 1) the front desk says Jeffries was never there, and 2) Chet Desmond has disappeared from Deer Meadow. Cooper and Gordon review the closed-circuit footage, determining that Jeffries was in fact present. "But where did he go?" says Cole. "And where is Chester Desmond?"

Exactly.

We have a few questions of our own . . .

Judy, Judy, Judy . . . *Twin Peaks* freaks love to ruminate over the identity of this mysterious character, mentioned here by Jeffries and only once again ever—at the end of the film, when the monkey briefly returns and says, simply, "Judy." She is never seen—not in the film and not in the series. Lynch's obsession with *The Wizard of Oz* is well documented (see *Wild at Heart*), triggering speculation that the character is named after Judy Garland (like Major *Garland* Briggs?). Robert Engels, who coscripted *FWWM* with Lynch, told *Wrapped in Plastic* in 2002 that Judy was named after his sister-in-law, and was intended to be Josie Packard's sister. According to Engels, Judy was in Buenos Aires with Jeffries prior to his disappearance, and Jeffries didn't want to talk about her because it evoked painful memories. Engels further mentioned that the film's original blueprint included a whole mythology centering on Josie, Judy, and Windom Earle, all dropped because the script was too dense already.

The "Missing Pieces" released in 2014 confirm some of Engels's comments: Prior to popping up in Philly, Jeffries checks into the Palm Deluxe, a swanky Buenos Aires hotel. "Do you have a Miss Judy staying here by any chance?" he asks. The desk clerk doesn't answer directly, but hands Jeffries an envelope. "The young lady, she left it for you," he says.

Next, Lynch cuts to the same telephone pole we've seen before, outside Fat Trout Trailer Park—a sure sign something strange and wonderful is about to unfold, and it does: we see a close-up of someone's mouth, followed by an extended version of the scene in the room above the convenience store, with strange, elliptical lines like "The chrome reflects our image" and "From pure air we have descended . . . from pure air. Going up and down. Intercourse between two worlds." Eventually, as in the theatrical cut, Bob claps his hands and he and the Man from Another Place exit through the red curtains, but here the scene is extended, so that, remaining in the Red Room, we see the Owl Cave ring sitting atop a table (thus at least giving *some* context to the Little Man's comment, "With this ring I thee wed"), followed by yet another strange image, of Laura Palmer's face superimposed onto the Red Room floor.

After a cutaway to a forest, we finally land in Philadelphia, where Jeffries emerges from the elevator and marches into Cole's office. This too is an extended scene, with multiple new references to Judy, including this one: "I found something in Seattle at Judy's. And then there they were. And they sat quietly for hours. And I followed." Jeffries groans, rests his head on Cole's desk, and says, "Oh. Oh. Oh. Ring. The ring."

Cole attempts to summon someone in to record Jeffries's recollections, but his intercom is busted; static builds and the fluorescent lights hum— electricity is a huge recurring theme in *Twin Peaks,* harking all the way back to the morgue scene in the pilot with the flickering lights. "Mayday," Cole says, prompting Jeffries's cryptic response: "May . . . February 1989"—the month and year, of course, of Laura Palmer's death, approximately a year into the future from when this scene unfolds. This leads to speculation that Jeffries has time-traveled, which would also explain his distrust of Cooper— *if* he has been to the Black Lodge following Cooper's entrapment there.

Jeffries then vanishes, as in the theatrical cut, but here we find out where to: back to the hotel in Buenos Aires, standing on a staircase, screaming. A freaked-out bellhop literally defecates himself, and a maid crawls across the floor, whimpering. "Are you the man?" the bellhop shouts. "Are you the man?"

Largely inscrutable, yes, but rife with possibilities. Is the "something" Jeffries found at Judy's the Owl Cave ring? Was he zapped to the room above the convenience store upon touching it? Was Desmond transported to the same room when *he* touched the ring (and if so, why don't we see him)? If Judy had the ring, was she Bob's next intended victim, equating her relationship to Jeffries with Teresa's to Desmond and Laura's to Cooper?

At the very least, Jeffries's reference to Seattle places Judy in the state of Washington, home also to Twin Peaks and Deer Meadow. Plus, remember that in the immediate aftermath of the burning of Packard mill and her attempt on Cooper's life, Josie departs for an extended stay in Seattle, for purposes never fully explained (though she does do a lot of shopping).

Not included in the "Missing Pieces" are two lines Jeffries delivers in the original *Fire Walk with Me* script, dated July 3, 1991, still presupposing that

Cooper would lead the Teresa Banks investigation. Immediately after commenting that "Judy is positive about this," the G-man says, "Her sister's there, too. At least part of her." These lines were dropped in the final script and never filmed, but they do raise the possibility that Judy was envisioned as Josie's sister (at the 1993 *Twin Peaks* fan festival, Frank Silva, who portrayed Bob, said that it was his understanding that Bob—whom Cooper sees in the immediate aftermath of Josie's death—takes Josie to the Red Room).

So now that we've settled all that, how about the monkey?

Honestly, no clue.

"Fire Walk with Me"

Eventually tapped for the title of the 1992 *Twin Peaks* prequel film, the phrase "Fire walk with me" was first heard by American television viewers on April 8, 1990, in the pilot episode of the television series, when Cooper and Truman come across a torn piece of newsprint in the derelict train car where Laura was murdered, with those exact words written on it in blood. The phrase is later repeated as part of a poem that is recited by the spirit Mike, in the guise of the One-Armed Man Gerard, and has attracted considerable attention among *Twin Peaks* fans, partly because of its inscrutability and partly because of inconsistencies in its articulation. Our first exposure to the poem is in episode two, during Cooper's Red Room dream, in a scene excerpted from the European ending to the pilot. In the Mark Frost/David Lynch-penned script, the poem appears as follows: "Through the darkness of futures past, the magician longs to see, one chance out between two worlds . . . fire, walk with me." Despite this, Al Strobel, who portrayed the One-Armed Man, told the fanzine *Wrapped in Plastic* that he memorized the poem not from the script, but from Lynch's handwritten notes, and that while the original poem contained the word "chance," Lynch had crossed it out and written "chants" before shooting the scene. This would mean simply that the correction was never noted in the episode-two script; remember, Strobel did not read the line while filming episode two, but rather while filming the European ending to the pilot. By episode thirteen, when Mike recites it for the second time, "chants" has become the official version.

The other inconsistency involves the articulation of the opening phrase, which appears variously as "Through the darkness of futures past," "Through the darkness of future past," and "Through the darkness, the future past"; Lynch's 1994 book *Images* uses "Through the darkness of future past," but Martha P. Nochimson, author of *The Passion of David Lynch: Wild at*

Heart in Hollywood (1997), wrote that Lynch specifically told her the version appearing in episode two ("futures past") was correct.

Peaks fans can obsess all they want over the precise phrasing—and they do—but more importantly, what does it mean? So much of *Twin Peaks* pivots on the concept of doubleness, evoked here by the reference to two worlds. We could argue forever over the delineation of those two universes—reality versus illusion? dreaming versus wakefulness? spirit versus material? good versus evil? White Lodge versus Black Lodge?—any one of which could be said to be appropriate.

Engels, who in addition to writing and producing for the series cowrote the *Fire Walk with Me* script with Lynch, has said that Bob, Mike, the Man from Another Place, and all the rest of the otherworldly spirits roaming about in *Twin Peaks* hail from another world, and were attempting to navigate their way back home. An extended version of the *FWWM* convenience-store scene, released among the "Missing Pieces" in 2014, includes the Man from Another Place saying, "Going up and down. Intercourse between two worlds."

Don't worry, none of this makes any sense to us either.

The identity of the magician is equally indecipherable—the only literal reference to a magician in either the series or the film is to the Tremond boy, whose grandmother says, after the creamed corn mysteriously disappears from her plate and winds up in his hands during the Meals on Wheels scene with Donna Hayward in the series, that he is studying magic. Reams of paper—virtual and not—have been spent attempting to unravel this riddle, with some arguing that the magician is Cooper, longing to see beyond the material world, so that he can identity Laura's murderer, and characters like Sarah Palmer and Maddy Ferguson—perhaps gifted, perhaps damned—also have visions, but really, who knows? And are we even meant to?

Finally, there is the phrase "Fire walk with me" itself, which Lynch deemed crucial enough to appropriate for his film title, yet also seems to defy comprehension. In recounting his episode-two dream to Harry and Lucy, Cooper reports that "They"—meaning Mike and Bob both—"had a tattoo . . . Fire Walk with Me." In Mike's case, the tattoo was on his left arm, which was severed once he saw "the face of God." The phrase is also spoken by Laura in *FWWM* during her scene with Harold Smith; the script reads "She allows the feeling of Bob to come over her" just before pronouncing it. The Man from Another Place also utters it, more than once, including in the series finale; many deconstructionists point convincingly to this as the moment when the setting shifts from the Red Room to the Black Lodge. The series and film make countless additional references to fire—the burning of Packard mill, Major Briggs's recollection of "stepping from the flames" following his abduction, Bob flicking matches at young Leland during summers at Pearl Lakes, all those active fireplaces—the list just goes on and on. While studying a chalkboard rendering of the Owl Cave petroglyph, which includes flames, in Truman's office in the series finale, Cooper contemplatively recites the "Fire walk with me" phrase twice, but it seems to lead him nowhere—just like the rest of us. In his Log Lady–delivered episode intros written when Bravo reran the series in 1993, Lynch frequently evokes fire. For the pilot, for example, Lynch wrote: "To introduce this story, let me just say it encompasses the all—it is beyond the 'fire,' though few would know that meaning."

Amen.

Let's leave the last word to the Log Lady, the Cassandra of Twin Peaks, who lost her lumberjack husband in a forest fire: "He met the devil. The devil took the form of fire. Fire is the devil, hiding like a coward in the smoke." It is as direct an explanation as we ever get . . . we *think*.

Ghostwood Forest

You know those thick, dark woods everyone keeps talking about? That's Ghostwood Forest, home of the towering, majestic Douglas firs Cooper obsesses over, but also twelve sycamores circling Glastonbury Grove—gateway to the Black Lodge—and Owl Cave, whose stone walls are adorned with Native American petroglyphs, including one that maps out the way to the lodge and indicates the period in time (the conjunction of Saturn and Jupiter) at which the gateway opens. Good old Sheriff Harry S. Truman, a sensible man if ever there was one, is convinced "There's a sort of evil out there, something very, very strange in those old woods. Call it what you want—a darkness, a presence. It takes many forms, but . . . it's been out there for as long as anyone can remember . . ."—an evil that Cooper ultimately identifies as the Black Lodge. The Bookhouse Boys, a secret society, was formed decades earlier to protect the town from that darkness; Truman, Hawk, and James and Big Ed Hurley all belong, while Hank Jennings, once "one of the best," went rogue.

Meanwhile, back on planet Earth, Ghostwood is where Ben Horne is desperately seeking to build a country club—the Ghostwood project. This entire storyline is impossibly convoluted and dense, though as best we can tell it comes down to this: Ben Horne and Catherine Martell are secretly conspiring to bankrupt the mill, so that Josie Packard will sell the land to Ben, who would use it for the Ghostwood development. Plan B—in the event Josie refuses to sell—is to burn the mill down, then lead investigators to suspect Josie had orchestrated the fire to defraud her insurance company (at which point Catherine would produce the mill's true ledger, showing that it was going under, rather than the cooked book, indicating everything was copacetic, to explain Josie's motivation). However, somewhere along the way, Josie, working for Andrew Packard's vengeful ex-business partner Thomas Eckhardt, who is out to ruin the Packard family, approaches Ben with a

Ben Horne: Sometimes a cigar *isn't* just a cigar.   *ABC/Photofest*

more appealing deal, offering him the land for $5 million. This plan too calls for setting the mill ablaze, with Catherine inside, as Josie has secretly arranged to become the sole beneficiary of a $1 million life-insurance policy for Catherine. Eventually, after Ben is arrested on suspicion of murdering Laura, he's blackmailed into signing both the mill and the Ghostwood project over to Catherine, in exchange for an alibi on the night of the murder (trysting), though even then Catherine doesn't deliver. Ben tailspins into staggering depression, involving Civil War hallucinations, and when he finally comes to (not soon enough, if you ask us), he launches a campaign to stop the Ghostwood development on the grounds that it would threaten the endangered pine weasel. Takes one to know one, Ben.

Glastonbury Grove

Glastonbury Grove shows up very late in *Twin Peaks*, at the conclusion of episode twenty-seven ("The Path to the Black Lodge"), when it is revealed as the gateway to the Black Lodge; this occurs as Bob materializes in the dark woods, just above an ash-covered circle of stones, in the center of which is a pool of black oil—the same oil that Jacoby, Ronette, and others have reported smelling when in proximity to Bob. The exact spot is marked by a circle of twelve sycamores, and it is here that Hawk found the bloody towel and the diary pages that Leland/Bob scattered in the wake of Laura's murder. Here too is where Earle drags the abducted Annie Blackburne, intending to leverage her fear to enter the Black Lodge himself; where Cooper eventually tracks them to; and where old faithful Sheriff Truman sits and waits for Cooper's return. It is also, in *Fire Walk with Me*, where Leland/Bob enters the Red Room and encounters Mike and the Man from Another Place, after having killed Laura and disposed of her body. As Cooper points out, the grove shares a name with Glastonbury Abbey, King Arthur's reputed burial place in England (likely inspired by Mark Frost's abiding interest in Arthurian legend); the story is that Arthur's tomb was uncovered by workers who were rebuilding Glastonbury Abbey in 1191, seven years after it had been destroyed by—get this, *Twin Peaks* fans—fire, though some historians suspect that this was just a hoax perpetrated by monks desperately seeking funds for the reparation of their church. There are those in the world of *Twin Peaks* fandom who see the Arthur-Guinevere-Lancelot triangle as analogous to the mess involving Windom Earle, Caroline Earle, and Dale Cooper, which would make Cooper Lancelot, though Earle, who is madly obsessed with chess, prefers to view Cooper as an opposing king, as he articulates in his tape-recorded message: "I'm even prepared to sacrifice my queen because, I assure you, dear Dale, my goal will be attained at any cost: the king must die!" This line of reasoning—if you want to call it that—also equates Lancelot's failure to pass the Holy Grail's purity test, due to his adulterous relationship with Guinevere, with Cooper's debacle in the Black Lodge and his affair with Caroline.

Mystery Men

There are three significant unexplained appearances by men (or so we assume) in black, or at least dark clothing, over the two-season run of *Twin Peaks*, and we're pretty sure none of them have anything to do with Johnny Cash or Walter O'Dim:

Appearance One: In episode two, Bobby Briggs and Mike Nelson head into the Twin Peaks woods in pitch blackness to pick up a stash of coke from Leo Johnson. The mood is tense: Bobby and Mike are shy $10,000, and a shotgun-toting Leo—no sweetheart to begin with—is especially grumpy because he's convinced his wife, Shelly, is fooling around with some guy, which she is (with Bobby), though Leo doesn't appear to know that part yet. Bobby spots a figure off in the distance, hiding behind a tree, scaring the bejesus out of him. "Who's that?" he asks. "Is there someone with you?" Leo dismisses the question with a hostile (Leo default mode) "Never mind," not even bothering to turn around and look, perhaps suspecting Bobby is trying to distract him. The script, by Mark Frost and David Lynch, makes no mention of this mysterious figure, but no surprise there, as the episode was helmed by Lynch, who was always revising on set. This man in black is never identified; we've always suspected it was Leland/Bob, keeping an eye on Leo, whom he had seen at Jacques Renault's cabin while stalking Laura the night of her murder, though of course none of this would be known to viewers when the series first aired, since the details of Laura's murder had yet to be revealed as of this episode's airing. At the 2015 Twin Peaks Festival, it was reported that this man in black was actually a production crew member who was standing in for Ray Wise, the actor who portrayed Leland. Bingo!

Appearance Two: An easy one: In the season-one finale ("The Last Evening"), Donna, Maddy, and James play a particularly cruel trick on Dr. Jacoby, conspiring to lure him from his office by trying to pass Maddy (in a blonde wig) off as her dead cousin Laura, so that they can search for an audiotape tape that Laura recorded for the mad doctor and that they believe will help them crack the case. This nasty little scheme works, and Jacoby agrees to meet Laura/Maddy at the town gazebo; while gazing at her from afar in disbelief, Jacoby is smacked over the head from behind and beaten by a ski-masked man in black. Though the fiend is never explicitly identified, the fairly obvious answer is Leland/Bob, for two reasons: One, as Maddy slips out of the Palmer house to rendezvous with the dynamic duo, she's unknowingly spotted by Leland, who's sitting alone in the dark in the living room with that creepy look on his face, suggesting Bob too is watching (though this is *not* apparent at the time either, since viewers had yet to discover Bob's possession of Leland), and that he had followed Maddy to the gazebo. Second, recalling the incident later to Cooper, Jacoby remembers smelling scorched engine oil, an odor associated with Bob and the Black Lodge, just prior to the attack. Plus, in his 1991 book *Twin Peaks: Behind-the-Scenes*, Mark A. Altman reported that Mark Frost had confirmed to him that the assailant was Leland, possessed by Bob. There—we buried the lede.

Appearance Three: At the tail end of episode seventeen ("Dispute Between Brothers"), Cooper and Garland Briggs are toasting marshmallows in the Twin Peaks woods while out night-fishing when the major asks Cooper if he's ever heard of the White Lodge. Negative, says Coop, who then excuses himself to answer "the call of nature." While Cooper is off urinating, there's a blast of white light; Briggs twice calls out to Cooper, and we see, for approximately two seconds, a hooded figure off in the distance, hiding behind a tree (the script calls him a "tall, dark, cloaked figure, face obscured by a cowled hood"). By the time Cooper returns to the campsite, the major is gone, as is hooded man. The major we see again, the mystery man we don't (at least not in person, though we do see static images of what may be the same character later on in the series). It seems safe enough to assume this guy has nothing to do with the man/men in black seen earlier—first because they are garbed differently and second because Leland is by now deceased, and hence no longer stalking men who appear to be interested in Laura or Maddy (or anyone else, for that matter). Since clues as to the identity of this figure are virtually nonexistent, anything we have to say about it is merely conjecture. Still, that hasn't stopped us before. Best guess: a monk from the White Lodge. Reasoning: Once Briggs returns, he tells Cooper he has come to believe he was taken to the White Lodge during his abduction. Plus, all that white light!

USAF Major Garland Briggs, a "deeply weird individual."

Project Blue Book

Project Blue Book was a bona fide U.S. Air Force initiative investigating unidentified flying objects, launched in 1952 and terminated in 1969—or so the government says. Not true! says Major Briggs, who reveals to Cooper that certain Air Force personnel have "unofficially" kept the flame burning, expanding their sphere of study to the woods surrounding Twin Peaks, in search of the White Lodge. The FBI loaned Windom Earle out to Project Blue Book from 1965 to 1967; bad move, gents. He became "destructively obsessive," per Briggs, raving about dugpas and the Black Lodge, so had to be booted from the project. This debriefing convinces Cooper that Earle's true purpose is not revenge for his dalliance with Caroline Earle, but access to the Black Lodge. Or maybe both?

Rings

Twin Peaks abounds with rings and ring references, but one ring rules them all, and that is the Owl Cave ring, from *Fire Walk with Me*. Teresa Banks wore it prior to her death, but by the time FBI agents Chet Desmond and Sam Stanley arrive to examine the body, the ring has vanished. Desmond is determined to find it, and eventually does, beneath the Chalfont trailer at Fat Trout park, but maybe that wasn't such a great idea, since he disappears while reaching for it. The Man from Another Place dangles it in front of

Laura Palmer in her dream; Agent Cooper warns her then not to take it, yet ultimately she ignores his advice, slipping on the ring in the final moments of her life. Nothing good ever seems to come of it, yet an argument can be (and has been) made that ultimately it liberates Laura, and hence Cooper was misguided in urging her to rebuff it.

The Owl Cave ring has no presence whatsoever in the television series, though Owl Cave does: here's where Cooper, Truman, and the rest of the law-enforcement gang uncover the petroglyph that guides them to Glastonbury Grove, portal to the Black Lodge. They're directed there by Annie Blackburne, who sees Cooper doodling on a paper napkin, connecting the shapes of the tattoos Major Briggs and the Log Lady brought back with them from separate abduction experiences, decades apart, and recognizes the symbol from an etching on Owl Cave's walls. This design—twin mountain peaks linked by a diamond—is identical to the one that appears on the Owl Cave ring.

Worth noting: While the Owl Cave ring does appear in the original version of the *Fire Walk with Me* script, in which Cooper (Kyle MacLachlan) runs the Teresa Banks investigation, it has nowhere near the prominence it finally assumes once Desmond gets the assignment. Remember that MacLachlan initially balked at reprising his role, so coscripters David Lynch and Robert Engels had to come up with a new character to handle the assignment, which evolved into Desmond. However, MacLachlan eventually relented, accepting a smaller, though still prominent, role, meaning Lynch and Engels were compelled to devise a plot mechanism by which Cooper would take over the investigation; hence, the disappearing act, triggered by the ring. This, however, turned out to be just the beginning of the reimagining of the ring.

Like so much of *Twin Peaks*, the Owl Cave ring is shrouded in mystery. How did Teresa Banks come to possess it? Why has it vanished by the time Sam Stanley performs the autopsy? What does the Man from Another Place mean, in the convenience-store scene, when he says, "With this ring I thee wed" (a line that appears in the film, but not the shooting script)? Why does Special Agent Phillip Jeffries, missing for almost two years before suddenly turning up at FBI offices in Philadelphia—a little whacked out, we might add—mutter, "The ring, the ring" (an extended scene released in 2014 *seems* to suggest that Jeffries may have found the ring himself at Judy's place in Seattle, and, like Desmond, was transported elsewhere, possibly to the meeting in the room above the convenience store). How does the ring eventually wind up with the One-Armed Man Gerard (inhabited by Mike), who flashes it at Laura and Leland while screaming, "It's him! It's your father!"? Is Cooper right or wrong to counsel Laura against accepting it? In the train-car scene, is Gerard purposely sharing the ring with Laura, or does he accidentally drop it? Finally, what exactly are the consequences of Laura's decision to wear the ring, just prior to her murder?

Looking for definitive answers? Forget it, Jake, it's *Twin Peaks*.

For us, the most compelling questions—and those generating the most chatter over the years—center on Laura's action in the train car, near the end of the film. Leland, possessed by Bob, has dragged her and Ronette there from Jacques's cabin, with horrific intentions. Mike, the ring-bearer, has been traipsing through the woods in pursuit. We know he wants to thwart Bob, but by this point his motives are murky—the Mike who seemed so intent on stopping Bob in the TV series because he had "seen the face of God" is not the same Mike we encounter in *Fire Walk with Me*. Ronette slips free of her bonds and slides the train-car door open; the ring either falls in accidentally or is tossed in by Mike (the actual act occurs off camera, and the script is no help here because the ring isn't even mentioned in the train-car scene). Laura slips the ring on, and is stabbed to death.

For whatever it's worth, Al Strobel, who portrayed Mike, is on record as saying his character wasn't deliberately trying to pass the ring to Laura. Mike's goal, according to Strobel, was not to save Laura but to stop Bob, which isn't necessarily the same thing. For Strobel, the ring is simply a talisman from the other world, whence he and Bob hail. Still, why revise the scene to include the ring if it didn't have some significance beyond that? Laura has had three previous exposures to the ring, and there's a scene about ninety minutes into *FWWM* where she pieces all of them together: sitting in her bedroom, she recollects, in order, the encounter with the One-Armed Man in the car, the dream sequence with the Man from Another Place, and her get-together at the Red Diamond Motel with Ronette and Teresa Banks, who wears the ring while brushing aside her bangs. "The same ring," Laura says, followed by a flash of blue light. Laura glances up at the ceiling above the window, from where Bob has breached her room, and her body, on so many occasions, and seethes: "Who are you? Who are you really?"

If Laura associates the ring with death—particularly Teresa's—the act of slipping it on is easily interpretable as her attempt to assert control, expediting her own death and liberating herself from a life of endless torment, abuse, and despair. It is specifically when Laura puts the ring on that Leland can be heard screaming: "Don't make me do this!" (In the script, though not the film, Laura responds, "No, you have to kill me!") This reading accords with Laura's diary entry, revealed in the television series, that she has to die because it is the only way to repel Bob, and also with Dr. Jacoby's comment to Cooper, also in the television series, that "maybe [Laura] allowed herself to be killed," to finally rest in peace (Laura places the ring on her finger soon after Ronette's guardian angel appears, perhaps giving Laura hope that redemption awaits for her as well). But Laura may be accomplishing something else here as well: In his death scene in the series, Leland reveals that Bob and his cohorts were desperate to inhabit more humans, including Laura, but she "was strong. She fought him. She wouldn't let him in." (Bob tells Laura directly in the train-car scene: "I want you!") Perhaps by choosing the ring, and death, Laura triumphs in the end by thwarting Bob's attempts to possess her.

As we learn from one of *FWWM*'s deleted scenes released in 2014, the Owl Cave ring eventually winds up on the finger of Annie Blackburne, who somehow acquires it during her sojourn to the Black Lodge in the series finale. However, the ring is then stolen by a nurse at the hospital to which Annie is transported. The script describes it thusly: "With an anticipatory smile, then a selfish laugh, she puts the ring on her finger."

To be continued.

Scorched Engine Oil

Crazy as it sounds, we'll go with it: Scorched engine oil is kind of like perspiration odor for Black Lodge spirits, since every time somebody smells it Bob is not only present, but all worked up over something. The list of unfortunate souls compelled to inhale this malodor in Bob's presence is blessedly short (though, sadly, not short enough): Maddy Ferguson (just prior to being attacked by Leland/Bob), Dr. Lawrence Jacoby (twice, poor guy—once while being attacked by the town gazebo and once while eyewitnessing Bob/Leland's murder of Jacques Renault), Ronette Pulaski (on the night of Laura's murder), and finally Laura herself (at least once, in *Fire Walk with Me*, when she and Leland are confronted by Mike in the traffic scene, though probably more than that, like in the train car on the night of her murder). The origins of this oil remain concealed until the series finale, when the Log Lady shows up at the sheriff's station with a jarful of it, which Ronette categorically identifies as the same stench she inhaled on the night of Laura's murder. Once again, it's the Log Lady to the rescue, providing a crucial clue linking the oil to the Black Lodge, where Windom Earle is headed as they speak with the abducted Annie Blackburne; Margaret tells Cooper her husband brought the oil home one night, shortly before his death, and called it "an opening to a gateway." As Cooper soon discovers, that gateway—to the Red Room and beyond—is situated in Glastonbury Grove, marked by a circle of twelve sycamore trees, inside of which is a circle of stones, inside of which is a shallow pool, inside of which is . . . you guessed it, oil.

White Horse

Critics who slammed *Fire Walk with Me* in 1992 had a field day with the white horse that pops up in the middle of the film, in Sarah and Leland Palmer's bedroom, flouting it as evidence of Lynch's supposed pretentiousness and self-conscious eccentricity. To each his own. The *equus* had an earlier cameo in episode fourteen of the television series ("Lonely Souls"), also directed by Lynch (from a teleplay by Mark Frost), and what the two appearances have in common is that on each occasion Leland/Bob apparently slipped Sarah a drug in order to incapacitate her during an upcoming act of transgression—the murder of Maddy Ferguson in the television episode and another sexual encounter with Laura in the film. The significance of the horse is never explained (naturally), but most likely it is a harbinger of death or danger. Interpreters typically cite the Book of Revelation 6:8, referencing the Fourth Horseman of the Apocalypse: "And I looked, and behold, a pale horse! And its rider's name was Death, and Hades followed him" (in the script of episode fourteen, the horse is referred to as "pale"; in the screenplay for the film the word "white" is used). In 1993, when the cable channel Bravo reran *Twin Peaks* to launch a programming bloc called "TV Too Good for TV," Lynch penned introductions for all thirty of the episodes, delivered on camera upfront by the Log Lady. The intro for episode thirteen ("Demons") ends with this line: "Woe to the ones who behold the pale horse," clearly a reference to the biblical citation above.

Here's what we think: In the 2007 documentary *Lynch*, the director talks at length about being blown away one day at the American Film Institute while watching *Le Sang des bêtes* (*Blood of the Beasts*), a 1949 ultrarealist documentary by French filmmaker Georges Franju, contrasting bucolic life in the outskirts of Paris with gruesome scenes unfolding in nearby slaughterhouses. The scene that made the strongest impression? The graphic depiction of the slaughter of a white horse.

"What Happened to Josie?"

Bob himself puts this head-scratcher to Agent Cooper—but it wasn't in the script.

The short answer is she died of fright and her soul apparently became trapped in a wooden knob on a Great Northern nightstand. This being *Twin Peaks*, the short answer only raises more questions (for instance: Wha? Huh? A . . . knob? Wait, what?). Of the many enigmas of *Twin Peaks*, Josie's fate ranks among the most puzzling. Why does her body weigh only sixty-five pounds at her autopsy? Why do Pete and Ben appear to see her face in different fireplaces in the Great Northern—moments that do not appear in the script? Why were scenes of Josie in the Red Room (hiding her head behind the curtain) filmed but not aired? And, of course, WHY DOES JOSIE GET STUCK IN A KNOB?

Don't ask Mark Frost. He has stated in interviews that, among the many outlandish occurrences in *Twin Peaks*, the resolution of Josie's storyline is one that he never understood.

So the strange death and afterlife of Josie Packard was a special project of Lynch's. Frustratingly, or hearteningly, depending on your point of view, definitive answers to the above questions will probably never come. The bizarreness of Josie's transformation, and her subsequent manifestations,

Body Double: Proof that Josie wound up in the Red Room?   *Photo by Richard Beymer*

may just have to be chalked up to the show's embrace of the ineffable, and its prioritization of sensation, emotion, and mood over narrative logic. There may be nothing to "solve." However, there are some tantalizing clues that suggest Lynch might have had further, as yet unrealized, plans for his mysterious femme fatale:

In *FWWM*, Agent Jeffries, reeling from a very strange experience in Buenos Aires, states that he will not talk about "Judy." Later, we see a monkey repeat the name. According to *FWWM* cowriter Robert Engels (who says that he supplied the name "Judy," courtesy of his sister-in-law), Judy was Josie's sister, and the two of them were involved in Buenos Aires with Windom Earle in some presumably unsavory fashion (considering Earle's penchant for disguises—maybe he was in a monkey costume?). An early draft of the *FWWM* script contained this intriguing line, in reference to Judy's sister (Josie): "Her sister's there, too. At least part of her."

OK, that sounds ominous. Did Josie lose some vital part of herself in Argentina? Does that account for her underweight condition at her autopsy?

At the 1993 *Twin Peaks* fan festival, Bob himself (Frank Silva) stated that Josie eventually wound up in the Red Room. Silva stunned the audience by revealing that a scene was shot for the series finale in which "Josie's" body (in actuality a body double, as Joan Chen was unavailable) is seen protruding from the Red Room curtains, dressed in the same nightgown she wore in her death scene at the Great Northern in episode twenty-three, her head stuck on the other side of the curtains. Robert Engels has confirmed that this scene was shot, though Lynch opted not to include it in the final episode, for reasons unknown (natch). In 2011, a website called The Twin Peaks Archive, run by Mischa C., posted six never-before-published stills of Josie's double, wearing the same nightgown. These photos were courtesy of actor Richard Beymer (Ben Horne), who documented the final days on the *Twin Peaks* set with a marathon shooting session.

Was the "headless" Josie in the Red Room indicative of her diminished state? Or was she caught between dimensions, her body in the Red Room, her head appearing in the fires of the Great Northern? What was her connection to Earle?

Like we said: more questions.

13

Guaranteed to Cause Some Sleepless Nights

Dossiers: Persons of Interest

Hank Jennings (Chris Mulkey)

A very busy bee in Twin Peaks' criminal underworld, Hank Jennings drives a lot of action in the series' plot. Hank is married to Norma, the long-suffering owner of the Double R, and his release from prison early in the series presents a major roadblock for her romance with Big Ed. Less prosaically, it was Hank who engineered the murder attempt on Andrew Packard, and Hank who shot Leo . . . in another unsuccessful assassination gambit. Some fans postulate that the domino Hank carries around and fetishistically

Chris Mulkey as rogue Bookhouse Boy/domino kid Hank Jennings.

gloats over represents the number of people he's killed, but in terms of in-series murder attempts, he's batting zilch. Mulkey deftly conveys both Hank's sullen menace and easy charm; it's understandable that level-headed Norma might once have fallen for him, and, indeed, Truman reveals that Hank was once a Bookhouse Boy, and "one of the best." Hank is one *Twin Peaks* villain who seems not so much truly evil as he does humanly weak and selfish. Still, he's a jerk, and one of the show's most deliciously satisfying moments is the beating administered to him by the supernaturally strong Nadine Hurley.

Leo Johnson (Eric Da Re)

Leo's trajectory over the course of the series is intriguing: he begins as an utterly hateful, degenerate, abusive bastard and ends up a pitiable Job figure—it's as if the character is an experiment designed to elicit sympathy from the unlikeliest source possible. Da Re (son of *TP* casting director Johanna Ray and veteran character actor Aldo Ray) vividly conveys the simmering rage just below Leo's cool, detached affect; he's one of the show's most chilling non-supernatural antagonists, a blandly handsome "regular guy" who insists on cleanliness and order when not otherwise engaged in various acts of sickening depravity or cold-blooded violence. Leo's a key player in Twin Peaks' drug trade, his truck-driving job a perfect cover for bringing cocaine in over the Canadian border. He is also a former sexual partner of Laura Palmer's, and indeed was engaged in a debauched orgy with her, Ronette Pulaski, and Jacques Renault (shudder) the night she died. The likeliest-looking suspect in Laura's murder, Leo certainly fits the bill of a sadistic killer: he tortured Laura in the course of their last encounter, physically and psychologically abuses his young wife Shelly, burns down the Packard mill with Catherine Martell and Shelly inside, and, perhaps most heinously, guns down Waldo the mynah bird in cold blood. He also attacks Bobby Briggs with an axe, but the kid arguably had it coming. Leo's fortunes take an abrupt plunge after he is shot in the head by Hank Jennings (tying up some pesky loose ends regarding that arson). Reduced to a conscious but semi-vegetative state, he is left in the care of Shelly . . . and Bobby, now openly flaunting their passion before the wheelchair-bound Leo's helpless eyes. Leo is repeatedly humiliated and abused by the couple, and it's hard to say he doesn't deserve it, but it's uncomfortable to watch nonetheless. Eventually escaping this domestic hell, he immediately lands in a worse one, conscripted by the demented Windom Earle to be his dogsbody and

Bad, bad Leo Johnson: Meanest man in the whole damn town?

whipping boy, controlled by a shock collar. The last we see of him, Leo sits helplessly in the woods, unable to move or open his mouth lest he activate a cruel trap devised by Earle involving a great number of poisonous spiders suspended above his face. Justice served?

Blackie O'Reilly (Victoria Catlin)

Elegant, imperious, and perfectly discreet, One Eyed Jacks madam Blackie O'Reilly (also known as "The Black Rose") rules her roost with sultry noirish élan. A former lover of Benjamin Horne, Blackie operates his brothel/casino and resents the hold he has over her; understandable, since his control is based on the heroin addiction he manipulated her into. She takes sadistic pleasure in returning the favor when Horne's daughter Audrey infiltrates the bordello, keeping the girl captive and forcibly injecting her with the opiate. Do things work out for Blackie? No, no they do not, as she is murdered by Jean Renault (at the behest of her own sister, ouch) after assisting him in the hostile takeover of OEJ. She's a bad egg, but she has style, and her arch flirting with Big Ed Hurley on the occasion of his undercover mission to the casino cracks us up every time.

Nancy O'Reilly (Galyn Görg)

Lord help the sister who comes between me and my man: Nancy is the sister of One Eyed Jacks boss lady Blackie O'Reilly, but let's just say there isn't a ton of sisterly love going around here. The reasons aren't fully explicated, though at least part of it has to do with Nancy's miscreant boyfriend Jean Renault, apparently Blackie's onetime squeeze ("What does she do for you I can't?" Blackie wants to know. "Well, something new," replies Renault, who nearly gets a shot glass of whiskey tossed in his face for that retort). Just how rancorous is their relationship? Well, very: Nancy urges Jean to kill her sister, and he eventually obliges. When last seen, Nancy is taking a nasty punch to the gut from Cooper; not very chivalrous, true, but after all, she *is* trying to kill him.

Renault Brothers (Jacques, Bernard, Jean) (Walter Olkewicz, Clay Wilcox, Michael Parks)

A singularly scummy fraternity, the Brothers Renault constitute some of *Twin Peaks'* most loathsome characters. Most crucial to the Laura Palmer arc is middle sibling Jacques (the self-proclaimed "Great Went"): a blackjack dealer, bartender, cocaine runner, and general reprobate who was (along with good buddy and partner in crime Leo Johnson) intimately and sickeningly involved with Laura Palmer (he both "partied" with her and pimped her out). Grossly overweight, slovenly and lecherous, and, in his own words, "blank as a fart," Jacques does manage a certain low, roguish charm—he's crudely entertaining, even after he takes a cowardly shot at Harry. Predictably, he comes to a bad end, smothered to death in the hospital by Leland Palmer after his (erroneous) arrest for Laura's murder.

Little brother Bernard mules dope from Canada for Jacques. He's a rather pathetic, weaselly figure, dispassionately disposed of by business partner Leo Johnson in the woods after getting picked up holding cocaine at the border by the law. Tidy Leo, always on the lookout for loose ends.

Oldest, and worst, brother Jean, played by legendary character actor and Tarantino favorite Michael Parks, presents himself as soft-spoken, elegant, and sophisticated, in contrast to his coarser siblings. This veneer hides pure ruthless avarice. A career criminal, Jean angles to take control of One Eyed Jacks, murdering the madam, Blackie (the creep is the lover of Nancy, Blackie's sister), and spearheads the scheme to ransom Audrey Horne back to her father, Benjamin, owner of the casino and brothel. Jean also plots revenge against Cooper, whom he blames for the deaths of his brothers (no great loss), and frames him for drug running, resulting in Coop's temporary suspension from the FBI. He's a vicious, hateful man, actively evil and sadistic (contrasted with Jacques's largely self-destructive sins of sloth, lust, self-indulgence, and moral weakness), and his death at Cooper's hands at Dead Dog Farm inspires no tears.

14

The Bookhouse

Twin Peaks in Print

There's things you can't get in books.

S till piqued? You might want to track down these publications, best enjoyed over coffee and pie:

Books

The Secret Diary of Laura Palmer (1990, Jennifer Lynch)

Penned by David Lynch's daughter Jennifer (just twenty-two at the time), *The Secret Diary of Laura Palmer* is the king (or queen, if you prefer) of all *Twin Peaks* books, spending ten weeks on the *New York Times* best-seller list, even as some retailers refused to stock it due to its graphic content ("'Secret Diary' peaks lusty curiosity," ran the *Chicago Sun-Times* headline). As the story goes, Jennifer Lynch was whisked into the offices of her dad and Mark Frost during the season's roller-coaster first season, informed of the identity of Laura's killer—making her one of just three people in the know—and tasked with writing the book, sprinkling clues throughout without actually revealing the killer's identity. The book, released on September 15, 1990, two weeks before the second-season premiere, introduces new characters like Harold Smith and the Tremonds, but also suffers from inconsistencies with the series and film, most notably the timeline, which is a year off (the last dated entry is October 31, 1989, eight months after Laura's death). Sheryl Lee has credited *Secret Diary* as a huge influence on her portrayal of Laura in *Fire Walk with Me.*

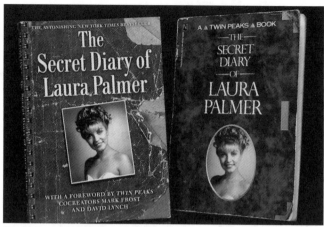

David Lynch's daughter Jennifer penned *The Secret Diary of Laura Palmer*, which cracked the *New York Times* best-seller list in 1990 even though some retailers refused to stock it because of graphic content. The book was reissued in 2011, with forewords by David Lynch and Mark Frost.   *Photo by Scott Ryan*

"Diane . . .": The Twin Peaks Tapes of Agent Cooper (1990, Scott Frost, others)

A forty-five-minute audio book performed by (Grammy-nominated) Kyle MacLachlan, "*Diane . . .*" comprises both monologues from the series and new material penned by Scott Frost, Mark's brother, all addressed to Cooper's never-seen assistant Diane, toiling away as always back in the Philly office. Released early in the second season (October 1990, to be exact), the tape opens with Cooper musing about his newest purchase—another $199.99 black suit (upping his total to five, one for each day of the work-week)—while anticipating his new assignment in Twin Peaks, and concludes about nineteen hours after the attempt on his life that ended the first season.

Welcome to Twin Peaks: Access Guide to the Town (1991, David Lynch & Mark Frost & Richard Saul Wurman)

Touted as "An Unforgettable, In-Depth Tour of the Town That's Captured America's Imagination!," this traveler-guide parody ladles out heaping help-ings of trivial information about the town of Twin Peaks—history, dining, lodging, fauna, religious worship, Norma Jennings's cherry-pie recipe, and so on. Included are brief bios of many of the characters (sample tidbit: Pete Martell is "the most uxorious man in Twin Peaks and can tie a Duncan Loop in the dark"). The book's assertion that the 1990 census revealed the town's population to be 5,120.1, rather than 51,201, as stated on the "Welcome to Twin Peaks" sign in the title sequence of the series, is a swipe at ABC, which insisted on the larger number. Richard Saul Wurman, who "coauthored" (a number of writers and researchers, including Harley Peyton and Robert Engels, are credited at the back of the book) with Lynch and Frost, produced the Access line of travel guides, but is better known today as founder of the TED (Technology, Entertainment, and Design) conference.

The Autobiography of F.B.I. Special Agent Dale Cooper: My Life, My Tapes (1991, Scott Frost)

Imagine this: Dale Cooper receives his first tape recorder as a Christmas gift in 1967, and has obsessively dictated his thoughts ever since (with some interruptions). Scott Frost does exactly that here, following Cooper from age thirteen all the way up to February 24, 1989, a date that should be familiar to *Twin Peaks* fans (final entry: "There's been a body found in Washington state, Diane. A young woman, wrapped in plastic. I'm headed for a little town called Twin Peaks"). Released in May 1991, just as *Twin Peaks* was ending its run, the book is burdened by multiple inconsistencies with the series and with *Fire Walk with Me*—the most glaring being Cooper's role as the lead agent on the Teresa Banks investigation, though in fairness to Scott Frost that was everyone's intention until Kyle MacLachlan initially balked at reprising the role of Cooper in the film. Look for suggestions that Bob had been keeping an eye on Cooper and his Mom as far back as 1969, and for the origins of the ring that Cooper winds up surrendering temporarily to the Giant.

Reflections: An Oral History of Twin Peaks (2014, Brad Dukes)

While not officially authorized by Lynch-Frost, this estimable oral history of *Twin Peaks*—the TV series, but not *Fire Walk with Me*—includes interviews with almost all of the major players, and many minor players as well, though among the missing are David Lynch and Lara Flynn Boyle.

Not Books

Twin Peaks Gazette (1991)

Officially licensed by Lynch-Frost, the *Twin Peaks Gazette* published four monthly issues beginning with a four-page "preview issue" in January 1991 ("Agent Cooper Makes Blacktie's Best-Dressed FBI Agent List" is the lead article), distributed via the Twin Peaks Fan Club; a fifth, "special edition" was produced by Worldvision to accompany the video release of the first season. Display ads appearing in *The New Yorker* in January 1991 offered twelve-issue subscriptions for $29.95 (plus an address for your own home in Twin Peaks and a Twin Peaks Sheriff's Department coffee mug for "that damn good cup of coffee"), but the plug was pulled upon cancellation of the series. Named after the town newspaper as identified in the series, the *Gazette* touted itself as "at once a small town newspaper, literary journal and mystery magazine," offering contests, interviews, editorials, letters, hard news about the show, and "mental and metaphysical stimulation."

Twin Peaks Collectible CardArt (1991)

"Relive the Mystery!" was the pitch for this set of seventy-six trading cards, issued by Star Pics and sold for $19.95 back in 1991. Though authorized by Lynch-Frost, the cards did contain factual errors (most notorious example: Card sixty-seven says Windom Earle is being dispatched to Twin Peaks to

Card Sharks: Star Pics released this set of seventy-six *Twin Peaks* trading cards for $19.95 back in 1991. Though authorized by Lynch-Frost, the cards included factual errors about some of the characters.   *Photo by Scott Ryan*

conduct an internal FBI investigation into Cooper's actions, when in fact Earle was—blessedly!—no longer with the FBI at this point, and it was Special Agent Roger Hardy who led the probe). Character cards included birthdates and astrological signs, plus "likes," educational background, accomplishments, strengths, and weaknesses, incorporating information from not only the show, but also the officially authorized companion books.

Wrapped in Plastic (1992–2005)

Wrapped in Plastic launched in October 1992 (less than two months after *Twin Peaks: Fire Walk with Me* premiered in the U.S.) and ran for seventy-five

Revered fanzine *Wrapped in Plastic* ran for thirteen years—eleven more than the TV series it celebrated. Here's the cover of its most famous issue, arguing that the entire *Fire Walk with Me* prologue was Cooper's dream.   *Photo courtesy of John Thorne and Wrapped in Plastic*

issues, finally shuttering in September 2005. A grassroots publication spearheaded by the heroic John Thorne and Craig Miller, the fanzine took its name from Pete Martell's memorable description of Laura Palmer's body on the shore at Black Lake on the morning of February 24, 1989, while out fishing, phoned in to Sheriff Harry S. Truman in the series pilot: "She's dead. Wrapped in plastic." Included were essays, episode analyses, and pages and pages of fan letters, all deconstructing the series in the minutest detail, plus interviews with members of the cast and creative team, including both David Lynch and Mark Frost. The fanzine's most famous essay, "Dreams of Deer Meadow" (issue 66), controversially interpreted the entire prologue of *Fire Walk with Me* as Cooper's dream. Sadly, Miller passed away in 2010, four years too early to learn that *Twin Peaks* would be returning to television.

15

The Only Thing Columbus Discovered Was That He Was Lost

Dossiers: Outsiders and Interlopers

Buck and Tommy (Chris Pedersen and Victor Rivers)

The less said about these two punks the better, but just so you know: They're the sleazeball truckers who pick up Laura and Donna at the Roadhouse in *Fire Walk with Me*, then take them to an iniquitous truck stop astutely named Partyland, where they meet up with Jacques and Ronette. Hard to decide which of these two guys is worse, though Buck's the one who slips Donna the depth charge, precipitating an outburst at Donna by Laura ("Don't ever wear my stuff!"), who is distressed at seeing her idealized friend corrupted in a manner hitting so close to home.

Thomas Eckhardt (David Warner)

This creep drops by for a three-episode arc late in season two, which ends rather badly for him, what with him being shot dead and all while sharing a bed with Josie Packard, who commits the deed. Once upon a time Andrew Packard and the Hong Kong–based Eckhardt were business partners and buds, but the arrangement soured over what Andrew cryptically refers to as a "piece of business," and eventually Eckhardt enlists Josie in a botched attempt to assassinate Andrew by blowing up his boat (Andrew and Catherine sussed out the plot, and wound up faking Andrew's death). We do know this: Eckhardt, who plucked Josie from the streets of Hong Kong when she was young, is, up until the time he dies, madly obsessed with her, or madly obsessed at least with "ownership" of her—"Josie is mine; she belongs to me," he tells Andrew—and, conversely, Josie is scared to death of Eckhardt and has no desire to return to him. Beyond this the facts are kind of murky. David Warner, who portrayed Eckhardt, appears in James Cameron's 1997 titanic hit *Titanic* as the churlish bodyguard to Cal Hockley, a character played by Billy Zane (John Justice Wheeler in *Twin Peaks*).

Madeleine "Maddy" Ferguson (Sheryl Lee)

Maddy Ferguson's arrival midway through the first season of *Twin Peaks* should come as no surprise; in a series so focused on duality and *doppelgängers* (down to its very title), it only stands to reason that Laura Palmer, the girl at the center of the mystery at the center of the story, should have a double. Maddy is Laura's cousin, and their identical appearances (aside from Maddy's dark hair and owlish glasses) can be read as a cheeky reference to the TV kitsch classic *The Patty Duke Show*, which put forth the idea that the existence of identical cousins may cause one to lose one's mind (Leland certainly does). Maddy, who has traveled from Missoula, Montana (David Lynch's actual hometown, hmmmm), to assist her bereaved aunt and uncle, is all sweetness, kindness, and light, an inverted reflection of her dark and tormented cousin. She shares with her aunt a touch of precognitive ability, not that it ends up benefiting her (or Mrs. Palmer) much. Maddy emerges as perhaps *Twin Peaks'* most tragic victim figure—unlike Laura, Maddy has a chance to connect with the audience over the course of many episodes, and her murder, at the hands of her uncle Leland, is graphically depicted in a nigh unendurable scene of primal horror and violation. It's the single most traumatic sequence in a show that never feared to confront the most lurid and depraved aspects of human nature, and one of the most disturbing murder scenes in the history of the medium. The death of Maddy Ferguson reestablished the seriousness of the stakes in the story of *Twin Peaks*; however eccentric, campy, and absurd the show could be, it derived its formidable emotional power from a deep undercurrent of sadness and outrage at the evil that men do.

Jones (Brenda Strong)

This South African giantess, executive assistant to the satanic Thomas Eckhardt, didn't do much except check in at the Great Northern and serve coffee until her diabolical employer was shot dead by Josie Packard, at which point Jones suddenly assumed a higher profile, first gifting Catherine with a mysterious black box on Eckhardt's behalf and then stripping down to her slip and stockings before trying to strangle Harry in his sleep (as Eckhardt, jealous of Josie's relationship with Harry, had instructed her to do prior to his death). Let's just say she didn't make a lot of friends during her brief sojourn in Twin Peaks. Flash-forward thirteen years and Strong lands her breakout role as the dearly departed Mary Alice Young, beyond-the-grave narrator of *Desperate Housewives*—a role originally given to Sheryl Lee, *Twin Peaks'* Laura Palmer.

Jonathan Kumagai: aka Mr. Lee aka Asian Man (Mak Takano)

Thomas Eckhardt's ponytailed lackey, a skilled martial artist and brute with an Interpol rap sheet "as long as your arm," per Albert Rosenfield, is dispatched to Twin Peaks to fetch Josie Packard and return her to Hong Kong, where Eckhardt waits with open arms, among other limbs. Unfortunately for Jonathan, the plan goes awry when Josie pumps three bullets into the back of his head in a car in Seattle, on their way to the airport. *Bāaibaai*, Jonathan! One interesting note about this character: About two-thirds of the way into episode six ("Realization Time"), which takes place prior to the Josie-Jonathan arc, Audrey Horne slips a note under Cooper's door (Room 315) at the Great Northern, then spots an Asian man checking in to Room 312; the man looks at her and bows his head, and that's that—no elaboration then, or ever. According to the script, this character is also named Jonathan (never spoken or credited on-screen), leading some to speculate that this was the original iteration of the later Jonathan, though this apparently is incorrect. This Jonathan was portrayed by Derick Shimatsu, who reappears, for two episodes, in season two as Mr. Tojamura's assistant, another uncredited role. Shimatsu's sister, Paula, was Mark Frost's assistant, in addition to being a unit publicist and on-set still photographer.

Royal Canadian Mountie Preston King (Gavan O'Herlihy)

King looks regal, first in the Red Serge and later, during his One Eye Jacks scene, in a monkey suit, but the guy's toxic. He first shows up midway into season two, barging into the Twin Peaks Sheriff's Station with Special Agent Roger Hardy of FBI Internal Affairs, whining that Cooper's unauthorized raid of Jacks upended his six-month operation to nail Jean Renault on drug charges. Truthfully, King is in cahoots with Renault in the coke biz, and eventually gets taken down along with him at Dead Dog Farm, where he is pummeled into submission by transgender DEA Agent

Dennis/Denise Bryson. Not a bad outcome, eh? King is named after the title character in *Sergeant Preston of the Yukon*, a fifties TV show, and his wonder dog King.

D.A. Daryl Lodwick (Ritch Brinkley)

Sad-sack prosecutor Daryl Lodwick spends two pitiable days in Twin Peaks: first his wallet is lifted by Hank Jennings at the Double R, where he's briefly mistaken for puissant eatery critic M. T. Wentz (sort of gives himself away by ordering burger, fries, and Coke), and then he strikes out twice before Judge Sternwood, once seeking bail for Leland Palmer and once advocating for the prosecution of Leo Johnson. Round-bellied and bearded, Lodwick was likened physically to Yukon Cornelius, the arctic prospector in the 1964 Rankin/Bass television special *Rudolph the Red-Nosed Reindeer*, by the *New York Observer*, rather brilliantly. Sternwood's distaste for the man is barely containable, as evidenced by his constant interruptions of Lodwick's pontification before the court. The thing is, if you really stop and think about it, Lodwick was right . . . both times.

Evelyn Marsh (Annette McCarthy)

Of all the TV shows on all the networks in all the world, she walks into ours. Almost universally dissed by *Twin Peaks* fans, Evelyn Marsh is the femme fatale in a noir-tinged five-episode arc (it just *seems* to go on forever) in the middle stages of season two, fitting squarely into a bloc of episodes properly derided as the worst of the series (also comprising the Little Nicky, Lana Budding Milford, Nadine-and-Mike, and Ben Horne Civil War storylines, not to mention Cooper walking around in flannel shirts). Distraught after Maddy Ferguson's murder, James Hurley climbs aboard his hog and leaves Twin Peaks (and Donna Hayward) in the dust, finally stopping at a roadside "hideout" named Wallies, where he encounters Evelyn Marsh at the bar sucking on olives and spouting ersatz noir dialogue like "Men are always all right. Right up until they pull the trigger." Evelyn is a sultry tigress, blonde and bitter, who wears low-cut blouses, black stockings, and short dresses, flashing plenty of thigh. It doesn't take long for her to persuade James to follow her home so that he can fix her rich husband Jeffrey's 1948 Jag (among other things), which she herself has wrecked, before he returns from a business trip. This all turns out to be a scheme to frame James for Jeffrey's murder, so that Evelyn and lover Malcolm Sloan can abscond with his dough; James being the sap that he is, it nearly works. Evelyn and Malcolm go to great lengths to convince James that Jeffrey is beating her—in one scene she appears with facial bruises (never mind that they have miraculously disappeared by the next time James sees her)—and before you know it she's bedding the Bookhouse Boy and declaring her love for him. In the end Evelyn wins some sort of redemption for herself by pumping a bullet into Sloan's heart, but hey, what about the rest of us? We'll never get those five hours back.

Jeffrey Marsh (John Apicella)

More MacGuffin than character, moneyed businessman Jeffrey Marsh appears briefly in two mid-second-season, James M. Cain–styled episodes, the victim of a murder plot concocted by wife Evelyn and her lover Malcolm Sloan, who are scheming to collect Jeffrey's money and frame James Hurley for the deed. Evelyn and Malcolm endeavor very hard to convince James that Jeffrey is an unmerciful wife-beater, but when James—and we—finally meet him, we discover that he's really just a friendly, balding, slightly over-weight bloke in a track suit with a passion for cars, who appears to be very much in love with his comely wife.

Gwen Morton (Kathleen Wilhoite)

Wilhoite, who would go on to recurring roles in *Gilmore Girls* and *ER*, appears in a single, second-season episode, as Gwen Morton, extremely loquacious and un-self-aware sister of Lucy Moran, visiting from Tacoma with her newborn babe (Andy, thinking it is Lucy's, and thus perhaps his, immediately passes out). Wilhoite's performance as Lucy's sibling is spot-on, with laudable support from hairdressing, makeup, and wardrobe. Gwen is far more invasive and opinionated than her sister, and rambles on about everything, from her own medical issues to the white man's treatment of Native Americans, but especially about men, whom she generally regards as "sperm guns running around loose." We have nothing more to add except to echo Lucy: "Shut up, Gwen."

Ernie Niles (James Booth)

The Professor! Though not in the eggheady, *Gilligan's Island* sort of way. Ernie earns the sobriquet thanks to his proficiency with numbers, which comes in handy considering he is helplessly addicted to gambling, which leads to thievery from a savings and loan and a stint in the hoosegow, where he buddies up with Hank Jennings (not a great judge of character, our Ernie)—none of which, believe it or not, has anything to do with his presence in Twin Peaks. Rather, Ernie is in town because his new wife, Vivian Smythe Niles, is showing him off (!) to her daughter, Norma Jennings. The visit turns into a nightmare for Ernie, who's lured first into dealing coke for Jean Renault, then into helping Cooper and DEA Agent Dennis/ Denise Bryson take Renault down, both of which he humongously botches, largely because the good Lord apparently neglected to bless him with a spine. Ernie is an inveterate liar and coward, thoroughly without grace, as evidenced when the wire he is wearing during the Dead Dog Farm coke buy short-circuits due to excessive perspiration (hyperdrosis—a "childhood condition" contracted during some heroic mission in Korea, explains Ernie, who can't even lie congruously). Still, Ernie is so staggeringly transparent and inept that you can't help but feel for the guy, and several of his scenes are downright funny.

Vivian Smythe Niles (Jane Greer)

Vivian is a frosty, sanctimonious crab who's found the perfect occupation for her personality type: restaurant critic. Vivian's three-episode arc in the middle of season two ends with the revelation of her secret identity, Seattle-based food and travel pundit M. T. Wentz ("M. T. Wentz c'est moi"), who drives her own daughter, Norma Jennings, to tears by panning the restaurant she owns and operates (the Double R diner), then scolding Norma for being melodramatic about it. ("This is just not a very good restaurant. I can't violate my professional ethics.") The irony, of course, is that what we have here is a critic who is totally blind to her own faults, which are bountiful, including not only her deplorable parenting skills but also her calamitous taste in men. Vivian was portrayed by Jane Greer, star of one of the great classic-period noir films of all time, *Out of the Past* (1947).

Sid (Claire Stansfield)

Quick, pick a number between three and five. That's how many lines of dialogue Sid has over her two second-season *Twin Peaks* episodes, none longer than four words. So why include her here? Because she's Sid. She's awesome! She's so awesome she doesn't even have a last name, at least that we know of. Here's what we do know: She's Judge Clinton Sternwood's law clerk/traveling partner (at least), drives a Winnebago, and is the go-to gal for black Yukon sucker punches (which, research informs us, is one shot each of Yukon Jack and blackberry brandy, mixed with a dash of bitters, all blended with ice). She's a statuesque brunette with a beguiling smile and a sharp fashion sense (dig those fringed pants, Sid). Leave it to Cooper to encapsulate the essence of this woman in three words: "Man, oh man."

Malcolm Sloan (Nicholas Love)

Initially introduced as Evelyn Marsh's brother, Sloan is eventually revealed to be her lover, and the mastermind behind the nefarious scheme to bump off Jeffrey Marsh and pin the blame on James. The *kindest* thing we can say about this black-hearted soul is that he is thoroughly despicable (unless you are of the mind that framing James for murder and threatening to kill Donna are good things, which, alas, many people are), a fact that even Evelyn comes to realize in the end, as evidenced by the fact that she shoots him dead.

Judge Clinton Sternwood (Royal Dano)

This silver-haired, silver-tongued jurist, who shares a surname with Philip Marlowe's millionaire client in *The Big Sleep*, emerges out of a dark and stormy night in duster and Indiana Jones hat in the fourth episode of season two, having arrived in town to preside over Leland Palmer's bail hearing (following his arrest for the murder of Jacques Renault) and Leo Johnson's competency examination. Sternwood—the "last of the frontiersman," Truman dubs him—is at least the most eloquent character in *Twin Peaks*, if not the wisest. For sheer eloquence, nothing beats Sternwood's homily delivered to Leland in season two, episode four: "Before we assume our respective roles in this enduring drama, just let me say that when these frail shadows that we inhabit now have quit the stage, we'll meet and raise a glass again together in Valhalla" (credited to "Jerry Stahl and Mark Frost & Harley Peyton & Robert Engels," this was one of the show's most controversial scripts—see the episode guide for more details). Sadly, Sternwood hangs around for just two episodes.

Mr. Tojamura (Fumio Yamaguchi)

Tojamura-san is the mysterious mustachioed Japanese businessman in town from Seattle who slips Ben Horne a phony cashier's check for $5 million in exchange for a stake in the Ghostwood project, except he isn't any of those things really. What he is is Catherine Martell—wrongly believed to have perished in the Packard mill fire at the close of season one—in disguise, masquerading as a squat, long-haired, utterly humorless representative of an unnamed Asian investment firm, in a scheme to fleece Ben Horne in retaliation for conniving with Josie Packard to burn the mill down . . . with her inside. The *Twin Peaks* production team went to great lengths to conceal this sleight of hand; Piper Laurie's on-screen credit as Catherine Martell was scrapped for the early episodes of season two, while Tojamura's name began appearing in episode eleven ("Laura's Secret Diary"), as portrayed by Fumio Yamaguchi, a completely fictitious being. This arrangement lasted through episode fourteen ("Lonely Souls"), when Tojamura finally reveals himself as Catherine to Pete Martell; after this Laurie gets double billing, as both Catherine and Tojamura, until episode seventeen ("Dispute Between Brothers"), when she finally ditches the disguise and becomes Catherine Martell once again, returning things to normal, at least by *Twin Peaks* standards.

Rusty Tomasky: aka Heavy Metal Youth (Ted Raimi)

Poor dumb Rusty Tomasky is force-fed Windom Earle's insufferable pontification about so many things, including the White and Black lodges, a story Rusty finds "cool," but what he really wants to know is, where's the beer, man? A heavy-metal musician who looks every bit the part—long hair, headband, earring—Rusty is en route to a gig in Knife River when a tire blows. Sadly, he's lured to Earle's woodsy getaway with promises of free-flowing beer, though Earle's real plan is to shoot him with an arrow and stuff his corpse inside a giant black pawn created especially for the occasion, then dump it at the Twin Peaks gazebo with a note for Cooper: "Next time it will be someone you know." By most accounts an ignominious ending for anyone, though perhaps we should look at it from the point of view of Earle, who tells the headbanger, "You have lived your short life in odium and obscurity, but now at last you will step upon the larger stage." Rusty was portrayed by Ted Raimi, brother of noted film director Sam Raimi, who appeared as Joxer the Mighty in *Xena: Warrior Princess* and *Hercules: The Legendary Journeys*.

M. T. Wentz (Jane Greer)

Pseudonymous Seattle-based travel writer/restaurant critic, the most power-ful in Washington State, who generates buzz by crisscrossing his/her beat incognito. A rave from Wentz can galvanize business, which explains why everyone at the Double R and the Great Northern is all aflutter upon hear-ing that Wentz is Twin Peaks-bound. For more on this mysterious pundit, see "Vivian Smythe Niles (Jane Greer)."

John Justice Wheeler (Billy Zane)

An enigma in a series with no shortage of them, Billy Zane's John Justice Wheeler, an associate of Ben Horne, has the distinction of remaining entirely pointless and uncompelling. Handsome, virtuous, and irredeem-ably bland, Wheeler serves as a romantic foil for Audrey after Agent Cooper declines her advances. Their romance is short and sweet, interrupted by a mysterious errand of revenge Wheeler must attend to in Brazil. And that's it. No follow-up, no consequences. Perhaps the affair was meant to act as counterpoint to the twisted, frequently fatal, always unhappy romantic entanglements endured by the rest of the characters; or maybe (probably) there was an interesting idea for the character that fizzled out somewhere along the way (Zane claimed in an interview that Audrey would discover she was pregnant with Wheeler's child in season three). Zane would go on to earn richly deserved hisses as *Titanic*'s villainous Cal Hockley and belly laughs as a walk-off judge in *Zoolander*, but Wheeler remains a smarmy, pouty-lipped mannequin of dullness.

16

I Feel Like I'm Going to Dream Tonight

Fire Walk with Me

She's filled with secrets.

Here's *How* It Happened: Background

Fire Walk with Me, the David Lynch–directed theatrical prequel to the television series, bombed spectacularly when released in 1992, though history has been much kinder to it. The world premiere, at the Cannes International Film Festival in France in May, was legendarily disastrous: critics crucified it ("shockingly bad . . . simpleminded . . . scornful of the audience," opined Roger Ebert of the *Chicago Sun-Times*, a longtime Lynch nemesis), then assaulted Lynch with censorious questions at a tense post-screening press conference, suggesting that he was a "perverse" director who glorified violence and drugs, among other things (just two years earlier, Lynch's *Wild at Heart* had won the Palme d'Or). Sample question: If Lynch loved the world of *Twin Peaks* so much, as he often maintained, "why do most of the characters have such miserable and fucked-up lives?" Years later, Lynch told interviewer Chris Rodley the experience made him feel like he was "made of broken glass." While Robert Engels, who coscripted the film with Lynch and was at Cannes, has vociferously repudiated reports that the film was literally booed at the festival, then-*Newsday* film critic Jack Mathews, also in attendance, reported that "there were a few cheers scattered among the rude catcalls for which Cannes press audiences are known," and another attendee, actor Walter Olkewicz (Jacques Renault), also reported booing.

Not disputed is this: filmmaker Quentin Tarantino, whose *Reservoir Dogs* also screened at Cannes that year and was a fervent fan of the television series, responded to *FWWM* by saying that Lynch "has disappeared so far up his own ass" that he had no desire to watch another Lynch film for the foreseeable future.

Stateside, *FWWM* bowed before a hospitable, capacity crowd at the inaugural *Twin Peaks* fan festival (Twin Peaks Fest '92) in the Seattle area on August 16, attended by Lynch and stars Sheryl Lee (Laura Palmer) and Ray Wise (Leland Palmer), among other cast members, and twelve days later was released publicly by New Line Cinema to commercial theaters—*without* advance press screenings, a typical tactic when distributors fear scathing reviews and hope to build audience by word of mouth instead. Sure enough, critics savaged it post-opening, notably Vincent Canby of *The New York Times* ("It's not the worst movie ever made; it just seems to be").

FWWM's opening-weekend gross: $1.8 million spread over 691 theaters, an average of $3,500 per screen. Not terrible, but the worst was yet to come: in the wake of those mostly brutal reviews, ticket sales tumbled at least fifty percent week to week for each of the first four weeks, and the film, which cost approximately $10 million to make, grossed just $4 million domestically before being yanked from general release just six weeks in (though the film did particularly boffo business in Japan, where *Twin Peaks* also was hugely popular, opening with the second-largest weekend box office in that country's history to date, after *Terminator 2: Judgment Day*).

Bottom line: *Fire Walk With Me* flopped unequivocally, both critically and commercially.

But guess what? Critics—and audiences—are often wrong, and in this case both were. Yes, *Fire Walk with Me* is a challenging film, and anyone demanding the same dollop of idiosyncratic (some might say "Lynchian")

"Clearly, there is no suspense involved in this story with a preordained outcome. Another significant drawback is that Laura Palmer, after all the talk, is not a very interesting or compelling character and long before the climax has become a tiresome teenager."

—Todd McCarthy, *Variety*, May 18, 1992.

"'Twin Peaks: Fire Walk With Me' is a deception. It's not the worst movie ever made; it just seems to be. Its 134 minutes induce a state of simulated brain death, an effect as easily attained in half the time by staring at the blinking lights on a Christmas tree."

—Vincent Canby, *The New York Times*, August 29, 1992.

"If you plan on seeing 'Twin Peaks: Fire Walk with Me,' bring a book. You won't be able to read it in the darkened theater, of course, but it should still provide more entertainment than what's on the screen. Feel the binding. Flip through the pages. Wear it on your head. By the time the movie—and calling it that presumes, wrongly, that it moves—ends, playing with your book will seems like high adventure."

—John Anderson, *Newsday*, August 31, 1992.

humor figuring so prominently in the television series is in for a rude surprise, but considered on its own terms *FWWM* is a profoundly heart-wrenching tale of an abused young woman's emotional, psychological, and, eventually, physical destruction, and in the years since its initial release, numerous critics have come to appraise it as among Lynch's most uncompromising films, a harrowing metaphorical journey into what the director himself has called "the loneliness, shame, guilt, confusion, and devastation of the victim of incest," plus the "torment of the father—the war in him."

But why stop there? *Fire Walk with Me* can be admired on so many levels—as a meditation on the nature of evil (human? transcendental? a little of this and a little of that?), say, or on the struggle within all of us between our light and dark impulses. *FWWM* can be viewed as a cosmic battle between two worlds, one good and one evil, or even as a metaphor for filmmaking: confronted with an existence so brutal and so terrifying, we concoct fictional scenarios as a defense, yet the real world keeps pecking away, refusing to stay submerged. What all these themes have in common is the concept of duality, a favorite Lynchian theme, evoked by both the title of the TV series—*Twin Peaks*—and by the abstruse comment first uttered by the One-Armed Man in Cooper's famous second-episode dream, from which the film's appellation is drawn: "One chants out between two worlds: 'Fire, walk with me!'" Finally, let's not underestimate the importance of this: *FWWM* is *huge* fun to deconstruct and decipher because of all the mind-bending, never-explained weirdness that transpires within it—talking monkey, white horse, creamed corn, green ring . . . trust us, we could go on and on.

Briefly, here's how *Fire Walk with Me* came to be: Shortly after ABC announced the cancellation of *Twin Peaks*, Lynch teamed with Robert Engels, a writer/coproducer on the TV series, to begin scripting a feature-film version, with Lynch to direct. Reports surfaced that it was the first of multiple planned *Twin Peaks* films. Mark Frost, who had cocreated the television series with Lynch and remained on board as showrunner and exec producer until the bitter end, was uninvolved in the feature film (despite his on-screen EP credit); rumors had circulated of a fractious relationship between the two during the series' troubled second season, and several years later Frost explained to *Wrapped in Plastic*, the revered *Twin Peaks* fanzine, that he and Lynch had disagreed over the direction of the film: Frost wanted to push the story forward, picking up from where the cliffhanging series finale left off; Lynch, on the other hand, was fixated on a prequel, focusing on the final week of Laura Palmer's life. Lynch's obsession with Laura Palmer is well known; as he told Chris Rodley in *Lynch on Lynch*, a

2005 compendium of interviews, "I was in love with the character of Laura Palmer and her contradictions; radiant on the surface but dying inside. I wanted to see her live, move, and talk" (novelist David Foster Wallace, writing about Lynch for *Premiere* magazine, commented that *FWWM* "sought to transform Laura Palmer from dramatic object to dramatic subject. . . . She now embodied, in full view, all the Dark Secrets that on the series had been the stuff of significant glances and delicious whispers.").

Lynch and Engels worked quickly, polishing off their script in July 1991, less than a month following the June 10 airing of the series finale. Then, a setback: Kyle MacLachlan's surprise announcement that same month that he wouldn't reprise his series role as FBI Special Agent Dale Cooper (explanations vary: fear of typecasting, discontent over season two, yada yada—history is such a bitch to accurately record), forcing Lynch and Engels to retool the script, inventing a new character, FBI Special Agent Chester "Chet" Desmond, to stand in for Cooper. However, by August, MacLachlan had relented, consenting to an abbreviated shooting schedule, meaning Lynch and Engels had to come up with some way to accommodate both characters (rockabilly musician Chris Isaak was hired to portray Desmond). Their solution, as reflected in the new script, dated August 8 (the "shooting script," subtitled *Teresa Banks and the Last Seven Days of Laura Palmer* and available in its entirety on the Internet): assign the film's opening investigation, into the death of a seventeen-year-old drifter waitress named Teresa Banks (whose body is discovered shrink-wrapped bobbing along Wind River in Deer Meadow, Washington, about a year before Laura Palmer's corpse is similarly discovered in Twin Peaks), to Desmond—and then, approximately twenty-seven minutes in, have Desmond vanish into thin air, never to be seen or heard from again.

Enter Cooper, dispatched to Deer Meadow to investigate Desmond's disappearance—a mystery never solved. For *Peaks* purists, the issue with this "Deer Meadow Prologue," as it has come to be called, is that it appears to contradict the series—Teresa's death is referenced as far back as the pilot, when Cooper speculates that she and Laura were victims of the same killer—which hinted strongly, though never stated outright, that Cooper was the head honcho on the Banks investigation, and unequivocally repudiates *The Autobiography of F.B.I. Special Agent Dale Cooper: My Life, My Tapes,* which definitely places the Banks probe in Cooper's hands. (The original, pre-Desmond script also positioned Cooper as top dog in Deer Meadow, though, of course, without his disappearance at the end of the segment.)

We viewers eventually learn that Teresa was bludgeoned to death by Laura's father, Leland, who had been paying her for sex, and who had already been revealed as Laura's killer in the TV series, although we are never entirely certain whether it is Leland himself who is committing these acts or a parasitic evil spirit named Bob (one particularly provocative choice Lynch makes in the film is that when Teresa is being killed, at no time do we see Leland transform into Bob, as we do when he murders Laura at the end of *FWWM* and when he kills Laura's look-alike cousin Madeleine Ferguson in the series, and it is this fact, along with the suggestion—confirmed in a deleted scene—that Teresa is blackmailing Leland, that leads to the suspicion that it is Leland himself who is responsible for Teresa's demise).

Regardless, Desmond and his dweeby FBI partner, Sam Stanley, never do get to the bottom of this mess, and following Desmond's disappearance, the film moves on to the bureau's Philly office. Here, Cooper and two characters from the TV series, the hearing-impaired Regional Bureau Chief Gordon Cole (portrayed by Lynch himself) and the masterfully sardonic forensics specialist Albert Rosenfield, are visited by long-lost FBI agent Phillip Jeffries. What follows surely is one of the more bizarre scenes in the history of American cinema: Jeffries recalls for the assembled agents a meeting occurring sometime and someplace inside a room above a convenience store, attended by a deliciously bizarre assortment of ominous characters—including Bob and the red-suited dwarf known as the Man from Another Place, well known to viewers of the TV series—all the while insisting that under no circumstances whatsoever would he talk about Judy, even though no one is suggesting he do so and no one seems to have any idea who Judy is, since she is never identified or even mentioned again during the course of the film—until the very end, where her name is enunciated by a talking monkey (who also shows up in the room above the convenience store). This hallucinogenic interlude ends with Bob and the Man from Another Place parting the curtains in the Red Room, a locale familiar to viewers of the TV series from Cooper's episode-two dream, and then again from the series finale (the convenience-store locale is itself a reference to a comment made in that same dream by the One-Armed Man, Phillip Gerard, who says that he and Bob "lived among the people—I think you say 'convenience store'").

FWWM then returns briefly to Deer Meadow, with Cooper searching futilely for Desmond, and finally arrives in Twin Peaks, where it resides for nearly the entirety of its remaining run time (otherworlds excluded), limning the final week of Laura Palmer's tragically tortured life, during which time she is raped either by her actual father or by her father as

Reunited and it feels so good: Mike reconnects with his severed left arm, in the embodiment of the diminutive Man from Another Place.   *New Line Cinema/Photofest*

possessed by Bob, depending on your interpretation: Is Bob merely Laura's invention, contrived as a buffer against an unbearable truth, but finally unraveling? Or, as the television series seems to prefer, a cosmic demon who inhabits human vessels to commit abominable acts, thus absolving the human host of blame? All the while Laura plummets deeper and deeper into debauchery and self-immolation fueled by drugs and promiscuity, until finally she is dragged out to a derelict train car in the woods and slaughtered, her body later washing ashore wrapped in plastic by Black Lake—the entry point for the television series. Interestingly, in the wake of all the violence and despair, the film wraps not on this grievous note, but with hope and redemption: Laura, fully manifesting the radiance Lynch rhapsodized about to Rodley, laughing blissfully while gazing up at her guardian angel, finally freed of the demons that had haunted her for so long, with Dale Cooper—whom she had never actually met, despite their intersecting dreams—standing beside her. (Worth noting: Though angels are hugely significant in the film, there isn't a single mention of them in the August 1991 shooting script, and there's ample reason to believe from interviews with Sheryl Lee that Lynch was inspired to insert them by on-set conversations between actor and director, which is, as Gordon Cole might say, Lynch's M.O.—modus operandi!)

The Palmer family: Sarah, Laura, and Leland pose for a family photo; it doesn't take a Sherlock Holmes to detect something very, very wrong going on here.

Lynch and crew spent two months filming *FWWM*, from September 4, 1991, through October (the gruesome train car scene was filmed, appropriately enough, on Halloween, the final day, and also the birthdays of both Frank Silva, who plays Bob, and Michael J. Anderson, the Man from Another Place), the first four weeks in the Snoqualmie Valley region of western Washington state, where the pilot too had been shot. According to Ron Garcia, the director of photography on both, Lynch had asked for an amber, woodsy tone on the pilot, but persistently overcast skies compelled them to manufacture the desired colors, while during the film shoot they had nothing but sunshine, so opted to exploit the contrast between the brilliant colors and exceedingly dark tone of the story. This was followed by four weeks in L.A., ending up with some five hours of footage. This eventually was cut by almost half (final run time: approximately two hours and fifteen minutes), meaning dozens of scenes were left on the cutting-room floor, several involving characters from the TV series who, as a result, are completely absent from the film. Most of the series' actors had agreed to return for the film, though Richard Beymer (Ben Horne), Sherilyn Fenn (Audrey Horne), and Lara Flynn Boyle (Donna Hayward) weren't among them. The reasons for their absences have been inconsistently reported over the years, with even, in some cases, the actors themselves providing differing accounts. Lynch himself has acknowledged that some of the actors in the television series felt abandoned by him and Frost during the second season of the show, which might have played a role, as might have conflicting work commitments. The Hornes could be dropped relatively easily due to their tangential relationship to Laura. Donna, however, was a different matter: as Laura's best friend, she was essential to the story, and when Boyle declined, Lynch wound up recasting the role with Moira Kelly.

The cuts, Lynch said, were necessitated not only by time constraints, but also because many of the scenes were extraneous to Laura's story and thus, in the director's opinion, diluted the driving narrative. Numerous critics cited the absence of so many familiar characters among their complaints, and *Twin Peaks* fans clamored for access to these deleted scenes for over two decades (deconstructing them over and over based on the shooting script), until finally they were released in July 2014 in a comprehensive *Twin Peaks* Blu-ray boxed set including also the full series, plus bonus material shot specifically for the occasion by Lynch. Even then the director stood by his original cut, segregating the deleted scenes into their own feature rather than integrating them into the film as originally written.

Still, the deleted scenes (some of them explored in detail elsewhere in this chapter) are elucidative for a variety of reasons, whether advancing the Laura Palmer story or not. Some strongly evoke the offbeat humor that was so integral to the television series, the absence of which in *FFWM* created, for many critics, a dissonance that they were unable—or unwilling—to overcome. (Ironically, as the film was released, it is the Deer Meadow Prologue that most resembles the TV series tonally, even while featuring an almost completely different cast of characters, with Gordon Cole being the lone exception up to the Philadelphia scenes.)

Clearly, Lynch was unfettered by the television series; rather, he seemed perversely intent on shattering any expectations created by it. The first image we see in *FWWM* is of blue static, appearing on-screen for two and a half minutes as the film's credits are superimposed. Eventually, the camera pulls back; the static is emanating from a television set, promptly smashed to smithereens, followed by a woman screaming and then shouting "No!," and finally by a thud (we

"Laura Palmer is exhumed most cruelly in David Lynch's 'Twin Peaks: Fire Walk With Me,' the perversely moving, profoundly self-indulgent prequel of the director's darkly comic TV series. Memorable moments and ludicrous ones collide in this psychic autopsy, a weirdly fundamentalist cogitation on the intersection of Heaven, Hell and Washington state. Fans of the dark comedy will find little to laugh about—unless it is Lynch's pretentiousness—in this horrific look at Laura's last seven days."

—Rita Kempley, *The Washington Post*, August 29, 1992

discover later, during a Leland Palmer flashback, that this is Teresa Banks pleading futilely for her life). For a director as elliptical as Lynch, the symbolism is anomalously blunt. By the time the series had so spectacularly flamed out, after a phenomenal first season, many members of the cast and creative team had grown resentful of the experience, but Lynch especially, irritated at ABC (and television critics) for badgering him to reveal the identity of Laura's killer way before he was ready. Lynch's involvement in the narrative of the series appeared to wane after that—much has been made of his chafing at Cooper's evolution in season two, when, temporarily suspended from the FBI, he began showing up in flannel shirts instead of dark suits and ties—and now, fully engaged once again and in complete creative control, Lynch was restaking his claim, warning viewers that what they were about to experience was a different *Twin Peaks,* unconstrained by the commercial imperatives of broadcast television.

The promotional material released by New Line and other companies involved in the film revel in this dissimilitude, touting *FWWM* as Lynch's true vision of Laura's story: "Nothing that happened in the series held a candle to the scenes in this picture, the TV censors saw to that," Lee is quoted as saying. One press release crowed: "Now . . . Lynch could finally film Laura's last tryst in a derelict railroad car as he's envisioned it . . . surrounded by macabre mirror images of Frank Silva as the hulking intruder, Bob, and Michael Anderson as the 'Man from Another Place.'" Lynch, in fact, was so invested in the film that, at his request, New Line sent the following correspondence to theater projectionists around the country, along with the film: "David Lynch, the director of *Twin Peaks: Fire Walk with Me,* has asked me to contact you regarding the sound level of his motion picture. Mr. Lynch has put a lot of effort into the soundtrack of *Twin Peaks,* and feels that the best reproduction of sound will be achieved by increasing the volume 2 decibels above normal. Your efforts to accommodate Mr. Lynch will surely result in greater audience enjoyment of the film and, therefore, greater box office sales."

Alas, it wasn't meant to be. But as time has moved on, *Fire Walk with Me,* like Laura Palmer, has, for many of us at least, finally won the redemption it deserves.

Here's What We *Think* Happens: Synopsis

FBI Regional Bureau Chief Gordon Cole puts in a call to Special Agent Chester "Chet" Desmond, who's in Fargo, North Dakota, arresting what appear to be a couple of prostitutes and a school bus driver in the middle of nowhere as screaming children look on (this scene does not appear in the original version of the script, in which Cole summons not Desmond but Agent Cooper, who is in the FBI's Philly office when the call comes). Desmond and Sam Stanley are dispatched to Deer Meadow, Washington, to probe the murder of Teresa Banks, a seventeen-year-old diner waitress/drifter whose body is found wrapped in plastic by Wind River—a so-called blue rose case, though only certain FBI agents seem to know what this means, and they're not sharing. Deer Meadow law enforcement officials . . . also not in a sharing mood; Sheriff Cable doesn't want any J. Edgars "sniffing around my neck of the woods," but Desmond pulls rank, and he and Stanley head out back to the morgue to examine Banks's body. The agents determine that a ring is missing from Teresa's possessions, and Sam uses a pair of tweezers to extract a piece of white paper with the letter "T" from under the ring finger of her left hand. Gross.

Desmond and Stanley grab coffee and chow at Hap's Diner, Teresa's place of employment up until her demise; fellow waitress Irene, a crusty old-timer with multiple chins, reports that Teresa's left arm went numb for three days just before her death. We have no clue what that means either. Next up: a trip to Fat Trout Trailer Park, where the gents check out Teresa's trailer. Lookee here: a photo in which Teresa is wearing the green Owl Cave ring on her left hand. Following an encounter with a mysterious old woman—the Curious Woman, as she is referenced in the credits—trailer park manager Carl Rodd lapses into a trance, and recites two lines of dialogue that seem to make no sense, to Desmond or to us. Plus, what's up with that telephone pole? Sam departs for Portland with Teresa's body, for more testing, while Desmond returns to Fat Trout for one last look around. Well, how about that: There's the ring on a mound of dirt underneath one of the trailers. Desmond reaches for it. Fade to black.

FBI headquarters, Philadelphia: Special Agent Dale Cooper marches into Regional Bureau Chief Gordon Cole's office, announcing that it's 10:10 a.m. on February 16 and he's worried because of a dream he had, also not shared. Ziggy Stardust—um, sorry, David Bowie, as Special Agent Phillip Jeffries—shows up, almost two years after having disappeared in the field, and it's difficult to ascertain whether Cooper is more agitated because of Jeffries's sudden reappearance or because Cooper himself has just turned up in the hallway live on the closed-circuit monitor even though he is no longer in the hallway, so that he is appearing in two places at once. Weird happenings all around. Jeffries won't talk about Judy, which seems unproblematic, since no one's asking him to—does anyone even know who Judy is? However, he *will* talk about some meeting he attended above a convenience store, which must have been a doozy because the attendee list includes Killer Bob, the Man from Another Place, the Tremonds/Chalfonts, an electrician, a Jumping Man, two woodsman, and a monkey. Yes, a monkey.

Jeffries vanishes. The front desk reports that he was never there. Word arrives from Deer Meadow that Desmond too has vanished. Lots of that going around. Cooper is dispatched to Deer Meadow to find him. The trailer at which Desmond was last seen? Also missing. What is this new devilry? According to Rodd, the latest residents of that trailer were named the Chalfonts, an old woman and her grandson, as were the residents before that. Cooper finds Desmond's car—the words "Let's Rock" are written on the windshield—but no Desmond. An old woman and her grandson should remind us of the episode of the television series where Donna Hayward delivers chicken and creamed corn to the Tremonds; "let's rock" is a quote from Cooper's Red Room dream, uttered by the dancing dwarf in red, also known as the Man from Another Place, probably because he's sure not from anyplace we've heard of.

End "Deer Meadow Prologue."

Twin Peaks, one year later. Comely high school coed Laura Palmer is balancing relationships with bad boy Bobby Briggs on the one hand and sensitive biker James Hurley on the other, snorting coke in bathroom stalls, and pondering life's mysteries with best friend Donna Hayward. Upstairs in her bedroom, Laura discovers that pages from her secret diary have been ripped out; shaken, she rushes off to confide in agoraphobe Harold Smith, a regular on her Meals on Wheels route. Laura's convinced the culprit is someone named Bob. But Bob isn't real, protests Harold. "Bob *is* real!" Laura lashes. "He's been having me since I was twelve." Bob "wants to be me or he'll kill me," Laura says. Spooky stuff! Laura turns almost vampiric ("She allows the feeling of Bob to come over her," the script reads), grabbing Harold by the lapels as she hisses, "Fire . . . walk . . . with . . . me!" Harold is freaked, but agrees to hide Laura's diary.

Philly Interlude: Cooper shares his premonition with Special Agent Albert Rosenfield that the next victim will be a blonde high school girl who is sexually active, using drugs, and crying out for help. Albert asks, what's she doing now? Cooper replies, "She's preparing a great abundance of food."

Back to Twin Peaks: Laura, a blonde high school girl who is sexually active, using drugs, and crying out for help, is preparing a great abundance of food, packing up the station wagon for a Meals on Wheels run, when she encounters an old woman and her grandson—known in the TV series as the

Laura bickers with boyfriend Bobby Briggs outside Twin Peaks High School as Donna looks on.

Tremonds, though here they are the aforementioned Chalfonts—outside the Double R diner. Mrs. Chalfont hands Laura a painting of an empty room with an open door, says it would look nifty on her wall. Laura, don't take paintings from strangers. Her grandson, here wearing a white mask with a conical nose, as he did at Jeffries's convenience-store meeting, reports cryptically (Tremond/Chalfont default mode) that "The man behind the mask is looking for the book with the pages torn out. He is going towards the hiding place. He is under the fan now." Freaked, Laura rushes home, finds Bob upstairs skulking around her room. Freaked even more, she makes a mad dash for the bushes outside, from where she spies dad Leland exiting the house.

Brutal, excruciating scene that night at the Palmer dinner table: Leland excoriates Laura for not washing her hands before sitting down to eat, even though it was Leland who told her to sit down to eat before washing her hands. He doesn't like that necklace she's wearing either, the one with a broken heart, acting like a jealous lover. Upstairs, Laura hangs the painting from Mrs. Chalfont on her bedroom wall, and dreams of the Red Room, the Man from Another Place, Cooper, and Annie Blackburne. The Little Man dangles the Owl Cave ring; Cooper urges her not to accept. Annie pops up in Laura's bed, all bloody: "My name is Annie. I've been with Dale

Leland Palmer delivers a lecture on the importance of hygiene in an intensely disquieting scene.

and Laura. The good Dale is in the Lodge, and he can't leave. Write it in your diary."

Following night, Palmer abode: Laura's all gussied up, prepping for a night out on the town. Donna wants to tag along; no way, José, says Laura, who's protective of Donna, seeing her as her idealized self. Outside the Roadhouse, Laura bumps into the Log Lady, who warns her to be careful, though not in so many words, because Margaret doesn't talk that way (though at least here she lays off the owls). God bless the Log Lady. We should all have one (at least) in our lives.

Inside, Julee Cruise sings "In a World of Blue," which is a pretty accurate description of Laura's mood. Donna is being a bit of a bad girl herself, having followed Laura. Laura spots her; then, as if to prove a point, nods at Jacques Renault, the bloated, degenerate barkeep, who sends two drooling bikers her way. "So, you wanna fuck the homecoming queen?" says Laura.

Yup. Money exchanges hands. Much hanky-panky, with Donna doing her best to keep up with Laura. Next stop: the aptly named Partyland, a truckers' dive north of the border, where the group runs into Jacques (moves pretty fast for a porky guy) and Ronette Pulaski, another debased teen from Twin Peaks High (this is known colloquially as the Pink Room scene, and while we cannot be sure why, it may have something to do with the fact that the music Lynch composed for it is called "The Pink Room," perhaps in reference to the effect achieved by the combination of strobe and other lighting, plus the pink paint that production designer Patricia Norris used on the white caulking that is holding the log walls together). Buck drops a depth charge into Donna's beer. Turns out Ronette, Laura, Jacques, and Teresa Banks were old-time buddies. Ronette reveals that Teresa was blackmailing someone; Jacques confirms, adding that she had called him seeking physical descriptions of Ronette's and Laura's dads. Jacques slobbers over his "high school sandwich," inviting the "party twins" to his cabin in the woods on Thursday. Gross again. Debauchery ensues, until Laura spots one of the bikers savoring a seminude Donna, which brings an abrupt, frantic halt to the evening.

Following morning: Leland and Laura, riding in Leland's open convertible, are pursued by another vehicle, driven erratically by Mike, aka Phillip Gerard, aka the One-Armed Man, aka the one-armer, who is furious at Bob, aka Leland, for stealing the corn he had canned in the room above the convenience store, aka garmonbozia. That's what the Man from Another Place calls it. Yes, corn. We have seen bowls of creamed corn before, in Phillip Jeffries's evocation of the meeting he attended above the convenience store, but who knew it was this important? Guess what's on Mike's right hand? Yup, Teresa's ring. "It's him! It's your father!" Mike yells at Laura. She and Leland are so freaked. Laura smells scorched engine oil. Leland is having flashbacks involving Teresa Banks: turns out he answered one of her ads in *Flesh World* and was having sex with her. In this flashback Leland suggests next time Teresa bring along a couple of her girlfriends, which she does, but Leland beats a hasty retreat upon realizing that those girlfriends are named Laura Palmer and Ronette Pulaski. Teresa gets suspicious. The little Tremond boy is jumping around the parking lot of the motel. We don't know why either.

That night, in her bedroom, Laura realizes she's seen Mike's ring before: once in her dream, dangled by the Little Man, and again on Teresa's finger. "The same ring," she says. Meanwhile, in the living room, Leland has a wicked, disturbing flashback, in which he bludgeons Teresa Banks to death.

One day more: Midnight approaches. Bobby and Laura head off into the Twin Peaks woods to score some coke, from an anonymous friend of Jacques's. Laura's high as a kite, and very giggly. Turns out the seller is Deputy Cliff Howard, one of Desmond's nemeses from the Deer Mountain Sheriff's Department; why are we not surprised? Deputy Dawg yanks out a gun, but Bobby's faster, gunning Cliff down. Laura is convinced the dead man not walking is not Cliff but someone named Mike—presumably Bobby's friend Mike Nelson—and finds this hysterically funny. Bobby, not so much.

Bobby one day, James the next: Biker boyfriend comes by Laura's to find out why she blew him off the night before. Leland stares, and broods. Nighttime, and Laura is upstairs in her bedroom snorting coke . . . again. Leland brings Sarah a glass of milk, gently forcing her to drink it down to the last drop. Clearly drugged, Sarah sees a white horse standing in the middle of her bedroom. Yes, we said "white horse standing in the middle of her bedroom." So what? Leland turns on that ominous ceiling fan above the Palmer staircase. Bob creeps in through Laura's window; midsex, Laura looks up and sees not Bob's face, but Leland's, and shrieks.

The final night of Laura's life begins like this: She hops on the back of James's bike and off they go into the night ("Nervous about meeting J. tonight," reads the last entry in Laura's nonsecret diary). At the famous stoplight at Sparkwood and 21, they argue; Laura gives James the finger, tells him she loves him, and runs off into the woods, meeting up with Jacques, Ronette, and Leo Johnson. The four party at Jacques's cabin in the woods, with Waldo the mynah as resident voyeur. The sex gets rough. Leland/ Bob watches from a window outside. Jacques leaves; Leland/Bob beats him unconscious. Leo drives off in his little red Corvette. Bob/Leland abducts the two girls, marching them to a derelict train car deep in the Twin Peaks woods, the One-Armed Man in hot pursuit, though we still don't know why. Ronette sees her guardian angel and tries to escape, but Leland/Bob catches her in the act, knocking her around and tossing her out the door as the One-Armed Man looks on. His Owl Cave ring falls inside the train car; Laura places it on her finger, and is stabbed to death by Leland/Bob. The One-Armed Man walks away.

Leland wraps Laura's body in plastic, sets in afloat in Black Lake, and heads for Glastonbury Grove, where he enters the Red Room/Black Lodge/ whatever you want to call it. There, Mike and the Man from Another Place sit waiting. Leland splits into two—"One half becomes Bob—opaque. The other half floats up and becomes Leland—transparent," the script reads. What the . . . ? Here Bob appears to heal Leland's wound (some interpret this as Bob extracting Leland's garmonbozia, which, we are about to learn via subtitling, translates to "pain and sorrow," from murdering his daughter): "Bob, I want all my garmonbozia (pain and sorrow)," Mike and the Little Man say in unison. We see a close-up of someone's mouth eating creamed corn, for fifteen seconds. The monkey is back! "Judy," it says. Finally, someone wants to talk about Judy! Next, a close-up of Sheriff Harry Truman's arm pulling back the plastic from Laura's face on the shore at Black Lake (this we know from the TV series). Then, back to the Red Room—empty this time, but we track in behind the curtain, and there is Laura Palmer, all made up, looking stunning, with Agent Cooper standing by her side, looking down at her and smiling (have we finally encountered the White Lodge?). Laura's face is illuminated by flashes of blue-white light as her guardian angel hovers above. Laura is smiling, deliriously happy, at long last.

Here's What Happened, Then Didn't, Then Did: The "Missing Pieces"

As originally cut by director David Lynch, *Fire Walk with Me* clocked in at a whopping three hours and forty minutes, way too long for theaters (on the other hand, not so bad when you consider reports that editor Mary Sweeney's first cut was five hours!). The version finally released, in 1992, ran two hours and fifteen minutes. With the shooting script available online, fans had a pretty good idea of what had been dropped (though Lynch famously disregards scripts when shooting anyway) and clamored for the "Missing Pieces." Finally, on July 29, 2014, their wish was granted, with the release of *Twin Peaks—The Entire Mystery*, a Blu-ray box set comprising the film, all thirty episodes of the TV series (plus the European ending to the pilot), numerous special features (including *Between Two Worlds*, in which Lynch interviews Ray Wise, Grace Zabriskie, and Sheryl Lee both in character, as Leland, Sarah, and Laura Palmer, and as themselves), and thirty-three missing and extended scenes totaling eighty-eight minutes. In short: the Holy Grail.

There are plenty of gems here, including appearances by fondly remembered characters from the TV show whose absence from the film was bitterly lamented by critics at the time. Scenes with Pete, Josie, Lucy, Andy, Big Ed, Norma, and others bubble with the quirky humor so intrinsic to the series, but missing from the dark, unrelenting final cut of the film. Other scenes

Fire Walk with Me "Missing Pieces" was finally released on Blu-ray in 2014, after more than two decades of fan clamoring, featuring many of the characters from the series who had been cut from the film.

pack a wallop, either literally (as when Special Agent Chet Desmond administers a beatdown to Deer Meadow's smug Sheriff Cable—the last scene cut from the film, according to coscripter Robert Engels) or figuratively (in one extended scene, a distraught Laura seeks refuge at Donna's, where the Haywards fawn over her, feed her huckleberry muffins, and exhibit melancholic symptoms as Laura waits for Leland to pick her up, establishing that they at least suspected something was amiss at the Palmer household). Still, Lynch has always stood by the theatrical cut, noting that many of the deleted scenes distracted tonally and narratively from the focus of the film: the harrowing final days of Laura Palmer's life. Lynch felt so strongly about this that when the "Missing Pieces" were finally released, they were edited into a stand-alone piece rather than integrated into the film, as originally intended.

As to whether or not any of the many mysteries consuming *Peaks* freaks for over two decades are finally, resolutely resolved, the answer is . . . not really, at least as far as we're concerned, though some may disagree (everyone has their theories). The blue rose is what now exactly? Who's Judy? Why is the good Cooper trapped inside the Black Lodge? What happened to Chet Desmond? What's up with Mike, who appears so different from his TV iteration? No solutions here, to these or many other questions. But the fun of *Twin Peaks* isn't knowing the answers; it's unraveling the clues (or trying to), and there's a fresh bounty here to enjoy.

Here are highlights of the "Missing Pieces":

"Epilogue": Much of the postrelease chatter centered on the final missing piece, which, unlike all the others, unfolds *after* the conclusion of the television series. Annie Blackburne, having survived her Black Lodge ordeal, is rushed to the hospital by Sheriff Truman; catatonic, she repeats the exact same dialogue she spoke earlier in *FWWM*, when she shows up in Laura's bed at the tail end of the Red Room dream: "My name is Annie. I've been with Laura and Dale in the lodge. The good Dale is in the lodge, and he can't leave. Write it in your diary." Annie now wears the Owl Cave ring, suggesting she may well have been Bob's (i.e., the bad Cooper's) next target, except that the ring is lifted from her finger by a nurse, who appears to desire it as nothing more than a flashy trinket. Over at the Great Northern, Harry and Doc Hayward break into the bathroom to check on Cooper/ Bob, who, having already created a bloody mess by banging his head against the mirror, is acting exceptionally weird, even for Coop. Meanwhile, the good Cooper is stuck in the Black Lodge with the Man from Another Place, wondering how he is ever going to get out. The Little Man, helpful as ever, responds, "You are here. Now there is no place to go but home!," then resorts to that nasty little habit of cackling maniacally and dancing. Cooper has deduced that Annie has the ring, and by the look on his face we can safely conclude that he comprehends fully the potential calamity of the situation.

"Cooper and Diane": More proof of Diane's identity, as we watch Cooper perform isometric exercises against a door frame at FBI offices in Philadelphia while flirting with his off-camera and unseen (as always) secretary.

"Stanley's Apartment": Cooper acts uncharacteristically peevish with dorky fellow agent Sam Stanley, the only scene in which the two of them appear together, though originally Cooper was supposed to be the lead agent on the Banks investigation (remember, in the series pilot Cooper specifically instructs Diane to share evidence with Albert Rosenfield rather than Sam, opining that "Albert seems to have a little more on the ball").

"Buenos Aires"/"Above the Convenience Store": We're gonna talk about Judy: One of the most baffling segments in all of *Twin Peaks* lore involves David Bowie's brief appearance as FBI Special Agent Phillip Jeffries, who, in *Fire Walk with Me*, shows up in the Philadelphia office after being MIA for almost two years. Jeffries refuses to discuss Judy—a woman who is never identified—evokes a meeting he attended at some unspecified time in a room somewhere above a convenience store, whose participants also included Bob, the Man from Another Place, and the Tremonds, and announces that we all live inside a dream. He points at Cooper and suggests he isn't who he appears to be. At the end of the scene Bob and the Little Man exit through a red curtain, suggesting some link to the Black Lodge. The "Missing Pieces" bookend the film's Jeffries sequence with two scenes set at a swank hotel in Buenos Aires, and also extend the convenience-store scene. We can confidently say we *still* don't know what the hell's going on: Jeffries, in the same white suit, print shirt, and red shoes he wears in *FWWM*, enters the Palm Deluxe hotel carrying a briefcase. "Do you have a Miss Judy staying here by any chance?" he asks the desk clerk. The clerk doesn't answer, but hands Jeffries an envelope. "The young lady, she left it for you," he says. Cut to a shot of the telephone pole with the number six on it—the same pole we've seen on a couple of occasions before, by Fat Trout Trailer Park, both times with weird consequences. Then, a close-up of a mouth, and we are inside the room above the convenience store. Strange, impenetrable lines are spoken by the various oddballs assembled in this room, also including two Woodsmen and an Electrician—"The chrome reflects our image" . . . "From pure air. We have descended . . . from pure air. Going up and down. Intercourse between the two worlds." . . . "Animal life." Eventually we arrive at the portion of the segment included in the original film. However, not in the film: the Owl Cave ring appears, atop a black table, and Laura's face is weirdly superimposed. Then, back to the room above the store, where we see blurred, ghost-like images of the characters in the background (though not Bob and the Man from Another Place, who have already exited). Next, a shot of Ghostwood Forest, and then Jeffries exiting the elevator in Philadelphia, as in the film. Some of what follows appears in the film, but some doesn't, including tantalizing new clues about Judy: "I sure as hell want to tell you everything, but I ain't got a whole lot to go on," Jeffries says. "But I will tell you one little bitty thing: Judy is positive about this." A line that was closed-captioned "Elga, baby, damn no" in the original DVD release of the film now reads "Hell, God, baby, damn, no." Oh, so that's what he meant! Then, this provocative comment: "I found something in Seattle at Judy's. And then there they were. And they sat quietly for hours. And I followed." Jeffries then groans, placing his head on the desk. "Oh. Oh. Oh. Ring. The ring." The lights start flickering and Gordon Cole's intercom malfunctions. When Cole says "Mayday," Jeffries replies, "May. February, 1989" (time travel, anyone?). Then, as in the film, he vanishes. Then, another close-up of a face in the room above the store, and finally we're back in Buenos Aires: Jeffries reappears on the staircase hotel, screaming, with burn marks on wall behind him. A maid crawls across the floor, whimpering. Shaken, the bellhop has literally defecated himself: "Santa Maria, where did you go?" he says. "Are you the man? Are you the man?"

"The Palmers": A funny, lovely scene of rare domestic bliss at the Palmer dinner table, where Leland instructs Sarah and Laura on how to greet the Norwegians Ben Horne is courting as investors for the Ghostwood project in their native language.

"2x4": Never met a Jack Nance scene we didn't like, and here's no exception: Pete patiently explains to Josie and Dell Mibbler—the creaky old loan manager who may very well be blown to smithereens in the series finale—why a two-by-four slab of wood isn't really two-by-four. Hilarious.

"Best Friends"/"I'm the Muffin": Nothing much to report on Gordon Cole's baffling blue rose, but Doc Hayward muffs a magic trick involving a red one; this is the aforementioned scene in which Laura, having just encountered Bob in her bedroom, and spied Leland exiting the Palmer house immediately after while hiding in the bushes, rushes to Donna for comfort, and spends a lovely interlude with the Haywards, the normal, loving family she aches for but will never have. The jolt here is when Doc, seeing that Laura is despondent, invents a message for her while reading from a piece of paper that in reality is a prescription: "The angels will return, and when you see the one that's meant to help you, you will weep with joy," injecting new meaning into the film's concluding scene, and also explaining what Laura means that night when she stares, fixated, at a painting of an angel on her bedroom wall and says, aloud to herself, "Is it true?" Like most of the major allusions to angels, including Ronette's guardian angel in the train car and Laura's angel at the end, Doc's quote does not appear in the *FWWM* shooting script.

"Bob Speaks Through Laura/Blue Sweater": Creepy! Laura, mounting the stairs to her bedroom, stops, with the portentous ceiling fan circling overhead, momentarily possessed by Bob, who says: "I want to taste through your mouth." Sarah unknowingly breaks the trance, demanding to know what Laura has done with her blue sweater, until Laura points out that she (Sarah) is wearing it.

"Fire Walk with Me": Super creepy! Mike (the One-Armed Man) sits shirtless on a floor by a ring of twelve candles, one by one extinguishing the flames.

Says "Fire walk with me" in that Red-Roomy voice. Twice. Because once is not enough? Further confusing us as to what exactly this guy's story is, when everything seemed so simple in the TV series.

"Smash Up": Big Ed Hurley, completely absent from the theatrical cut, turns up in a couple of "Missing Pieces"—one where Nadine storms out of the Double R after coming face-to-face with Norma, but far more charming is this scene, absent from the script, in which he and Norma, both apparently a little tipsy, hang out, hook up, and listen to Badalamenti tunes in the back of Ed's pickup truck as they ponder the existential implications of their frakked-up relationship.

"Party Girl": Hooray for Teresa Banks, who gets some extra screen time, first fielding a phone call from Leland, who's answering her *Flesh World* classified ad, then informing Laura and Ronette that their John (Leland) has skipped, then calling Jacques to request physical descriptions of Ronette's and Laura's dads, and finally placing the fateful blackmail call to Leland. All of this is referenced second-hand in the final cut (by Jacques and Ronette), but a couple of interesting things transpire here. One, Teresa doesn't appear to be wearing the Owl Cave ring when she fields the first call from Leland, raising the possibility that it was a gift from Leland/Bob or perhaps even from Mike, who might have tracked her down knowing of Bob's interest. Two, Leland's reaction to Teresa's blackmail call—stewing silence—further fuels speculation that it is he, and not Bob, who kills her.

"Waiting for James": As we already knew, on the last night of her life Laura sneaks out her bedroom window and meets up with James, who pulls up in front of the Palmer abode on his motorcycle. What we didn't know was that Leland arrives home just before James gets there, and that Laura hides in the bushes, hoping he doesn't see her and that he disappears inside the house before James arrives. Tense! Of course, Leland eventually finds Laura that night in Jacques's cabin, suggesting that he did in fact see her leave with James and that he followed her throughout the night. Maybe.

"Bobby and Laura in the Basement": Major Briggs, whose strangeness knows no bounds, spends a quiet evening at home with his wife, Betty, reading from the Book of Revelation.

"Distant Screams": Alone in her cabin in the woods on the night of Laura's death, an anguished Log Lady clutches her slab of ponderosa pine close to her chest as screams pierce the night ("My log saw something that night," she will later tell Cooper in the series). Heart-wrenching.

17

Morons and Half-Wits

Dossiers: Deer Meadow

Teresa Banks (Pamela Gidley)

Though never actually appearing in the television series (she is referenced on multiple occasions), Teresa Banks plays a huge role in *Twin Peaks* mythology, since it is Dale Cooper's conviction that she and Laura Palmer were victims of the same madman that brings the G-man to town (once the FBI is alerted to the case because Ronette Pulaski stepped out over the state line, that is). Teresa's murder, in Deer Meadow, Washington, a little over a year before Laura's, is the eruptive crime that drives the opening segment of *Fire Walk with Me*; like Laura's, Teresa's corpse is found wrapped in plastic, by Wind River, and Cooper's suspicions are fortified when he finds a tiny piece of white paper with the letter "R" wedged under one of Laura's fingernails (in Teresa's case it was a "T"). Like Laura, Teresa is dead before we meet her, and it is only through flashbacks and remembrances by other characters that we come to know anything about her sad, lonely existence: a striking young woman with platinum blonde hair worn short and piercing blue eyes, Teresa is described as a "drifter," living alone at Fat Trout Trailer Park, and following her death no one comes forward to claim the body. A waitress on the night shift at Hap's Diner, where she was chronically late for work, Teresa, it is suggested, had a coke problem, and supplemented her income with sex for hire. It was her particularly bad fortune to hook up with Leland Palmer, Laura's dad, who—one way or another—is responsible for both of their deaths (either as Leland himself, or Leland as possessed by the evil spirit Bob). Teresa and Laura traveled in the same debauched circles, as we discover when Teresa, at Leland's request, sets up a foursome (and here we speak not of a golf outing), and Laura turns out to be one of the gang, along with Ronette Pulaski (Leland beats a hasty retreat before Laura spots him). Vexing question: were Laura and Teresa really victims of the same killer? A sticky wicket. We actually see Leland transmogrify into Bob during Laura's murder, but not during Teresa's.

G-men Sam Stanley (left) and Chet Desmond are summoned to Deer Meadow to investigate the murder of Teresa Banks.

New Line Cinema/Photofest

And yet, how else to explain the plastic wrapping and those letters under the fingernails? Plus, there's that matter of the mysterious green ring, which, at one time or another, each of them possessed. Deleted scenes released in 2014 confirm what Jacques Renault and Ronette Pulaski both hint at during the Partyland scene in *FWWM:* Teresa, having become suspicious of Leland once he skipped out on the orgy, had discovered that he was Laura's dad, and hoped to make a fortune by blackmailing him, which might very well have been the direct cause of her demise.

Footnote: Banks's first name is spelled Teresa in the pilot and *Fire Walk with Me*, but Theresa four different times in the script of Episode 1002 ("Zen, or the Skill to Catch a Killer"). We've made the executive decision to go with the *FWWM* spelling, for obvious reasons.

Sheriff Cable (Gary Bullock)

Obstructive and belligerent, Sheriff Cable (*FWWM* only) is the reverse image of his Twin Peaks counterpart: while Harry S. Truman welcomes Cooper to town to oversee the Laura Palmer murder probe, Cable dismisses

Desmond as "little fella" and warns him that "I don't like you people sniffin' around my neck of the woods." Though not too sharp on the uptake, Cable does possess an idiosyncratic skill, as Desmond discovers from a framed newspaper photo of the sheriff hanging on the office wall, captioned "Cable Bends Steel," in which the loutish lawman is seen bending a rod of steel into an inverted U. Tempers flare when Cable attempts to stop Desmond and Stanley from transporting Teresa Banks's body to Portland for more sophisticated forensics testing, triggering a brawl in which Desmond kicks Cable's butt (this scene was shot but cut from the final film, and photos floated among fans for years before it was finally included among the deleted scenes in the 2014 Blu-ray release).

Curious Woman (Ingrid Brucato)

This old hag makes one brief appearance in *Fire Walk with Me*, lasting approximately thirty seconds, never uttering a word, yet *Twin Peaks* fans love to hypothesize about her because there's almost nothing to go on. Many have pointed out the character's resemblance to David Lynch, speculating that it was the director himself in drag, but in reality the Curious Woman (as referenced in the end credits) is portrayed by Ingrid Brucato, who spent two hot summer days on set with her hair drenched in Vaseline and dust to enhance the effect, which we would describe, as succinctly as possible, as "bizarro." Her appearance outside Teresa Banks's trailer as it is being searched by Agents Desmond and Stanley appears to trigger an extreme reaction in Carl Rodd, manager of the trailer park, who lapses into a trance. The scene is so remarkable that it bears deconstructing: Desmond, Stanley, and Rodd are standing around drinking coffee when Lynch abruptly cuts outside, dollying in toward the trailer from a subjective POV. Cue the spooky sound effects. The screen turns black, and upon fade-up we are back inside the trailer, with the Curious Woman peeking through the open doorway, an ice pack pressed against her face with her right hand, a walking cane gripped in her left. Her face and hair are filthy, and she wears a pendant with a cross around her neck. She never enters, and when Desmond asks if she knew Teresa Banks, the woman gets the shakes, then backs away and out of sight, forever. Desmond glances over at Rodd, who looks distant. Lynch then cuts to a telephone pole outside, with the numbers 24810 on it (there's at least one additional number, blocked from sight), and a large 6 underneath them (this is the same pole that Desmond stares at later, immediately before heading to the Chalfont trailer, where

Carl Rodd (left) and Cooper contemplate the mystery of Desmond's disappearance at Fat Trout Trailer Park.

he reaches for the ring and disappears). Back to Rodd, who takes a drag on his cigarette. "See, I've already gone places," he says. "I just want to stay where I am." Desmond says nada, but looks concerned (as he should, since no one has any idea what Rodd is talking about). And there you have the curious case of the Curious Woman.

Deputy Cliff Howard (Rick Aiello)

Howard, who appears in *FWWM* only, is a boorish bozo who, when first encountered, is intent on preventing Desmond and Stanley from meeting with his boss, Sheriff Cable, but ultimately fails, when Desmond grabs hold of his nose and pinches a nerve, inflicting the buffoonish lawman with considerable pain. Imagine Will Ferrell parodying a sheriff's deputy and you get a pretty good picture of the hulking, mustachioed Howard, who is habitually laughing or snorting derisively (and cluelessly) at Desmond and Stanley. Like Teresa Banks, Howard lives at Fat Trout, and it is while approaching Howard's trailer that Desmond, according to the *FWWM* script, "gets a strange feeling" and detours instead to a neighboring unit, where he eventually discovers Teresa's ring, leading to his disappearance. Howard makes one last, fateful appearance in *FWWM*, meeting up with Bobby and Laura in the Twin Peaks woods, carrying a bag of what is supposed to be cocaine (though later determined to be baby laxative, which we discover in a deleted scene), and is fatally shot by Bobby after pulling a pistol on them. Laura is mistakenly convinced the dead man is not Howard, but someone named Mike—presumably Bobby's friend Mike Nelson, though this is never explained—which for some indecipherable reason Laura finds hilarious (probably because she is high as a kite).

Irene at Hap's (Sandra Kinder)

A crusty, white-haired hash-slinger on the graveyard shift at Hap's Diner in Deer Meadow, Irene (*FWWM* only) is visited by agents Desmond and Stanley as they prowl around for info on Teresa Banks, who worked nights at Hap's during the month leading up to her death. Outfitted in a pink waitress uniform similar to the one Teresa wore the night she was killed, with matching fingernails, Irene isn't much help with the Banks investigation—she calls Teresa a "nice girl" with a coke problem who never could get to work on time, and hypothesizes that her death was a "freak accident"—but reveals to the gents that shortly before her death, Teresa's left arm went completely numb for three days; Sam then suggests transporting the body to Portland for more sophisticated tests, which leads him to depart Deer Meadow while Desmond remains behind for one last, fateful look-see at Fat Trout Trailer Park. Asked by Desmond if she snorts cocaine, Irene, cigarette dangling just north of her upper chin, replies, "I don't do drugs." When Sam chimes in that "Nicotine is a drug. Caffeine is a drug," Irene's retort to Desmond is priceless: "Who's the towhead?"

Jack (C. H. Evans)

Jack, the manager at Hap's Diner, has only a handful of lines, but sometimes that's all it takes. The guy is irresistible, maybe because of his voice, which sounds like his larynx is made of sandpaper, though maybe it's the cigarettes, since he is holding a lighted one in his hand as he instructs Agents Desmond and Stanley to direct their questions about Teresa Banks not to him but to Irene, her fellow waitress. We know almost nothing about Jack (or, for that matter, the actor who portrayed him, C. H. Evans, who has only one other credit that we can find—a long-forgotten 1991 TV movie titled

Dead in the Water) from the version of the film released in theaters, though he gets a little more attention in the "Missing Pieces" and in the script; according to the latter, he and Irene are "united in holy matrimony." This makes sense, as Jack appears to be intimately familiar with Irene's temper, warning the agents not to make any jokes at her expense because of her name and the fact that she works at night ("Now Irene is her name, and it is night. Don't go any further with it. There's nothing good about it."). These unscripted lines would appear to reference the song "Goodnight Irene," which includes the lyrics "I'll see you in my dreams." *Wrapped in Plastic* has pointed (rightly) to this as one of numerous references to dreams in the Deer Meadow prologue, arguing (wrongly) that this is proof that the entire segment is itself a dream. Dream on, guys.

Carl Rodd (Harry Dean Stanton)

Carl Rodd, who appears in *Fire Walk with Me* only, is the manager of Fat Trout Trailer Park, which Teresa Banks, Deer Meadow Deputy Cliff Howard, and the Chalmonts all called home. Portrayed by character actor Harry Dean Stanton, who had worked with Lynch in the 1988 French short *Le Cowboy et le Frenchman* (*The Cowboy and the Frenchman*) and again in *Wild at Heart* (1990), Rodd appears in just three scenes—two with Desmond and one with Cooper, all at Fat Trout, and we never learn much about him, though we do know this: he likes to sleep in ("DO NOT EVER DISTURB BEFORE 9 A.M.—EVER," reads the sign on his trailer) and brews a wicked cup of coffee, which he calls "Good Morning, America" (with the "sting of the forty-eight-hour blend," per Desmond). Rodd is a scruffy, flannel-on-flannel sort of guy, who sports an adhesive bandage above his right eye, dried blood visible. Relentlessly beleaguered, he's a straight-shooter who does what he can to help Desmond and Stanley out. He has the distinction of being the last person to see Desmond before his disappearance, but his most notorious scene occurs when Desmond and Stanley are searching Banks's trailer and Rodd lapses suddenly into a trance, announcing, "See, I've already gone places. I just want to stay where I am," totally out of context. Those lines—the meaning of which is never explained—do not appear in any version of the script, and *FWWM* cowriter Robert Engels has speculated that they emerged from an impromptu on-set collaboration between Lynch and Stanton.

18

I'm Ready to Lay the Whole Thing Out

A *Twin Peaks* Timeline

Sometimes, things can happen just like this.

What Happened, When, and to Whom

Confused about what happened when? Join the club. The following timeline *should* help. Be advised: the information contained herein derives only from the TV series and *Fire Walk with Me*—not from any of the companion books, which often present conflicting accounts. Life in Twin Peaks is complicated enough.

We include events that we see transpire, but also those that are referenced as having happened.

The events in the series occur in 1989, which is when the episodes were filmed rather than when they aired.

The Deer Meadow prologue of *Fire Walk with Me*, including Teresa Banks's death, transpires in 1988. The bulk of the film, unfolding in the days leading up to Laura's death, occurs in 1989.

Most *Twin Peaks* episodes happen over the course of a single day, though multiple episodes straddle two days, and it is sometimes difficult to ascertain whether we are in the pre- or postmidnight hours. But we do our best.

1985

Windom Earle stabs his wife, Caroline, to death. Cooper is severely wounded. Earle is institutionalized. (In *The Autobiography of F.B.I. Special Agent Dale Cooper: My Life, My Tapes*, this occurs in 1979, one of numerous inconsistencies with the series.)

1987 or 1988

Josie Packard, working for Thomas Eckhardt, hires Hank Jennings to kill Andrew Packard in a boat explosion. Catherine and Andrew suss out the plot; Andrew fakes his death and goes into hiding. To deflect suspicion, Hank commits vehicular manslaughter, is convicted, and goes to jail. (There are conflicting references in the series as to when these events occur.)

1988

February

Leland Palmer hooks up with Teresa Banks after answering her ad in *Flesh World* (she looks like Laura, at least to Leland). At Leland's urging, Teresa arranges a foursome, but Leland skips out after spying Laura in the motel room (along with Ronette Pulaski) on his way in.

February

Teresa, after figuring out that Leland is Laura's dad, begins blackmailing him.

February 9

Teresa is murdered (this date is established in the series, though it conflicts with information in the *Fire Walk with Me* script, which, while ambiguous, establishes a later date—but in any event that line never made it into the film).

February

Agents Chet Desmond and Sam Stanley are dispatched to Deer Meadow to investigate Teresa's murder.

February

Desmond disappears while reaching for the Owl Cave ring.

1989

February 5 (Sunday)

Laura shares her necklace with James.

February 12 (Sunday)

The famous picnic: Laura, James, and Donna.

February 16 (Thursday)

Cooper tells Gordon Cole he is worried about his dream.

Phillip Jeffries shows up at FBI offices in Philadelphia after being missing
　　for almost two years, then vanishes again.
Laura brings her secret diary to Harold Smith for safekeeping.

Laura Palmer, small-town sweetheart and tragic victim.

February 17 (Friday)

Cooper tells Albert the killer will strike again.

Mrs. Tremond/Chalfont presents Laura with a painting.

Laura finds Bob upstairs in her bedroom, searching for the secret diary. Hiding in the bushes outside immediately after, she sees Leland leave the house.

At the Palmer dinner table, Leland harasses Laura for not washing her hands.

Laura has the first of two Red Room dreams, involving the Tremonds, Cooper, Annie, and the Man from Another Place, who holds up the Owl Cave ring.

February 18 (Saturday)

Bobby arranges a drug buy with Jacques Renault.

Laura encounters the Log Lady outside the Roadhouse. Donna follows her there. They hook up with Tommy and Buck, then head to Partyland, where they meet Jacques and Ronette. Donna is drugged. Laura learns that Teresa was blackmailing someone, and had asked Jacques what her father looked like.

February 19 (Sunday)

Mike (One-Armed Man) confronts Leland and Laura during a traffic backup, freaking both of them out.

Laura experiences an epiphany regarding the ring.

February 20 (Monday)

FWWM appears to skip this day altogether.

February 21 (Tuesday)

Laura has her second Red Room dream, which we never see but is later recounted in the diary entry Harold leaves for Donna—the same dream that Cooper has in episode two of the series.

February 22 (Wednesday)

During a botched drug buy, Bobby shoots and kills Deer Meadow Deputy Cliff Howard (this probably happens postmidnight, so we list it here instead of on the previous day).

Bobby hands Laura the $10,000 he was planning to use at the drug buy; this money eventually winds up in Laura's safety deposit box, where Cooper and Truman find it.

Leland drugs Sarah, who sees a white horse.

Bob creeps into Laura's bed; during sex she looks at him and sees Leland.

High school romance finds sensitive biker James Hurley and dutiful Donna Hayward.

February 23 (Thursday)

Laura tutors Josie Packard in English.

Laura records an audiotape for Dr. Jacoby, telling him she's in "kind of a weird mood."

Laura receives a phone call from James, agrees to meet him. Laura writes in her diary that she is "nervous about meeting J tonight." Before leaving the house she sees an angel in a painting in her bedroom disappear.

Laura meets up with James, hops on his bike. Leland watches.

February 24 (Friday)

(First day of the television series): Very early morning: Laura and James fight. She gives him the finger, then tells him she loves him. She leaves him at the intersection of Sparkwood and 21 at about 12:30 a.m., running into the woods, where she meets up with Ronette, Jacques, and Leo.

Laura, Jacques, Leo, and Ronette (and Waldo the mynah bird) party at Jacques's cabin.

Leland/Bob marches Laura and Ronette to the train car, where he kills Laura (sometime before 4:00 a.m.). He leaves an R under her fingernail, wraps her body in plastic, and sets it adrift in Black Lake. He enters the Red Room, encountering Mike and the Man from Another Place.

TV show starts here: Pete Martell finds Laura's body while out fishing, and calls it in to Sheriff Harry Truman.

Ronette, in shock, is found wandering across a railroad bridge.

FBI Special Agent Dale Cooper arrives in Twin Peaks.

Deputies locate the train car where Laura was murdered; after arriving on the scene, Cooper and Truman come across Laura's half of the necklace and a note saying, "Fire walk with me."

At the bank, Cooper and Truman find the $10,000 in Laura's safety deposit box, plus a copy of *Flesh World* with Ronette's photo.

Roadhouse brawl.

Donna and James bury James's half of Laura's necklace, which Dr. Lawrence Jacoby later digs up.

Traumatized and semicatatonic, Ronette Pulaski makes her slow return from the hellish train car in the woods.

February 25 (Saturday)

Doc Hayward delivers autopsy report to Cooper and Truman.

Pete finds a fish in the percolator.

Sarah Palmer has a vision of Killer Bob.

The Log Lady tells Cooper her log saw something the night of Laura's
murder.

Ben Horne's brother Jerry returns from Paris with incredible butter-and-
brie baguettes. Ben and Jerry drown their sorrows at One Eyed Jacks.

Audrey Horne slips a note under Cooper's door: "Jack with one eye."

Bobby sees the mysterious man in black in the woods while meeting up
with Leo.

February 26 (Sunday)

Cooper introduces Harry, Lucy, Hawk, and Andy to the Tibetan rock throw.

Audrey dances by herself at the Double R, dreaming of Agent Cooper.

Albert Rosenfield arrives in town.

Cooper dreams about the Red Room.

February 27 (Monday)

Madeleine Ferguson comes to town.

Harry and Albert come to blows in the morgue.

Laura's funeral.

Cooper meets the Bookhouse Boys.

Leo helps Jacques get across the border.

Cooper encounters Dr. Jacoby at Laura's gravesite.

Cooper and Hawk discuss souls, and help a broken Leland get home.

February 28 (Tuesday)

Andy sketches Bob, based on Sarah's description.

Hawk tracks the One-Armed Man to the Timber Falls Motel, where he
claims to be a shoe salesman and denies knowing Bob.

Cooper and the gang visit Dr. Robert Lydecker's veterinary clinic, discovering a file on Waldo, the mynah bird belonging to Jacques Renault.

Hank Jennings is paroled.

Leo kills Bernard Renault.

Ben hires Leo to burn down Packard mill.

March 1 (Wednesday)

Hank Jennings returns to Twin Peaks.

Audrey gets a job at the perfume counter of Horne's department store.

Searching Jacques's apartment, Cooper and the gang find a photo of a cabin with red curtains, familiar to Cooper from his dream, plus proof that Ronette and Laura were receiving sexual solicitations mailed to Jacques's post office box.

Cooper, Truman, Hawk, and Doc Hayward visit with the Log Lady, then search Jacques's cabin in the woods, and find Waldo.

Audrey spies Ben and Catherine discussing plans to burn down the mill, then having angry sex.

Maddy tells Donna she's discovered a stash of Laura's audio recordings.

Hank beats up Leo.

Shelly shoots Leo (who's obviously having a bad day).

Audrey shows up in Cooper's bed, buck naked; Cooper goes for malts and fries.

Thursday, March 2 (Thursday)

Leo shoots/kills Waldo.

At One Eyed Jacks, Audrey ties a cherry stem into a knot with her tongue, and is hired on the spot.

Cooper and Big Ed Hurley go undercover at One Eyed Jacks, to chat with Jacques Renault, who deals there.

James, Donna, and Maddy lure Jacoby from his office, so James and Donna can look for the missing tape Laura made for him. Jacoby is attacked, probably by Leland/Bob.

Jacques is ambushed and arrested.

Leo torches the mill, trapping Shelly and Catherine inside (he thinks).

Nadine ODs; Ed finds her and calls an ambulance.

Lucy's pregnant.

Leo attacks Bobby with an ax; Hank shoots Leo.

Leland smothers Jacques to death with a pillow at Calhoun Memorial Hospital.

Josie puts three bullets in Cooper's gut.

March 3 (Friday)

Cooper is visited by a Giant, who leaves three clues.

Leland's hair turns white.

He's baaaaack! Albert returns to Twin Peaks.

Donna starts smoking.

Major Briggs shares his "veranda of a vast estate" speech with Bobby.

Cooper and Albert are convinced Laura's killer is the "Third Man."

Josie's MIA, supposedly in Seattle; Catherine's MIA, supposedly dead.

An atypically sunny Norma Jennings pours Bobby Briggs a damn fine cup of coffee.

At the Hayward Supper Club, Leland sings "Get Happy" and collapses.
Ronette stirs, remembering the night of Laura's murder.

March 4 (Saturday)

Albert tells Cooper that his ex-partner, Windom Earle, has escaped from a
    mental institution.

Donna delivers a Meal on Wheels to the Tremonds, who suggest she visit
    with Harold Smith.

Ronette ID's Bob from Andy's sketch.

Leland recognizes Bob; he lived next door to his grandfather's summer
    home on Pearl Lakes.

Ben Horne reports Audrey missing.

Emory Battis tells Audrey he recruited Laura and Ronette for One Eyed
    Jacks, and that Laura was caught using drugs so they kicked her out.

Major Briggs delivers a message to Cooper: "The owls are not what they
    seem."

Donna gets a call from Harold Smith, who's willing to meet.

Maddy sees Bob.

Cooper is woken from a dream by a phone call from Audrey, who is caught
    by Blackie O'Reilly.

March 5 (Sunday)

Bob tries to kill Ronette by tainting her IV, and leaves the letter B under her fingernail.

Cooper tells Harry and Albert he's been visited by a Giant.

Dick Tremayne arrives at the station to take Lucy out for lunch.

Donna visits Harold Smith.

Leland tells Cooper and Truman that he recognizes Bob from the sketch.

The One-Armed Man sees the sketch of Bob and gets dizzy, heads for bathroom. Mike emerges.

Nadine thinks she is eighteen.

Jacoby IDs Leland as Jacques's killer.

Cooper and Truman arrive to arrest Leland for the murder of Jacques.

Donna sees Laura's secret diary at Harold's.

March 6 (Monday)

Judge Clinton Sternwood comes to town.

Leland admits to Jacques's murder.

Travel/restaurant critic M. T. Wentz is coming to town!

Donna enlists Maddy in a plan to lift Laura's diary.

Jean Renault demands ransom for Audrey, kills Battis.

Anyone up for pie?   *Photo by Pieter Dom*

Josie returns from Seattle. Jonathan tells her Mr. Eckhardt wants her back in Hong Kong now that her work in Twin Peaks is complete.

March 7 (Tuesday)

Cooper finally finds Audrey's note saying she is going to One Eyed Jacks.
Leland has hearing, is released.
Tojamura offers Ben phony $5 million check for Ghostwood Estates.
Cooper, Truman, and Hawk rescue Audrey.
Jean Renault kills Blackie.
Maddy and Donna are caught by Harold, but rescued by James, though they are forced to leave the diary behind.

March 8 (Wednesday)

Leo comes home.
Donna tells Truman about the secret diary.
David Lynch makes his first on-screen appearance, as FBI Bureau Chief Gordon Cole.
Maddy tells James she is leaving tomorrow.
Coop gets Earle's first chess move.
Harold Smith hangs himself.
One-Armed Man questioned, reveals information about Bob.

March 9 (Thursday)

Gordon Cole leaves for Bend, Oregon—"hush, hush mission."
Cooper and Truman take Mike to the Great Northern to look for Bob; lots of bouncing balls, but no Bob.
Hawk finds Harold Smith hanging from the rafters of his greenhouse, plus the secret diary.
Maddy tells Leland and Sarah she is leaving.
Audrey confronts her dad about Laura and One Eyed Jacks. He admits sleeping with Laura and says he loved her.
Cooper and Truman take Ben Horne in for questioning.
Log Lady tells Cooper there are owls in the Roadhouse.
"It is happening again," the Giant tells Cooper.
Sarah sees the white horse again.
Leland/Bob kills Maddy, puts an O beneath her fingernail.

March 10 (Friday)

Ben and Jerry flashback: Louise Dombrowksi flashlight dance!
Leland learns of Ben's arrest.
Vivian and Ernie Niles arrive in Twin Peaks.
Pete delivers Catherine's message to Ben.

Ben is officially charged with Laura's murder.

Maddy's body found.

March 11 (Saturday)

Albert returns, linking Maddy's murderer to Laura's.

The new Mrs. Tremond hands Donna a missing page from Laura's diary; Cooper and Laura shared the same dream.

Tojamura reveals him/herself to Ben, bribes him into turning over the mill and Ghostwood.

Donna shares the news with James that Maddy is dead.

Cooper assembles the suspects at the Roadhouse; the Giant returns his ring.

Captured, Leland/Bob confesses to murdering Laura.

Leland dies; Bob escapes.

Cooper and the guys wonder: What *is* Bob?

March 12 (Sunday)

Nothing

March 13 (Monday)

Nothing

March 14 (Tuesday)

Nothing

March 15 (Wednesday)

Leland buried.

Coop suspended.

M. T. Wentz revealed: Vivian Niles; Norma kicks her out of her restaurant and her life.

Ernie and Hank meet with Jean Renault.

Josie returns.

Major Briggs abducted.

March 16 (Thursday)

James meets Evelyn Marsh, who takes him home.

The gang meets Little Nicky.

Hawk fills Cooper in on the Lodges.

Dennis/Denise Bryson arrives in town.

Ben watches home movies.

Cooper hears from Windom Earle.

Lana and Dougie Milford wed.

Josie begs for mercy from Catherine, who takes her back as her maid.

Andrew Packard lives!

March 17 (Friday)

Cooper checks out Dead Dog Farm.

Dougie Milford dies.

Ben has a nervous breakdown, involving Civil War delusions.

Under pressure, Ernie Niles agrees to help Cooper and Bryson bring down Jean Renault.

Major Briggs returns.

March 18 (Saturday)

Harry deputizes Cooper.

Nadine beats up Hank.

Cooper kills Jean Renault.

Leo's awake. Shelly stabs him. Leo escapes into the woods.

Earle takes a pawn.

Blackout.

March 19 (Sunday)

Cooper cleared of drug charges.

Jeffrey Marsh dies.

Cooper shares details of the Pittsburgh tragedy with Harry.

Eckhardt and Jones check into the Great Northern.

Donna tracks down James, helps him escape.

Leo meets Windom Earle.

March 20 (Monday)

Dixie!

Ben (finally!) comes to his senses.

Evelyn kills Malcolm Sloan.

Cooper hears from Earle.

March 21 (Tuesday)

John Justice Wheeler arrives in town, captivates Audrey.

Earle draws Donna, Audrey, and Shelly to the Roadhouse.

Exit James.

Josie dies, winds up a wooden knob on a nightstand.

March 22 (Wednesday)

Annie Blackburne arrives in town, captivates Cooper.

Donna spies an intimate moment between Ben and her mom.

The Log Lady and Major Briggs bond over symbols.

Fashion show debacle.

Jones delivers puzzle-box present from Eckhardt to Catherine, tries to kill Harry.

March 23 (Thursday)

Gordon Cole returns, with news that Earle once worked on Project Blue Book. Digs Shelly.

Donna and Audrey spy on Ben and Eileen Hayward.

Cooper, Truman, and the gang go spelunking in Owl Cave.

Earle discovers petroglyph.

March 24 (Friday)

Cooper and company return to Owl Cave, find petroglyph.

Windom Earle kills a headbanger inside a giant papier-mâché chess piece that he later leaves in a crate at the gazebo with the message "Next time it will be someone you know."

Coop kisses Annie; Cole kisses Shelly, then leaves.

March 25 (Saturday)

Donna tracks down her birth certificate; no father listed.

Cooper assembles Donna, Audrey, Shelly at the sheriff's station to talk about Windom Earle.

Major Briggs finds out that Earle's stint at Project Blue Book didn't go so well.

Donna times three, one for each "You're my daddy!"   *Photo by Richard Beymer*

Earle abducts, drugs, tortures Briggs.

Coop, Pete, others get the shakes.

Jack deflowers Audrey, leaves for Brazil. Audrey and Pete go fishing.

Annie decides to enter Miss Twin Peaks pageant.

"No, no," Giant warns Coop.

Earle deduces that petroglyph is a map to the Black Lodge.

Bob is back! At Glastonbury Grove.

March 26 (Easter Sunday)

Leo frees Major Briggs. Save Shelly!

Bedtime for Annie and Cooper.

Andrew shoots Eckhardt's box open and finds a key inside.

Cooper deduces that the Black Lodge opens during the conjunction of Jupiter and Saturn.

Andy knocks over a bonsai, revealing Windom Earle's bug.

Lucy wants Andy to be the father of her baby.

Annie, crowned Miss Twin Peaks, is abducted by Earle.

Annie, Earle, Cooper enter the Black Lodge via Glastonbury Grove.

Nadine regains her memory (bad news for Mike).

Unfortunate "You're my daddy!" outburst from Donna.

Doc Hayward punches Ben Horne, who hits his head against the fireplace.

March 27 (Monday)

Civil disobedience! Audrey chains herself to the vault at Twin Peaks Savings and Loan, to protest bank's ties to Ghostwood development.

Andrew and Pete, in search of Thomas Eckhardt's parting gift, track down safety deposit box at bank; bomb goes off.

At Double R, Sarah delivers message to Major Briggs: "I'm in the Black Lodge with Dale Cooper."

Bob kills Windom Earle, possesses Cooper's evil half.

Cooper/Bob and Annie resurface at Glastonbury Grove.

March 28 (Tuesday)

"How's Annie?"

19

I Have No Idea Where This Will Lead Us

A *Twin Peaks* Episode Guide

There are clues everywhere—all around us. But the puzzle-maker is clever.

Speaking of puzzles, referencing *Twin Peaks* episodes by number is—surprise!—tricky. Lynch/Frost Productions employed its own numbering system, which differs from the sequencing used on numerous popular websites, like Netflix. The Lynch/Frost method designates the two-hour premiere (airing on Sunday, April 8, 1990) not as episode one, but as the pilot, and the first one-hour installment, airing four days later, on Thursday, April 12, as episode one. Unofficially, the pilot often appears as episode one, and the first one-hour installment as episode two. Yet another numbering system lists the pilot as episode #1000, the first hour-long installment as #1001, and so on. Under this system, the second-season premiere appears as episode #2001, and the two-hour series finale as #2021 (or the twenty-first episode of the second season, which is actually two episodes cobbled together).

So why not simply dispense with all this numerical nonsense and simply refer to episode titles only? Here's why: Lynch/Frost never used episode titles. The designations you find on sites like Netflix, Wikipedia, and Amazon are English-language translations of the titles invented for the German telecasts. Hence, these titles are unofficial, and *Twin Peaks* purists are loath to use them.

Our compromise is to use the Lynch/Frost numeric designations, but to include titles as well, to avoid any confusion.

Just sayin'.

Season One

The Pilot ("Northwest Passage")

Aired: Sunday, April 8, 1990
Twin Peaks Time: Friday–Saturday, February 24–25, 1989
Written by Mark Frost + David Lynch. Directed by David Lynch.
Rating: The best. 10 out of 10 damn fine slices of pie. 🥧🥧🥧🥧🥧🥧🥧🥧🥧🥧

If trivia's your thing, look for Lucy Moran's (Kimmy Robertson) name in the end credits: it appears as Lucy Morgan.

Out fishing, Pete Martell spots a woman's body washed up on shore at Black Lake. Pete, a sensible guy, does what any sensible guy *would* do: he rings up local law enforcement, in this case Sheriff Harry S. Truman, telling him, "She's dead. Wrapped in plastic." Three of the most famous words ever spoken on *Twin Peaks*, and we're only five minutes in.

Harry rounds up the team, including Doc Hayward and Deputy Andy Brennan, who converge at the lake. Andy's supposed to shoot photos, but he's a sensitive guy and can't stop crying at the site of the lifeless body. Harry and Doc flip the corpse over and clear away the plastic: good God, it's young Laura Palmer.

Meanwhile, over at the Palmer abode, Laura's mom Sarah attempts to summon her daughter downstairs for breakfast, so as not to be late for

Sob Story: Deputy Andy Brennan cries . . . a lot . . . including here at the site of Laura's murder.

school. No luck there. Sarah treks up the stairs to Laura's bedroom, but still no sign of Laura. Getting angsty, she checks in with Beth Briggs (full name Elizabeth, and known as Betty in every subsequent episode), the mother of Laura's boyfriend Bobby, and also with her own husband, Leland, in-house counsel to local nabob Benjamin Horne, owner of the Great Northern hotel. Neither, however, has any clue as to Laura's whereabouts. Leland takes the call in the hotel lobby, his back to the glass door, so he doesn't see Sheriff Truman pulling up in his squad car. We do. This Lynch fella knows something about directing, huh? Slowly it dawns on Leland that Harry is there to see him, and the news isn't good. On the other end of the telephone line, Sarah emits a gut-wrenching scream.

Whither Bobby Briggs? Double-timing Laura at the Double R diner, that's whither. The object of his affection is lithesome waitress Shelly Johnson. Never mind that Shelly is married to a trucker named Leo, who's supposed to be in Butte, Montana, but clearly isn't, judging by the presence of his truck outside the Johnson residence as Bobby and Shelly approach. Bobby skedaddles.

At Twin Peaks High School, Ben Horne's daughter Audrey switches from saddle shoes to red heels while sneaking a cigarette at her locker, which may seem insignificant but is nevertheless unforgettable, even without all the symbolism attached (young woman straddling the line between

Shelly Johnson and Bobby Briggs: just a couple of crazy kids in love.

adolescence and adulthood). Sensitive biker James Hurley, Laura's other, secret boyfriend, drops by the locker of Donna Hayward, Laura's best friend, looking for LP, but Donna too hasn't a clue. Ominously, deputies are everywhere; we spot them traversing the hallways, and when one asks to speak privately to Laura's homeroom teacher, Donna sees a female student scampering across the schoolyard screaming at the top of her lungs. One by one people turn their gaze to Laura's empty chair, and before you know it Donna is sobbing. Bobby finally shows up at school, where everyone seems to be looking for him, including Sheriff Truman, who shares the news that Laura's dead. Bobby can't believe he's a suspect. Principal Wolchezk barely gets through the announcement over the public-address system before he too breaks down. Music ("Laura's Theme") swells; cut to the famous framed photo of Laura as homecoming queen in the high school trophy case.

No rest for the weary: Sheriff Truman's next stop is the Palmer home, where he interviews a sedated Sarah, who last saw Laura the night before at approximately 9, after she returned from Bobby's and headed up to her room. Deputy Hawk finds a diary and a camcorder, taking both into possession as evidence. Laura's phone rang once after 9, says Sarah. Receptionist Lucy Moran calls from the sheriff's station to report that another Twin Peaks teen, Ronette Pulaski (known here as Ronnette, though Ronette on every other occasion), also didn't come home last night and has been reported missing by her parents.

At the Packard mill, Josie Packard and Catherine Martell (Pete's wife, known here at Katherine, with a K, but in every other episode as Catherine) lock horns; Josie wants to close up shop for the day in deference to Laura and to Ronette, whose father is a Packard mill employee, but Catherine is adamantly opposed (all about the money, honey). Josie, widow of the mill's previous owner, Andrew Packard (Catherine's brother), wins when Pete follows her wishes.

Ronette isn't missing for long; she turns up walking across a bridge ("Ronette's Bridge," as fans call it) on her way back into Twin Peaks, wearing only a white slip smeared with blood, in a severe state of discombobulation.

James drops by Big Ed's Gas Farm, run by his Uncle Ed, who's in love with Double R diner proprietor Norma Jennings but married to a patch-wearing crazy lady named Nadine, who's obsessed with silent drapes. We wish Nadine would be silent. James leaves a note for Donna, asking her to meet him at the Bang Bang Bar, a local dive known among locals as the Roadhouse, later than night.

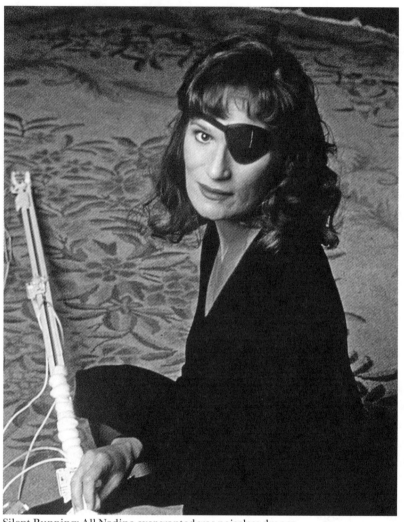

Silent Running: All Nadine ever wanted was noiseless drapes.

Here cometh our protagonist, FBI Special Agent Dale Cooper, who's dispatched to Twin Peaks to head up the investigation, for two reasons:

One, Ronette Pulaski at some point stepped out over the state line, making this a multijurisdictional case.

Two, Laura's murder, as we'll soon learn, bears certain striking resemblances to the death of another young woman, Teresa Banks, about a year earlier in a town called Dear Meadow, Washington, a case with which Cooper was somehow involved (for more on the Banks investigation, see the chapter on *Twin Peaks: Fire Walk with Me*).

Cooper approaches Twin Peaks in a rented sedan, chattering away in his stream-of-consciousness style about everything from the weather to the trees to the tuna fish sandwich he had for lunch, speaking into his omnipresent mini-tape-recorder and addressing his remarks to someone named Diane.

He and Harry hit it off famously, and proceed to Calhoun Memorial Hospital, where they are told that Ronette was raped multiple times and is currently in shock and unavailable for questioning. The lawmen share an elevator with a strange one-armed man, then encounter a possibly even stranger two-armed man named Dr. Lawrence Jacoby, town shrink, whose patients included Laura Palmer. From there it's on to the morgue, where Cooper plucks a little piece of white paper with the letter "R" on it from under Laura's left ring finger. "It's the same thing," Cooper says to Diane. "I told you I had a feeling we'd see this again." Throughout the morgue scene the fluorescent lights flicker overhead, which, as ardent *Twin Peaks* fans know by now, was not called for in the script, but happened by chance, and Lynch liked the effect so much he issued instructions not to fix it (he actually wound up flicking the lights on and off himself manually to duplicate the effect, according to reports).

Cooper pries Laura's diary open and discovers that the final entry is dated February 23, the eve of her death. "Nervous about meeting J tonight," she wrote. Cooper flips back eighteen days to day one; taped to the page is a plastic envelope with the remnants of a white powdery substance, plus what looks to be a key from a safety deposit box. Cooper suspects the residue is coke, but Harry is incredulous. "You didn't know Laura Palmer," he says. That's what he thinks! The deputies locate the abandoned train car where Laura was killed, which naturally has Andy crying again, and who can blame him? Harry and Cooper give Bobby the third degree; he tells them Laura was studying at his house until about 9:30 the previous night, but then drove herself home, and that was the last he saw of her. Cooper slips Truman a note that says, "He did not do it," and they let Bobby go.

Mischievous Audrey Horne directly disobeys Daddy's orders by sharing news of Laura's murder with a group of Norwegians who are on the verge of investing huge sums of money in Ben's Ghostwood development project, but who can't get out of town fast enough after hearing about Laura. Bobby and good buddy Mike "Snake" Nelson plot to beat up James for his dalliance with Laura.

Next on the hot seat: Donna, whom Cooper and Truman interrogate while screening the video from the camcorder Hawk found in Laura's room, which shows Laura and Donna picnicking somewhere up in the mountains,

Audrey Horne contemplates mischief, wears the hell out of that sweater.

and having a swell time of it. Cooper wants to know who's doing the taping; Donna is cagey, and claims it was just a stranger passing by, but she's way out of her league, because Cooper's already got it figured out, having spotted the reflection of a motorcycle in Laura's iris and therefore deducing that the third member of their group was a biker.

Cooper and Harry take a road trip to the derelict train car, where they find a gold necklace with a heart pendant that's been snapped in half, as well as a torn piece of newsprint on which written in blood are the words "Fire walk with me." Cooper wants to know who has the other half of that pendant.

Over at the Hornes, Audrey is sitting at the dining room table with her mom, Sylvia, while nearby her emotionally handicapped twenty-seven-year-old brother Johnny, who's wearing an Indian headdress, bangs his head against a toy house repeatedly, upset that Laura isn't coming over to keep him company, which is something she apparently did on a regular basis.

Harry and Coop excavate the contents of Laura's safety deposit box over at the bank, where a severed buck's head adorns the conference-room table, for no other reason than that it fell off the wall and no one has gotten around to replacing it. More significant is what they find inside the box: $10,000 in cash and one issue of a rag unambiguously titled *Flesh World*, which includes a photo of Ronette Pulaski within the classifieds, plus a snapshot of Leo Johnson's truck, though Cooper and Harry don't know enough yet to make that connection.

Speaking of Leo, the greasy-haired, ponytailed trucker demands an explanation from Shelly as to why there are two different brands of cigarette butts in the ashtray at their abode. If he ever sees two different brands of cigarette butts in their abode again, he is going to snap her neck like a twig, he tells her. Prince of a guy, Leo. Norma calls Big Ed at the gas farm and says she *needs* to see him; they plan to meet later at the Roadhouse. We suspect something is brewing at the Roadhouse, as everyone seems to be headed there.

Concerned for the safety of the young women of Twin Peaks, Cooper hastily arranges a town meeting and, while waiting for it to begin, gets a crash course from Truman on some of the more distinctive townsfolk, including the Log Lady, so called because she carries around a stump of ponderosa pine wherever she goes. The Log Lady is first glimpsed turning the lights on and off in an attempt to bring the meeting to order, evoking the morgue scene from earlier in the episode and foreshadowing the strobe lights that will play so crucial a role in the so-called Red Room sequences beginning in episode two.

Cooper tells the assembled crowd that a year earlier almost to the day, in the southwest corner of the state, the body of a young drifter named Teresa Banks was found. There are "irrefutable similarities" between the two deaths, leading Cooper to suspect that Laura and Teresa were victims of the same killer.

Later that night, Donna overhears Pops—Doc Hayward, that is—commenting that Cooper and Truman believe that whoever possesses the missing half of the necklace is the killer. She sneaks out to meet James at the Roadhouse. Mike, who apparently was very recently Donna's boyfriend and thinks he still is, shows up at the Haywards looking for her, along with Bobby, who is grossly intoxicated. "Don't take any oink oink off that pretty pig," Bobby tells Mike, which strikes us as a pretty weird thing for anyone to say, but can be accounted for by the fact that the network nixed the original comment, which was, "Don't take any more crap from that pretty bitch."

Coop and Harry stake out the Roadhouse, waiting for their biker to show. Inside, Norma tells Big Ed she's leaving her husband, Hank Jennings, who's serving time in prison for manslaughter. Julee Cruise sings "Falling." A huge brawl breaks out between the bikers and the jocks when Mike tries to manhandle Donna, and James's biker friend Joey slips Donna out of the Roadhouse and into the woods, where she meets up with James, who is on edge because he doesn't have an alibi for the night of Laura's death. Actually, he was with Laura for part of the night, an experience he characterizes as "kind of like a nightmare" (dream references are common in *Twin Peaks*), since half the time Laura "wasn't making any sense" and no matter what he did James couldn't calm her down. Finally, when they pulled up at the stoplight at Sparkwood and 21 after midnight, Laura hopped off the back of James's bike, screamed that she loved him, and scurried off into the woods. Before you know it, Donna and James are locking lips. Turns out James has the missing half of the necklace, and he and Donna decide to bury it right there in the woods.

On the way back into town, James is taken into custody for questioning. He's placed in a jail cell downstairs at the sheriff's station, within eyesight of Bobby and Mike, who inexplicably feel a compulsion to start barking like dogs.

Harry, that sly dog, pays a late-night visit to Blue Pine Lodge to see Josie, and let's just say it has nothing to do with police business. Catherine Martell and Ben Horne, both married to other people, arrange a tryst of their own.

Sarah Palmer awakes screaming from a vision in which a gloved hand digs up the necklace that James and Donna have buried in the woods (note Bob's very briefly glimpsed reflection in the mirror above Sarah's head—a production gaffe that Lynch liked so much he decided not to excise; for more on this, see the segment on Bob in Chapter 11). As if her day hasn't been bad enough already.

End pilot—American version, that is.

Doing the Continental (or the European Version of the *Twin Peaks* Pilot)

In reeling in financial backing for Twin Peaks, David Lynch and Mark Frost contracted to produce a closed-end version of the pilot for the European home-video market, offering one solution at least to the mystery of who killed Laura Palmer. While at variance with the resolution eventually revealed in the series, this eighteen-minute appendage forges crucial elements of *Twin Peaks* mythology, establishing Bob as the killer (though without establishing any connection to Leland Palmer) and the One-Armed Man (Mike) as his nemesis, and also introducing the Red Room and all of its esotericism, including the Man from Another Place (the "dancing dwarf") and the aberrant dialect spoken within its red curtains (the characters actually articulate their lines backward, but the film is reverse-printed, so that they come out sounding somewhat intelligible, yet still odd enough to benefit from subtitling). Lynch has estimated that 50 percent of *Twin Peaks* as it evolved was created because of the financial commitment to produce the closed ending for Europe.

Scenes from this ending were eventually repositioned for Cooper's Red Room dream in episode two, though not all of it, resulting in one of the more famous quirks of the series: when Cooper recounts his dream for Lucy and Sheriff Truman the following morning, he includes scenes that appear in the European ending but not in the dream as viewers of the previous episode just witnessed it.

By all accounts, Lynch and Frost didn't spend much time pondering this deus ex machina until zero hour approached, at which point they had to do some pretty quick thinking. Lynch has acknowledged that he initially forgot about the commitment and was just "winging it" at first. Al Strobel, who portrayed the One-Armed Man, told the *Twin Peaks* fanzine *Wrapped in Plastic* that he had no advance knowledge of the alternate ending, but was asked by Lynch to stay on for a few days after the U.S. version wrapped. Lynch handed him a two-page monologue, including the famous "Fire walk with me" poem, recited for the first time here.

Here's a closer look at the European ending:

Following the shot of the red stoplight at Sparkwood and 21, we cut to Sarah Palmer, asleep on the living room couch, like in the American iteration. In the ABC-TV version, Sarah wakes with a fright after experiencing a vision in which a gloved hand (later revealed to be Jacoby's) dislodges a rock in the woods and uncovers James's half of Laura's necklace. The American pilot ends there.

In the European version, Sarah's vision takes her instead inside Laura's bedroom, where she spies Bob crouching at the foot of Laura's bed, and awakes screaming. Leland Palmer shares Sarah's vision with Lucy, who informs Sheriff

Truman (super-weird Lucy-Andy scene here, in Lucy's home, where Lucy bangs away on a wooden paddle ball while Andy blasts out "Taps" on the trumpet, or at least tries to). Deputy Hawk is summoned to the Palmer house to sketch the killer, based on Sarah's description.

Meanwhile, over at the Great Northern, Cooper's sleep (it's 2:30 a.m.; why wouldn't he be sleeping?) is interrupted by a call from the One-Armed Man, whom he has never officially met, though he and Truman did share an elevator ride with him at Calhoun Memorial Hospital earlier in the pilot. Mike tells Cooper he knows who killed Teresa Banks, and "there's more I think you'd enjoy hearing." They agree to rendezvous at the hospital. (Note: The One-Armed Man also volunteers that he knows about "the stitches with the red thread"—a comment never explained here, in the series, or in *Fire Walk with Me*, and thus another in a long line of unanswered *Twin Peaks* mysteries. Unknown is whether this comment is related in any way to the One-Armed Man's rant at Leland in *FWWM*, "The thread will be torn, Mr. Palmer! The thread will be torn!")

Next, Cooper gets a call from Lucy, filling him in on the goings-on over at the Palmer abode. Cooper's pumped, sensing resolution is near; he instructs Lucy to tell Truman to grab the sketch from Hawk as soon as possible and meet up with him at the hospital. The One-Armed Man, waiting for them in a dark room, recites the "Fire walk with me" poem, then launches into his "convenience store" recollection, also later repositioned for the series. There's some unfamiliar dialogue here, about Bob's affection for hospitals, since he preys on the infirmed, but also more repositioned commentary, about how Mike used to hang with Mike, until he "saw the face of God" and severed his entire left arm. Mike tells Cooper and Truman Bob is "right here. He's downstairs in the basement."

Next, Cooper and Truman confront Bob, in a room with a ring of twelve burning candles (evocative of the twelve sycamore trees encircling Glastonbury Grove). Truman asks what the letters under the fingernails are meant to spell, and Bob replies, "Robert, that's my proper name" (in the TV series, it is Cooper who deduces this, but not for many episodes). At this point Mike appears, fatally shooting Bob, then crying out in pain himself while sinking to the floor, suggesting some weird sort of symbiosis. "You got a nickel," he says. "It hurts something terrible! Well, you took your turn, Bob!"

"Make a wish," says Cooper, and all of the candles blow out. The scene ends; fade up on a shot of the older Cooper in the Red Room, with the caption "TWENTY-FIVE YEARS LATER" (this caption is missing from the U.S. version, though in the series finale, Laura tells Cooper, "I'll see you again in twenty-five years"). Everything from here on is virtually, though not completely, identical to the series version of the Red Room sequence, though it's worth noting that unlike the American iteration, the European version of the Red Room sequence is never explicitly presented as a dream.

Variations (I)

Fifteen differences between the original version of the pilot and the one that aired:

1. Original title was *Northwest Passage*.
2. Catherine Martell was Katherine Martell.
3. Josie Packard was Giovanna Pasqualini Packard, whom Andrew met in Italy, not Hong Kong; was originally to be portrayed by Isabella Rossellini (David Lynch's then-girlfriend), forced to bow out due to modeling commitments to Lancôme.
4. Sheriff Harry S. Truman was Sheriff Dan Steadman (too similar to *thirtysomething*'s Michael Steadman?).
5. One of the most famous lines of the series—"Wrapped in plastic," delivered by Pete Martell to describe Laura's corpse at Black Lake in the aired pilot— never appears in the original script.
6. The Norwegians pulled out of Ghostwood, and Twin Peaks, not because Audrey Horne tells them about Laura's murder, but because they saw it on the news (in fact, Audrey Horne doesn't have a single line in the original script, and appears, silently, in just two scenes).
7. Deputy Hawk, a Native American, was Deputy Bernie Hill, an African American.
8. Ronette Pulaski was Sharon Pulaski.
9. Douglas firs were ponderosa pines, as in the Log Lady's log (and also, reportedly, the subject of a PhD thesis once upon a time by Lynch's dad, a research scientist for the U.S. Forest Service).
10. Originally, events unfolded in November rather than February; Laura was killed on November 14 rather than February 24.
11. Laura was murdered inside a cave, rather than a derelict train car.
12. *Flesh World* was *Sex Toys*.
13. "Don't you take any oink oink off that pretty pig," Bobby's line to Mike (about Donna), was originally "Don't take any more crap from that pretty bitch" (network intervention).
14. No Dr. Jacoby (while an unidentified gloved hand does dig up James's half of the necklace at the end, it was not identified as Sarah's vision).
15. Unbelievably, no Log Lady!

Episode 1 ("Traces to Nowhere")

Aired: Thursday, April 12, 1990
Twin Peaks Time: Saturday, February 25, 1989
Written by Mark Frost + David Lynch. Directed by Duwayne Dunham.
Rating: Still hummin'.
9 out of 10 damn fine slices of pie. 🥧🥧🥧🥧🥧🥧🥧🥧🥧◳

Cooper swills his first "damn fine" cup of coffee at the Great Northern, joined by Audrey Horne as he orders eggs over hard, super-crispy bacon, and freshly squeezed grapefruit juice, precipitating a sight gag centering on Audrey's breasts. Next, Coop heads over to the sheriff's station for Doc Hayward's autopsy report: Laura died between midnight and 4:00 a.m. on Friday from a loss of blood, facilitated by multiple shallow wounds. She had bite marks on her shoulders and tongue, the latter likely self-inflicted, plus lesions on her wrists, ankles, and upper arms, all likely areas of binding. Drug report: pending, but within the last twelve hours of her life Laura had had sex with at least three different men. Poor old Doc Hayward aches just saying it aloud.

Over at the Johnson abode, Shelly discovers a bloody shirt in Leo's laundry, and hides it.

Cooper and Truman pump James for info, with some success: James reveals that Laura had briefly conquered her coke habit, but resumed shortly before her death because she was spooked by someone or something she wouldn't reveal to him. On the eve of her death (meaning Thursday), Laura snuck out of her house at 9:30 to meet up with James; three hours later he stopped his bike at the intersection of Sparkwood and 21, site of the famous Twin Peaks stoplight; Laura hopped off and disappeared into the woods, never to be seen by James again. The guilt is killing him, but then again when *isn't* James tormented?

Mike and Bobby, not so much. They're still locked up at the sheriff's station, but that might be a blessing, since they owe Leo $10,000 (reasons unspecified for now) and the cash is stashed away in Laura's safety deposit box at the bank, which they have no access to.

Something strange happens here: We see video of Laura and Donna at the picnic, freezing on a close-up of Laura, who says "Help me," though her lips never move and we have no idea who's playing the video or who's watching it or how Laura can be talking to us when the video is frozen and she has been dead for two days. Spook-y!

Like James, Donna is tormented: she *should* be sad, and she is sad, but she's also happy, because she has come to the realization that all that time she, Laura, and James were hanging out together during Laura's secret romance with James it was really she and James who were falling in love, which was a betrayal of Laura, wasn't it? Teen life is so complicated. "It's like I'm having the most beautiful dream and the most terrible nightmare all at once," Donna tells her mom. Welcome to *Twin Peaks*.

Nadine is obsessed with inventing the world's first completely noiseless drape runner.

Cooper and Truman pay Josie a visit at Blue Pine Lodge, where Cooper tells Pete he takes his coffee "black as midnight on a moonless night." "Pretty black," says Pete. The mood sours all around when Pete discovers a fish in the percolator. To Harry's astonishment, Coop intuits that he and Josie are romantically entwined ("body language," Cooper explains).

Here's what pillow talk between Catherine Martell and Ben Horne sounds like: she's impatient waiting for the Packard mill to go bankrupt; he suggests arson. Sweet couple, no?

Donna checks in on Sarah Palmer, who freaks everybody out with another of her visions, this one of a creepy-looking guy with flowing gray hair crouching at the foot of Laura's bed. We're not sure which is spookier: this or the superimposition of Laura's face onto Donna's body, which Sarah also sees.

Sitting vigil outside their daughter's hospital room, the Pulaskis tell Hawk that Ronette peddled perfume at Horne's department store on weekdays after school, so they weren't surprised that she didn't come home after school on Thursday afternoon. Hawk's distracted by the One-Armed Man, who's snooping around the ICU, but he loses him in the stairwell, which is unusual because Hawk hardly ever loses sight of anyone.

Back at the Great Northern, Audrey admits to Pops that she deliberately scared off the Norwegians before they could commit to the Ghostwood project by sharing news of Laura's brutal murder. Ben is unamused, threatening to pack her off to a Bulgarian convent if she ever pulls a stunt like that again.

Things are equally unpleasant at the Briggses, where the major slaps Bobby across the face for popping in a cigarette during a lecture on rebelliousness. The offending butt lands smack in the middle of Mrs. Briggs's meatloaf.

At the Double R, Coop has his first slice of Double R cherry pie (huge episode for Coop, culinarily speaking). Norma informs the boys that Laura not only assisted her with Meals on Wheels, but actually organized it herself.

The Log Lady tells Cooper her log "saw something" on the night of Laura's murder, but when he hesitates to follow up with the log directly, she walks out in a huff, lugging the ponderosa pine with her.

Leo slips a bar of soap into a sock and prepares to smack Shelly around when she tells him she has no idea where his shirt is.

James dines with the Haywards.

Oh, and that missing necklace that Donna and James buried in the woods in the pilot, and then was dug up by someone's gloved hands? That would be Dr. Jacoby, Laura's shrink. We know this because we witness him fondling the necklace while listening to an audiotape Laura made for him on February 23, on which she tearfully refers to James as sweet but dumb, says she knows "I'm going to get lost in those woods again tonight," and makes an obscure reference to a "mystery man" whom she apparently had told Jacoby about at least once before. The whole thing is too much for the mad doctor, who breaks down and cries like a baby.

The Mad Dr. Jacoby wasn't in the original version of the pilot or the final episode.

Episode 2 ("Zen, or the Skill to Catch a Killer")

Aired: Thursday, April 19, 1990
Twin Peaks Time: Saturday–Sunday, February 25–26, 1989
Written by Mark Frost + David Lynch. Directed by David Lynch.
Rating: Dreamy.
      10 out of 10 damn fine slices of pie. 🥧🥧🥧🥧🥧🥧🥧🥧🥧🥧

David Patrick Kelly bows as Ben Horne's depraved brother/business partner Jerry (Ben & Jerry, get it?), and Miguel Ferrer as FBI Special Agent Albert Rosenfield, master of mordancy.

Jerry Horne returns from Paris with succulent gifts—"the best damn sandwich I ever ate" (brie and butter on baguette)—nearly triggering an orgasm from Ben as he scarfs one down. Still, so much bad news to share! Jerry is seriously bummed by word of the Norwegian exodus, plus that nasty little business aboutLaura Palmer, so Ben arranges a jaunt to One Eyed Jacks, a casino/brothel located just north of the Canadian border, where they flip a coin to see who gets to play with the new girl (Ben, natch).

James and Donna make out on the Haywards' living-room couch, guilt being no match for teen hormones.

Back at the hotel, Cooper fields a call from Hawk, who tells him about the one-armed man roaming the hospital hallway, but when Cooper asks what Hawk learned from the Pulaskis, the deputy replies that Ronette had recently quit her day job, at Horne's department store, which is curious because the Pulaskis had specifically told Hawk they assumed they didn't see Ronette Thursday after school because she had gone straight to work. Never mind. Coop answers a knock at the door; no one's there, though he does find a note saying, "Jack with One Eye." Lovely handwriting.

Bobby and Mike drive deep into the woods to consummate a drug deal with Leo, who's toting a shotgun and a lousy attitude because 1) they still owe him ten grand, and 2) he's convinced Shelly is two-timing him right in their own home (though twice he ignores Bobby when he asks if Leo has any idea who the culprit is). Hey, who's that masked man hiding over by the tree? Bobby sees him, Mike sees him, we see him. Leo may or may not see him, but tells Bobby "never mind" when he asks about it.

So ends Saturday.

On to Sunday: Ed accidentally drips grease onto Nadine's cotton balls, which infuriates her, because, really, what good are greasy cotton balls?

Plenty, as it turns out: greasy cotton balls are the secret ingredient to 100 percent noiseless drape runners, making Nadine a very happy woman.

Cooper assembles Harry and the gang in the woods to school them on the Tibetan rock throw, a deductive technique "involving mind-body coordination operating hand and hand with the deepest level of intuition," which came to him in a dream (it's a doozy, all right, but nothing compared with the one coming up). Essentially this involves tossing a rock at a glass bottle situated sixty feet, six inches away while someone—in this case Truman— pronounces the names of each of the suspects, and then recording any significant outcomes. In this case the significant outcomes are as follows: Cooper hits the bottle when Harry says "Dr. Jacoby" and breaks the bottle when Harry says "Leo Johnson." He also accidentally hits Andy in the head with a rock, but this does not strike anyone as nearly as significant.

Invitation to Love, the faux soap opera *Twin Peaks* characters are periodically observed viewing, makes its debut, watched here by Shelly Johnson, who is visited by Bobby, who is infuriated by the bruises on her face. This would appear to be a continuity error, since daytime soaps don't typically air on Sundays.

Donna and her folks—what happened to Harriet?—drop by the Double R after church, as does Audrey, who can't stop thinking about Agent Cooper, who presumably is in her thoughts as she dances dreamily by herself on the diner floor.

Too dreamy . . . Audrey Horne.

Cooper and Truman search for clues along the railroad tracks, near the scene of Laura's murder.

Harry shows Cooper a bloody white towel that Hawk found half a mile down the tracks from the derelict train car where Laura was murdered.

FBI Special Agent Albert Rosenfield arrives, quickly alienating everyone (except viewers) with his blistering wisecracks, most of which are directed at this "sinkhole" of a town and the "bumpkins" who inhabit it. Albert is a brilliant forensic scientist who lacks "in some of the social niceties," as Cooper so politely explains to Truman just before playfully pinching the sheriff's nose, in a completely anomalous moment for both of them. Translation: Albert is a bastard, yet so fun.

At Blue Pine Lodge, Pete slips Josie a key to Catherine's "secret" safe, where she discovers two sets of ledgers for the mill. So much duality!

Meanwhile, Leland and Sarah teeter on the brink of madness: Leland, clutching a photo of Laura, dances to "Pennsylvania 6-5000"; Sarah attempts to seize the photo from him, but they struggle and the frame breaks, so Leland winds up smearing the photo with blood (unscripted and completely spontaneous).

Now, about that dream: Here we come to Cooper's infamous Red Room dream, so referenced because of the dominant color scheme: the curtains are red, and the dwarf who appears in the dream—the so-called Man from Another Place—is garbed in a red suit. The first image we see is of Cooper himself, but it is an older, wrinkly Cooper who is sitting in a chair. Then we see the back of the head of the Man from Another Place, who is shaking and saying "Laura." Sarah Palmer also appears, as does a woman who looks like Laura, plus the silver-haired man seen crouching by Laura's bed in Sarah's vision from the previous episode and the one-armed man from the hospital, who recites the following line, which one day in the not too distant future will lend the theatrical-film prequel to *Twin Peaks* its name: "Through the darkness of future pasts the magician longs to see. One chants out between two worlds: 'Fire, walk with me!'" These last four words appeared in the pilot, you might recall, on the note discovered in the abandoned train car where Laura was murdered. The One-Armed Man, who identifies himself as Mike, has a lot more to say, mostly about how he and Bob—that silver-maned dude—used to live together above a convenience store and hung out together doing all sorts of nefarious things, but then Mike saw the face of God and was transformed, severing his entire left arm, which apparently

You the Man (from Another Place): Lynch and Michael J. Anderson.

Photo by Richard Beymer

liberated him from his satanic ways. Bob speaks, too, though just briefly, promising to kill again.

The Man from Another Place is chatty in his own way when not dancing, but it's not like we have any idea what any of it means:

> "I've got good news: that gum you like is going to come back in style."
> "She's my cousin, but doesn't she look almost exactly like Laura Palmer?"
> "She's filled with secrets."
> "Where we're from the birds sing a pretty song and there is always music in the air."

At the end of the dream the woman who resembles Laura moseys over to Coop and plants a kiss on his lips—a nice long one—after which she whispers something in his ear that we viewers are not privy to. Immediately upon awakening, Cooper rings up Harry, telling him he knows the identity of Laura's killer, and instructing him to meet him at the hotel restaurant at seven o'clock in the morning.

Yes, it *can* wait till then, Coop says.

Such a tease.

Episode 3 ("Rest in Pain")

Aired: Thursday, April 26, 1990
Twin Peaks Time: Monday, February 27, 1989
Written by Harley Peyton. Directed by Tina Rathborne.
Rating: Mourning becomes electric.
        10 out of 10 damn fine slices of pie. 🥧🥧🥧🥧🥧🥧🥧🥧🥧🥧

Helmer Tina Rathborne had, in 1988, directed a feature film titled *Zelly and Me*, starring Lynch's then-paramour, Isabella Rossellini (who was originally intended to fill the *Twin Peaks* role that eventually mutated into Josie Packard and went to Joan Chen), and featuring Lynch in a minor role.

This is the first script not contributed by Frost and Lynch.

Walter Olkewicz debuts as porcine reprobate Jacques Renault, a crucial player in *Twin Peaks* mythology as things turn out (note that his surname is misspelled Oklewicz in the opening credits). So does Clay Wilcox as Jacques's doomed brother Bernard. Maddy Ferguson, Laura's look-alike cousin, also bows, portrayed, like Laura herself, by Sheryl Lee.

Audrey Horne, who may or may not be stalking Cooper but definitely has a Nancy Drew complex, confesses to having crafted the "Jack with One

Eye" note, and informs the G-man of her salient discovery: Laura, like Ronette, worked the perfume counter at daddy's department store.

Cooper shoos Audrey away and welcomes his next guests, the always entertaining Harry and Lucy, filling them in on the specifics of his dream, and as he does so it occurs to us that the dream we actually saw is only a segment of the dream he is here describing, and this is where a little *Twin Peaks* background comes in handy: in fact Cooper is describing the ending of the European version of the pilot, of which only a small portion is excerpted in the dream scenes we saw at the conclusion of the previous episode (worth noting: the original script for the previous episode contained the entire Euro ending, so at the time the script for this episode was written, Cooper was accurately and fully describing the dream that viewers would have seen).

Whatever he's describing, Cooper buries the lead, which is that he can't remember the identity of the killer as it was whispered to him by Laura Palmer. "Harry, my dream is a code waiting to be broken," Cooper says. "Break the code, solve the crime." Lucy dutifully jots this down, but Harry is bummed.

Still, Cooper *can* recall crucial details from portions of the dream that we never saw, like the fact that the One-Armed Man's name is Mike and that the killer, named Bob, is the silver-haired man Sarah Palmer saw in her vision (yes, we now have two Mike and Bob tandems). Mike had a tattoo on his right arm that said "Fire Walk with Me," but cut off the arm as a ritual of repentance, and when Bob vowed to kill again, the One-Armed Man shot him.

Enough! Cooper and Harry are summoned to the morgue, where Albert is ready to drill a hole in Laura's head—so much to do, so little time!—but Doc Hayward won't allow it, insisting that the body be released for the funeral as is. Harry wallops Albert in the face, and Albert comes in for a crash landing atop Laura. Forced to choose a side, Cooper picks Doc's, which irritates Albert, though honestly it's tough to tell the difference with him.

Harry and Cooper pay a visit to Leo, who lies serially, even claiming he didn't know Laura.

Major Briggs, bless his heart, tries again to connect with Bobby, this time over the funeral, but with similarly disastrous results.

Albert may be a hard-ass, but the guy is good. Here he reports to Cooper that the plastic envelope discovered in Laura's diary contained traces of cocaine, which also turned up in Laura's body during the autopsy (or, in Albert-ese: "The little lady had a habit"). On the night of the murder, Laura was tied up twice, at two different locations, and traces of pumice were found in standing water outside the railroad car—industrial-strength soap, also found on the back of Laura's neck. Conclusion: the killer washed his hands and then leaned in for a kiss. Distinctive wounds found on Laura's neck and shoulders appear to have been claw marks plus bites of some sort. Finally, a small plastic fragment containing the letter J was found inside her stomach, partially dissolved by digestive acids. Who the heck knows what that means?

Cooper refuses to endorse Albert's assault charge against Harry, kvelling about the "decency, honor, and dignity" he has found in Twin Peaks since arriving. Albert takes it in stride, retorting: "Sounds like you've been snacking on some of the local mushrooms."

Laura's funeral is a humdinger: Bobby blows up, lashing out at all the hypocrites who knew Laura was a mess but never did anything about it. He and James nearly come to blows, and Leland leaps onto Laura's casket as it is being lowered into the ground (Ray Wise's idea), shouting and wailing all the while.

Bobby Briggs's outburst disrupts Laura's funeral, nearly triggering a brawl with James Hurley.

Following the funeral, Ed, Hawk, and Harry break bread (or, more accurately, pie) with Cooper over at the Double R, where they chat about a drug bust they've been running for the past six months, targeting Roadhouse bartender Jacques Renault as the middleman in a scheme to run drugs into Twin Peaks from Canada. Harry tells Coop "there's a sort of evil out there, something strange in the hills. It takes different forms, but it's been there for as long as anyone can remember. And we've always been here to fight it." Coop digs this secret-society speak, so they take him over to the Bookhouse Boys' hangout, where James and biker boy Joey are holding Jacques's brother Bernard captive after nabbing him with an ounce of cocaine as he crossed the border. Just about this time Jacques is on his way to the Roadhouse, but reconsiders upon spotting a warning light emanating from the bar, and calls Leo to get him the hell out of Twin Peaks and back to Canada.

Shelly, having had her fill of Leo, brings home a gun.

Josie fears Catherine and Ben Horne are out to get her, warning Harry, "Something horrible is going to happen."

During a nocturnal visit to the cemetery, Coop spies Jacoby placing flowers at Laura's grave; turns out the mad doctor was hopelessly in love with her.

In one of our favorite scenes, Cooper and Hawk ponder the existence of the soul over drinks at the Great Northern, while out on the dance floor Leland searches desperately for a partner, his grief once again overwhelming him. Touched by his despair, Cooper and Hawk gently console him, and offer to escort him home.

In a show with so much brutality, it is such tender moments as these that stay with you forever.

Episode 4 ("The One-Armed Man")

Aired: Thursday, May 3, 1990
Twin Peaks Time: February 28, 1989
Written by Robert Engels. Directed by Tim Hunter.
Rating: The mystery deepens, some funny stuff happens, some sexy stuff also
    happens, and there is a llama.
    7 out of 10 damn fine slices of pie. 🥧🥧🥧🥧🥧🥧🥧▱▱▱

Palmer place: So Andy *is* good for something: his sketch, based on Sarah Palmer's description, is a more than adequate likeness of Bob. A bedraggled

Leland mockingly suggests his wife also describe her vision of Laura's broken necklace, which she does. Her audience seems intrigued.

At the sheriff's, Lucy is catching up on her favorite soap opera, *Invitation to Love*, when Harry enters and asks for an update. She gives a detailed rundown on all of the outré plot twists of her program, and it's a description maybe just three shades more ludicrous than the storyline of *Twin Peaks* itself. Maybe two shades. Critics watching at the time perked up like dogs at the dinner bell, because this meant they could wax on at length about *postmodernism*, a super-hot concept at the time that everyone later got tired of, sort of like *The Real World*. Anyway, Harry wanted a summary of events at the station, duh.

Cooper questions Jacoby, who obliquely references Laura's dark secrets and reveals that he, in the course of his own investigation of her murder, followed a man in a red sports car. Cooper and Harry instantly connect this to Leo. Are Jacoby's mismatched sunglass lenses a subtle nod to the show's preoccupation with duality, or is he just annoying? His smarmy departing patter and extreme golf-focus favor the latter interpretation.

Bureau Chief Cole calls to report that Albert 1) determined the marks on the shoulders of Laura's body were made by a bird and 2) wants Harry thrown off the force. Cooper stalwartly defends his new friend, further endearing himself to the local law.

Josie takes photos, private-eye style, of the motel in which Ben Horne and Catherine Martell are burning up the sheets and making plans for burning down the mill. Hawk, meanwhile, has tracked the One-Armed Man from Cooper's dream to the very same establishment, a few rooms down. Harry and Cooper arrive to brace the man, learning he's a shoe salesman named Gerard (Andy spills his sample case and accidentally discharges his weapon during the visit, to Cooper's hilarious consternation) whose missing arm, lost in a car accident, bore a tattoo reading "Mom." Gerard does in fact know a Bob, a veterinarian. As Ben leaves the motel, he drops a poker chip from One Eyed Jacks, which Catherine finds. Keeping score, that's a One-Armed Man, a One-Eyed Jack, and a half-wit deputy.

At school, Audrey and Donna kibitz in the ladies' room about that dreamy new guy in town and share their information about Laura's secrets, resolving to team up Hardy Boys style to investigate her murder. Audrey is particularly intoxicated by the idea of Laura at One Eyed Jacks—and boy is she headed for a rude awakening on that score—and she tells Donna that both Laura and Ronette Pulaski worked the makeup counter at her father's department store. That's a thread you want to think twice about pulling on, Audrey.

Norma testifies on Hank's behalf at his parole hearing with all the enthusiasm of someone facing root canal. Hank promises to change his ways. If he's working on an incentive plan involving Norma's pies, he might just mean it.

Cooper and Harry visit Bob Lydecker's veterinary clinic (look *real* close and you can see the reflection of a cameraman in the Indian Head ethyl gas pump outside the clinic—don't thank us; that's what we're here for). Lydecker does a bustling and varied business, as evidenced by the llama in the waiting room (according to director Tim Hunter's DVD commentary, Kyle MacLachlan was instructed to put a piece of chewing gum in his mouth, so that the smell would attract the llama's attention, which worked, because he and the llama practically wind up locking lips). Cooper barely acknowledges the beast, as he's interested in another species of patient: birds. Shoulder-nibbling birds, to be exact.

Shelly and Bobby maul each other's faces in Leo's kitchen, but Bobby frets about the man of the house's whereabouts. Shelly tells him not to worry, he's off with his creepy friend Jacques Renault. Bobby postulates that Leo and Jacques are running drugs into Twin Peaks, prompting Shelly to show Bobby Leo's bloody shirt. He's excited about it, but even more excited about Shelly's gun, which she slides seductively over her half-clothed body. Fade to black, damn it.

More gun talk at the sheriff's: While Lucy goes through Lydecker's files, the boys repair to the range to instruct Andy in the proper use of his firearm. Hawk and Harry shoot competently, Andy shoots like Andy (completely missing his target), and Cooper deals hot lead with unearthly precision. Conversation about Andy's romantic troubles with Lucy prompt some philosophical thoughts on women from the group, including Cooper, who alludes to a clearly painful memory of lost love.

At the Double R, Shelly and Norma similarly commiserate about love trouble. They decide to seek catharsis at a spa . . . men have their guns and women have their mud packs, apparently. James is around and doing or saying something, but before he can bore anyone too severely, a stranger enters: a young woman, identical, save her dark hair and enormous spectacles, to Laura Palmer.

She is Maddy Ferguson, Laura's identical cousin (You can lose your mind/When cousins are two of a kind), perhaps the series' clearest iteration yet of its doubling/light-and-dark motif.

Hank is granted parole. Norma reacts like she's been handed a sentence.

Audrey approaches Ben for a father-daughter heart-to-heart. Audrey claims to have turned over a new leaf and wishes to help the family—maybe she could work behind the cosmetics counter at the department store? We know it's a position with excellent opportunities for advancement.

At the sheriff's, the men learn that Laura's bird-inflicted wounds were made by a parrot or a mynah bird—a mynah bird such as Waldo, a patient of Lydecker's belonging to one Jacques Renault. It feels like things are coming together, huh? That's a feeling you should learn to ignore.

Cooper, Harry, and Hawk head to Renault Manor (a seedy apartment), startling Bobby, who appears to be visiting sans invitation. He hops out a window before being discovered. It transpires that Bobby came not to steal, but to donate: Leo's bloody shirt, a piece of evidence of high interest to the investigators. And where is Leo, anyway? Attending a business meeting in the woods with ol' Ben Horne, that's where. *Arson* business.

Donna and James are also in the woods, discussing Sarah Palmer's seemingly psychic knowledge of Laura's necklace. They start getting lovey-dovey or something, but it's so boring it's difficult to *zzzzzzzzz*.

Josie makes the avuncular Pete a sandwich as they agree to participate in a fishing competition. There is more erotic heat and dramatic tension in this innocuous exchange than in the entirety of Donna and James's relationship. Pete heads to bed and Josie reacts strangely to a strange piece of mail, a drawing of a domino, identical to the one Hank carries around. Hm. Probably a coincidence. Then the phone rings, and speak of the devil, it's Hank! He promises to see her later, sucking on his domino all the while. We can't imagine prison dominos are particularly sanitary, but to each his own. Josie hangs up, looking like she wants to vomit. He's a real catch, our Hank.

Episode 5 ("Cooper's Dreams")

Aired: Thursday, May 10, 1990
Twin Peaks Time: March 1, 1989
Written by Mark Frost. Directed by Lesli Linka Glatter.
Rating: Short on watercooler moments but smoothly firing on all cylinders . . .
    7 out of 10 damn fine slices of pie. 🥧🥧🥧🥧🥧🥧🥧◇◇◇

Cooper is awakened at 4:28 in the damn a.m. by singing Icelandic junketeers at the Great Northern. He requests Diane send him his earphones.

At breakfast, Audrey approaches and informs him that she is newly employed and wishes to help in the investigation. Cooper pointedly asks her how old she is. Cooper, you dog.

Jerry Horne is having a blast with the Icelandic guests, partying into the wee hours, pitching woo at a Nordic goddess named Hepa, and brandishing an enormous leg of lamb. Ben suggests they take their potential investors out for a night at One Eyed Jacks, a plan to which Jerry enthusiastically agrees. Seems like kind of a risky assumption that a group of foreign real estate investors would be excited about visiting a sleazy bordello, but we don't claim to understand the ways of business. A disheveled Leland staggers in offering to pitch in, much to Ben's exasperated disgust.

Cooper and company continue to search Jacques Renault's apartment. Among their discoveries is a hidden *Flesh World* porno magazine, which contains both a mash note to Ronette Pulaski from a bearded transvestite ("no Georgia peach" is Harry's assessment of the included photo) and, printed in the magazine itself, a picture of Leo's vehicle. Hmmm.

Back at Leo's, Shelly and Bobby play house and pantomime an imagined showdown with the abusive trucker, with Shelly's gun in a starring role . . . and let's just say Mark Frost has read his Chekhov. Andy stops by to ask about Leo's whereabouts, but Shelly is able to get rid of him with some lies and evasions. She also could have tossed a stick into the yard. Perhaps feeling his ears burning, Leo calls to announce his imminent return. Yay.

Norma stops by Big Ed's Gas Farm to inform Ed of Hank's parole. Ed explains that due to Nadine's problems, he can't leave her. Norma curses the both of them for being too kind to just take what they want. It's a point to consider.

Audrey's meeting with Mr. Battis, the department store bureaucrat, begins nicely enough, but Battis is living in a fool's paradise if he thinks he can fob Audrey Horne off on the gift wrap department. She'll get the perfume counter or falsely charge Battis with attempted rape. He quickly demurs, and we see the effectiveness of not being too nice.

James tells Donna a sad story about his mom and cries. This happens in a gazebo. Gazebo is a funny word. What were we talking about, again?

More discoveries at Renault's apartment: a photo of a cabin with red curtains, familiar to Cooper from his dream. Proof that Ronette and Laura were receiving sexual solicitations mailed to Renault's post office box. Suspiciously large amounts of heating oil for an apartment dweller—does Jacques have a secret cabin? The boys head to the woods to investigate.

Maddy meets Donna and James at the Double R, where they confide their intention to solve the murder and ask for Maddy's help in uncovering Laura's storied hiding place. She agrees. Hank has been eavesdropping on their conversation; as they leave he sucks up to Norma for a job and is named dishwasher. Shelly looks pretty uneasy about the development as she catches a few seconds of *Invitation to Love* on the kitchen's TV.

Dr. Jacoby's family therapy session with the Briggses goes off the rails immediately, so he asks to speak to Bobby alone. He may dress like a brain-damaged art teacher, but Jacoby appears to be an effective therapist—he quickly breaks down Bobby's defenses and the two come to understand that Laura was driven to corrupt others by her own profound self-loathing, and that it was she who pushed Bobby into criminal activity. We don't learn who convinced him to wear his hair that way.

Cooper and company find a cabin, but it belongs to the Log Lady. She invites them in for tea and cookies and relates her log's report of the night of Laura's murder. It perceived three men and two women, laughing, and horror. Our heroes postulate that the two women were Laura and Ronette, two of the men Jacques and probably Leo, but who was the Third Man? Spoiler: not Harry Lime.

Further searching turns up a second cabin, and it looks like pay dirt. Red curtains, a self-resetting record player (music is always in the air), and Waldo the mynah bird. Dream prophecy jackpot! Also on offer are a camera on a tripod loaded with film and a cuckoo clock that dispenses a One Eyed Jacks chip with a chunk missing from the side. They must be pretty excited; you can't take two steps in the joint without tripping over a clue.

Party time at the Great Northern. Josie sits alone in a room, smoking from an elegant cigarette holder. One wonders what she makes of the inn's rustic decor, particularly the nightstands.

The action is happening in the ballroom, with the Icelanders making merry as the Horne brothers schmooze with oily aplomb. Catherine Martell pours her drink on Ben's shoe, subtly indicating her displeasure. He hustles her off to his office as Audrey surreptitiously follows. From her spy hole, she witnesses the pair discussing arson plans and having angry sex. Somehow, this strikes her as terribly funny.

She's not laughing minutes later when a clearly distraught Leland arrives, interrupting Jerry Horne's speech with a heartbreaking solo dance routine. Ben forces Catherine onto the floor with Leland to cover, and soon the entire crowd is happily bopping around the disintegrating Leland, misinterpreting his anguished gestures as novel dance moves. Sickened by the spectacle, Audrey cries from the corner.

Maddy calls Donna, reporting her discovery of Laura's hidey-hole and the tape it contained.

Ben joins Josie. She gives him some sort of notebook, and they plan to proceed with something the following night. All the duplicity and double-dealing seems exhausting—aren't these people all already pretty rich? We guess there is only so much pie and woolen outerwear a person can buy.

Leo arrives home and is immediately punched out by Hank, which marks Hank's single likable moment in the series. Leo has apparently let his ambition get a little out of control. Bloody and humiliated, he charges into the house and starts knocking Shelly around. She responds by drawing her gun and shooting him. All the drama majors in the audience can exhale.

Finally, Cooper returns to his room to find a naked Audrey Horne in his bed. The Great Northern may have a lax noise policy, but service like that really must be saluted.

Episode 6 ("Realization Time")

Aired: Thursday, May 17, 1990
Twin Peaks Time: March 2, 1989
Written by Harley Peyton. Directed by Caleb Deschanel.
Rating: Loads of fun . . . a prime example of peak Twin Peaks. Cooper in a tux!
    8 out of 10 damn fine slices of pie. 🍰🍰🍰🍰🍰🍰🍰🍰▱▱

Cooper very gently and kindly lets Audrey down, but you can tell it's a struggle. He instead offers his friendship, and the scene is actually very sweet. MacLachlan and Fenn have great chemistry, and it's a shame they have so little time together on-screen.

Lucy gives Andy the very cold shoulder when he arrives at the sheriff's, and a serious-sounding phone call from her doctor does little to improve her mood. Doc Hayward, Harry, and Cooper examine Waldo (Cooper keeping his distance, as he doesn't like birds; don't let the owls hear you say that), theorizing he will resume vocalizing after returning to full avian health. Cooper sets up a voice-activated tape recorder to capture anything he might say, hoping he might have picked up some informative phrases during Laura's murder.

Albert exposits that forensic evidence proves both Laura and Ronette spent time at Jacques's apartment and that the plastic fragment found in Laura's stomach came from the One Eyed Jacks chip found in the cuckoo clock. A trip to the casino seems in order, but unfortunately it lies outside Twin Peaks' jurisdiction. Cooper says not to worry, they're going in their capacity as Bookhouse Boys. Not sure that's a legal distinction the courts would recognize, but they agree to proceed.

Leo, still recovering from Hank's beating and Shelly's bullet, spies on his house through binoculars, and comes unglued when he sees Bobby Briggs arrive and sweep his wife into a tender embrace. He's a louse, but the guy is having a *really* bad day. Inside, Bobby assures Shelly he will handle everything. When Bobby is your rock, it's time to reevaluate your life course.

Leo overhears Lucy discussing the Waldo situation over some kind of police scanner he has in his pickup. We hope the Sheriff's Department didn't shell out too much for birdseed (we know they skimped on the grapes, per Doc).

Donna, Maddy, and James listen to the tape Maddy found in Laura's hiding place. It's an audio missive to Dr. Jacoby, full of heavy innuendo. Another tape case from the stash is empty, and James suggests breaking into Jacoby's office to find it. It's weird when James threatens to become interesting. They hatch a plan to draw Jacoby out, leaving his hypothetical tape stash unprotected.

Audrey's first day at the perfume counter (adorned with a sign reading "Invitation to Love"—both a clever reference to Twin Peaks' favorite soap opera and the secret function of the cosmetics department) goes about as well as one would expect; she insults a difficult customer, sneaks into Battis's office, steals a cigarette, and spies on him ushering her counter-mate Jenny into the elegant, charming world of Northwoods prostitution.

Hank sucks up to Shelly at the Double R. She seems to be warming to him, which is classic Shelly. Hank subtly pumps her for information about Norma's recent activities and learns that Big Ed has been a real help to her during Hank's incarceration. Ouch. Cooper and Harry arrive and brace Hank, but he fails to take the bait. He's in a good mood because he just stole a customer's silver lighter. Cooper also suggests he and Harry give themselves a present, but in this case he means a cup of coffee. Oh Cooper, someday you'll be a Real Boy.

Audrey cons the One Eyed Jacks madam's phone number out of Jenny. She's a Horne, it's in her genes.

Josie Packard and Catherine Martell bask in the warmth of sisterhood and close friendship.

Ed returns home to find a disconsolate Nadine eating bonbons and watching *Invitation to Love*. He assures her that someday they will find a patent attorney who appreciates noiseless drape runners. Sometimes we feel sorriest for Ed.

Harry visits Josie and admires Pete's new taxidermied fish. Josie tells him about her motel snooping. She produces incriminating photos of Ben and Catherine and reveals their arson plans. Harry promises to look into it.

Cooper and Ed prepare for their visit to One Eyed Jacks. Cooper looks replete in a glossy tuxedo, but he directs Ed to don a hideous curly wig and false mustache for his disguise as a swingin' oral surgeon from out of town. Again, sometimes we feel sorriest for Ed. Cooper distributes $10,000 in gambling money, courtesy of the FBI. He expects to return it with interest, including his winnings. We wonder if he thinks there will be a game involving throwing a rock while not looking. He is good at that.

En route to One Eyed Jacks herself, Audrey desperately tries to contact Cooper, to no avail. She slips a note under his door. Probably not reading "Do you like me? Check Yes or No," but maybe.

Catherine is visited by insurance man Mr. Neff. We have seen *Double Indemnity* and know where this is going. He wants her signature on the new insurance policy taken out on her life by Josie and Ben. Funny, they didn't mention it to her. So thoughtful, those two.

Waldo has begun to metaphorically sing. Not for long, though. A gunshot comes through the window. Leo's pickup speeds off as blood from Waldo's swinging cage spatters a tray of doughnuts. Leo, you MONSTER. Those doughnuts looked good! What did the tape record? "Hurting me, stop it, Leo, no."

Blackie O'Reilly greets Cooper and Ed at the casino, and some excruciating flirting ensues (she remarks Cooper looks like Cary Grant; MacLachlan would play Grant in the 2004 comedy *Touch of Pink*), but she seems charmed. She digs gangling, tonsorially disastrous gas station–owning oral surgeons, apparently.

Maddy sneaks out of the house for Project: JacobyTape and doesn't notice Uncle Leland brooding alone in the dark. Creepy.

Ben has reached his limit of Icelandic caroling; Jerry reassures him the investors are on the verge of signing the contracts, and want to conclude their business at One Eyed Jacks. Ben agrees, first calling Josie to arrange for Catherine's presence at the mill. Oh, there's Hank! Josie seems about as pleased by his presence as the rest of the female characters on the show.

Audrey's job interview with Blackie gets off to a rocky start when the madam catches her in some obvious lies—that "Hester Prynne" alias is too clever by half, kid—but our girl wins the position with a display of her oral cherry stem knot-tying prowess, in a scene that immediately became iconic and inspired many parodies. It's an impressive trick, but it seems Audrey's "Elizabeth Taylor's hotter little sister" looks would be sufficient for employment here.

Cooper and Ed play blackjack. Their dealer is, appropriately, "Black" Jacques Renault. He is . . . not an attractive figure. Cooper is winning, as expected. Ed is losing, as was inevitable.

Donna, James, and Maddy proceed with their plan, luring an angrily incredulous Jacoby to the gazebo with a phone call and videotape of Maddy in Laura drag holding a current newspaper. So that works, but! That scoundrel Bobby Briggs is afoot, planting a large bag of drugs in James's unattended motorcycle. Mean, but funny-mean.

Back at the gazebo, we see a clearly nervous Maddy awaiting her rendezvous with Jacoby. A heavy-breathing figure stalks her from the bushes. Is it the wary psychologist or . . . someone else?

It's probably James doubling back to look for his dropped retainer or something. Derp.

Episode 7 ("The Last Evening")

Aired: Wednesday, May 23, 1990
Twin Peaks Time: March 2–3, 1989
Written and directed by Mark Frost.
Rating: We don't really learn anything and the cliffhanger is brutal, but we're in
the groove here. . . .
8 out of 10 damn fine slices of pie. ▰▰▰▰▰▰▰▱▱

Donna and James search Dr. Jacoby's tiki-themed office, accidentally setting off an automated Hawaiian music player and eventually finding Laura's necklace and another tape in a coconut shell. Bobby watches from the shadows. At the gazebo, the good doctor himself gasps in shock when he sees Maddy done up as Laura. His astonishment is short-lived, as he is immediately assaulted by a masked man and suffers a heart attack.

Ed continues to lose at One Eyed Jacks, but Cooper's card-counting skills keep him in the chips. He tips his dealer, Jacques, with the broken chip found in the corpulent degenerate's apartment, and tells him he knows Leo. Meanwhile, Audrey's first-day orientation involves drawing a playing card from Blackie's deck; she gets the Queen of Diamonds.

Cooper snows Jacques, claiming to be Leo's money man. He offers Jacques a cool ten thousand for a night's work and makes plans to meet him later with the details. Jacques explains the broken chip: it was placed in a bound Laura Palmer's mouth as she was helplessly pecked on the shoulder by Waldo. Fun place, Jacques's cabin.

Shelly washes her hair in the sink and is seized by an enraged Leo, who tells her his actions are all her fault. Yes, that Shelly is a real scourge. Poor Leo.

Harry and his men ambush Jacques at the meeting point and arrest him, but he manages to grab an officer's gun and draws a bead on Harry. Andy, with steely reserve, draws and shoots Jacques, putting the big man down. Time on the range: well spent.

Donna, James, and Maddy listen to Laura's tape, and there is a wonderful moment in which they hear Laura describe James as "sweet, but so dumb." Laura goes on to describe a dangerous mystery man in a red sports car who both nearly killed her and really turns her on. Sigh. The prettiest girls always go for guys like that.

Shelly, for instance, is tied up by her husband at the mill next to a timer attached to an incendiary device. Hey . . . Leo's been seen in a red sports car!

Nadine, resplendent in a ball gown, attempts suicide with pills. How many lives will patent attorneys destroy before someone takes action?

Hank bugs Josie again, hanging around all menacingly even after she gives him $90,000—his payoff for his role in Andrew Packard's death. Seems Hank isn't ready to dissolve their partnership, and he cuts their thumbs and mingles their blood to symbolize their bond-for-life. We figured out Hank: It's all abandonment issues with this guy.

Speaking of odd couples, Catherine tears her place apart looking for a secret ledger when Pete arrives. In a rare moment of warmth between the two, they reminisce about the passionate early days of their relationship, and he pledges to help her. Pete rhymes with sweet, and that's no coincidence.

At the sheriff's, the men enthusiastically recount Andy's heroism, emboldening the deputy to plant a big old kiss on the sour-faced Lucy. She tells him she's pregnant, and he furiously stalks off. Ulp. Someone has some 'splaining to do. Bobby calls soon after, claiming to be Leo and dropping a dime on James re: the drugs in his bike.

Cooper and Harry question the injured Jacques in the hospital, learning that the *Flesh World* ads were Laura's idea and that on the night of the murder Leo inexplicably knocked Jacques unconscious and disappeared with the girls. It was probably Shelly's fault!

Jacoby's recovering, too, and has filled Doc Hayward in on his call from and meeting with "Laura."

As Catherine and Pete continue to search for the ledger, Catherine receives a call from Hank, informing her that the ledger is at the mill. What a coincidence. Hank is a busy bee this episode: he also finds time to sweet-talk Norma about starting over, and she accepts his kiss. Grody.

Ed returns home to find a prostrate Nadine, and mysteriously does not moonwalk right back out of the house and over to Norma's, but instead calls an ambulance.

James visits Cooper at the sheriff's, and the G-man is very curious about the Bland Biker's shenanigans with Jacoby and, in particular, about the bag of drugs found in James's motorcycle. James goggles in mute befuddlement, because he's James.

Ben Horne FINALLY gets the Icelandic investors to sign the contracts and decides to celebrate with the new girl in Blackie's stable of hostesses. Good news/bad news there, Ben: She is beautiful, but this isn't Mississippi.

Bobby winds up his night with a visit to Shelly's, but of course she's not there. Leo is, and he promptly attacks Bobby with an axe. Also Shelly's fault?

Bobby is saved by the timely arrival of Hank (the one time anyone has ever been happy to see him), who shoots Leo through the window.

Catherine arrives at the mill to continue her ledger search and discovers the bound and whimpering Shelly. Right in the proverbial nick, too, because the timer goes off and the two are quickly surrounded by flames. Catherine cuts Shelly free, but the door appears to be blocked by a roaring sheet of fire.

In a clever bit of editing, we cut to someone engaging a fire alarm, but we're now at the hospital. In the resulting confusion, we see a man smother Jacques to death with his own pillow. It's Leland.

At the mill, Pete heroically enters the inferno to search for the still-missing Catherine. The man is a brick, an absolute brick.

Finally, an exhausted Cooper returns to his room at the Great Northern, finding Audrey's note. There's not much he can do about it, though, because a mysterious figure knocks on his door and straight up shoots him three times at close range.

Fade to black, end season one.

Season Two

Episode 8 ("May the Giant Be with You")

Aired: Sunday, September 30, 1990
Twin Peaks Time: Friday, March 3, 1989
Written by Mark Frost (who also appears briefly as the reporter at the site of the burned-down mill). Directed by David Lynch.
Rating: The critics griped. Who cares?
   10 out of 10 damn fine slices of pie. 🥧🥧🥧🥧🥧🥧🥧🥧🥧🥧

Close Encounters of the Twin Peaks Kind? Here's the episode that Steven Spielberg *almost* directed, at the behest of Mark Frost and Harley Peyton, who visited him at his home to extend the offer. Spielberg, a huge *Twin Peaks* fan, was keen on the idea, but David Lynch nixed it, saying *he* would direct instead: this was a special two-hour (commercials included) episode airing at 9:00 p.m. on a Sunday before the series moved to its new, controversial 10:00 p.m. Saturday time slot. ABC had rerun the entire first season over the summer, hoping to reignite passion, and was pressuring Frost and Lynch to reveal the identity of Laura's killer in the season-two opener.

So do they?

They don't.

Lynch with Hank Worden (the Waiter) and Carel Struycken (the Giant): One and the same?

Photo by Richard Beymer

The episode opens with an incongruously languorous scene in which Cooper, bleeding profusely from the three gunshots to the gut that closed the book on season one, lies prostrate on the floor of his Great Northern hotel room as an antediluvian room-service waiter shuffles in with a glass of warm milk and, oblivious to the medical emergency before him, asks Cooper to sign the bill; Coop obliges, then asks if gratuity is included. Nothing much happens beyond that, yet the scene lasts three minutes before the Waiter (portrayed by Hank Worden) finally disappears into the hallway—without offering Cooper any assistance. And what happens then? He returns . . . twice, before finally exiting for good. Dissatisfied with Worden's initial pacing, Lynch surprised everyone assembled by instructing Worden not to speed it up, but to make his way across the room to Cooper as if he were a hundred and twenty years old.

Following the Waiter's third and final farewell, a Giant materializes out of thin air; turns out the big fella is one of the good guys (we think): "Think of me as a friend," he tells Cooper. "We want to help you," though he's tightlipped about who "we" are. The Giant offers Cooper three cryptic kernels of wisdom, to jump-start the investigation:

1. "There's a man in a smiling bag."
2. "The owls are not what they seem."
3. "Without chemicals, he points."

Before vanishing, he asks Cooper for his ring, promising to return it once "you find these things to be true."

Like all Lynch-directed episodes, this one is stellar, loaded with memorable, even iconic moments. At One Eyed Jacks, Ben Horne tries to bed the "new girl," unaware she's his daughter Audrey (masked). Over at the Palmer home, Sarah and Maddy are shocked to discover Leland's hair has turned white overnight, a radically different reaction from the one Leland gets when he returns to work at the Great Northern crooning "Mairzy Doats": the Horne brothers dig the sound, with Ben dancing along atop his desk (the hoofing wasn't in the script; Lynch spotted Richard Beymer shuffling during a lull in the shooting to break in a new pair of shoes, and appropriated it for the scene). Searching the grounds outside Leo's house, Andy accidentally dislodges a loose plank of wood, which jumps up and smacks him in the face, knocking him woozy but uncovering a huge stash of cocaine in the process; you can just imagine how much fun the newly-returned-to-Twin Peaks Albert Rosenfield has with this. Donna begins her transmutation from good girl to Laura Palmer postulate, donning her late friend's sunglasses, taking over her Meals on Wheels route (to be fair, in service of her investigation into Laura's death), and taking up smoking, triggering a very seductive and/or very funny (we're still not sure) exchange with James between the bars of a jail cell (James on the inside, Donna on the out).

Andy and Lucy hilariously leaf through copies of *Flesh World* for a photo of Teresa Banks, and Dr. Jacoby, from his hospital bed (seems like half of Twin Peaks is bunking at Calhoun Memorial Hospital in this episode), proves that he may be weird, but he *can* be perceptive, telling Cooper and Truman that the last time he saw Laura he was convinced she was finally at peace—not because her torment had ended, but because she was ready to die, and may even have allowed herself to be killed. Jacoby also reports having smelled scorched engine oil the night Jacques Renault was murdered as both lay recuperating in ICU. Big Ed recalls his and Nadine's tragic backstory for Cooper, who deciphers the first of the Giant's clues when he spots an unzipped body bag drooping from the wall of a hospital washroom—the heretofore mentioned "smiling bag," which earlier had carried Jacques's body.

At the Double R, Major Garland Briggs shares his "veranda of a vast estate" vision with Bobby, one of *Twin Peaks'* most beloved scenes (and one of Mark Frost's favorite scenes in the entire series), leaving Briggs junior in tears. Over coffee and doughnuts (goes without saying) at the sheriff's station, Coop and Albert bring the rest of the team (plus viewers, and probably the network as well) up to speed on the investigation, with much ado about the mysterious "Third Man," now believed to be Laura's killer. Here we encounter a vexing continuity error: the G-men reveal that the Third Man left behind a note—"Fire Walk with Me"—written in blood, since determined to be AB Negative, a rare type not matching any of the four people known to have been in Jacques's cabin that night. Hence, Albert concludes, the note must have been written in the killer's own blood. However, in episode five from the first season ("Cooper's Dreams"), Doc Hayward had reported to Cooper that Jacques's blood was AB Negative.

Whoops.

And where exactly is the curiously MIA Josie Packard during all of this? Inquiring minds want to know; this includes an enigmatic "Asian Man" who calls Blue Pine Lodge asking for her. Purportedly off on a business trip to Seattle, Josie really "wanted to put a little distance between her and the smell of smoke" in the aftermath of the mill fire, Hank Jennings confides to the Hornes.

As the episode winds down, we meet precocious Gersten Hayward, another of Donna's younger sisters, whose existence had heretofore been unknown to us. Dressed in a pink fairy princess outfit, Gersten tickles the ivories as the Palmer and the Hayward clans assemble for dinner. Leland, inexplicably dressed in a tuxedo, insists on singing "Get Happy," but passes out before he can finish. Back at One Eyed Jacks, the imperiled Audrey Horne can't understand why her "special agent" hasn't rescued her, unaware that Cooper was about to open her note when he was shot and has since forgotten about it. Meanwhile, Coop sleeps soundly in Room 315 at the Great Northern—until the Giant pops back in for another visit, this time telling Cooper: "One person saw the Third Man. Three have seen him, yes, but not his body. One only. Known to you. Ready now to talk." Translation: Ronette has stirred at last. Over at Calhoun Memorial, she is having horrific visions of her last moments with Laura, and we fade out on Bob, his bloodcurdling scream piercing the night.

MIA: Catherine Martell, presumed dead from the fire. Attentive viewers will note that Piper Laurie is no longer listed in the opening credits.

Episode 9 ("Coma")

Aired: Saturday, October 6, 1990
Twin Peaks Time: Saturday, March 4, 1989
Written by Harley Peyton. Directed by David Lynch.
Rating: Creamed corn, corny James, and a jolly Giant.
    9 out of 10 damn fine slices of pie. 🍰🍰🍰🍰🍰🍰🍰🍰🍰◻

Back-to-back episodes from Lynch—never a bad thing. Standout scenes: Cooper and Truman take sixty seconds to adjust the stools at Ronette Pulaski's hospital bedside, while Ronette—having finally woken from her coma—waits to be questioned (unscripted, but improvised by director Lynch); James strums guitar and warbles the Angelo Badalamenti-David Lynch composition "Just You" with Donna and Maddy, until Donna freaks out at the googly eyes James and Maddy are exchanging.

The episode opens with vexing news, as Albert reports that batty ex-G-man Windom Earle has escaped from the madhouse and is nowhere to be found: "Your former partner flew the coop, Cooper," he says, our first reference to Earle, soon to become a very Big Baddy.

Donna's first Meals on Wheels client we know of is a real doozy, the elderly Mrs. Tremond, who grows excessively agitated upon discovering creamed corn on her plate. The corn magically winds up in the hands of her tuxedoed young grandson, Pierre, an aspiring illusionist, then disappears altogether. Mrs. Tremond denies having known Laura well, but directs Donna to the agoraphobe next door, Harold Smith, who doesn't answer his door, so Donna leaves a message.

Over at Calhoun Memorial Hospital, Cooper and Truman finally stop futzing around with those stools long enough to show Ronette a sketch of Bob, triggering a tizzy of epileptic proportions, during which she is able to articulate only one word cleanly: "train." "Have You Seen This Man?" posters of Bob go up around town; Leland spies one in Ben Horne's office and says he knows the man, from when he was a youngster visiting his grandfather's summer home on Pearl Lakes, then dashes out to share the news with Harry.

The Log Lady translates a metamessage from her log to Major Briggs—"Deliver the message." Andy too has a message, for Lucy: he's sterile, so the baby she's carrying can't be his.

Ben Horne, very possibly the worst father in television history, finally reports Audrey missing, "for as much as maybe two days." Doc Hayward gives Shelly the 4-1-1 on Leo's medical condition, which isn't good—or *is*

Maddy, Donna, and James compare notes on their investigation. Donna looks annoyed at James, just saying.

good, depending on your POV: possible permanent paralysis and vegetation. Bobby cooks up a scheme to collect Leo's disability checks, but it only works if Leo lives at home with him and Shelly, meaning he can't go to prison for the Packard mill fire.

At One Eyed Jacks, Audrey barges in on Emory Battis's kinky sex party—he's bound and blindfolded, his toenails polished red—eliciting key info in her quest to help Cooper with his murder investigation: One Eyed Jacks is owned by her Pops, and Battis's role is to funnel "girls" over by hiring them to work the perfume counter at Horne's department store, Ronette and Laura included. Asked if Ben knew Laura was at Jacks, Battis replies: "Mr. Horne makes it his business to entertain all the girls." Yikes!

As night settles over Twin Peaks, Major Briggs heeds the log's advice and delivers a message to Cooper, confiding that his military job includes monitoring deep-space communication, most of which turns out to be gibberish, though two decipherable messages were received at more or less the same time Cooper was being shot: one, "The owls are not what they seem," and two, the word "Cooper" repeated over and over.

Meanwhile, Maddy, James, and Donna are jamming over at the Haywards when Donna gets all worked up over those pining looks James and Maddy are sharing. Their spat is interrupted when Donna gets a call from Harold Smith, who's willing to meet, and Maddy freaks over a sudden vision of Bob climbing the living-room couch and heading right for her, before suddenly disappearing.

Guess who pays Coop another bedtime visit? Yep, the big guy. There follows a jumble of images, all apparent visions from another Cooper dream: Ronette thrashing about, Bob's face transforming into an owl's, Sarah Palmer calling for Laura as she heads downstairs, ceiling fan circling overhead—all sorts of scary stuff like that. Coop's fitful slumber is interrupted by a call from Audrey Horne, but she's disconnected before she can share her whereabouts, by One Eyed Jacks doyenne Blackie O'Reilly, who's in a pretty nasty mood. It's not nice to fool den mother Blackie.

Episode 10 ("The Man Behind Glass")

Aired: Saturday, October 13, 1990
Twin Peaks Time: Sunday, March 5, 1989
Written by Robert Engels. Directed by Lesli Linka Glatter.
Rating: Awesome Albert, plus crucial plot developments.
        8 out of 10 damn fine slices of pie. 🥧🥧🥧🥧🥧🥧🥧🥧

A trio of series debuts: Dick Tremayne, Jean Renault, Harold Smith (not counting his eyes, briefly seen last episode peeking out from venetian blinds).

Lynch steps away, succeeded by Lesli Linka Glatter. We miss him.

Along with all his other faults, James has the worst luck of any two-timer ever: every time he even touches Maddy, Donna shows up.

The episode opens at Calhoun Memorial Hospital, where Cooper plucks the letter B from beneath Ronette's left ring fingernail. For those keeping score, the tally is now three letters (including Laura's R and Teresa's T), and four people still alive are known to have laid eyes on Bob at one time or another: Cooper, in his dream; Ronette, in the train car on the last night of Laura's life; and Sarah Palmer and Maddy Ferguson, both in visions.

Coop finally feels the time is right to fess up about his visit from the Giant, providing bountiful ammunition for Albert ("And you gave him the beans you were supposed to use to buy a cow?"). Harry and Albert nearly come to blows, but Albert sermonizes about nonviolence, invoking Gandhi and Martin Luther King and professing (platonic) love for Harry. Donna finally meets up with shut-in Harold Smith, whose deep bond with Laura is kind of spooky; that's a Cypripedioideae (lady slipper orchid) he presents to Donna to place at Laura's grave. Dick Tremayne, an ascot-wearing dandy, shows up at the sheriff's office for a lunch date (Dutch) with Lucy, stopping to admire his reflection on the way. At the Double R, Lucy blows a gasket, furious that Dick hasn't so much as called in the six weeks since their last date, when he took her to Pancake Plantation family night and they wound up, two bottles of champagne later, frolicking in a display bed at Horne's department store, where Dick works in men's fashions.

Back at the sheriff's office, Leland recalls his youthful summer encounters with Bob, who lived in a white house on the other side of a vacant lot, went by the name of Robertson, and liked to flick lit matches at the young Leland, taunting him with, "You wanna play with fire, little boy?"—more or less the same words James, two episodes earlier, had remembered Laura saying to him one night in the woods. Coop's convinced Bob is leaving behind letters to spell out the word ROBERTSON.

At the Double R, James confides to Maddy that he's disturbed by Donna's tough-girl act . . . and Donna walks in on the two of them holding hands. Over at One Eyed Jacks, Audrey rides the white tiger, doped up on heroin by Blackie, who's planning to ransom her back to Ben Horne for a ton of cash, 30 percent of which will go to Jacques Renault's equally (at least) miscreant brother Jean, who's out to avenge his brothers' deaths (and holds Cooper responsible).

One-armed Phillip Gerard is peddling work boots to Harry at the sheriff's station, but nearly passes out upon spotting another of those Bob posters, retreating to a men's room stall, where he shoots up with some sort of drug, emerging disheveled and discombobulated. Coop, remembering that Bob and Gerard knew each other in his season-one dream, goes looking for him, but Gerard has disappeared, though Cooper does find the unused hypodermic needle the One-Armed Man left behind and makes a connection to the Giant's third clue: "Without chemicals, he points."

Nadine finally wakes up from her coma, convinced she's eighteen and back in high school, somehow gifted with superhuman strength.

Under hypnosis, Jacoby recalls that it was Leland who snuck into the ICU and smothered Jacques with a pillow, forcing Cooper and Harry to, sadly, arrest him (Leland, that is). Donna places the lady slipper at Laura's grave, soliloquizing about how much she resents her friend for dying, and also her fear of losing James. Over at the Palmer house, James confides his Mommy issues to Maddy . . . and Donna walks in on the two of them smooching. Dude! Donna runs off to Harold Smith's house, where the two of them share a laugh recalling one of Laura's favorite sayings: "Donna Madonna there's always manana." Harold steps out of the room for a moment, which is all the time it takes for Donna to stumble upon the secret diary of Laura Palmer.

Episode 11 ("Laura's Secret Diary")

Aired: Saturday, October 20, 1990
Twin Peaks Time: Monday, March 6, 1989
Written by Jerry Stahl and Mark Frost + Harley Peyton + Robert Engels. Directed by Todd Holland.
Rating: Great opening, Sternwood arrives, poignant Ray Wise, stormy weather, and . . . Sid! 8 out of 10 damn fine slices of pie. 🥧🥧🥧🥧🥧🥧🥧🥧🥧🥧

"When these frail shadows we inhabit now have quit the stage, we'll meet and raise a glass again together in Valhalla." Meet Clinton Sternwood (surname no doubt appropriated from Raymond Chandler's *The Big Sleep*, given the Frost-Lynch devotion to classic Hollywood noir), silver-haired/silver-tongued jurist who crisscrosses his district in a Winnebago with a pulchritudinous law clerk named Sid, dispensing grandfatherly advice and aphorisms of just the sort as this one, delivered at Leland's bail hearing. Sternwood is one of several additions to the *Twin Peaks* cast of characters here, also including D.A. Daryl Lodwick and mysterious Japanese business-man Mr. Tojamura, in town from Seattle for still-unspecified purposes, though we don't like the looks of it.

Never mention the words "Jerry Stahl" to Mark Frost: credited as a coscripter of this episode, Stahl had heretofore penned installments of *ALF*, *thirtysomething*, and *Moonlighting*, but would gain his greatest fame as the author of *Permanent Midnight: A Memoir*, a harrowing account of drug addiction published in 1995 and subsequently adapted into a motion picture. By his own admission Stahl was in the throes of addiction during his brief tenure on *Twin Peaks*, an experience Frost later described to Brad Dukes, author of *Reflection: An Oral History of Twin Peaks*, as an "absolute car wreck." Note the anomalous listing of four names as the authors of this episode, including Frost's.

Whatever, the episode has plenty of merit, beginning with the artful opening sequence conceived by director Todd Holland, at this point a young up-and-comer with TV credits including *Max Headroom* and *Amazing Stories*. Holland devised the notion of starting the shot inside the acoustic tiles on the wall of the jail cell in which Leland is imprisoned, to give the impression of being inside Leland's mind as he stares ahead at the wall. Under questioning from Harry and Cooper, he admits to suffocating Jacques Renault in retaliation for Laura's murder, convinced Jacques was her killer. Ray Wise masterfully conveys Leland's dolor, telling his interrogators they have no concept of what it's like to lose a daughter: "Every cell screams. You can hear . . . nothing else." Cooper is uncharacteristically cranky over Doc Hayward's suggestion that Leland's action is not without justification: "You approve of murder, Dr. Hayward?"

Andy calls mulligan on the sperm test, providing copious comic relief. Hawk reports from Pearl Lakes that the last known residents of the white house were the Kalispells, which is one of those things you expect to go somewhere, but never does. Coop notices that Andy's work boots are the same brand as those discovered outside Leo's house—"Circle"—which may or may not mean anything, though it does speak to the circular theme running throughout *Twin Peaks*, notably in the significance of rings, but also the orb of twelve sycamore trees in Glastonbury Grove that frame the entrance to the Black Lodge in the series finale.

Word spreads that famous travel/restaurant critic M. T. Wentz is coming to town; such a fuss! Jean Renault pays Ben Horne a visit, bringing along video of a bound-and-gagged Audrey and demanding two things: a stake in One Eyed Jacks and a commitment that Cooper will be the one delivering the ransom ($125,000 in cash). Donna craves unfettered access to Laura's secret diary, but Harold isn't giving it up, so she enlists Maddy in a scheme to lift it.

Bye-bye Battis: Jean shoots Emory dead in the chest, either because he was sick of the sound of his voice or just because he felt like it . . . we're not sure. Josie returns from Seattle, but she's gaming Harry now, acting all offended by his insinuation that she may have had something to do with the mill fire. Harry's a real patsy, but who can blame him, the way Josie flashes those gams?

The mysterious "Asian Man" finally has a name, which isn't very mysterious at all: Jonathan, introduced to Pete as Josie's cousin. Sure you are. Josie and Jonathan conspire: he says her task in Twin Peaks—disposing of the Packard holdings—is nearly complete, and that a Mr. Eckhardt anxiously awaits her return to Hong Kong; she assures him Sheriff Truman "means nothing to me." Ouch!

A storm brews over Twin Peaks, lightning and thunder and all that. Very spooky. Dick offers Lucy $650 to "take care" of the pregnancy; outraged, she gives him the boot. Coop and Harry meet up at the Roadhouse, prepping for an undisclosed mission—maybe something to do with Audrey Horne? And Hank Jennings takes a well-deserved beating, from Jonathan, though we're unsure whom to root for.

Episode 12 ("The Orchid's Curse")

Aired: Saturday, October 27, 1990
Twin Peaks Time: Tuesday, March 7, 1989
Written by Barry Pullman. Directed by Graeme Clifford.
Rating: Taut, expertly choreographed last-act toggling between Donna and
      Maddy's scheme to purloin Laura's diary from Harold and Cooper and
      Harry's daring rescue of Audrey at One Eye Jacks . . .
      8 out of 10 damn fine slices of pie. ▰▰▰▰▰▰▰▰▱▱

Musician Van Dyke Parks appears as Leo's lawyer, Jack Racine, who shares a last name with the lawyer portrayed by William Hurt in the *Double Indemnity*-inspired movie *Body Heat*.

Cooper begins another day—his twelfth in Twin Peaks—in Room 315 at the Great Northern with a headstand, which might seem inconsequential except that it is during this exercise that he finally rediscovers, hidden under his bed, the note from Audrey Horne, addressed to "My Special Agent" and cryptically advising him that she has "gone North. Jack may have the answer."

Lucy heads to Tacoma for a few days, to visit her sister.

Since Twin Peaks apparently is without a courtroom, Leland's pretrial hearing is held at the Roadhouse, where he pleads not guilty to a first-degree murder charge and is released on his own recognizance.

Donna tricks Harold into revealing the location of Laura's diary.

Judge Sternwood declares Leo unfit to stand trial for multiple crimes, including the murder of Laura Palmer, ordering that he be sent home. Over black Yukon sucker punches ("They sneak up on you," Sternwood warns), the judge advises Cooper to "keep your eye on the woods. The woods are wondrous here, but strange." This is what lit professors call "foreshadowing." Nadine returns home from the hospital, but really, who cares?

Mr. Tojamura drops in on Ben Horne, claiming to represent an Asian investment firm offering $5 million for the Ghostwood project, even though the Hornes already have accepted a payment from Icelandic investors. Ben likes.

Jean Renault calls in, instructing Ben and Cooper to deposit the ransom money at midnight beside a headless horse on a carousel in a derelict amusement park north of the Canadian border. Ben, expecting Jean to kill Cooper, orders Hank to follow the G-man, making sure that Audrey—and the briefcase full of money—is safely returned. Scoundrel that he is, Renault is already planning a double cross of his own, involving the murders of both Audrey and Blackie O'Reilly, egged on by his jealous lover Nancy, who also happens to be Blackie's sis.

Comic relief: Andy calls for results of the sperm test. Diagnosis: "They're not just three men on a fishing trip; they're a whole damn town." "Woohoo!" says Andy.

Cooper and Harry plot their top-secret raid of One Eyed Jacks. Hawk enters, reporting that the One-Armed Man Gerard is staying at the Robin's Nest Motel over on Highway Nine, but hasn't been seen or heard from in over a day. Hawk departs, clearly suspicious that something is up.

At Harold's, Donna shares a provocative story involving her and Laura, short skirts, three guys, dancing by a stream in the woods, and skinny-dipping, though who knows how much of it is true and how much is Donna trying to overheat Harold? Regardless, it overheats us. After discussing orchids and pollinating insects, they kiss; once again Harold excuses him-self for a moment—will this guy never learn?—giving Donna a chance to signal Maddy, who is waiting outside, to come look for Laura's diary while Donna keeps Harold otherwise occupied, if you get our drift.

Meanwhile, over at One Eyed Jacks, Coop punches a woman (Nancy) in the stomach, though in fairness she *is* trying to kill him. Blackie bites the dust, stabbed by Jean, who exchanges gunfire with Harry as Coop heads for the exit, Audrey draped over his right shoulder. Not so fast, boys. A One Eyed Jack gunsel thwarts them, but just momentarily, as Hawk makes a sur-prise appearance, tossing a knife in the big lug's back. You go, Hawk! Hank, watching from outside, is accosted by Jean, who sticks a gun in his ear.

Maddy does find Laura's diary, but clumsily, making a racket so doing. Harold threatens the girls with a hand rake: "Are you looking for secrets?" he demands, Donna and Maddy cowering. "Is that what all this is about? Do you know what the ultimate secret is? You want to know? Laura did. The secret of knowing who killed you." Unstable fella that he is, Harold turns the rake on himself, leaving a trio of blood marks across his cheek . . . and we fade out.

Episode 13 ("Demons")

Aired: Saturday, November 3, 1990
Twin Peaks Time: Tuesday–Wednesday, March 7–8, 1989
Written by Harley Peyton + Robert Engels. Directed by Lesli Linka Glatter.
Rating: The pace quickens, plus Gordon Cole!
    8 out of 10 damn fine slices of pie. 🔪🔪🔪🔪🔪🔪🔪🔪▱▱

David Lynch makes his first *intentional* on-screen appearance (after a couple of occasions when his reflection is inadvertently captured on camera as he directs), as hearing-impaired FBI Regional Director Gordon Cole, Coop's boss, named after a minor character in the classic Hollywood noir *Sunset Blvd.*

Picking up where the prior episode left off: Donna and Maddy are rescued by James, who suspected something was up and furtively followed Maddy to Harold's, although the diary is left behind in the scuffle. James's passionate rapprochement with Donna pains Maddy, but Harold aches too, letting forth screams of despair from the greenhouse. Is it fair to hate James for lines like, "It's like if we could put our hearts together and just keep them that way forever, we'd be safe no matter what"? Or should we blame the writers?

Coop has a crisis of conscience upon realizing that Jean Renault was dangling Audrey as bait to hook the G-man and exact revenge for the deaths of his two brothers. "Harry, this isn't the first time my actions have brought suffering to someone I care about in the name of doing what I had to do," says Coop, tantalizing us with another hint of his tragic past. Harry neatly encapsulates the essential difference between the two of them, telling Coop he's the best lawman he's ever known, "but sometimes you think too much." No one's ever accused Harry of that!

Bobby and Shelly get the first of Leo's monthly disability checks, but for $700 instead of the $5,000 they were expecting. Leo utters his first word since the shooting: "Uhh"—not much, but enough to spook them.

Donna shares news of Laura's secret diary with Harry, who promises to dispatch a deputy to Harold's house as soon as possible.

Gordon Cole pops in with news from Albert, who found fibers from a vicuna coat in the hallway outside Cooper's hotel room in the aftermath of the shooting. We suspect this is important. Also from Albert: sheets of paper found near the bloody towel down the train tracks from the scene of Laura's murder were ripped from a diary. We *know* this is important.

Nadine's in a frisky mood with Big Ed, but let's not go there.

Speaking of frisky, Josie two-times Harry with Jonathan, though doesn't seem real pleased about it. Jonathan tosses her a one-way ticket to Hong Kong and says they're leaving that night, and Josie doesn't seem real pleased about that either—she still hasn't collected from the insurance company for the fire or from Ben Horne for the impending sale of the Packard property, but Jonathan suspects it's more than that, and threatens to kill Harry if she isn't aboard the plane by midnight.

Lakeside, James and Maddy talk heart-to-heart, and Maddy, acknowledging her dalliance with James is over, announces that she's leaving Twin Peaks and returning home.

Josie pays Ben a visit, hoping to collect, but the meeting gets off to a rocky start as Ben reveals that he has compiled a "fascinating" dossier connecting Josie to a series of prosecutable transgressions, including her late husband Andrew's "little boat that went boom." Josie counters that if anything suspicious should happen to her it would lead authorities to a safety deposit box "inside of which there is enough evidence to lock you away for three lifetimes." Humbled, Ben signs over Mr. Tojamura's "check" to Josie as a gesture "of good faith."

Bobby and Shelly celebrate Leo's "freedom" with a party, but the celebration is interrupted when Leo's head moves.

Speaking of heads, Gordon is worried Cooper may be getting in over his, as he did once before, in Pittsburgh, but Coop assures him everything is "A-OK" on that front. More vexing is the anonymous note Gordon produces, addressed to Cooper at the home base: "P-K4," which Cooper recognizes as an opening chess move from Windom Earle. (Frost conceived of the chess match between Earle and Cooper but soon lost interest in it, according to Harley Peyton, leaving it up to the rest of the writers to plot the moves, which some chess experts criticized as unimaginative and even dumb, eventually prompting an apology from Peyton.)

Harry shows up at Blue Pine Lodge to see Josie, catching her just as she is about to bolt with Jonathan, introduced this time as her assistant, Mr.

Lee. Twice Harry says he loves her, but twice is not enough, and Josie walks out anyway.

Ben and Mr. Tojamura conduct business over dinner at the Great Northern, but they're interrupted by Leland, who decides to perform "Getting to Know You" for the assembled diners. Ben tries to put a halt to that, but winds up duetting. Mr. Tojamura ends up at the bar discussing musicals with Pete.

Hawk hauls in an agitated Gerard, who's craving a fix, but Cooper plays it tough, refusing to dole out the dope. The one-armer, as Gordon calls him, eventually calms down and delivers the goods: Bob, he says, is "my familiar," a parasite who requires a human host, feeding on fear "and the pleasures." Once upon a time he and Bob were partners, but Mike "saw the face of God, and was purified," cutting off his arm but continuing to inhabit Gerard's body for one purpose and one purpose only: to stop Bob. Sometime during this confession he recites the chant from Cooper's early first-season Red Room dream, Cooper at first speaking the words along with him: "Through the darkness of future past, the magician longs to see. One chants out between two worlds: 'Fire walk with me.'" Only two types of people can see the true face of Bob, says Gerard: the gifted and the damned. Asked if Bob is somewhere nearby, Gerard replies yes, for nearly forty years. Where exactly? "A large house made of wood, surrounded by trees. The house is filled with many rooms, each alike, but occupied by different souls night after night."

Next stop: the Great Northern hotel.

Episode 14 ("Lonely Souls")

Aired: Saturday, November 10, 1990
Twin Peaks Time: Thursday, March 9, 1989
Written by Mark Frost. Directed by David Lynch.
Rating: Awesome episode! Killer revealed.
    10 out of 10 damn fine slices of pie. 🍴🍴🍴🍴🍴🍴🍴🍴🍴🍴

HUGE, HUGE episode, as Laura's killer in finally revealed, crafted by the two people most responsible for *Twin Peaks'* greatness: Mark Frost (script) and David Lynch (direction).

Frost and Lynch were so determined to keep the killer's identity secret until the episode aired that they filmed three different versions of the scene, each with a different killer (once with Leland, once with Bob, and once with Ben Horne)—even most of the crew members didn't know who the real killer was. When sound-mixing the episode, Lynch insisted on putting up curtains, so that passersby from other shows couldn't peek in.

Lynch briefly directs himself, in the opening scene, as Cole, who's off to Bend, Oregon, on "real hush-hush" business.

A touch of Lynchian brilliance: As Andy parades the Great Northern guests and staff before the One-Armed Man, hoping to expose Bob, dozens of sailors (no explanation offered) pass the time by bouncing pink rubber balls against the wooden lobby floor, making a racket (neither the sailors nor the bouncing balls were in the script, but were added by Lynch). The only one to get a rise out of Mike is Ben Horne, who storms in demanding an explanation; the one-armer points and collapses.

Meanwhile, Hawk drives out to Harold Smith's house with a warrant for Laura's secret diary, but finds the poor soul hanging from the rafters of his greenhouse.

With Louis Armstrong warbling "It's a Wonderful World" on the phonograph, Maddy breaks the news to Aunt Sarah and Uncle Leland that she's heading back to Missoula, Montana; they are sad but understanding.

Harry and Coop meet up with Hawk at Harold's, discovering a suicide note that reads, "J'ai un homme solitaire," translated by Coop as "I am a lonely soul." This is not our first exposure to the line: Mrs. Tremond's grandson Pierre spoke the same words five episodes earlier, during Donna's Meals on Wheels visit, another Lynch-directed installment, although at the time nobody knew what the hell he was talking about.

Hawk—who else?—discovers Laura's secret diary amid the mess at Harold's. "Pay dirt," says Coop. Indeed.

Over at the Johnsons', trouble in paradise: Shelly and Bobby do the math, and it isn't pretty: $42 in monthly living expenses after all the bills are paid. Things are getting a little testy between Bobby and Shelly. Exacerbating matters is that Leo appears to be slowly coming around, judging by his sporadic spitting and babbling, which includes the words "new shoes," convincing Bobby Leo has money stashed away in a pair of shoes somewhere.

Audrey confronts her dad with everything she learned at One Eyed Jacks. Ben is uncharacteristically forthcoming. Asked if he slept with Laura, Ben says yes. Asked if he killed her, he replies, "I loved her."

A distraught Shelly tells Norma she has to quit waitressing at Double R to care full time for Leo. Norma, celestial being that she is, assures Shelly she is always welcome back.

This Nadine-Big Ed stuff is really, *really* starting to annoy us.

Mike Nelson makes his first appearance of season two, as he and Bobby find a minicassette concealed beneath the heel of Leo's boot.

Coop peruses the remains of Laura's diary, finding repeated references to Bob, a threatening presence in her life since early adolescence, with intimations of repeated abuse and molestation. On multiple occasions he is referred to as a friend of Leland's. In an entry dated less than two weeks before her death, Laura writes: "Someday I'm going to tell the world about Ben Horne. I'm going to tell them who Ben Horne really is."

Just then Audrey Horne drops by with her own news of Ben, informing Cooper that her dad owns One Eyed Jacks and slept with Laura.

Meanwhile, it's business as usual for Horne, who's meeting with Mr. Tojamura as Cooper and the team barge in, demanding that Ben accompany them to the sheriff's office for questioning in the murder of Laura Palmer. Ben's dismissive, and has to be corralled.

Over at the Palmer residence, foreboding signs: an LP has finished playing but skips unattended on the phonograph; Sarah crawls arduously down the stairs, suggesting the possibility that she has been drugged.

At the sheriff's station, the Log Lady waits for Cooper with another of her cryptic messages: "We don't know what will happen, or when, but there are owls in the Roadhouse" (the original dialogue, changed by Lynch, was, "You must go to the Roadhouse. Everything points that way").

A full moon hangs over Twin Peaks.

At Blue Pine Lodge, Tojamura reveals his (her?) true identity to Pete: he/she is really Catherine Martell ("Dummy, it's me!").

Back at the Palmers: Sarah sees the white horse materialize out of thin air in the middle of the living room, then conks out. Close-up on skipping record. Leland straightens his tie in the mirror.

Uh-oh.

On stage at the Roadhouse, ethereal chantoosie Julee Cruise performs "Rockin' Back Inside My Heart" before a set of red curtains, redolent of the Red Room. Donna and James share a booth. Enter Cooper along with Harry and the Log Lady, who proceeds to devour peanuts with impressive gusto. Seductively, Donna lip-synchs; we think this may be her finest moment (another of Lynch's revisions to the script, which had Donna and James leaving the Roadhouse before any of this happens).

Dissolve. Song changes: "The World Spins." Bobby is tossing down shots over at the bar. (Dana Ashbrook wasn't even supposed to be in the scene, but came by the set that day to hang out, and Lynch told him to go sit over at the bar and act sad, even though the actor had no clue why.)

Owls hang here.   *Photo by Pieter Dom*

Donna cries; James consoles her. Suddenly, a bright light; Cruise vanishes, supplanted by the Giant. Everyone freezes, except for Cooper, the Giant . . . and Margaret, the Log Lady—look closely and you'll see her hands move. Says the Giant: "It is happening again. It is happening again." Dissolve to phonograph in the Palmer living room. Leland is *still* staring at himself in that blasted mirror.

This time, Bob stares back.

Leland pulls on a pair of rubber gloves. Maddy hurries downstairs; she smells something burning—there's that "scorched oil" motif again, evoking Jacoby's reference to the night Jacques was murdered. Leland/ Bob—from this point on they keep switching back and forth from one to the other—rushes at her, and they disappear from the living room, the camera stubbornly staying behind. Off camera, Maddy screams. Leland/ Bob drags her back into the room by the throat, then wallops her in the face. Maddy breaks free, screaming for help, but there's no escaping Bob tonight. He punches her in the face again, then Leland picks her up, hugging her, moaning, kissing her. "Laura, my baby," he says. The truly awful thing is that Maddy never loses consciousness—her eyes are open throughout. She is aware of everything that is happening to her. Finally, Bob bashes her face first into the glass frame of a picture hanging on the wall.

Maddy is dead.

Leland plants an "O" under her left ring fingernail.

Back at the Roadhouse, the Giant vanishes into ether once again, and Julee Cruise is back on stage performing. From over at the bar, the antediluvian room service waiter at the Great Northern trudges over to Cooper, pats him on the shoulder, and says, "I'm so sorry." Are he and the Giant two sides of the same coin?

Donna sobs. Over at the bar, Bobby looks so sad.

Cut to Cooper. Dissolve to red curtains.

The end.

Episode 15 ("Drive With a Dead Girl")

Aired: Saturday, November 17, 1990
Twin Peaks Time: Friday, March 10, 1989
Written by Scott Frost. Directed by Caleb Deschanel.
Rating: So many great scenes, but how about that woodpecker? 9 out of 10 damn fine slices of pie. 🥧🥧🥧🥧🥧🥧🥧🥧🥧▱

Piper Laurie finally reclaims her opening credit, as "Tojamura and Catherine Martell." James Booth debuts as Ernie Niles, and Jane Greer—from the great 1947 Hollywood noir *Out of the Past*—as Vivian Smythe Niles. This episode is scripted by Scott Frost, Mark's brother.

Leland, nattily garbed in a business suit, is hitting golf balls . . . lots and lots of golf balls . . . in the Palmer living room. Not exactly normal behavior, but a far cry from the homicidal maniac we last saw.

Donna and James drop by to bid Maddy farewell, but Leland says he dropped her off at the bus station earlier that morning. Maddy's bloody corpse is stowed in Leland's golf bag, which he tosses into the trunk of his blue convertible as he motors off to work humming "The Surrey with the Fringe on Top."

Guess who's representing Ben Horne, with Leland himself up on a murder charge? Jerry Horne, counselor at law, though Cooper is unwowed by his credentials: Gonzaga University, 1974, last in his class of 142; barred from practicing in four states. Ben's alibi—that he was with Catherine Martell on the night of Laura's murder—isn't exactly foolproof, since Catherine is missing and presumed dead (thanks to Ben). Ben and Jerry reminisce, leading to a magic *Twin Peaks* moment, the so-called Louise Dombrowksi Flashlight Dance: a childhood flashback (only referenced in the script, but choreographed by director Deschanel) in which young Louise (portrayed by Emily Fincher, the sister of noted film director David Fincher) dances in the dark on a hook rug in bobby socks, flashlight in hand, as the two young, nerdy-looking Horne brothers look on, part mesmerized, part terrified, all set to a seductive score by Angelo Badalamenti. This leads to an equally unusual moment of self-reflection from Jerry: "Lord, what's become of us?"

Lucy's back in town with sister Gwen and Gwen's baby, whom Andy mistakes as Lucy's, and thus possibly his, and so passes out.

At the Great Northern, Harry breaks the news of Ben's arrest to Leland, who retreats to another section of the lobby, where he and Bob do their folie a deux thing (Ray Wise calls this his favorite *Twin Peaks* moment), and then, something interesting happens: Cooper follows him into the room, ostensibly at least to ask Leland to give him a call should he remember anything strange about Ben's behavior on the night of Laura's murder. Note the similarity here between the shot of Leland from the back, seen from Cooper's vantage point, facing the red curtains, and our first glimpse of the Man from Another Place in Cooper's episode-two dream. When Cooper rejoins Harry, Truman inquires if everything's OK, to which Coop replies, "I'm not sure," subtly suggesting—at least to us—that Cooper, for the first time, suspects something is amiss with Leland.

Bobby, listening to the minicassette, overhears Ben and Leo plotting the mill fire, with visions of blackmail dancing in his head.

Norma's hypercritical mom Vivian arrives in town, towing along new husband Ernie Niles, who looks like he wandered in from the set of *Guys and Dolls*. What is it, the loud sport coat? The half-unbuttoned shirt? The

Lucy has some 'splaining to do after Andy erroneously deduces that she has given birth.

gold necklaces? All those rings? The discarded newspaper with handwritten annotations suggesting he's a gambler? All of the above?

At the Great Northern, Gerard's stump twitches; the one-armer pronounces Bob near at hand. The next thing we know he's overpowering a deputy and escaping out the window.

Harry spots a pileated woodpecker. Just sayin'.

Pete drops by the sheriff's office and commiserates with Harry over Josie's departure, confessing that he too loved her. Their suspicions are aroused when they compare notes on Jonathan, since Josie introduced him differently to each of them. Harry and Coop get word that Gerard is MIA, so depart to find him, leaving Pete free to fulfill his true mission: delivering a message, via cassette recorder, to Ben from Catherine, who offers to confirm his alibi only if he signs over the mill and Ghostwood Estates. Ben freaks: Pete's in clover.

Back in his convertible warbling "The Surrey with the Fringe on Top," Leland is swerving all over the road and nearly crashes head-on into Cooper and Truman. Left momentarily alone with Cooper as Harry returns to the car to answer a radio call from Lucy, Leland *volunteers* to show Coop his new golf clubs, opening the trunk and pulling out an iron that he appears on the verge of smacking Cooper over the head with, until Harry returns to report that Hawk—who else?—has tracked down Gerard.

Andy shares the good news about his sperm with Lucy.

Gerard sniffs around Ben and reports that Bob is close, but "not here now." Jerry demands that Truman either charge Ben or let him go; Truman chooses the former. Well played, Jerry. Cooper takes Harry aside and tells him he thinks they have the wrong man, but Harry's had it with Cooper's "mumbo jumbo" and says he's locking Ben up—a rare moment of tension between the two. Cooper yields: "It's your backyard."

Turns out Hank and Ernie were prison buddies, while Ernie was doing time for ripping off a savings-and-loan company to bankroll his gambling addiction. Ernie swears he's gone straight, but hey, what about that newspaper? Hank smells leverage.

Over in Room 315, Audrey pays Coop another late-night visit, wondering if her tip had anything to do with Pop's arrest, though this time she keeps her clothes on (however, she does climb onto Coop's bed). Their conversation is halted abruptly by a phone call—another body has been found: Maddy Ferguson, wrapped in plastic, just like cousin Laura.

Episode 16 ("Arbitrary Law")

Aired: Saturday, December 1, 1990
Twin Peaks Time: Saturday, March 11, 1989
Written by Mark Frost + Harley Peyton + Robert Engels. Directed by Tim Hunter.
Rating: Mother of mercy, is this the end of Leland? 10 out of 10 damn fine slices of pie. 🍰🍰🍰🍰🍰🍰🍰🍰🍰🍰

A superlative episode, in which we say goodbye to Leland Palmer and wrap up the Laura Palmer arc. For many, *Twin Peaks* ends here, but what do they know?

Good news (and we need it): Albert is back, reporting that Maddy's murderer is "the same ghoul who killed Laura." Cooper asks Harry to hold off for twenty-four hours before contacting Maddy's relatives. Albert surprises again, telling Cooper: "I don't know where this is headed, but the only one of us with the coordinates for this destination in his hardware is you. Go on whatever vision quest you require. Stand on the rim of the volcano. Stand alone and do your dance. Just find this beast before he takes another bite." Damn, this guy is good!

James presents Donna with a ring, the significance of which we are unsure, though he says they should be together all the time, "if that's OK with you." It is. *Some*-thing transcendent seems to have happened between them last night; we can only imagine.

Donna overhears Andy reciting the line from Harold Smith's suicide note; making the connection to Pierre Tremond, she dashes off to tell Cooper, and together they head over to the Tremonds' to investigate. However, the Mrs. Tremond Donna met previously is nowhere to be found now, supplanted by a middle-aged woman who has no idea who Donna is or what she's talking about, though she does have a note for her, found in her mail the morning after Harold's death.

So instructed by Cooper, Donna unseals the envelope, discovering a page from Laura's secret diary. The first entry, dated February 22, describes a dream from the night before, which, we recognize as Donna reads on, is identical to Cooper's Red Room dream from early in the first season. We know this too because we actually see images from the dream as Donna reads, superimposed over Cooper's eye, leading us to conclude that Cooper is coming to the same realization. Laura reports in her diary that Bob is afraid of just one person—a man named Mike—and wonders if Mike is the older man in her dream, though *we* know this is, rather, an older iteration of Cooper. The diary resumes with another entry the next night, February 23: "Tonight is the night that I die. I know I have to, because it's the only way to keep Bob away from me, the only way to tear him out from inside. I know he wants me. I can feel his fire. But if I die he can't hurt me anymore."

Coop seeks guidance from Gerard—now Mike—hoping desperately to unlock the secret of his dream. "Bob and I, when we were killing together, there was this, this perfect relationship: appetite, satisfaction, a golden circle," Mike says. The ring! Mike's familiar with the Giant—he's "known to us here"—and says the big guy can help him find Bob. "You have all the clues you need," Mike says.

Outside, in the hallway, Cooper has another encounter with the room-service waiter, who tells him the milk is "getting warmer now."

Tojamura visits Ben in jail, revealing his/her true identity. With corroboration of his alibi dangling before him, Ben signs the mill and Ghostwood projects over to Catherine. Oh, how the mighty have fallen.

Donna drops in on Leland, bringing a cassette of the song she and Maddy recorded a few nights earlier with James, hoping Leland will forward it on. Leland gets a call from Maddy's mom, saying she never arrived back in Missoula. Leland/Bob comes seriously close to offing Donna, but is interrupted by Truman, who arrives with news of another murder, though not revealing the identity of the victim. Donna figures it out. Distraught, she arranges a meeting with James to break the news that Maddy is dead; she begs him not to leave, but he drives off on his hog—so much for being together "all the time."

Thunder and lightning, lightning and thunder. Ben, Cooper, and Albert congregate at the otherwise empty Roadhouse, and are soon joined by Big Ed, Hawk, Leo, Bobby, and, finally, Major Briggs and the room-service waiter from the Great Northern. Yes, a strange aggregation. It's classic locked-door mystery, with Cooper announcing: "I have reason to believe that the killer is in this room." When the old Waiter offers Coop a stick of gum, Leland pipes up, saying he chewed the same brand as a kid. The waiter repeats the words of the Man from Another Place in Cooper's dream: "That gum you like is going to come back in style."

Everything freezes. Cooper is revisiting his dream: the Man from Another Place dances; Laura whispers the magic words into Cooper's ear: "My father killed me." The Giant appears—he seems to dig the Roadhouse—offering Cooper back his ring.

Cooper orders Ben to accompany them back to sheriff's station, suggesting he bring Leland along as his attorney. Once there, Cooper whispers something into Harry's ear; Truman nods.

Hawk takes Ben downstairs, but just as he's about to enter the interrogation room, Harry pushes Ben aside and he and Cooper toss Leland in instead, slamming the door behind him.

Leland/Bob goes berserk.

Under interrogation, Leland/Bob confesses to killing both Laura and Maddy. "I have this thing for knives, just like what happened to you in Pittsburgh that time, huh, Cooper?" he says. Cooper's visibly shaken by this evocation of his past. "Does Leland know what you've done?" he asks. "Leland's a babe in the woods, with a large hole where his conscience used to be, and when I go, children, I will pull that ripcord and you watch Leland remember. Watch him!"

What's amazing here is that the episode actually cuts away for an interlude with Andy, Dick, and Lucy, who tells the two rivals that she's keeping the baby and will authorize a blood test to determine paternity once the child is born. Dick lights up a cigarette (in a holder, of course), in what seems like a throwaway joke, but the smoke wafts up to the sprinkler above his head; this will have repercussions. Everything's connected. ("A golden circle.")

The Dweller on the Threshold: Leland Palmer's shadow self.   *Photo by Richard Beymer*

Back downstairs, Harry still can't get over what he's witnessed, even after Cooper patiently explains everything (for the network, perhaps?). "Now this Bob, he can't really exist?" Harry asks. "I mean, Leland's just crazy, right?" No one even attempts to answer.

From inside the locked room, Leland/Bob recites the familiar "Fire walk with me" chant when the sprinkler bursts, spewing water everywhere. Leland slams himself against the door, over and over. Cooper, Harry, Hawk, and Albert hurry back inside, but too late: Leland lies dying on the floor, begging for forgiveness, Bob finally having departed his body. Cooper gently guides his soul "into the light," where Laura waits for him, offering redemption.

Outside in the woods, the guys huddle up, profoundly pensive. The storm has passed; it is a calm, sunny day. Somehow Major Briggs is not only there but seems to know exactly what's been going on. "Gentlemen," he says, paraphrasing Hamlet, "there's more in heaven and earth than is dreamt of in our philosophy." Harry still can't wrap his head around it: "I've seen some strange things, but this is way off the map. I'm having a hard time believing." "Harry," Coop counters, "is it any easier to believe a man would rape and murder his own daughter? Any more comforting?" Adds Albert: "Maybe that's all Bob is: the evil that men do."

Leave it to Harry to ask the practical question: If Bob *was* real, and he got away, where did he go?

The answer, judging from the final scene of the episode: inside an owl.

Episode 17 ("Dispute Between Brothers")

Aired: Saturday, December 8, 1990
Twin Peaks Time: Wednesday, March 15, 1989
Written by Tricia Brock. Directed by Tina Rathborne.
Rating: Trouble brewing, though the ending rocks.
7 out of 10 damn fine slices of pie. 🥧🥧🥧🥧🥧🥧🥧▱▱▱

Clarence Williams III, Peggy Lipton's teammate in the sixties generation-gap cop show *The Mod Squad,* makes his *Twin Peaks* debut, as FBI Special Agent Roger Hardy of Internal Affairs, as do Tony Jay (Dougie Milford) and Gavan O'Herlihy, as Royal Canadian Mounted Police Sergeant Preston King.

Contains one of our favorite *Twin Peaks* moments, when Cooper tells the distraught Sarah Palmer he'd be honored to drive her to Leland's funeral (Coop's empathy is so crucial to his singular brand of heroism).

Three days have passed; Cooper and Doc Hayward are in the Palmer living room, attending to Sarah. Cooper assures her it wasn't Leland who committed these horrific acts—at least "not the Leland that you knew"—but rather someone who had fallen prey to "dark and heinous" forces, victimized by his own innocence. He tells her Leland had visions of Laura in the final moments of his life, and he's convinced Laura forgave him. Bob, he assures her, is "gone, forever." But is he?

Seems like everyone in town shows up at the Palmer home after the funeral with the exception of James, who apparently rode his motorcycle straight out of town after leaving Donna.

Coop isn't sure what's next, but with a few weeks of vacation time stockpiled he accepts Major Briggs's invitation to go night fishing.

The battling Milford brothers, Dwayne (the mayor) and Dougie (the newspaper owner), nearly come to blows in the middle of the gathering; the root of the argument is unclear but has something to do with the fact that Dougie is engaged to be married, for the fifth time, to a teenage babe. We are not feeling so good about this new storyline.

Nadine re-enrolls at Twin Peaks High, with special permission from the principal, and auditions for the cheerleading squad. It goes badly.

Audrey makes one last attempt to pierce Cooper's armor, popping in on him in Room 315 as he packs up his boxers, but Coop is ever steadfast and upright, and refuses to become romantically involved with someone who 1) is a teenager and 2) was involved in his investigation. He shares with Audrey details from his tragic past, in which a woman he loved—and was supposed to protect—was killed, an outcome for which Cooper accepts complete responsibility. "She died in my arms. I was badly injured, and my partner lost his mind," said partner being Windom Earle.

Audrey tells Cooper there's only one thing wrong with him: "You're perfect."

The unctuous Dick Tremayne is back, assuring Lucy he's ready to take parenthood seriously, even joining a big-brother program called Happy Helping Hands.

Coop drops by the sheriff's station to bid adieu; Harry presents him with a Bookhouse Boys patch and a green-butt skunk. With Hawk, Andy, and Lucy lined up to wish Cooper farewell, the scene resembles Dorothy's goodbye to the Scarecrow, Tin Man, and Lion in *The Wizard of Oz*, one of David Lynch's favorite films, but they're rudely interrupted when FBI Special Agent Roger Hardy of Internal Affairs barges in with Canadian Mountie Preston King, announcing that Cooper has been suspended sans pay for crossing into Canada twice during the Palmer investigation without consulting the FBI or Canadian authorities.

More on this to come.

Bobby, having already mailed Ben Horne the incriminating recording of him and Leo plotting the Packard mill fire, shows up for an unscheduled job interview with Ben, who has him physically removed from the room. Instead he winds up going for ice cream with Audrey, which seems like a better idea to us anyway. Audrey prefers cone to cup: "I like to lick," she says. She *does* know how to use her tongue, that girl.

Hardy reveals to Coop that the Mounties were working on a six-month drug sting to nail Jean Renault, but the One Eyed Jacks raid upended that plan, with Renault and the drugs now missing. Harry, ever loyal to Cooper, refuses to answer questions without a warrant, telling Hardy and King to "take their cooperation and stuff it."

Shelly's had it with Leo, and pleads with Bobby to put him in a home.

The Double R gets a scathing review from M. T. Wentz, who turns out to be Vivian Niles. Mommy dearest! Norma boots her out of her restaurant and her life.

Ernie and Hank cross over into Canada to discuss business opportunities with Jean Renault at One Eyed Jacks. Hey, what's Mountie King doing there? Other than conspiring with Renault to "crucify" Cooper, we mean.

You'll never guess who turns up on Harry's doorstep: Josie Packard. Wait, didn't she leave town? The reunion is passionate.

Over a campfire in the woods, Major Briggs inquires if Cooper has ever heard of a place called the White Lodge. Coop doesn't think so. Their philosophical dialogue is interrupted so that Cooper can take a leak—"nothing quite like urinating out in the open air." Bright lights and owl close-ups: two signs that something ominous is about to happen in Twin Peaks. Plus, what's up with that hooded figure off in the distance? Never seen him before. Briggs yells out to Cooper, who dashes back to the campsite, but too late. Major bummer. Briggs is gone.

Episode 18 ("Masked Ball")

Aired: Saturday, December 15, 1990
Twin Peaks Time: Thursday, March 16, 1989
Written by Barry Pullman. Directed by Duwayne Dunham.
Rating: We wish our invitation to the wedding had gotten lost in the mail. But Bryson is a plus, and there's lots of lodge stuff, and best of all the Linc-Julie reunion . . . 7 out of 10 damn fine slices of pie. 🥧🥧🥧🥧🥧🥧🥧▱▱▱

David Duchovny, almost three years shy of his breakout role in *The X-Files*, debuts as transgender Special Agent Dennis/Denise Bryson of the DEA, who has a history with Cooper (uh, not that kind). Also bowing: Robyn Lively as Lana Budding Milford and Annette McCarthy as Evelyn Marsh. Plus Joshua Harris as Little Nicky and Dan O'Herlihy as . . . well, it's a secret. We take no pleasure in reporting these additions to the cast.

Gordon Cole rings up from Bend, Oregon, offering Cooper his full support in the IA investigation. Gordon's parting advice: "Let a smile be your umbrella."

Cooper tells Hardy he's been doing a lot of thinking lately and has started to "focus out beyond the edge of the board, at a bigger game. . . . The sound wind makes through the pines, the sentience of animals, what we fear in the dark, and what lies beyond the darkness."

Hardy's response: "What the hell are you talking about?"

The suspension sticks.

Nadine thinks Mike Nelson has "the cutest buns."

James pulls into a roadside bar called Wallies, a couple of hours west of Twin Peaks, where he encounters the aforementioned Evelyn Marsh, possibly the most hated woman in *Twin Peaks* fandom. Directionless, James accepts her offer to fix her husband Jeffrey's 1948 Jag, and live in a room above the garage.

Sadly, Dick Tremayne refuses to go away, showing up at the sheriff's station with his new Little Brother, Nicky, a real monster.

In our fave scene of the episode, mostly because it is so full of foreboding, Harry and Hawk fill Cooper in on the White Lodge, a local legend going way back. There are "other worlds" out there, Hawk says, reminding us of the "Fire walk with me" recitation ("One chants out between two worlds . . .").

"My people believe that the White Lodge is a place where the spirits that rule man and nature here reside," says Hawk. Unfortunately legend also speaks of a place called the Black Lodge, the shadow self of the White Lodge, through which every spirit must pass on the way to perfection, confronting their own shadow self. "It is said, if you confront the Black Lodge with imperfect courage, it will annihilate your soul," says Hawk.

We suggest you remember all of this.

Dennis Bryson arrives, to aid in the investigation into charges that Cooper stole drugs being used in a sting operation during his raid of One Eyed Jacks. Cooper says they worked together in Oakland and calls him "one of the finest minds in the DEA." Except that he is now a she, and prefers Denise to Dennis. Cooper, empathetic fellow that he is, obliges.

Josie too obliges, after Harry demands answers, but she's a tough one to trust these days. She tells Harry she used to work in Hong Kong for a man named Thomas Eckhardt, who rescued her from the streets when she was sixteen, though he sounds like a bastard. "He was my father, my master, my lover," she says. Josie's late husband Andrew was once Eckhardt's business partner, and Eckhardt wasn't thrilled about losing Josie to him; Josie tells Harry she believes Eckhardt was responsible for Andrew's death. Now he wants Josie back in Hong Kong, which is where she was headed with Jonathan when she escaped from the Seattle airport and returned to Twin Peaks.

Hardy has a slice of pie at the Double R—Linc and Julie reunited!

Reprobates Hank and Ernie are back from One Eyed Jacks, and dealing coke for Jean Renault.

Disheveled and unshaven, Ben wistfully watches home movies of the Great Northern groundbreaking, when he was just a kid. Hank drops in with harsh news, alerting Ben that he has switched allegiances to Jean Renault, who has taken over control of One Eyed Jacks. Ben tells him he's "dancing with the devil"—pot calling the kettle black?—but Hank swaggers out, oblivious to Ben's warnings. Ben makes shadow puppets on the movie screen (a Richard Beymer improvisation, as director Dunham kept the camera rolling even after Hank left the room, when the scene was supposed to end).

Cooper receives a package from Windom Earle, with another chess move and a threatening message, delivered via audiocassette: "My goal will be attained at any cost: The king must die."

Lana and Dougie Milford wed; not *Twin Peaks'* finest hour. Cooper and Bryson meet for drinks at the Great Northern bar; Bryson reveals finding traces of the missing cocaine in Cooper's car. Both smell frame.

Josie returns to Blue Pine Lodge, telling Catherine that Eckhardt was responsible for Andrew's death, and that she herself is in serious danger with nowhere else to go. Catherine isn't in a forgiving mood; she allows Josie to stay, but only as her maid.

Hiding in the next room is none other than Andrew Packard: "Everything is going exactly as we planned," he tells his sister.

Episode 19 ("The Black Widow")

Aired: Saturday, January 12, 1991
Twin Peaks Time: Friday, March 17, 1989
Written by Harley Peyton + Robert Engels. Directed by Caleb Deschanel.
Rating: Too much time in the Marshes. Plus, Little Nicky is a big drag.
    6 out of 10 damn fine slices of pie. 🥧🥧🥧🥧🥧🥧▱▱▱▱

Nicholas Love debuts as Malcolm Sloan—painful for us to say even now.

Cooper in a flannel shirt; mother of mercy, is this the end of *Twin Peaks?*

The wit and wisdom of Ben Horne: "Admiration is for poets and dairy cows." Bobby Briggs doesn't get it, either, but Horne hires him to follow Hank Jennings around, snapping photographs.

Cooper checks out vacation homes, opting for an abandoned property known as Dead Dog Farm.

Little Nicky's caseworker, Judy Swain, informs Lucy, Andy, and Dick that the boy has been victimized by "persistent random misfortune," including the murder of his parents.

We don't care.

Dougie Milford dies of a heart attack on his wedding night.

We don't care.

Nadine pins Mike in front of the wrestling team.

We don't care.

James meets Evelyn's brother Malcolm Sloan, who drives her husband Jeffrey around. Jeffrey beats Evelyn, Malcolm says.

We don't care.

Cooper and real estate agent Irene Littlehorse drive out to Dead Dog Farm; Irene says nobody's been up to see it in at least a year, yet Cooper notices fresh tire tracks outside and cigarette butts inside, along with traces of baby laxative in the sink and cocaine in the kitchen.

We care, but only a little.

Colonel Riley, overseeing the Air Force investigation into the missing Garland Briggs, wants to know if Cooper noticed any owls in the area before the major disappeared. Coop says yes, he heard an owl just before Briggs vanished. Riley says the messages they received the night Cooper was shot came not from deep space, but from right there in the Twin Peaks woods. Might this have something to do with the White Lodge, Coop asks? "That's classified," Riley answers.

Now we care.

James and Evelyn make out in the front seat of the Jaguar. Ben, under siege, retreats into the innermost recesses of his twisted mind, somehow leading to an obsession with the Civil War, as he adopts a Southern accent and recreates battles with toy soldiers—the writers themselves had become fixated on the War Between the States thanks to Ken Burns's PBS documentary series *The Civil War*, which aired in September 1990. This is not their finest hour.

Audrey shows Coop a series of Bobby Briggs–snapped photographs of Jean, Hank, Ernie, and Sergeant King of the Mounted Police assembling outside Dead Dog Farm.

Dick is convinced Little Nicky is the Devil, or at the very least homicidal in the first degree.

Threatened with parole-violation charges for palling around with Jean Renault, the craven Ernie Niles becomes a reluctant front-line soldier in the DEA sting targeting Renault and King. Ernie sets up the meeting at Dead Dog Farm; Bryson poses as a big-time buyer in from Seattle.

James overhears what appears to be a violent argument between Evelyn and Jeffrey.

Another dark and stormy night in Twin Peaks. The lights in the Briggs house momentarily falter; Major Briggs reappears suddenly, inexplicably dressed in vintage aviator garb.

"Is everything alright?" Betty asks.

"No dear," he says. "Not exactly."

Episode 20 ("Checkmate")

Aired: Saturday, January 19, 1991
Twin Peaks Time: Saturday, March 18, 1989
Written by Harley Peyton. Directed by Todd Holland.
Rating: Some nifty work by Holland, but these storylines!
   6 out of 10 damn fine slices of pie. ▰▰▰▰▰▰▱▱▱▱

A stellar opening from director Holland: the cosmos, as a disembodied voice eerily intones a single word: "Cooper." A yellow, triple-triangular object hurdles toward us, bursting into flames; dissolve to Major Briggs, sharing his meager recollections of his abduction: "I remember stepping from the flames, a vague shape in the dark, then nothing, until I found myself standing by the cold remains of our campfire two days later."

Anything else? Yes, a single disturbing image, of a giant owl.

Doc Hayward spots three triangular scars behind Briggs's right ear, in perfect proportion.

Atypically, Briggs shares, telling Doc, Harry, and Cooper about Project Blue Book, the military's investigation into unidentified flying objects, officially disbanded in 1969, though certain members of the Air Force "unofficially" continue to examine not only the heavens, but also, in the case of Twin Peaks, the earth below, in search of the White Lodge. That's as far as Briggs gets before being whisked away by military bozos.

Holland stages another nifty trick here: as Cooper peruses a photo of the scars on Briggs's neck, a drop of water falls onto the photo, and Cooper, Harry, and Doc all gaze up at the leaky sprinkler overhead, evoking Bob's confession and Leland's death in episode sixteen.

Invitation to Love returns to *Twin Peaks* after a long absence, as Shelly has it playing in the background while trying to feed Leo. Meanwhile, Shelly's got soap-opera problems of her own: Bobby, ego bloated by his courtship of the Hornes, disses her on his way out the door; she sends him on his way with a hard slap to the face.

James dishes to Evelyn about Laura, inspiring another smooch session. My, what big sunglasses Evelyn has—the better to cover her bruises.

Nadine continues her relentless pursuit of Mike Nelson.

Hank spies Norma sneaking out of the Double R in the middle of the day for a tryst with Ed, and follows.

Harry wants Josie to move in with him, but she's afraid Eckhardt will kill them both if she leaves Blue Pine Lodge.

Ben's Civil War fantasy persists, so Audrey calls in the cavalry, here meaning Uncle Jerry and Dr. Jacoby, God help us all.

Norma wants to be with Ed no matter what.

Harry deputizes Cooper, empowering him to partake in the Renault sting. Harry is such a mensch.

Dick and Andy sneak into the Dorritt Home for Boys, looking for records that will prove Little Nicky murdered his parents.

Thanks to Ed, Donna learns that James is hiding out near Wallies, and heads off to find him.

Hank sneaks into Ed's house and beats him, until Nadine gets home and pulverizes Hank.

Catherine visits Ben at the Great Northern; despite everything, she still pines for him.

James and Evelyn get it on.

The Dead Dog Farm sting goes amiss when Ernie's excessive perspiration short-circuits the wire, causing Ernie to smoke. Literally. Renault and King demand safe passage to the border, taking Ernie and Denise (now Dennis again, though just temporarily) hostage, though Cooper swaps himself for them.

Something tells us Evelyn and Malcolm aren't *really* brother and sister, unless they're Lannisters.

Back at Dead Dog, Renault explains why Cooper's death is so important to him: "Before you came here, Twin Peak was a simple place. My brothers deal dope to the teenagers and the truck drivers. One Eyed Jacks welcomed the businessmen and the tourists. Quiet people live a quiet life. Then, a pretty girl die, and you arrive, and everything change. My brother Bernardo, shot, and left to die in the woods. A grieving father smother my remaining brother with the pillow. Kidnapping, death. Suddenly, the quiet people, they're quiet no more. Suddenly, the simple dream become the nightmare. So, if you die, maybe you will be the last to die. Maybe you brought the nightmare with you. And maybe the nightmare will die with you."

Impersonating a waitress, Denise arrives at the front door with a tray of food. King lets her in. Cooper grabs a gun from Denise's garter, gunning down Renault while the DEA agent subdues King.

Game over. Good guys win. Good guys win!

Leo wakes up. Shelly screams.

The sheriff's department receives an anonymous call, reporting that a bomb has been placed in the woods, followed by an explosion that blacks out Twin Peaks.

Inside Truman's office, Cooper finds a murdered man sitting by a chessboard, a buck's severed head by his arm. What is it? Truman asks. "It's a chess game," says Cooper. "Windom Earle's next move."

Episode 21 ("Double Play")

Aired: Saturday, February 2, 1991
Twin Peaks Time: Saturday–Sunday, March 18–19, 1989
Written by Scott Frost. Directed by Uli Edel.
Rating: *Twin Peaks* fanzine *Wrapped in Plastic* ripped this episode as the series' "lowest point," and it's hard to argue, given the Ben Horne-Dr. Jacoby "Dixie" duet and the excruciating scene in which Doc Hayward drives Andy and Dick to tears recounting Little Nicky's woebegone past, plus new and equally grievous developments in the insufferable Lana Milford and Evelyn Marsh sagas. 4 out of 10 damn fine slices of pie. 🥧🥧🥧🥧🥧🥧🥧🥧🥧🥧

German director Edel had made a splash in the fall of 1989 with his feature film *Last Exit to Brooklyn*.

Two long-gestating villains finally show: Windom Earle (Kenneth Welsh) and Thomas Eckhardt (David Warner). Brenda E. Mathers appears very briefly as Caroline Earle, her image flashing on-screen as Cooper recalls the tragic events in Pittsburgh, and Brenda Strong as Eckhardt's assistant Jones.

Cooper's convinced Windom Earle is behind the blackout and the murder of the vagrant found in Harry's office with a pawn stuffed inside his mouth: "He's taken his first pawn in a very sick game."

Audrey and Bobby huddle over how to bring Ben back from, as Audrey's phrases it, "limbo land, before he melts away and leaves us with a handful of nothing."

Shelly is locked inside her house with a fully alert (in a manner of speaking)—and aggressively angry—Leo (still no lights, making the scene even creepier). Kudos to Bobby, who nearly dies trying to save her, instead of turning tail and bolting when he realizes what is going on (the yin and yang of Bobby Briggs). Shelly to the rescue, stabbing Leo in the leg. He limps off into the night like a wounded puppy.

Andy and Dick are convinced Little Nicky murdered his own parents at the age of six; Lucy thinks they're both nuts.

James finally meets Jeffrey Marsh, who seems like a nice enough fellow if a bit of a schmo, though a rich one. Jeffrey takes the spiffed-up '48 Jag out for a spin, and crashes almost instantly. Close-up on Ev; very suspicious.

Cooper comes clean to Truman, admitting he's "brought some baggage to town I haven't told you about," finally laying out the details of the Pittsburgh tragedy: the brilliant Windom Earle was Cooper's first partner and taught him everything he knows about being an agent. Four years earlier they were assigned to protect Windom's wife Caroline, a material witness to a federal crime (which Coop now believes was committed by Earle). Unfortunately Cooper did more than protect her; he fell in love, and she with him. One night, he says, "I failed in my vigilance"; Caroline is attacked and stabbed, and dies in Cooper's arm. The killer was never identified, but Cooper's convinced it was Windom Earle. Following the attack, Earle supposedly goes mad and is institutionalized, though Cooper thinks the whole thing may have been an act.

On a tip from Big Ed, Donna tracks James to Wallies, where she runs into Evelyn Marsh, who fibs by saying James has left town.

Major Briggs stumbles into the sheriff's office, collapses, comes to, and tells Cooper and Harry he believes he was taken to the White Lodge during his abduction, though he has no specific recollection of it. He has a vague, intuitive sense that trouble lies ahead, and if they need him he'll be lurking "in the shadows." Isn't he always?

Mayor Dwayne Milford pulls a shotgun on Lana, but winds up smitten, just like every other guy she encounters. Yet somehow she can't win over a single *Twin Peaks* fan.

Pete learns Andrew is alive and kicking. Andrew explains that Josie was working with Eckhardt, his former business partner, who schemed to murder him after Andrew bettered him in a "business deal." Hence, the exploding boat. However, Andrew sussed out the scheme beforehand and escaped unharmed, though pretended to be dead for devious purposes of his own. After all, he is Catherine's brother.

Eckhardt and Jones check in to the Great Northern; flames from the lobby fireplace reflect in his sunglasses, leaving little doubt of his satanic purposes.

News of Jonathan's death in Seattle arrives; Harry, worried Josie may have had something to do with it, asks Coop to investigate.

James, wracked with guilt for cuckolding a swell guy like Jeffrey, is itching to ankle, but Evelyn pleads with him to stay, breaking the news that Jeffrey is dead. When James accuses her of setting him up—naturally people will suspect him, since he had just repaired the car—Evelyn comes clean, saying it was Malcolm's idea to implicate James in a scheme to kill Jeffrey. She admits they aren't really brother and sister. Duh. This is classic noir territory, all right. Cops arrive; James skedaddles, with help from Donna, who's waiting for him outside.

Leo, meanwhile, has apparently been wandering around the woods for the entire episode (lucky for him, as he didn't have to sit through some of these storylines), but finally happens upon a shack, from whence emanates melodic flute music. Entering, he encounters a rather diabolical-looking man, who identifies himself as Windom Earle. Even Leo can't be that dumb, can he?

He can.

Episode 22 ("Slaves and Masters")

Aired: Saturday, February 9, 1991
Twin Peaks Time: Sunday–Monday, March 19–20, 1989
Written by Harley Peyton + Robert Engels. Directed by Diane Keaton.
Rating: We're back on track.
8 out of 10 damn fine slices of pie. ◥◥◥◥◥◥◥◥▷▷

After a frustrating, rather rudderless clutch of episodes, *Twin Peaks* regains some authentic menace and mystery with this installment, which features Cooper's nemesis Windom Earle stepping up his campaign of psychological warfare and director Diane Keaton (in her sole outing as *TP* helmer) effectively nodding to Lynch's distinctive visual style with unsettling slo-mo insert shots and eerily strange tableaus, including a group of uniformed policemen frozen in profile along the bar at Wallies, and the episode's stately opening tracking shot through Earle's chessmen.

The plot, as ever, bubbles with incident: James is framed for the murder of Evelyn's husband and is nearly killed himself by Malcolm before Donna interrupts and Evelyn kills Malcolm herself. The resolution of this storyline is mourned by no one.

Windom Earle, when not skulking around town in an absurd disguise (did he use Catherine's guy?) hangs out with the escaped and still groggy Leo, fitting the abusive trucker with a shock collar and setting him to some as yet undefined nefarious purpose.

An effervescent and affectionate Albert Rosenfield visits the sheriff's station to deliver some warm hugs, fashion observations, and news of Earle's sinister doings.

Big Ed and Norma finally log some pillow time, joined by Nadine, who takes this development in stride, as she still yearns for the gormless Mike.

Ben Horne regains his senses after Audrey, Jerry, Bobby, and Dr. Jacoby stage a revisionist telling of Appomattox. So many cigars.

Scheming Catherine and her not-dead brother welcome the treacherous Thomas Eckhardt, dangling a traumatized Josie as bait. Pete turns out to be a whiz at chess, which will probably come in handy.

And in the standout scene, Cooper returns to his room at the Great Northern to find Caroline's death mask and a recorded message from Earle, informing the lawman that it's "his move." Suddenly it feels like season one again: a mystery is afoot, the night is dark and full of portents, and the owls are not what they seem.

Episode 23 ("The Condemned Woman")

Aired: Saturday, February 16, 1991
Twin Peaks Time: Tuesday, March 21, 1989
Written by Tricia Brock. Directed by Lesli Linka Glatter.
Rating: A sort of pokey episode until that final crazy sequence, so: 6½ out of 10
    damn fine slices of pie. 🥧🥧🥧🥧🥧🥧🥧🥧🥧🥧

In which perhaps the most terrifying interloper of all enters our story: we speak, of course, of Billy Zane, whose smarm levels could stun an ox at 50 feet. Mr. Zane, playing an associate of Ben Horne's called John Justice Wheeler, immediately catches the eye of the restless Audrey, who is eager to shed her virginity and considers Wheeler the top prospect for the job.

Horne *fils* continues his evolution into an all-around swell guy, abjuring his customary stogies in favor of nutritious celery stalks and taking up the cause of the endangered pine weasel. If this newfound environmental zeal complicates Catherine's plans for Ghostwood, all the better.

Big Ed sweetly proposes to Norma, prompting her visit to husband Hank, ensconced in a jail cell under suspicion of the attempted murder of Leo Johnson. Hank takes the news poorly, calling Norma Ed's "whore," which elicits the response "I'd rather be his whore than your wife," an utterance that caused a riot of colorful flowers to spontaneously blossom on the grave of Jacqueline Susann, probably.

Pete coaches Cooper on his next chess move with Earle. Earle has been a busy bee, choosing a sadly less outré disguise for his sorties into town as he draws Audrey, Shelly, and Donna—the iconic three beauties of early *TP* promotional efforts—to the Roadhouse, via mysterious notes intimating grave consequences should the girls not attend. All three show up, of course, because these gals LOVE mysterious threats and clearly have no reason to worry about their personal safety in the warm, comforting environs of this sleepy mountain town.

James leaves town.

James leaves town. That sentence made us so happy we had to type it twice. Happy travels, oh wooden one.

The episode's biggest development is the conclusion of Josie's storyline . . . and we can't help but feel that Joan Chen's character, while very beautiful and creditably performed, never seemed all that significant or interesting, despite serving as Harry's love interest and playing a key role in the Eckhardt/Packard feud (which, as the pertinent events in that storyline occurred before the start of the series, is a little difficult to feel too strongly about). Coop learns that it was Josie who shot him back in season one; he's pretty nice about it. He and Harry track Josie and Eckhardt to the Great Northern, but are too late: Eckhardt is dead, and a hysterical Josie soon joins him.

And then, SWEET HOLY OH MY GOD, Bob appears, slithering over the bed and doing his terrifying thing, The Man from Another Place pops in for a little soft shoe, and Josie, in the weirdest computer-generated effect in the history of television, turns into a wooden pull on the bedside bureau. This somewhat surprising turn of events is unexplained.

It was Lynch's idea.

Episode 24 ("Wounds and Scars")

Aired: Thursday, March 28, 1991
Twin Peaks Time: Wednesday, March 22, 1989
Written by Barry Pullman. Directed by James Foley.
Rating: Weird laughs and sultry pseudo-noir . . .
　　6 out of 10 damn fine slices of pie. 🥧🥧🥧🥧🥧🥧▱▱▱▱

James Foley, director of the celebrated neo-noir *After Dark, My Sweet*, helms this installment, opening, appropriately enough, with a whiskey-soaked, mournful saxophone-scored montage of Harry and Josie's sexy, sexy love.

Harry's in a bad way, drunkenly tearing up the Bookhouse and waving a gun around until Cooper is able to talk him down—an impressive feat, considering Coop also drops the news that the erstwhile Mrs. Packard was a prostitute in addition to being a murderer. And now she's a knob on a nightstand. An interesting journey for ol' Josie, indeed. Let her go, man.

Norma's lovely sister Annie arrives in town, sporting a troubled past and troubling scars on her wrists. Cooper is smitten anyway, and practically levitates with schoolboy ardor after she serves him coffee at the Double R. Windom Earle looks on, disguised this time as a biker, and takes the time to encourage Shelly to enter the Miss Twin Peaks pageant. Shelly protests that she doesn't think of herself as pretty, which leads one to wonder if perhaps she is an idiot, which, considering her taste in men, seems likely.

Windom Earle has trained the quasi-feral Leo like a dog: the big lug fetches the G-man his slippers, pipe, and newspaper with vacant obedience. Earle gets very upset when he realizes Cooper is angling for a stalemate in their chess match, clearly coached by an outside ringer. That is NOT ON in Earle's book, and many people will be very sorry.

Strange bedfellows: Donna spies an intimate moment between her mother and Ben Horne, and is visited by Earle in the guise of her father's deceased schoolmate; the Log Lady and Major Briggs compare postabduction skin markings; Ed and Nadine receive counseling from Dr. Jacoby; Nadine and Mike catch the bad disguise fever sweeping Twin Peaks and get a room; and Audrey and John Justice Wheeler go on a picnic and bask in having won the genetic lottery. Such lush, fulsome feminine beauty. Audrey is also pretty.

The episode's big set piece is a fashion-show fund-raiser for the endangered pine weasel. Andy and Lucy are the principal models, Dick Tremayne handles the MC duties, and David Lander's twitchy Tim Pinkle is on hand with an actual living pine weasel for educational purposes. What can go wrong? (Hint: everything, spectacularly.)

Finally Eckhardt's former associate, Jones, who bears a striking resemblance to Oh Henry! heir Sue Ellen Mischke, confronts Catherine, presents her with a featureless, sealed black box, and later slips into bed beside a drunkenly unconscious Harry. His luck with women is consistent, anyway.

Episode 25 ("On the Wings of Love")

Aired: Thursday, April 4, 1991
Twin Peaks Time: Wednesday–Thursday, March 22–23, 1989
Written by Harley Peyton + Robert Engels. Directed by Duwayne Dunham.
Rating: Place-setting, mostly, with some decent laughs . . .
    5 out of 10 damn fine slices of pie. 🥧🥧🥧🥧🥧▱▱▱▱▱

The action commences with Jones amorously interfering with Truman's unconscious body; after performing a weird sort of ritual, touching perfume to both their lips, she breaks the mood by attempting to strangle the snozzled sheriff with a length of piano wire. He fights her off and knocks her out. Harry, perhaps you should look into taking a little "me" time. Audrey brings Wheeler's breakfast to his room and smolders at him. The earnest young businessman bats his luxurious lashes back at her and informs her it's reaching the "put up or shut up" point, and invites her on a proper date. She gleefully accepts, and they both seem to feel pretty swell about everything.

Lots happening at the sheriff's station: Cooper aids Truman's hangover recovery with a vomit-inducing description of a vile home remedy, and all and sundry gather to admire a newly delivered bonsai tree, a mysterious anonymous gift that almost certainly does not contain a radio transmitter monitored by Windom Earle. David Lynch makes a delightful appearance as the aurally challenged Bureau Chief Cole, newly returned to Twin Peaks to deliver a confidential dossier on Earle to Cooper. It transpires that Earle was part of the Air Force's UFO-centric Project Blue Book, linking him to the phenomena experienced by Major Briggs. After mulling this over for a moment, and being officially welcomed back as an armed and credentialed member of the FBI, Cooper suggests that the group adjourn for a hearty breakfast. No wonder everyone loves this guy.

Back in their kozy kabin, Earle and Leo check out some playing cards that have been altered to portray Donna, Audrey, and Shelly as queens. There's a King Cooper, too, and a king with no face. These cards are displayed in close proximity to a flyer for the Miss Twin Peaks pageant. Probably nothing to worry about there.

Donna and Audrey spy on Ben Horne and Eileen Hayward having some kind of intimate, emotionally fraught meeting. Maybe Mrs. Hayward is profoundly moved by the plight of the pine weasel?

At the Double R, Cole takes an intense shine to the lovely Shelly, and he discovers that her voice alone registers normally to his failing hearing. Cooper all but gulps, stutters, and blushes like a hormone-addled schoolboy during his exchanges with nature-loving Annie; Truman wryly notes his friend's goner status. Getting down to business, Cooper's doodle of the weird tattoo markings remind both Truman and Annie of a painting in the ominously named Owl Cave ("the owls are not," etc.). Cooper decides they should probably check this cave out posthaste.

Donna gets a postcard from James. Stay gold, baby.

Earle contrives to run into Audrey, disguising himself this time as a poetry professor. Catch him if you can. This guy's wig/beard budget must be insane.

Andy, preparing for the jaunt to Owl Cave, practices spelunking in the office, prompting pleas from Lucy that he be careful. Oh, Lucy. Andy go boom. That's what he's here for.

Ben and Wheeler discuss the difficulties of leading a good life, and Wheeler discloses his romantic interest in Audrey. Ben hands him a carrot, which doesn't bear much thinking about, metaphorically speaking.

Finally, in Owl Cave, Andy, surprise surprise, promptly takes a pratfall. The group studies the painting in question and is dive-bombed by owls; Andy swings at one of them with a pickax and strikes the heart of the painting: a flame symbol. A bright light flashes and a cylinder begins extending from the wall, bearing a pictogram resembling a bird in flight. Cooper remarks, "Harry, I have no idea where this will lead us, but I have a definite feeling it will be a place both wonderful and strange." No kidding.

Later, Cooper runs into Annie and they talk, getting a little closer. He offers his help with whatever is bothering her, and she accepts. Brave man.

Earle enters Owl Cave and sees the extended cylinder. He grasps and twists it, which precipitates a cave-in. So that happened.

Episode 26 ("Variations on Relations")

Aired: Thursday, April 11, 1991
Twin Peaks Time: Friday, March 24, 1989
Written by Mark Frost + Harley Peyton. Directed by Jonathan Sanger.
Rating: A weird, funny, unsettling one, with some gorgeous images . . .
8 out of 10 damn fine slices of pie. 🥧🥧🥧🥧🥧🥧🥧🥧

Series cocreator Mark Frost cowrites this strong late installment, which ratchets up the menace of Windom Earle while generously serving up strange and amusing character details and interactions. This one gets the proportions right, and it's proof that the magic was still very much intact.

Cooper and co. reenter Owl Cave, discovering the "petroglyph" (an obscure symbol, because we were running low on those) and shoe prints, quickly deduced by Cooper as belonging to the troublesome Mr. Earle. They make a copy of the symbol and arrange to meet Major Briggs at the station.

Whither Windom? Back at the Cabin in the Woods with obedient Leo and a new friend, some unholy approximation of Pauly Shore in full party-dude mode. Party dude came for the promise of beer, but Earle instead holds forth on a Manichean concept (familiar to us from Major Briggs) involving a "White Lodge," a source of primal goodness, and its opposite number, a "Black Lodge" thrumming with evil vitality. Earle intends to harness the energies of the Black Lodge for his own purposes. Party dude thinks it's a cool story and all, but would still like that beer.

Casa Martell: Catherine interrupts Pete's mooning over Josie and asks for his input on the mysterious black box given to her by Jones. Pete recognizes it as a puzzle box and warns that it could take years to discover the secret to opening it. Historically, it is a terrible idea in supernatural stories to open ominous puzzle boxes. Just putting that out there.

At the Double R, Bobby encourages Shelly to enter the Miss Twin Peaks pageant, the first step in his new plan to exploit the plucky waitress's stunning beauty for fun and profit. As Shelly is at least pretty enough to inspire a minor religion, he might be on to something.

Cooper asks Annie on a date, sort of . . . he invites her to join him for afternoon "nature study," and, such is the winning charm of Kyle MacLachlan, this comes off as adorable rather than creepy. Overhearing Shelly reciting the portion of the poem she received from Earle, Cooper learns that she, Donna, and Audrey have all been getting some Earlemail special deliveries.

The meeting with Briggs is fruitful: the major recognizes the petroglyph, perhaps from a dream, and some handwriting analysis indicates that the poem fragments received by the girls were transcribed by the hand of one Leo Johnson. Dun dun dun!

One of the most arresting visuals in a series famous for them occurs as Briggs speaks: we see a foreboding cloaked figure superimposed on the slide of the petroglyph. Stars are visible through the figure's garment, and a fierce owl appears as the figure bursts into flame. It's a moment of inexplicable cinematic poetry, beautiful, inscrutable, and bracing.

Dick Tremayne, his nose still swaddled after his encounter with the endangered pine weasel, asks for and receives compensation from Ben Horne, who rues his recent evil-denying change of heart when confronted by the oily menswear salesman.

Back at the love shack, party dude finally gets some beer—the downside is that he has to drink it while standing in a giant papier-mâché chess piece Earle is building. We all make sacrifices, I guess, and it probably seems like a reasonably good deal until the moment Earle shoots and kills him with a crossbow.

And then some levity at the Roadhouse, where the Miss Twin Peaks pageant is getting under way. Ben Horne implores the judging committee to let their better natures guide them. Mayor Milford isn't listening, as he's putting the fix in to get his squeeze Lana the crown. Nadine is keen to compete, and Mike finally gets a chance to explain their relationship (to an incredulous Bobby): "Do you have any idea what a combination of sexual maturity and superhuman strength can result in?"

Truman visits Catherine to discuss Josie. Boy's got it bad. Pete comes in and clumsily drops the puzzle box, which opens to reveal a smaller box inside, inscribed with symbols relating to the Zodiac and the phases of the moon. Yep, I'd leave it alone now, guys. This ain't a box of Cracker Jack.

Cooper and Annie share confidences and a sweet kiss during "nature study," but the moment is darkened by a spying Windom Earle, who, whatever else you might say about the guy, really has tremendous energy and drive. Whatever his plan is, he is INTO it.

There follows an amusing sequence in which Dick Tremayne's wine-tasting seminar is undone by the uncouthness of Andy and Lucy, and a funnier one in which David Lynch's delightful Bureau Chief Cole bids farewell to Twin Peaks in his inimitable style, demolishing a cherry pie while pitching courtly woo at Shelly and charmingly kissing her despite Bobby's indignant protests.

SO MUCH HAPPENING: Donna angrily presses her mother on her relationship with Ben Horne as her parents dissemble; Cooper and Wheeler commiserate about the sweet agony of new love (and what was the point of Wheeler? Anyway, it appears he's leaving. Maybe he'll run into James and they can start a support group for useless supporting characters); again we see the haunting, frightening image of the hooded figure, the moon, and the owl.

Finally, Cooper and the TP lawmen find Earle's latest clue, a large crate left on a gazebo. After some fancy sharpshooting from Coop (to open the crate from a safe distance), the contents are revealed: the papier-mâché chessman, with party dude's dead head sticking out of it, bearing the words "Next time it will be someone you know."

(Not Josie, she's already a nightstand.)

Episode 27 ("The Path to the Black Lodge")

Aired: Friday, April 19, 1991
Twin Peaks Time: Friday–Saturday, March 24–25, 1989
Written by Harley Peyton + Robert Engels. Directed by Stephen Gyllenhaal.
Rating: Moving around pieces on the chessboard, gearing up for the bitter end . . . 6 out of 10 damn fine slices of pie. ▰▰▰▰▰▰▱▱▱▱

The giant chess piece containing the dead party dude is removed from the gazebo, and we learn from his devastated friend (played by Willie Garson, who would go on to face much greater horrors on *Sex and the City*) that they were on their way to a gig when Earle approached them and lured Rusty (party dude) away with the promise of free beer. Kids, don't accept offers of alcohol from weird guys skulking around in the woods. It's the first rule of crossbow safety and just good common sense.

The ranks of the Miss Twin Peaks contestant pool continue to expand as Lucy announces her intention to run, and to choose a father for her child—between Andy and Dick, we suggest she go with the pine weasel.

John Wheeler continues the most protracted hotel checkout in history, telling Ben Horne he must away to Brazil to avenge the murder of his friend, or whatever. Doc Hayward gives Ben a physical and warns him to stay away from his wife. No lollipop for Ben.

Donna is interrupted while studying her birth certificate—which does not list a father (and, curiously, lists her mother's maiden name as Eileen Hayward, which we always kind of assumed was, you know, her *married* name)—by a summons to the sheriff's station, where Cooper has also gathered Audrey and Shelly. They quickly piece together Earle's various disguised visits, and Shelly recognizes the handwriting on the divided poem as Leo's.

Cooper also meets with Major Briggs, who reveals that Earle was Project Blue Book's top man until the focus of their investigation shifted from outer space to the woods around Twin Peaks, at which point he completely flipped out, and when Briggs says you're weird, buddy, you're WEIRD. We see a video of Earle in this period, ranting about the Black Lodge and evil sorcerers called "dugpas" who use the Lodge's energies for their magic. Cooper has an epiphany: Earle's revenge scheme is a smoke screen, masking his true purpose, which is mastery of the Black Lodge. Briggs decides all this heady stuff requires a restorative walk in the woods. Guys. The woods. Is nobody paying attention? Ixnay on the oodsway.

Earle hears all of this, of course (bonsai-phone), and decides a meeting with Briggs tops the day's agenda. He and Leo set out for the woods, but not before Leo surreptitiously slips his shock collar controller into his pocket. Bad Dog!

At the Double R, a patron is distressed by a strange palsy in her hand. This malady will also befall Pete and Cooper in the course of the episode. Mayor Milford and Bobby Briggs coach their respective paramours for the pageant. Shelly's speech needs work, and Lana needs to go find James and start a chinchilla farm or something far away from Twin Peaks, please.

Pete rushes Audrey to the airfield to intercept the departing Wheeler (relax, this guy moves like frozen molasses when leaving town). They succeed and Audrey sacrifices her virginity to the pouty-lipped mannequin before he jets off for Brazil, leaving her with only an offer of a fishing trip with Pete for consolation.

Annie and Cooper flirt and blush and make goo-goo eyes as Cooper encourages her to enter the Miss Twin Peaks pageant (at this point we expect Denise Bryson to return and go for the crown as well).

Briggs's constitutional in the woods is interrupted by the arrival of a pantomime horse, which promptly shoots him with a tranquilizer dart, and we again marvel at the depths of Windom's costume closet. Briggs wakes up strapped to a target on the wall of Earle's cabin and stoically refuses to answer any of the madman's questions about the symbols in Owl Cave, despite Earle's pesky habit of playing with crossbows indoors. So, Earle injects him with a truth serum and learns of a fated meeting between Jupiter and Saturn. Worth it? Probably!

Meanwhile, Catherine and her brother fuss with the puzzle box some more, and Andrew discovers a third sealed box inside when he susses out the trick of opening the star sign–embossed layer, tapping out sequences on the celestial illustrations relating to his and Eckhardt's birthdays. Apparently unsatisfied with his prize, Andrew unceremoniously smashes this container to reveal a metallic brick. Worth it? Probably!

Cooper and Annie have a sweet date at the Roadhouse, dancing, smooching, falling in l-u-v, when an address by Mayor Milford announcing the opening of the Miss Twin Peaks pageant goes very weird: Milford, vexed by microphone feedback, is suddenly replaced on stage by the Giant. Only Cooper seems to see him, as the rest of the room appears frozen in time. The Giant seems to be warning Cooper of something, emphatically waving his arms and shaking his head "no." Some would consider this development a bad omen.

Why, and so it is: Earle cackles in his cabin as Leo screams mindlessly. Earle's cracked the code and discovered the petroglyph is not only a snazzy cave decoration but a map to the Black Lodge, located right here in Twin Peaks. And, in even worse news, a weird light appears in the woods, from which who should satanically materialize but Bob, bright-eyed and bushy-haired. Maybe he wants to enter the Miss Twin Peaks pageant too?

Episode 28 ("Miss Twin Peaks")

Aired: Friday, June 10, 1991
Twin Peaks Time: Sunday–Monday, March 26–27, 1989
Written by Barry Pullman. Directed by Tim Hunter.
Rating: When the going gets weird, the weird get pie . . . 8 out of 10 damn fine slices of pie. 🥧🥧🥧🥧🥧🥧🥧🥧▱▱

With ratings continuing to plunge, ABC held off on airing this episode for almost two months, and eventually paired it with the series finale as an *ABC Movie of the Week*.

Windom Earle returns to the cabin to discover Major Briggs has escaped, and initiates a new game with Leo as a means of conveying his displeasure. Earle, having just communed with the Black Lodge, strikes a particularly sinister figure here: teeth blackened, skin blanched, wild-eyed and raving, this version of Earle makes jean-jacketed Bob look about as threatening as Otto from *The Simpsons*. It's a legitimately terrifying vision of evil and madness, and a hell of a jolt to start this penultimate chapter.

At the Double R, former Miss Twin Peaks (and a real contender should she want to run again, in our book) Norma expresses her support for Shelly and Annie in the contest. This year Norma's contribution to the festivities is a selection of pies, and *now* we get it: Miss Twin Peaks pageant = pie time. No wonder everyone is so excited.

Audrey meets with her father, Ben, to discuss her discovery of the Packards' plan to funnel money into the Ghostwood project via some banking calumny. New boring Ben is more interested in a stack of religious texts and Audrey's potential use of the Miss Twin Peaks crown as a platform for political activism. The pine weasel population continues to dwindle, apparently. Remember when this guy smarmed around with giant cigars, running a brothel? That was fun.

Back at the sheriff's station, Cooper and the boys ponder Briggs's whereabouts and speculate as to the nature of Bob's connection to Josie's death and the Black Lodge. Earle listens in on his shrub mic, looking now less like the demonic figure from the opening scene and more like Phyllis Diller after a really long flight. It's . . . an improvement?

Anyway, Earle agrees with Cooper's theory that fear is the key to accessing the Lodge's power. Much enthused by the epiphany, he makes haste to put the final stages of his plan into action. Leo seems less than fully engaged by Earle's psychotic monologue, perhaps distracted by the bag of spiders

Earle has suspended over his head. Note: Do not invite Windom Earle over for Game Night. His understanding of the term is skewed at best. At the Roadhouse, Mr. Pinkle (this guy's *résumé* must be insane) rehearses the contestants in his inimitable sclerotic manner. Lana gets Dick Tremayne alone in a storage room and aggressively lobbies (blatantly seduces) the unctuous pageant judge for his support in the competition.

Annie visits Cooper at the Great Northern for some help on her speech for the pageant, but they end up undressing each other and falling into bed. Annie, that's Lana's move. Get your own material.

Ed and Norma somehow manage to get through an awkward and bizarre meeting with Nadine, Mike, and Dr. Jacoby, in which their various romantic entanglements are resolved, wrestling highlights are recounted, an engagement is announced, and Mike's hand is crushed. In Twin Peaks, this qualifies as a pleasant evening in.

Hawk brings in a dazed and incoherent Major Briggs, discovered wandering along the roadside. He's full of Earle's drugs and much the worse for wear after bumbling through the underbrush. The gang kindly wrap him in a snappy Navaho blanket and continue strategizing re: the Black Lodge.

In mysterious-box news, Pete and Andrew are still struggling with the latest recalcitrant container when Andrew decides to just start shooting at it. Success! A key is extracted. Worth it? Probably!

Donna again confronts her folks about Ben Horne and is again rebuffed. Donna's mad-face is truly on point and an inspiration to thwarted teens everywhere. Seriously, that thing could cut glass.

Cooper and his retinue study the petroglyph some more, deducing that the symbols indicate a significant planetary conjunction. Briggs, still stoned to the epaulets, makes some gnomish pronouncements about "protecting the queen," which Cooper interprets to mean Miss Twin Peaks. The reliably clumsy Andy makes his affliction pay off again by knocking over the bonsai tree and exposing Earle's bug. Good boy! In our fantasy, Andy and Leo wind up together on a beautiful farm upstate, romping through fields and digging up soup bones and chasing rabbits without a care in the world.

Finally, the pageant. It's a real scene: cheesy choreographed dance numbers (including a number in which the contestants are costumed in transparent vinyl raincoats: pretty girls wrapped in plastic for the delectation of the audience. Pretty sick joke, guys); Cooper and Truman desperately arranging for increased security; Lucy tap-tap-tapping her adenoidal little heart out (honestly, she's really good and surprisingly sexy), and Pinkle maybe hitting on an uninterested Log Lady.

Or maybe not! The Log Lady in attendance turns out to be Earle's latest, and greatest, disguise. Earle introduces Pinkle's head to the business end of his log and knocks him out.

Lucy concludes a long-running storyline no one cares about by selecting Andy as the father of her baby. Tremayne is relieved, as is the audience at the prospect of not having to hear about this anymore.

Annie's speech is a triumph, and she is crowned Miss Twin Peaks. Pity she didn't get first runner-up, because her prize is a swift kidnapping by Earle, amidst smoke bombs and a blackout and all manner of chaos. In this moment of stunned defeat and hopelessness, Andy provides a potential ray of sunshine: the petroglyph, he has discovered, is, among other things . . . a map.

Episode 29 ("Beyond Life and Death)

Aired: Friday, June 10, 1991
Twin Peaks Time: Friday–Saturday, March 24–25, 1989
Written by Mark Frost + Harley Peyton + Robert Engels + David Lynch (uncredited). Directed by David Lynch.
Rating: The mind-bending, soul-twisting, doppelgänger finale . . . 10 out of 10 damn fine slices of pie. 🥟🥟🥟🥟🥟🥟🥟🥟🥟🥟

Andy and Lucy, recovering from the chaotic events of the pageant, declare their love for one another. It's sweet. Cooper, desperate to rescue Annie, furiously studies the petroglyph as Pete arrives to lodge a complaint of grand theft auto (and trout): the Log Lady stole his truck and drove it into the woods! That was no Log Lady, Cooper explains, but the diabolical Earle. Cooper and Harry realize that the petroglyph depicts Glastonbury Grove in Ghostwood, the site where Hawk found the bloody towel and missing diary pages and which shares a name with the mythical burial place of King Arthur. Pete protests that Arthur is buried in England, contributing the single useless tidbit of information to the conversation. We love him so.

The unfairly impugned Log Lady arrives with a jar of oil her husband referred to as "an opening to a gateway." All agree it smells scorched, including Ronette Pulaski, brought in to give her olfactory two cents. She cowers at the aroma. Good thing she never tried Pete's fish coffee. Away to Glastonbury!

. . . Where Earle is already dragging Annie towards the white circle on the ground marking the gateway. He tells her they have an appointment at the end of the world (that is also Time Warner Cable's standard installation policy). Red curtains appear behind the trees, and Earle and Annie pass between them before they disappear.

Doc Hayward tends to Nadine and Mike, who were injured at the pageant. Tragically, a sandbag to the head has restored Nadine to her middle-aged, hysterical, curtain-runner-obsessed senses, seriously derailing the romantic plans and potential happiness of Mike, Ed, and Norma.

As awkward as this little domestic contretemps is, it doesn't compare to the scene at the Hayward house, where Donna tearfully confronts Ben Horne and her mother *again* about the truth of her paternity. Donna, you've seen your best friend horribly murdered, dated the world's most boring bad boy, been stalked by at least one lunatic bent on revenge, and driven an agoraphobe to suicide. Maybe have a little perspective here. Things happen.

Like Doc Hayward arriving home and exploding into rage at the sight of Ben Horne, assaulting and possibly killing him before sinking to his knees and screaming inconsolably at the wreckage of his family. Okay, that's pretty bad.

Andrew Packard, the old scamp, surreptitiously takes the key discovered last episode from Catherine's hiding place, recognizing it as a safe deposit box key. Curiosity something something cat.

Cooper and Harry arrive at the grove, oil in hand. Cooper insists on proceeding alone, and vanishes behind the ghostly red curtains, just as Earle and Annie did.

He emerges in the Red Room, where legendary jazz crooner Jimmy Scott, famed for his unsettling androgynous voice, serenades the FBI agent with a haunting ballad referencing Glastonbury Grove's sycamore trees. The lights begin to strobe and the Man from Another Place ambles in and takes a seat. Buckle up!

Outside, Andy and Harry have an exhausted conversation about breakfast; it appears they have been waiting for Cooper to return for some ten hours.

A similarly sleepy scene at the Twin Peaks Savings and Loan: an elderly receptionist sleeps soundly at her desk, and an even more elderly loan manager (Dell Mibbler) reacts with bemused equanimity when Audrey Horne arrives and handcuffs herself to the vault, protesting the bank's involvement with the Ghostwood farrago. Andrew and Pete arrive, brandishing the safe deposit key. It indeed opens a box, revealing a note from Eckhardt ("Got you, Andrew. Love, Thomas") and a bomb, which promptly explodes. It's unclear whether anyone survives, but a shot of broken spectacles landing in a tree amidst a shower of blasted currency doesn't inspire much confidence.

Damn it, Andrew, Pete is a treasure and Audrey is exquisite and WHAT DID WE TELL YOU ABOUT OPENING MYSTERIOUS BOXES? A rosier scene takes place at the Double R, where the sight of Major Briggs blissfully canoodling with his wife inspires Bobby to propose to Shelly. She's delighted, but points out she's still legally married to Leo. Cut to Leo in the woods, shivering with terror at the venomous spiders suspended over his head. We're not saying this is a commentary on the institution of marriage, but somebody might. Sarah Palmer enters the diner and approaches Briggs, telling him, "I'm in the Black Lodge with Dale Cooper" in a spooky, demonic voice—we believe it to be the voice of one Windom Earle. You're looking well, Sarah, all things considered.

And so back to the Red Room, and the most defiantly surreal and perplexing sixteen or so minutes in broadcast television history (discounting that time Rob Lowe and Snow White duetted at the Oscars). In all sincerity, it bears mentioning that with some simple set design, basic camera and lighting tricks, brilliant staging, and the talents of the ensemble cast, Lynch and company create here a sequence of enduring, iconic power and mystery, conjuring a unique and unforgettable atmosphere of atavistic dread out of what looks to be a budget of about fourteen dollars. Like the man said, it's easy if you're a genius.

Cooper has exchanges with the Man from Another Place, Laura Palmer (who periodically hisses and screams in a truly horrific manner), Maddy, and the Giant. Cooper struggles with a cup of coffee (or is it burnt engine oil?) of variable viscosity and loses his way wandering through identical corridors and rooms. The conversations consist of typical Red Room non sequiturs and portentous koans, but a theme begins to emerge: the MFAP exclaims, "Wow, Bob, wow," a palindrome, and after the gaunt old waiter from the Great Northern transforms into the Giant, he proclaims, "One and the same." At the end of this sequence, the MFAP very emphatically intones, "Doppelgänger."

The dwarf's eyes are a filmy, iris-less blue as he says it, and now we meet a succession of similarly cataracted familiar faces: doppelgängers, the shadow sides of characters we have come to know well.

Suddenly bleeding from the abdomen, Cooper meets doppel-Laura, who is as horrifyingly screamy as Original Flavor Laura. Cooper finds Annie, who transforms into Caroline (Earle's wife) and back again. Earle himself appears and offers Cooper Annie's life in exchange for Dale's soul. He agrees, and is stabbed by Earle, but, hoo boy, Bob is back, and he declares the transaction void. He's happy to take Earle's soul, though (why not? He's not using it), and does, causing the demented schemer's head to burst into flames. This prompts the entrance of doppel-Cooper, who joins Bob in hysterical laughter. Uh oh.

Regular Cooper meets doppel-Leland, who protests he never killed anyone, in a corridor. Doppel-Cooper herds our hero back into the first room, sharing another big old laugh with Bob. These guys may be unspeakable expressions of man's basest impulses, but their senses of humor are undeniably well developed.

Harry sees the red curtain reappear in the woods and hurries to the site to find Cooper and Annie on the ground.

The next morning, Doc Hayward (guess Ben got better) and Harry visit Cooper at the Great Northern. Cooper asks after Annie and learns she is recovering well in the hospital. Cooper very emphatically wishes to brush his teeth, makes several announcements to that effect, and retires to the washroom to do so. Apparently he has a change of heart, squeezing the entire tube of toothpaste into the sink before smashing his head into

"How's Annie?" Cooper's evil doppelgänger bonds with Bob in the bathroom at the Great Northern.   *ABC/Photofest*

the mirror. In the shattered glass, we see not Cooper's reflection but Bob's, grinning maniacally through the blood coursing down his face. Bleeding and matching Bob's predatory leer with an even more chilling one of his own, Cooper begins to repeat, with escalating hilarity, his question to Harry and Doc: "How's Annie? How's Annie? How's Annie?"

Fade to credits, superimposed over a cup of, presumably, damn fine coffee. On its surface floats the reflected image of Laura Palmer.

Variations (II)

Fifteen differences between the scripted version and aired version of the series finale:

1. The Log Lady never appears in the scripted version; in the aired version she brings the scorched engine oil to the sheriff's station.
2. In the aired version, Pete says there were twelve rainbow trout in his truck, which is what reminds Harry of the twelve trees at Glastonbury Grove. No such line in the script.
3. Ronette Pulaski in the aired version confirms that the burnt oil is what she smelled on the night of Laura's murder; Ronette never appears in the script.
4. Donna's extremely unfortunate "You're my Daddy!" outburst: not in the script.
5. In the aired version, Doc Hayward punches Ben Horne, who hits his head against the fireplace; in the script, Doc is merely trying to push Ben out of the house when he falls and hits his head.
6. Great Scott! Jimmy Scott (performing "Sycamore Trees"): not in the script.
7. In the aired version, Cooper enters the gateway to the lodge, arriving in the Red Room, which may or may not be the Black Lodge proper. In the script, he very specifically goes directly to the lodge—a "dark space, limitless," which then becomes a shabby motel office, the Great Northern, and then the Red Room.
8. In the script, Major Briggs and Hawk go searching for Leo, and eventually locate him in Earle's cabin; never happens in the aired version, as the major is too busy chowing down at the Double R.
9. In the script, Cooper encounters a man who looks like his father in the motel office; again, never happens in the aired version.
10. In the script, it's Catherine, not Pete, who's inside the Twin Peaks Savings and Loan with Andrew when the bomb goes off.
11. Both Sarah Palmer and Dr. Jacoby are missing from the script; in the aired version Jacoby escorts Sarah to the Double R so she can deliver a message

to Major Briggs. (Heidi the diner waitress and Sylvia Horne also appear briefly in the aired version, but not the script—old homecoming week!)

12. In the script, Truman, waiting for Cooper at Glastonbury Grove, sees a tall, dark woman holding a white shield and a silver sword, who then vanishes, none of which happens in the aired version.

13. No Man from Another Place, Giant, or Waiter in the script; Lynch brings all three back in the aired version.

14. In the script, Earle warbles Cole Porter's "Anything Goes," in top hat and tails. In the aired version, this *didn't* go.

15. In the scripted version, Earle takes Cooper to a dentist's office, where Annie is trapped behind glass in a medicine cabinet (presumably a large one), Bob shows up in a white dentist's smock, and Laura intervenes, thwarting whatever nefarious action Bob had planned for Cooper. Not in the version that aired.

20

There Was a Fish in the Percolator

Memorable Moments in *Twin Peaks*

A place both wonderful and strange

Everyone remembers the dancing dwarf, the cherry stem knot, the girl wrapped in plastic—but *Twin Peaks* contains a plethora of equally memorable moments that have not quite risen to iconic status (Audrey's dance arguably has, but we just wanted to mention it again). Below we enumerate some of our favorite (and least favorite) less-celebrated *Twin Peaks* moments that have helped to lodge the show so deeply in our dreams.

The Best

Audrey's Dance

Audrey and Donna sit chatting in the Double R when the strains of Badalamenti's "cool jazz" drift from the jukebox. Audrey seems pulled to her feet by an unseen force as she enters a swooning reverie, commenting the tune is "too dreamy" and dancing alone to the insinuating melody. It's a magical scene: Audrey's sexual charisma is off the charts, though she does nothing explicitly provocative, and the entire universe of the show seems to hold its breath as she sways. It's a tableau that feels oddly suspended in time, mesmerizingly erotic, faintly nostalgic, and mildly unsettling, though it's hard to put your finger on just why—in other words, it's pure *Twin Peaks*, and we love it.

"Just You"

Teenage romance and murder investigations are tough . . . sometimes you just have to take a break and record a retro-fifties doo-wop tune in the living room for a while. At least, that's apparently the thought process behind this exceedingly odd but strangely compelling scene, in which James, Donna, and Maddy commit the pop confection "Just You" to tape. The song is in the Badalamenti/Lynch mode: pretty-verging-on-syrupy, full of early rock ballad clichés, and kitschy to the point of uncanniness. There is no context given for this sudden veer into music-making, the attitude of the performers is funereally serious, and James sings lead in a chillingly androgynous falsetto—like so many of *Twin Peaks'* most memorable scenes, it all feels like a dream. This one happens to be lovely. Weird, but lovely.

Father and Son

The straight-arrow, philosophical Major Garland Briggs would seem to have little in common with his wayward son, Bobby. But in an extraordinary scene, the military man recounts a dream to his son in which he sees a

James, Donna, and Maddy perform Lynch and Badalamenti's "Just You," an eerie love ballad, in one of *Twin Peaks'* most memorably odd sequences.   *ABC/Photofest*

bright future and noble purpose for Bobby, and expresses a profound love for the troublesome boy that reduces Bobby to incredulous tears—and we have to admit it gets a little dusty in our eyes every time we see it. Amidst all of the depravity and terror, there is a deep well of love in *Twin Peaks*, never expressed more poignantly—or unexpectedly—than in this moving sequence, which complicated our understanding of both characters and deepened our emotional connection to the series as a whole.

Cooper's Tibetan Zen Deduction Technique

In the second episode of the series, Agent Dale Cooper reveals his spiritual side with the introduction of a curious deductive technique, derived from the practices of Zen masters: Cooper listens to a list of suspects, throwing a rock at a bottle without looking as each name is read. When the rock hits the bottle, that name is considered "of interest." The scene is hilarious— Truman and Andy are gobsmacked by the oddity of the whole situation— but the interlude actually tells us quite a lot. Primarily, we learn Cooper is a little stranger than we thought, but the scene also underscores the idea that *Twin Peaks* will upset our genre expectations, and that the path to truth will be a winding and confusing journey. Located so early in the story, it's a warning viewers would do well to heed.

Albert Rosenfield, Man of Love

Cooper's colleague Albert Rosenfield is a pill, a superior, insulting city slicker who alienates half the town immediately upon arrival and provides the show with its wickedest one-liners. It is therefore a complete shock when Rosenfield later passionately defends himself as a "hatchet man in the fight against violence" who chooses to live his life "in the company of Gandhi and King." Furthermore, he proclaims his love for Sheriff Truman, whom he had earlier so offended that the level-headed lawman punched his lights out. It's a funny reversal and instance of *Twin Peaks* delightfully upending our expectations (it's also damn adorable).

Donna Hayward, Bad Girl

Donna, a sensible and well-behaved girl, attempts to reckon with the wild, transgressive dark side of her murdered friend Laura by trying on a new persona: she dons Laura's shades, takes up cigarettes, affects a sullen demeanor, and ups her dialogue game with some choice noirish deadpan tough talk, as in this exchange with Maddy, who fears their actions led to Jacoby's beating: "Maybe. Maybe the sun won't come up if you wash your hair. Think like that and you're gonna go crazy. What's done is done." Robert Mitchum couldn't have delivered it better, and Boyle is a hoot as a Chandleresque dangerous dame in schoolgirl sweaters and Mary Janes. Noir Donna is our favorite Donna.

Cooper's Hangover Cure

"You take a glass of nearly frozen, unstrained **tomato juice**.
You plop a couple of **oysters** in there, you drink it down.
Breathe deeply.
Next, you take a mound, and I mean a mound, of **sweetbreads**.
Sauté them with some **chestnuts** and some **Canadian bacon**.
Finally, **biscuits**. Big biscuits, smothered in **gravy**.
Now, here's where it gets tricky, you're gonna need some **anchovies**."

We know Cooper is an odd bird; he can seem at times shockingly guileless and savant-like in his manner and technique, and his sincere wonder at the beauty of the forest and the deliciousness of pastry is rather childlike. But Coop possesses a surprisingly sly wit, never better displayed than in this scene, in which he induces vomiting (Harry is miserably hung over) in the most charming way possible.

Gordon Cole, Pickup Artist

Lynch's turn as hearing-impaired Bureau Chief Cole is a consistent joy—the director's celebrated eccentricity finds hilarious expression in Cole's odd pronouncements and braying voice. His best moment comes when he meets Double R waitress Shelly Johnson, who so enchants the G-man with her (considerable) wiles that his hearing improves (though only in relation to her voice), and he shamelessly flirts with her in a manner reminiscent of Jimmy Stewart in *It's a Wonderful Life* . . . or maybe like a Martian's approximation of Jimmy Stewart ("My socks are on fire!"—now that's a line). He goes so far as to boldly kiss her in front of her stunned hotheaded boyfriend, Bobby Briggs, and we can't help but think that Mrs. Johnson's difficult life would improve dramatically if she were to run away with the oddball fed.

Hanks a Lot, Nadine

Hank Jennings is a grade-A jerk who enjoys intimidating women, so it is immensely gratifying to witness his comeuppance at the hands of the superhumanly strong Nadine Hurley, who arrives home to find Hank assaulting Ed (Hank's miffed about Ed's affair with his wife, Norma; for once he has a semi-valid grievance, but what the hell). Nadine bops in, resplendent in her cheerleading uniform, and proceeds to take Jennings apart, walloping him with a pom-pom, punching him repeatedly in the head, and ultimately throwing him across the room through a set of shelves. There's not much more to say about the scene except that it's BEAUTIFUL. We love Nadine.

Save the Last Dance for Leland

When a grief-stricken Leland Palmer wanders into a party at the Great Northern (Ben Horne is greasing potential investors), we hold our breath: his recent behavior has been bizarre, to put it mildly, and his presence

Strange bedfellows: A memorable moment indeed—from a *Wizard of Oz*-themed promo spot in which Cooper wakes, à la Dorothy, surrounded by . . . family? And friends?

Photo by Richard Beymer

promises extreme discomfort (best-case scenario). He begins to dance, alone, weeping and clutching at his temples in psychic agony, and it's about what we expected. But quick-thinking Ben pushes Catherine Martell onto the floor, and she begins mimicking Leland's odd movements as though they were the steps to an obscure dance; soon, everyone has joined in, having a high old time. The sequence is incredibly rich, making the most of that funny/horrifying tension *Twin Peaks* perfected, and it speaks thematically to the idea that public personas are a form of performance: beneath an ostensibly benign surface (fun party!) can lurk unimaginable horror. It's tragic, funny, moving, slightly grotesque . . . in other words, another night in Twin Peaks.

The Worst

Look Away: "Dixie"

Benjamin Horne's depressive spiral into delusion, which left him believing himself to be a Civil War general, was a drag; Richard Beymer's sly performance as the licentious, avaricious Horne had been a series highlight, and it was precisely zero percent fun watching him moon around in silly costume ruing the War of Northern Aggression. We get the thematic appropriateness—the Civil War is a neat metaphor for a body divided against itself—but the scene in which Dr. Jacoby leads Horne in a cathartic rendition of "Dixie" skirts minstrelsy and is the show at its most cringe-inducing re: forced wackiness.

A Little Nicky Is Too Much

Oof. The entire love triangle story involving dopey Andy, ditzy Lucy, and dastardly Dick Tremayne was a nonstarter, but this regrettable narrative dead end reached its nadir with the introduction of "Little Nicky," a pathetic orphan whose cause is taken up by Tremayne in an effort to demonstrate his suitability as a father. Nicky is dim and irritating (no wonder he caught Tremayne's eye), but the single worst scene in this misbegotten thread finds Doc Hayward delivering an insufferably maudlin soliloquy about the tyke's travails . . . if it's meant to be satirical, it doesn't land, and if it's supposed to be dramatic . . . ouch.

No Justice: Audrey and Wheeler

Audrey Horne and Agent Cooper were meant to have a romantic relationship, but behind-the-scenes pressures nixed that plan, so a replacement was needed for "the older man" half of the equation. Enter Billy Zane as John Justice Wheeler, a handsome, slightly older guy who . . . was just sort of Audrey's boyfriend for a while. Healthy relationships don't flourish on *Twin Peaks*, and their largely conflict-free liaison is mostly a snooze (Zane is usually a flavorful character actor, but here he seems weirdly anesthetized); the very, very attractive couple moon at each other for a while, and then Wheeler has to suddenly leave on a mysterious errand to Brazil. Their worst moment comes during an al fresco date: the scenery is pretty, the actors are pretty, the dialogue is forgettable, and nothing happens. It could be a filler scene from any conventional soap opera, and that's the last thing we want to see on *Twin Peaks*.

Double Indumbnity: James and Evelyn

After Laura Palmer's murder was solved, there was absolutely nothing left for her ex-boyfriend, James Hurley, to do on the show, so . . . they gave him his own very involved plotline, totally separate from the action of the rest of the show? Yes, they did. Never one of *TP*'s most dynamic characters (Hank's domino displays more personality), James finds himself enmeshed in a generic film noir plot, sexually manipulated by a scheming femme fatale, Evelyn Marsh (they couldn't even give her an evocative last name). The entire storyline flails pathetically for *something*—drama, eroticism, sly pastiche?—and comes up short in every department. Specifically, we find it difficult to watch any instance in which Evelyn must pantomime consuming lust for the vanilla pudding-like James; it's like watching a dog trying to ride a bicycle.

Sorry for Budding In: Lana Milford

Irresistible succubus, incorrigible schemer, heartless mercenary: she sounds like fun, right? Nope. Lana Budding Milford sows chaos, killing the elderly Dougie Milford with excessive passion, hooking up with his equally enfeebled brother, and attempting to fix the Miss Twin Peaks pageant, but the "comedy" of these shenanigans is labored and irritating. Frankly, introducing Lana as a bombshell who makes every man in her presence a slavering

Twenty-five years later: Kimmy Robertson (Lucy Moran) and Ian Buchanan (Dick Tremayne) are reunited at the 2015 Twin Peaks Festival.   *Photo by Pieter Dom*

fool makes little sense in a community already boasting the likes of Josie Packard, Audrey Horne, Shelly Johnson, and Annie Blackburne. Actress Robyn Lively is game in the role, but the elements just don't come together, and Lana remains an annoying distraction. Worst moment: her seduction of Dick Tremayne, because ewwwwwwwww.

Give 'em Hell, Harry: Truman's Bender

Sheriff Harry Truman is such a steady, comforting presence throughout the madness of the series that it comes as a most unwelcome shock to see him unravel so calamitously in the wake of Josie's death. Drunk as a lord, brandishing a firearm, Harry nearly self-destructs before being talked down by Cooper. In *Twin Peaks* we are seldom on solid ground, and we rely on Harry as a bastion of reason and sanity to keep our bearings; we like him bemused, slightly awed, healthily sardonic, and steady as a rock. Happily, the interlude ends quickly, and our man is soon back in the saddle with his head on straight.

The Mickey Rooney Award for Offensive Asian Stereotypes Goes To . . . Catherine Martell

After her apparent death in the Packard mill fire, Catherine Martell sows mischief in the guise of visiting Japanese businessman "Mr. Tojamura," a new player in the Ghostwood real estate imbroglio. In a series obsessed with masks and disguises, Mr. Tojamura is easily the most ridiculous; the makeup is high school play caliber, and Piper Laurie, a remarkable actress with an enviable list of credits, is simply not convincing as a laconic Asian man with weird hair (How could she be?). Ben Horne falls for it, though . . . what exactly is in those cigars he smokes?

Unhappy Birthday: Leo's Party

Leo Johnson, a consummate scumbag, is left in his abused wife Shelly's care after suffering brain damage (Hank Jennings, world's worst assassin, shot him in the head). Shelly and her boyfriend, Bobby Briggs, scheme to steal Leo's benefit money, which Shelly definitely deserves, but the pair take things into a positively sadistic direction with their mockery and abuse of the once-fearsome Leo, throwing the semi-comatose man a birthday party featuring copious petty humiliations. The scene effectively builds tension—is Leo faking?—but it's disheartening to see Shelly, a largely sympathetic character, so gleefully embrace cruelty. Like we said, Leo had it coming, but Shelly seems better than this.

Jonesin'

"Jones" is a striking woman, tall and regal, an associate of Thomas Eckhardt's who delivers a fateful puzzle box to Catherine Martell. That's cool. But then she strips down to her skivvies, crawls into bed with a black-out-drunk Harry Truman, applies perfume (Josie's?) to her lips and his, and begins to strangle him. We get that Eckhardt put a hit on Harry—for sleeping with Josie—but the arch weirdness of Jones's attack doesn't really land, registering as mere gratuitous strangeness. In a series with a tranquilizer-dart-shooting pantomime horse, we don't need more gratuitous strangeness.

Adventures in Modern Banking

It hurts just to type it: Andrew Packard, having wrested the safety deposit box key from the final puzzle box, takes a trip to the bank to see what surprise is waiting for him. It's a bomb, courtesy of Eckhardt: boom. Andrew apparently joins the Choir Invisible, and really, who cares, but HE BROUGHT PETE WITH HIM. Sweet, lovely Pete, who never hurt anybody (aside from some trout) and brightened every scene he graced. Damn you, Packard. Damn you, Eckhardt. RIP, noble fisherman.

21

You Remind Me Today of a Small Mexican Chihuahua

Twin Peaks Ephemera, Tributes, and Homages

Gentlemen, when two separate events occur simultaneously pertaining to the same object of inquiry, we must always pay strict attention.

Television

Twin *Peaks* hit the cultural landscape like a blazing comet from deep outer (or inner?) space—it was *the* topic for the proverbial water-cooler in its heyday, a watershed moment in the television medium that electrified and engaged its audience in ways few previous programs had. The show demanded a level of commitment and active participation unusual for products of the "idiot box," and fans eagerly parsed every new shred of information, every symbol and allusion, every tantalizing mystery with an intensity that represented a new way of engaging with TV: *Twin Peaks* encouraged communal viewing parties, inspired nascent Internet discussion groups, and paved the way for programs like *The X-Files*, *Lost*, and *True Detective*—series that share many structural, thematic, and aesthetic elements with Twin Peaks and elicit a similarly obsessive, detective-like approach to the material.

So it's not surprising that other TV creators delighted in referencing this most reference-heavy of shows; a *Twin Peaks* nod indicated membership in a special tribe, a cohort of hip, sophisticated pop culture consumers and makers who "got it." Below we have collected some of the most noteworthy homages, mentions, parodies, and the like. And yes, Scooby Doo really did visit the Red Room.

Wiseguy, various episodes (1990)

You know you have something special when the (possible) homages begin before the show even debuts. The groundbreaking crime series *Wiseguy* featured, in its third season, an arc taking place in the small Washington town of Lynchboro (get it?), which was served and protected by a weeping deputy. The Lynchboro arc aired before the debut of *Twin Peaks*—weird, right? For a brief time writer Robert Engels was concurrently employed by both series, but he has denied any responsibility for this confluence.

Northern Exposure, "Russian Flu" (1990)

This quirky series about a rustic Alaskan community and the bemused reactions of a recent interloper often played as a more benign, gentle version of *Twin Peaks*, as eccentric locals philosophized in the cold north woods (the shows were contemporaries, and many writers drew comparisons, including Timothy Egan of *The New York Times,* who referenced both shows, in addition to novelist Tom Robbins, filmmaker Gus Van Sant, and cartoonist Matt Groening, in a 1991 article titled "Northwest Noir: An Art of the Seriously Goofy"). *Northern Exposure* made the connection explicit in the episode "Russian Flu," in which a tour to a waterfall in Snoqualmie Falls (site of the Great Northern) includes multiple references to *Twin Peaks*, including mentions of cherry pie and coffee, gratuitous finger snapping, Julee Cruise on the soundtrack, and the Log Lady glimpsed through a telescope.

The Fresh Prince of Bel-Air, "Knowledge Is Power" (1990); "Someday Your Prince Will Be in Effect (Part 2)" (1990)

Somewhat surprisingly, ditzy Hilary Banks was a very plugged-in pop culture consumer, making wry references to the show in a couple of episodes.

Saturday Night Live, Kyle MacLachlan/Sinead O'Connor (1990)

Such was the cultural cachet of *Twin Peaks* in 1990 that star MacLachlan was tapped to host the first installment of *Saturday Night Live* in its sixteenth season. The inevitable *Twin Peaks* spoof featured MacLachlan as Cooper, who obstinately refuses to accept Leo Johnson's (played by Chris Farley?!) confession to the murder of Laura Palmer. Phil Hartman essays an eerily accurate Leland Palmer, Victoria Jackson gets a shot at the cherry stem trick, and then-writer Conan O'Brien stands in for Deputy Andy Brennan.

Sesame Street (1991)

The Muppets are not what they seem when Cookie Monster (as "Agent Cookie") finds himself conducting an investigation in "Twin Beaks." While there, he encounters "David Finch" and "The Log Bird," and regularly reports in to Diane. Basically, *Twin Peaks* just owned pop culture circa 1990, and not even adorable puppets were safe from its sinister influence.

The Simpsons, "Who Shot Mr. Burns? (Part 2)" (1995); "Lisa's Sax" (1997)

Springfield is a pretty weird town, full of pretty weird people, so *Twin Peaks* homages feel perfectly appropriate in *The Simpsons*, another series that revels in mischievous pop references. In "Who Shot Mr. Burns?" (note the title's nod to the central mystery of *Twin Peaks*), Chief Wiggum's efforts to solve the eponymous puzzle include a dreamy visit to the Red Room, where Lisa dispenses cryptic clues in the classic *Twin Peaks* manner.

A later episode, "Lisa's Sax," finds Homer watching an episode of *Twin Peaks* on television (specifically, a scene in which the Giant dances with a horse). He is nonplussed, to put it mildly.

Friends, "The One with the Fake Party" (1998)

Rachel attempts Audrey's cherry stem trick, with less than seductive results.

Fringe, "Northwest Passage" (2010); various episodes

The sci-fi series *Fringe* made its affection for *Twin Peaks* evident in its many references to the show: the character Walter wears glasses similar to Dr. Jacoby's, and even mentions Jacoby, "from Washington state," as a friend; Joan Chen appears as an otherworldly other woman; a Dr. Silva (a nod to Frank Silva, aka Bob) orders coffee and cherry pie; a young blonde girl is murdered, and her inconsolable mother weeps by a mantelpiece photo;

characters patronize Peggy's malt shop (the Double R diner was run by Norma Jennings, played by Peggy Lipton).

The episode "Northwest Passage" directly draws the comparison, as that title was the original name of *Twin Peaks*. The installment finds lead character Peter in a small community in Washington, where he visits a diner, orders pie, and assists the local sheriff in her investigation of the murder of a young woman.

Psych, "Dual Spires" (2010)

The lighthearted mystery series *Psych* launched a full-blown *Twin Peaks* reunion with its affectionate homage "Dual Spires." The outing is an explicit (from the title down) homage, with music (Roadhouse songbird Julee Cruise contributed an original theme song), cinematography, set design, etc., lovingly re-creating the atmosphere of its inspiration.

Detectives Shawn and Burton attend a cinnamon festival (uh, sure) in the odd little northwestern enclave of Dual Spires. A dead girl, wrapped in plastic, is found. She is identified as one Paula Merral (an anagram of Laura Palmer), and Shawn and Burton are drawn into the mystery of her murder.

Twin Peaks cast members Sheryl Lee, Sherilyn Fenn, Dana Ashbrook, Robyn Lively, Lenny Von Dohlen, Catherine Coulson (log included), and

The Little Girl from Another Place (Springfield): *The Simpsons*, the other show that transformed television in the early nineties, lampoons *Twin Peaks*.

Ray Wise all appear in the episode, which is so rife with references to and re-creations of *Twin Peaks* tropes that a full accounting would require a chapter of its own.

Scooby Doo! Mystery Incorporated, "Stand and Deliver" (2013)

Yep, this happened. In the episode "Stand and Deliver," the snack-happy pooch finds himself in the Red Room, where he encounters a strange-talking little person bearing a strong resemblance to the MFAP. The resemblance is made even stronger by the fact that the character is voiced by *Twin Peaks'* Michael J. Anderson, talkin' backwards.

Go Forth and Multiply

In the years since *Twin Peaks* left the air, creators have taken inspiration from its tone, aesthetic, and approach to story, producing a crop of programs that bear a clear family resemblance to Lynch and Frost's landmark series, often explicitly citing *TP* as a direct influence. *The X-Files, Lost,* and *True Detective* are the highest-profile descendants; below, we list some other shows that have most directly carried on that deliciously dark and weird tradition.

Eerie, Indiana (1991)

Premiering just three months after *Twin Peaks* shuttered, this short-lived NBC series centered on a teenager who moves with his family to a small Midwestern town where he has all sorts of, well, *eerie* encounters with bizarro people and creatures. The "Eerie, Indiana Pop. 16, 661" road sign certainly evoked its "Welcome to Twin Peaks" correlative, and one episode ("Mr. Chaney") even included a reference to the Log Lady.

Push, Nevada (2002)

Ben Affleck cocreated this *Project Greenlight* offshoot, which concerned a mild-mannered government functionary (who regularly reported in to his enigmatic secretary, Grace) investigating a mystery in remote Push, Nevada, an insular community of eccentrics with a big secret. The series had an odd hook: viewers could win cash by solving the central mystery. Comparisons to *Twin Peaks* were instantaneous (and unfavorable); the show was canceled after seven episodes.

Happy Town (2010)

In the remote town (sensing a pattern here?) of Haplin, Minnesota, a series of kidnappings is attributed to a possibly supernatural "Magic Man." The premise and general tenor of the show inescapably recalled *Twin Peaks*, with the general consensus being *Happy Town* was a weak imitation. It lasted eight episodes.

The Killing (2011)

Zero points for subtlety: A murder in the Washington woods, the young female victim's body discovered by a river. Morbidly disconsolate parents. Moody synth score. A catchphrase: "Who killed Rosie Larsen?" *The Killing* was a critical darling when it debuted, but narrative clumsiness quickly alienated viewers and reviewers, and the show was canceled after its third season (only to reappear on Netflix for an abbreviated, unheralded fourth season). Much critical hay was made over creator Veena Sud's obvious debt to Lynch—unfortunately, that debt included a less than masterful grasp of coherent storytelling, and did not include an ameliorating degree of artistic genius. Still, the excoriation Sud was subjected to by indignant critics when she declined to resolve the mystery of Rosie's murder on *their* schedule (meaning the concluding episode of the first season) seemed rude and excessive, and we couldn't help but be reminded of the similar beating Lynch and Frost took—in some cases, from the same critics—for taking their own sweet time in exposing Laura's killer. Some people never learn.

Gravity Falls (2012)

Creator Alex Hirsch describes this Pacific Northwest-set animated Disney show as *Twin Peaks* meets *The Simpsons*, even volunteering that his design choices are influenced by his admiration for the Lynch-Frost show. The premise? Twelve-year-old Dipper Pines and *twin* sister Mabel spend their summer vacation with "Grunkle" (Great Uncle) Stan in the fictional town of Gravity Falls, Oregon, encountering all sorts of supernatural mysteries. Even the title seems a tribute to *Twin Peaks'* Snoqualmie Falls.

Hemlock Grove (2013)

This small-town werewolf horror/drama was explicitly described by creator Eli Roth as "*Twin Peaks* with a monstrous edge." The critics certainly responded with a monstrous edge, with *Time* magazine calling it "one of the worst ten things on television in 2013."

Bates Motel (2013)

This well-received *Psycho* prequel came from *Lost* cocreator and avowed David Lynch superfan Carlton Cuse, who admitted "we pretty much ripped off *Twin Peaks*" when describing the series' lurid tone, lush visuals, and undercurrent of psychosexual horror. The charming Bates family— ensconced in California in the original film—has been relocated in this series to a coastal town in the Pacific Northwest. Mm hm.

Hannibal (2013)

Another serial killer story, and another prequel, from another Lynch fan: series creator Bryan Fuller remarked, upon taking on Thomas Harris's iconic titular elegant cannibal for television, "When I sat down to write the script, I was very consciously saying, 'What would David Lynch do with a Hannibal Lecter character?'" What Fuller did was continue *Twin Peaks'* traditions of striking, cinematic visuals, a beguiling tone that simultaneously seduces and repels, and a pervasive, romantic atmosphere of exquisite dread. The show was a hit with critics, and has inspired a devoted cult following ("Fannibals") similar to that enjoyed by *Twin Peaks* in its heyday.

Wayward Pines (2015)

Wayward Pines, you say? Is that possibly the name of a small town, say in the western United States? Is there an eerie, possibly supernatural conspiracy at play? A general air of uncanny small-town creepiness? An outside investigator determined to uncover the awful truth? Oh yes, yes on all fronts. But here's where *Wayward Pines* differs from *Twin Peaks*: star Matt Dillon is no Kyle MacLachlan, and co-executive producer and director M. Night Shyamalan is *really* no David Lynch. Still, the series was largely well regarded, and proof that there is still plenty of appeal to be mined from the basic elements of *Twin Peaks*.

Music

Musicians dig *Twin Peaks*. It's too dreamy.

10 Band Names Inspired by *Twin Peaks*

- Agent Cooper
- Dale Cooper and the Dictaphones
- Laura Palmer
- Laura Palmer Featuring Twin Peaks Killer
- Audrey Horne
- Windom Earle
- The Bookhouse Boys
- ArmsBendBack
- Garmonbozia
- One Eyed Jacks

10 Album Names Inspired by *Twin Peaks*

- Aborym, *Fire Walk with Us* (2001)
- Yasume, *Where We're from the Birds Sing a Pretty Song* (2003)
- Berkowitz Lake & Dahmer, *Without Chemicals He Points* (2002)
- The Future of Color, *White Lodge Black Lodge* (2007)
- Gallows, *The White Lodge* (2007)
- PinkySqueak, *The Owl Ring and the Smiling Bag* (2007)
- Amanda Palmer, *Who Killed Amanda Palmer?* (1998)
- V/VM, *There Was a Fish . . . in . . . the Percolator* (2008)
- Zynic, *Fire Walk with Me* (2011)
- Matt Skellenger, *The Owls Are Not What They Seem* (2013)

10 Songs Inspired by *Twin Peaks*

1. Anthrax, "Black Lodge" (1993)
   Thrash metal maestros Anthrax pledged allegiance to *Twin Peaks'* dark majesty with the pummeling "Black Lodge." Of course, Anthrax sings about the Black Lodge, but we would have liked to hear their take on Nadine's noiseless drape runners. Among the young hellions involved in the song's composition was one Angelo Badalamenti—keep an eye on that boy.

2. Marilyn Manson, "Wrapped in Plastic" (1994)
   Shock-rocker Manson penned this meditation on the sickness of family dynamics as played out in the Palmer home, including screams sampled from the final episode of *Twin Peaks*.
3. Superdrag, "Garmonbozia" (1994)
   Cheeky Brit-poppers Superdrag celebrated the spoils of pain and sorrow—garmonbozia—in this surging anthem. Bob would likely identify with the lyric "Somebody screams/And I'm gushing my load," but we're guessing he's more of a metal fan.
4. Camper Van Beethoven, "That Gum You Like Is Back in Style" (2004)
   The college-rock stalwarts borrowed a line from the MFAP for the title of this languid shuffle, included on the band's *New Roman Style*, a concept album about a future dystopian America. According to band leader David Lowery, *Twin Peaks* apparently fits into the album's labyrinthine narrative in some obscure way as a "crypto-key"; sounds appropriately enigmatic to us.
5. Surfer Blood "Twin Peaks" (2010)
   This indie-rock anthem, positing *Twin Peaks* as a backdrop to an ambivalent collegiate sexual encounter, is the rare musical tribute to treat the show as a cultural object rather than a direct aesthetic inspiration. The narrator displays questionable prudence selecting the show as a romantic mood setter (but hey, we don't judge).
6. Kool AD, "Eroika" (2013)
   Rapper Kool AD mentions watching *Twin Peaks* and Laura Palmer. He's down.
7. The Icypoles "Just You" (2014)
   The Melbourne, Australia, girl group the Icypoles (containing members of hipster fave Architecture in Helsinki) are such *Twin Peaks* fans that they covered the treacly-but-disturbing "Just You" from the *Twin Peaks* soundtrack—the number performed by Donna, Maddy, and James (affecting a chilling falsetto croon) in the Hayward living room.
8. Ben Frost, "Leo Needs a New Pair of Shoes" (2009)
   This moody instrumental—reminiscent of Angelo Badalamenti's foreboding score—quotes the redoubtable Leo Johnson in its title. Those Circle Brand boots are quite appealing. Fun fact: The track's source album, the critically acclaimed experimental/industrial piece *By the Throat*, also contains a two-part tribute to *Ghostbusters*' Peter Venkman.

Sky Ferreira channels Laura Palmer in *Night Time, My Time.*

9. Bastille, "Laura Palmer" (2011)

Moody Brit-poppers Bastille penned this sensitive ode to the trials of *Twin Peaks'* doomed central character. While many of the band's videos strongly reflect band leader Dan Smith's fascination with David Lynch, the clip for this song deliberately avoids Lynchisms, as a visual tribute combined with the lyric's specific reference would have been too on the nose.

10. Skye Ferreira, "Night Time, My Time" (2013)

Laura Palmer's evocative credo provides the title for both this song and its source album. The lyrics quote liberally from Laura's dialogue, and the track's sinister electronica pays fitting homage to *Twin Peaks'* dark glamour.

Twin Peaks Timeline

1986: David Lynch and Mark Frost first collaborate, on *Venus Descending*, film adaptation of Anthony Summers's *Goddess: The Secret Lives of Marilyn Monroe* (never filmed).

1988: Over a period of ten days, Lynch and Frost write *Northwest Passage*, the original pilot script for *Twin Peaks*.

February–March 1989: Lynch and Frost film *Northwest Passage* in Snoqualmie, Washington, and surrounding areas.

Summer 1989–early 1990: Lynch is off filming *Wild at Heart*.

August 1989: *Connoisseur* publishes first major *Twin Peaks* magazine article, a cover story hyping it as "the series that will change TV forever" (September issue, August release).

October–December 1989: Seven additional first-season episodes filmed.

November 1989: European version of the *Twin Peaks* pilot is released on home video in the United Kingdom, with alternate ending.

January 1990: *Twin Peaks* is previewed for press in Hollywood; ABC announces that pilot may air without ads (still no airdate).

March 7, 1990: ABC announces that *Twin Peaks* will debut as two-hour movie on Sunday, April 8, then move to regular time slot: 9 p.m. Thursdays beginning April 12.

March 9, 1990: Museum of Broadcasting (now The Paley Center for Media) salutes *Twin Peaks* with preview screening of the pilot at Seventh Annual Television Festival, followed by panel with Mark Frost, Chad Hoffman, Greg Fienberg, Kyle MacLachlan, Joan Chen, and Michael Ontkean.

March 26, 1990: ABC airs *Twin Peaks* ads during Academy Awards telecast.

April 6, 1990: *Entertainment Weekly* prints *Twin Peaks* cover story.

April 8, 1990: *Twin Peaks* pilot airs, becoming most watched TV movie of the year.

April 19, 1990: Cooper's Red Room dream airs, introducing viewers to the dancing dwarf, Mike, and Bob.

April/May 1990: *Time, Newsweek,* and *TV Guide* all publish major articles on *Twin Peaks*.

May 1990: *Wild at Heart* premieres at Cannes; wins Palme d'Or.

May 12, 1990: Julee Cruise appears as musical guest on *Saturday Night Live.*

May 21, 1990: *Donahue* honors *Twin Peaks,* with Mark Frost and six cast members appearing on panel: Mädchen Amick, Dana Ashbrook, Eric Da Re, Piper Laurie, Sheryl Lee, Peggy Lipton. ABC announces second-season renewal; Frost breaks the news live on *Donahue.*

May 23, 1990: First-season finale airs, with major cliffhanger—Who shot Agent Cooper?—but without resolution of the Laura Palmer murder, annoying many television critics.

July 1990: Second season begins filming.

August 1990: *Esquire* features Laura Palmer (Sheryl Lee) on the cover of its annual "Women We Love" issue.

August 2, 1990: Academy of Television Arts & Sciences nominates *Twin Peaks* for fourteen Emmy Awards, more than any other series that year.

August 5, 1990: ABC begins repeating entire first season of *Twin Peaks.*

September 1990: *The Secret Diary of Laura Palmer* and the *Twin Peaks* soundtrack are released; *American Chronicles,* a Lynch-Frost documentary series, premieres on Fox.

September 14, 1990: Alan Thicke hosts ABC special looking at upcoming second season, plus Steven Bochco's new musical drama *Cop Rock.*

September 16, 1990: *Twin Peaks* is shut out of all the major awards at the Emmys.

September 29, 1990: Kyle MacLachlan hosts *Saturday Night Live.*

September 30, 1990: Second season premieres.

October 1, 1990: *Time* magazine publishes Lynch cover story; *Diane . . . The Twin Peaks Tapes of Agent Copper* is officially released.

October 4, 1990: *Rolling Stone* publishes "Women of *Twin Peaks,*" with Lara Flynn Boyle, Sherilyn Fenn, and Mädchen Amick on cover.

October 7, 1990: *The Secret Diary of Laura Palmer* cracks the *New York Times* best-seller list.

November 10, 1990: Leland Palmer exposed as Laura's killer, in David Lynch–directed episode featuring the murder of Maddy Ferguson, one of the most powerful death scenes in television history.

December 31, 1990: Laura Palmer makes *People*'s list of twenty-five most intriguing people of 1990 ("Even in Death, the Daddy's Girl of *Twin Peaks* Stole Television's Most Bizarre Show").

January 19, 1991: *Twin Peaks* wins three Golden Globe Awards: drama series, lead actor (Kyle MacLachlan), supporting actress (Peggy Lipton).

February 1991: First full issue of *Twin Peaks Gazette* published.

February 16, 1991: With ratings tumbling, *Twin Peaks* begins a six-week hiatus.

The magic of "Hollywood": Twede's Café is transformed into the Double R diner for the Showtime relaunch.   *Photo by Mischa Cronin*

February 22, 1991: Lynch and Frost hold a press conference on the set of the Great Northern, urging fans to rally behind the show.

March 4, 1991: Series finale begins filming.

March 28, 1991: *Twin Peaks* returns.

April 1991: Star Pics releases *Twin Peaks* collector cards.

April 1991: Final issue of *Twin Peaks Gazette* published.

May 1991: Scott Frost's *The Autobiography of F.B.I. Special Agent Dale Cooper: My Life, My Tapes* is published.

May 1991: ABC announces the cancellation of *Twin Peaks*.

May 27, 1991: *Variety* reports that Twin Peaks will be returning as a feature film.

June 10, 1991: Series finale airs, with the good Cooper trapped in the Black Lodge.

August 8, 1991: *Twin Peaks: Fire Walk with Me* "shooting script" completed by Lynch and Robert Engels.

September 1991: *FWWM* filmed.

May 1992: *FWWM* has disastrous premiere at Cannes.

August 14–16, 1992: First *Twin Peaks* fan festival held, in Snoqualmie, Washington; includes the U.S. premiere of *FWWM*, attended by Lynch and members of the cast.

August 28, 1992: *FWWM* officially released in U.S.

June 11, 1993: Bravo begins rebroadcasting entire series, with new intros penned by Lynch and delivered on-screen by Log Lady.

July 29, 2014: "Missing Pieces" Blu-ray released.

October 3, 2014: Lynch and Frost simultaneously Tweet the news that *Twin Peaks* is returning to TV, as a nine-episode limited series on Showtime: "Dear Twitter Friends: That gum you like is going to come back in style! #damngoodcoffee." The new series picks up twenty-five years later, with all of the installments to be scripted by Lynch and Frost and directed by Lynch.

April 5, 2015: Lynch Tweets that he is dropping out of the Showtime revival, saying, "After 1 year and 4 months of negotiations, I left because not enough money was offered to do the script the way I felt it needed to be done."

May 15, 2015: He's back! Lynch announces, via Twitter again, that he is back on board: "Dear Twitter Friends, the rumors are not what they seem . . . . It is!!! Happening again. #TwinPeaks returns on @SHO_Network."

Summer 2015: Lynch, Frost, and team begin shooting the new version of *Twin Peaks* in and around Snoqualmie.

Appendix
Two Thumbs-Up

Awards and Nominations

Primetime Emmy Awards (1990)

Won: Outstanding Costume Design for a Series (Patricia Norris) (pilot episode)

Won: Outstanding Editing for a Series, Single Camera Production (Duwayne Dunham) (pilot episode)

Nominated: Outstanding Drama Series (Mark Frost, executive producer; David Lynch, executive producer)

Nominated: Outstanding Lead Actor in a Drama Series (Kyle MacLachlan, Special Agent Dale Cooper)

Nominated: Outstanding Lead Actress in a Drama Series (Piper Laurie, Catherine Martell)

Nominated: Supporting Actress in a Drama Series (Sherilyn Fenn, Audrey Horne)

Nominated: Outstanding Directing in a Drama Series (David Lynch) (pilot episode)

Nominated: Outstanding Writing in a Drama Series (Harley Peyton) (episode three)

Nominated: Outstanding Writing in a Drama Series (Mark Frost, David Lynch) (pilot episode)

Nominated: Outstanding Music and Lyrics (Angelo Badalamenti, composer; David Lynch, lyricist, "Into the Night," episode five)

Nominated: Outstanding Music Composition for a Series (Dramatic Underscore) (Angelo Badalamenti, composer) (episode two).

Nominated: Outstanding Main Title Theme Music (Angelo Badalamenti, composer; David Lynch, composer)

Nominated: Outstanding Art Direction for a Series (Patricia Norris, production designer; Leslie Morales, set decorator) (pilot episode)
Nominated: Outstanding Sound Editing for a Series (John A. Larsen, supervising sound editor; Matt Sawelson, sound editor; John Haeny, sound editor; Pat McCormick, sound editor; Albert Edmund Lord III, sound editor; Fred Cipriano, sound editor; Bruce P. Michaels, supervising ADR editor; Lori L. Eschler, supervising music editor) (episode seven)

Primetime Emmy Awards (1991)

Nominated: Outstanding Lead Actor in a Drama Series (Kyle MacLachlan)
Nominated: Outstanding Supporting Actress in a Drama Series (Piper Laurie)
Nominated: Outstanding Sound Editing for a Series (Richard Taylor, supervising editor; Pat McCormick, sound editor; Richard F. W. Davis, sound editor; Thomas DeGorter, sound editor; Albert Edmund Lord III, supervising ADR editor; Lori L. Eschler, supervising music editor) (episode twenty-five)
Nominated: Outstanding Sound Mixing for a Drama Series (Don Summer, production mixer; Gary Alexander, rerecording mixer; Adam Jenkins, re-recording mixer) (episode twenty-five)

Television Critics Association Awards (1990)

Won: Outstanding Achievement in Drama
Won: Program of the Year

Casting Society of America, USA (1990)

Won: Best Casting for TV, Dramatic Episode (Johanna Ray)

Golden Globes (1991)

Won: Best TV Series Drama
Won: Best Performance by an Actor in a TV Series-Drama (Kyle MacLachlan)
Won: Best Performance by an Actress in a Supporting Role in a Series, Miniseries, or Motion Picture Made for TV (Piper Laurie)
Nominated: Best Performance by an Actress in a Supporting Role in a Series, Miniseries, or Motion Picture Made for TV (Sherilyn Fenn)

Peabody Awards (1991) (for pilot episode)

American Society of Cinematographers, USA (1991)

Nominated: Outstanding Achievement in Cinematography in Movies of the Week/Pilots (Ron Garcia)

Directors Guild of America, USA (1991)

Nominated: Outstanding Directorial Achievement in Dramatic Series—Night (Lesli Linka Glatter) (episode five)

Grammy Awards (1991)

Nominated: Best Instrumental Composition Written for a Motion Picture or for Television (Angelo Badalamenti) (Soundtrack)

Selected Bibliography

Books

Altman, Mark A. *Twin Peaks Behind-the-Scenes: An Unofficial Visitors Guide to Twin Peaks*. Las Vegas: Pioneer Books, 1990.

Breskin, David. *Inner Views*. Boston: Faber and Faber, 1992.

Bulwer-Lytton, Sir Edward, *Zanoni*. London: Saunders & Otley, 1842.

Chandler, Raymond. *The Simple Art of Murder*. New York: Houghton Mifflin, 1950.

Dukes, Brad. *Reflections: An Oral History of Twin Peaks*. Nashville: short/Tall press, 2014.

Frost, Scott. *The Autobiography of F.B.I. Special Agent Dale Cooper: My Life, My Tapes*. New York/London/Toronto/Sydney/Tokyo/Singapore: Pocket Books, 1991.

Hayes, Marisa C., and Boulègue, Franck (Eds.). *Fan Phenomena: Twin Peaks*. Bristol, UK: Intellect Books, 2013.

Lim, Dennis. *David Lynch: The Man from Another Place*. Boston: New Harvest, 2015.

Lynch, David. *Catching the Big Fish: Meditation, Consciousness, and Creativity*. New York: Jeremy P. Tarcher/Penguin, 2006.

Lynch, David, Frost, Mark, and Wurman, Richard Saul. *Welcome to Twin Peaks: Access Guide to the Town*. New York: Pocket Books, 1991.

Lynch, Jennifer. *The Secret Diary of Laura Palmer*. New York: Pocket Books, 1990.

Mundy, Talbot. *The Devil's Guard*. Indianapolis: Bobbs-Merrill, 1926.

Nochimson, Martha P. *The Passion of David Lynch: Wild at Heart in Hollywood*. Austin: University of Texas Press, 1997.

Olson, Greg. *David Lynch: Beautiful Dark*. Lanham, MD: Scarecrow Press, 2008.

Rodley, Chris (Ed.). *Lynch on Lynch (Revised Edition)*. London: Faber and Faber, 2005.

Periodicals

Anonymous, "'Twin Peaks' Finale Draws Low Ratings," *The New York Times*, June 12, 1991.

Canby, Vincent, "One Long Last Gasp for Laura Palmer," *The New York Times*, August 29, 1992.

Carter, Bill, "At ABC, Several Motives for Keeping 'Twin Peaks,'" *The New York Times*, May 21, 1990.

Gelman, Morrie, *Laura* Review, *Variety,* January 31, 1968.

Givhan, Robin, "Clues to 'Twin Peaks' Cast Could Rest in Their Costumes,' *The Milwaukee Sentinel*, May 16, 1990.

Gould, Jack, "Crashing In on Crashing Bores," *The New York Times*, February 4, 1968.

Gould, Jack, "TV: Theme Song Is Still the Best Asset of 'Laura,'" *The New York Times*, January 25, 1968.

Grow, Kory, "Dream Team: The Semi-Mysterious Story Behind the Music of 'Twin Peaks,'" *Rolling Stone*, July 24, 2014.

Guider, Elizabeth, "Not a Peep from ABC re Getting a Peek at Lynch's 'Twin Peaks,'" *Variety*, February 28, 1990.

Harris, Mark, "Will 'Twin Peaks' Get a Second Chance?" *Entertainment Weekly*, March 8, 1991.

Hastings, Deborah, "'Secret Diary' Peaks Lusty Curiosity," *Chicago Sun-Times*, October 12, 1990.

Knight, Bob, "'Peaks' Gets Surprising Slot on ABC's Spring Sked; 'News,' 'Justice' Added Too," *Variety*, May 7, 1990.

Krupnick, Jerry, "Can You Wait?" *The Star-Ledger*, October 26, 1990.

Ledwon, Lenora, "*Twin Peaks* and the Television Gothic," *Literature/Film Quarterly*, Volume XXI/No. 4, 1993.

Macuson, Vinnie, and Grant, Drew, "Revisiting 'Twin Peaks' 2X4: Secret Diary Proves Laura Palmer Created Blogging," *New York Observer*, February 6, 2015.

Mathews, Jack, "A Walk on the Wild Side," *Newsday*, May 18, 1992.

Rodman, Howard A., "The Series That Will Change TV Forever," *Connoisseur*, September 1990.

Wallace, David Foster, "David Lynch Keeps His Head," *Premiere*, September 1996.

Weinstein, Steve, "The Other Peak: As a Lad, Mark Frost Sensed the Secrets of Small-Town Life; Now He and David Lynch Are Unmasking Them on 'Twin Peaks,'" *Los Angeles Times*, July 29, 1990.

Woodward, Richard B., "When 'Blue Velvet' Meets 'Hill Street Blues,'" *The New York Times*, April 8, 1990.

Websites

Blassmann, Andreas, "The Detective in *Twin Peaks*," http://www.thecityofabsurdity.com/papers/detective.html, April, 1999.

Buchanan, Brett, "Exclusive: Twin Peaks Writer Bob Engels Reveals Planned Followup to Cliffhanger Ending & 1950's Backstory," alternativenation.net, August 13, 2014.

Ebert, Roger, "*Storyville* Review and Film Summary," rogerebert.com, October 9, 1992.

Fraisse, Charlotte, "*Twin Peaks: Fire Walk With Me* Official Shooting Diary: Excerpts from a Shooting Diary," dugpa.com, undated.

Gleiberman, Owen, "*Twin Peaks: Fire Walk with Me* Review," ew.com, September 11, 1992.

Horne, Jerry, "Between Two Worlds: Josie's Fate," twinpeaksarchive.blogspot.com, July 23, 2011.

Lynch, David, and Engels, Bob, "Twin Peaks: Fire Walk with Me, Teresa Banks and the Last Seven Days of Laura Palmer," lynch.net, August 8, 1991.

Serrao, Nivea, "11 'Twin Peaks'-Inspired Cultural References Worth Checking Out," community.ew.com, April 10, 2015.

Index

THE FAQ SERIES